MY FRIEND HITLER

AND OTHER PLAYS OF YUKIO MISHIMA

modern asian literature

MY FRIEND HITLER

AND OTHER PLAYS OF

YUKIO MISHIMA

translated by **hiroaki sato**

COLUMBIA UNIVERSITY PRESS   NEW YORK

Columbia University Press

Publishers Since 1893

New York Chichester, West Sussex

Library of Congress Cataloging-in-Publication Data

Mishima, Yukio, 1925–1970

   My friend Hitler and other plays of Mishima Yukio / translated by Hiroaki Sato.

      p.   cm. — (Modern Asian literature)

   Includes bibliographical references.

   Contents: The Rokumeikan; Backstage essays; The decline and fall of the Suzaku; My friend Hitler; The terrance of the leper King; The flower of evil: kabuki; A wonder tale: the moonbow.

      ISBN 0-231-12632-8 (cl. : alk paper)—ISBN 0-231-12633-6 (pa. : alk. paper)

   I. Sato, Hiroaki, 1942–   II. Title.   III. Series.

PL833.17 A6 2000

895.6'25—dc21   2002067259

Columbia University Press books are printed on permanent and durable acid-free paper.

Designed by Chang Jae Lee

Printed in the United States of America

c 10 9 8 7 6 5 4 3 2 1

p 10 9 8 7 6 5 4 3 2 1

CONTENTS

PREFACE   VII

THE ROKUMEIKAN   1

BACKSTAGE ESSAYS   55

THE DECLINE AND FALL OF THE SUZAKU   63

MY FRIEND HITLER   113

THE TERRACE OF THE LEPER KING   161

THE FLOWER OF EVIL: KABUKI   219

A WONDER TALE: THE MOONBOW   241

PREFACE

Yukio Mishima (1925–70) was prolific—amazingly so when you consider he took the grand theatrical step of dying by disembowelment and decapitation at forty-five, an age most writers would regard as the starting point for mature work. As a playwright alone, from 1949, when his first play was published, to the year before his death, he wrote more than sixty works, and nearly all of them were staged in his lifetime. He was also an active participant in theatrical production and directed several of his own plays, among them the kabuki translated here as *A Wonder Tale: The Moonbow*. He wrote, produced, directed, and acted in the film *Yūkoku* (Patriotism). The movie is notable for a graphic depiction of the disembowelment of an aggrieved army officer who takes the step, in Mishima's fictional construction, because of his failure to be part of the 2/26 Incident, the attempted coup d'état of 1936.

Mishima saw dramatic characters everywhere. The play he wrote as a teenager, which lay undiscovered until the fall of 2001, was about the Archangel Gabriel.[1]

---

1. Titled *Rotei* (The passage), the four-act play deals with the Annunciation, opening with Gabriel speaking of the birth of Christ and closing with the archangel saying, "Go, go! The path is open for you." A notebook Mishima kept shows he finished writing the play on September 28, 1939—that is, when he was fourteen years old. Professor Satō Hideaki, who collated the manuscript from jumbled papers for the Mishima Museum, says the play is solidly structured with well-delineated characters (twenty-eight in all), adumbrating the dramatic talent Mishima would demonstrate in abundance in coming years. The play went on display on October 20, 2001, at the museum. At the time of this writing, it has not seen print. But it will undoubtedly be part of the forty-two-volume "definitive complete works" of Mishima Yukio, being published by Shinchōsha.

His last, a puppet play (a partial rewrite of the kabuki just mentioned), concerned the Japanese bowman-warrior Minamoto no Tametomo (1139–1170?). To list only some of the foreign characters he dealt with, there are, in addition to Gabriel, the Magi (depicted in his first published play), Brazilian aristocrats, Greek gods, Orpheus (based on Cocteau's film), Saint Sebastian, the Marchioness de Sade, figures from the *Arabian Nights,* and, as seen in this collection, Adolf Hitler and the twelfth-century Cambodian king Jayavarman VII.

Mishima once said, "I started writing dramas just as water flows toward a lower place. In me, the topography of dramas seems to be situated far below that of novels. It seems to be in a place which is more instinctive, closer to child's play" *(Gikyoku no Yūwaku,* "The temptation of drama"). Brought up with a great affinity for theater, he wrote plays with the kind of natural ease that prompted him to express disbelief at his friend Tennessee Williams's complaint that he could write "only a line or two" a day. As Mishima explained in a brief essay on Williams, "a play is above all based on a structural logic and once a structure is built with precision, you write it in one stretch." If you write only a few lines a day, "the flow of drama will die," Mishima wrote, pointing to "the structural weakness of Williams's drama" ("Tennessee Williams no Koto" [On Tennessee Williams]).

Perhaps because of this ease, the prevailing view for some years was that his plays were more "transient"—to use his own word—than his novels and short stories. More recently, however, there has been a move to reassess them—from the standpoints of theatrical language and dramatic structure. Today some critics even rate his drama above his fiction.

Mishima wrote four of the five plays translated here in the last three years of his life and saw three of them produced in a single year, 1969. Although I did not make the selection with a particular theme in mind, these four plays may be viewed in relation to what some critics have called Mishima's theology, an amalgamation of the "politics of death"—a "carefully premeditated death which is part of his work," as Marguerite Yourcenar has put it in *Mishima: A Vision of the Void*—with the notion of what Mishima himself called "the Emperor as a cultural concept."

The Decline and Fall of the Suzaku has to do with loyalty to the Emperor that is unreciprocated. *My Friend Hitler* is an attempt to suggest that in Europe Hitler could do what he did—simultaneously disposing of the left and the right to take the middle road—but in Japan the Emperor would have to side with the kind of army Mishima wanted. (Or at least that is an interpretation advanced by one biographer of Mishima, Inose Naoki.) *The Terrace of the Leper King* is a farewell to the youthful male body with the paradox that it is the body that survives, not the soul. And *A Wonder Tale: The Moonbow* is a fantasy of imperial succor.

All Mishima's plays—except for the recently discovered one—are assembled in the two-volume set *Mishima Yukio Gikyoku Zenshū* (Shinchō Sha,

1990). Individual plays are also in paperback editions either singly, as in the case of *Chinsetsu Yumiharizuki* (Chūō Kōron Sha, 1975) and *Raiō no Terasu* (Chūō Kōron Sha, 1975), or severally, as in the case of *Rokumeikan* (Shinchō Sha, 1984), which appears with three other plays, and *Waga Tomo Hitler* (Shinchō Sha, 1979), which is published with one other play. The separate paperback editions are mostly accompanied by Mishima's commentaries.

Of the three essays translated in this book, the originals of what I call "Backstage Essays" are included in *Geijutsu Dansō* (Fragmentary thoughts on art), the fourth in the paperback series called "Mishima Yukio's Essays" (Chikuma Shobō, 1995). If the original of "The Flower of Evil: Kabuki" has been collected in a Mishima volume since its publication in a magazine in 1988, I don't know of it. However, the publication of the forty-two-volume "definitive complete works" of Mishima is under way, and the transcript of the talk will likely be made part of the set.

In this book, all Japanese names, Mishima's on the cover and title page, and the translator's excepted, are given the Japanese way, family name first.

I thank Ronald H. Bayes, a recipient of the North Carolina State Award for Literature, and Frank Gibney, president of the Pacific Basin Institute. Mr. Bayes started the whole thing by asking me to translate *My Friend Hitler* in the late 1970s. He then asked me to translate Mrs. Mishima's favorite play, *The Terrace of the Leper King*. He published both in the magazine he founded and edited, *St. Andrews Review*. Mr. Gibney gave me a grant to translate a small group of Mishima's writings that included *The Rokumeikan* and "The Flower of Evil—Kabuki." M. E. Sharpe published the main portion of that grant work, the novel *Kinu to Meisatsu* (Silk and insight), in 1998.

I thank J. Thomas Rimer for promoting my translations and writings for more than a quarter of a century; Yajima Mieko for helping assemble the photographs to illustrate this book; Ishii Tatsuhiko for explaining a number of kabuki terms and providing me with information on various actors; Chia-ning Chang for his suggestions to improve the translations; Marie Squerciati and Wolcott Wheeler for reading some of the plays in translation; and Anne R. Gibbons for copyediting this book.

Finally, I thank the poet Robert Fagan and my wife, Nancy Rossiter. Without their help, no part of this work would have been possible.

Hiroaki Sato

MY FRIEND HITLER

AND OTHER PLAYS OF YUKIO MISHIMA

THE ROKUMEIKAN

The Rokumeikan (the Deer Cry Pavilion), from which this play gets its title, is a British-designed Renaissance-style social center built by the Japanese government in 1883 for the explicit purpose of encouraging social intercourse between foreign dignitaries and members of the Japanese aristocracy. An unabashed instrument of Westernization, it became the greatest tangible symbol of the Meiji slogan *bunmei kaika,* "civilization and enlightenment." The ball on the night of November 3, 1886, on which Mishima bases this play, was a grand affair. Seventeen hundred guests attended the gala, which was hosted by the foreign minister Count Inoue Kaoru (1835–1915) and his wife.

The appeal of the Rokumeikan as a place for socializing with foreign representatives did not last long. In April 1887 the prime minister, Count Itō Hirobumi (1841–1909), hosted another grand ball, this time a masquerade, but it turned into a scandal—"an orgy of ribaldry, bawdy and ridicule," as Pat Barr puts it in *The Deer Cry Pavilion* (Macmillan, 1968), her somewhat jaundiced report on foreigners' views of Japan. In the summer of the same year, Inoue, who had instigated the construction of the extravagant building, was forced to resign as foreign minister. These two incidents apparently had a sobering effect on the government-led copycatting of European manners and customs. In 1893 an earthquake damaged the building, and the government was unable to come up with the money needed for repair.

The building survived as a social club for Japan's high society until 1933. By the time Mishima first heard about it as an adolescent, it had become an object of nostalgia—a dazzling example of the aristocratic flowering of a bygone era. At least he wished it had; in his characteristically blunt manner, he noted: "The

Age of the Rokumeikan, according to contemporary paintings and senryū, was truly ridiculous and *grotesque,* a kind of monkeys' theater for enlightenment," in which "bucktoothed midget Japanese men wearing ill-suited swallowtails bobbed their heads to foreigners and dwarf-like women wearing party dresses like wolves' clothes danced in the clutches of foreigners twice as tall."

One historical event mentioned in the play deserves comment. It is what the character Kiyohara Einosuke, in act 2, refers to as "the *Maria Luz* incident."

The Meiji government was preoccupied with reducing or removing extraterritoriality and other unequal provisions forced upon Japan as the country opened itself under external pressure to international commerce and concluded various treaties. In the face of powerfully armed nations, the Japanese government in the best of circumstances felt hemmed in and followed a *naigō gaijū* policy—to be tough on its citizens' demands but submissive to those made by foreign countries—which necessarily fanned a great deal of nationalistic resentment. Conversely, any occurrence suggesting Japan's diplomatic independence was exaggerated.

In July 1872 one of the coolies being transported by the Peruvian ship *Maria Luz* escaped while the ship lay at anchor in Yokohama. This led to a chain of events that in the end impelled Foreign Minister Soejima Taneomi (1828–1905) to force the Peruvian ship to "liberate" all the coolies. Ōe Taku (1847–1921), then governor of Kanagawa, who served as chief judge in the tribunal convened, handed down the decision that the 231 coolies on board were being treated inhumanely and had to be freed and returned to their homeland, China. Ōe was, incidentally, among the first to recommend to the new government that the untouchable class of people—the *eta* and *hinin*—be abolished. He had done so a year earlier, in 1871.

The incident was touted as a case where Japan acted independently in an international situation for the first time and, besides, honored human rights over diplomatic considerations such as the absence of a treaty relationship with Peru. In reality, the Japanese government, which had initially arrested the escaped coolie and returned him to the ship, took the final action only after it was pressured by Great Britain and the United States. It was hardly a shining example of "independent diplomacy," as Kiyohara argues.

In one of those paradoxical statements he loved to make, Mishima said of *The Rokumeikan:* "During the ball on the Emperor's Birthday, on November 3, of the nineteenth year of Meiji, nothing remotely resembling the incident seen here [in the play] happened. However, the flaw of history is that what is written is about things that happened, but not about things that did not. That's the crack through which novelists, playwrights, poets, and other frauds slip in."

Mishima also mentioned in one program note, "Butōkai" (The ball), a short story written in 1919 by Akutagawa Ryūnosuke (1892–1927) to describe the gathering at the Rokumeikan, and the account or accounts by Pierre Loti (Julien

Viaud, 1850–1923) of the same affair, which the French writer attended as a naval officer. (Mishima identified Loti's work in question differently on two occasions—as "Edo no Butōkai" [The ball in Edo] in a short essay for a newspaper during the first production of the play, and as "Nihon no Aki" [Japan's autumn] in a program note when the play was produced again in 1962. The original title of the latter is *Japoneries d'automne*.) It is somewhat amusing to reflect that Akutagawa, who had a strong sense of the absurd, more or less idealized the ball while basing his story on Loti's apparently cynical description of it.

Mishima was commissioned by the Bungaku-za (Literary Theater) to write this costume drama to mark the theater group's twentieth anniversary. The role of Countess Asako was to be played by the theater company's lead actress, Sugimura Haruko, and Mishima characterized the play as "a piece for the actor's art." In an article for the 1986 Mishima special of the monthly *Kokubungaku* (Japanese literature), the poet-critic Ishii Tatsuhiko called *The Rokumeikan* Mishima's first theatrical masterpiece in which "artistry and popular appeal are perfectly merged." The play was printed in the December 1956 issue of the monthly *Bungakukai* (The literary world) and was staged from November 27 to December 9 of the same year, with Mishima himself appearing in the walk-on role of the carpenter.

The essays that follow the play are two of the four pieces that Mishima evidently wrote during the first production of *The Rokumeikan* and then published under the overall title *Gakuya de kakareta Engeki-ron* (Essays on theater written backstage) in the January 1957 issue of *Bungei Shinchō* (New tides in literary arts).

THE ROKUMEIKAN

A Tragedy in Four Acts

On the night of the ball, COUNT AND COUNTESS KAGEYAMA, played by Nakamura Nobuo and Sugimura Haruko, receive the Chinese ambassador and his entourage. Daiichi Seimei Hall, December 1956. *Courtesy of Waseda University's Tsubouchi Memorial Theatre Museum. By permission of Bungaku-za.*

Time: November 3, 1886 (nineteenth year of Meiji)
   From morning to midnight of the Emperor's birthday

Place:
   Act 1: Senkantei Hut in Count Kageyama's Mansion
   Act 2: Same as Act 1
   Act 3: Grand Ballroom of the Rokumeikan
   Act 4: Same as Act 3

Characters
   Count Kageyama Hisatoshi
   Countess Asako
   Marchioness Daitokuji Sueko
   Sueko's daughter, Akiko
   Kiyohara Einosuke
   Einosuke's son, Hisao
   Tobita Tenkotsu
   Head maid, Kusano
   Army general Miyamura
   General's wife, Noriko
   Baron Sakazaki
   Baroness Sadako
   Headwaiter, Yamamoto
   Waiters: Kawata, Konishi, etc.
   Carpenter, Matsui
   Maids: A, B
   Photographer

   Itō Hirobumi and his wife, Umeko
   Ōyama Iwao and his wife, Sutematsu
   Vice Admiral Hamilton, of the British Royal Navy, along with some
      officers
   The Ch'ing ambassador and his entourage
   Many other guests for the ball

ACT 1

November 3, 1886; ten o'clock on the morning of the Emperor's birthday.
   The tearoom Senkantei atop a hillock in the spacious garden of Count Kageya-
ma's mansion. There is a rivulet this side of the hut—hence the name senkan,
"purling"—along with chrysanthemums, stepping stones, a stone washbasin, and a

bamboo water pipe. To the right of the tearoom, you look down on a rear gate and a guard's hut at the foot of the hill, and there is the suggestion that you can see the Hibiya army parade ground in the distance at stage left. The path with stepping stones starts from stage right, goes around the tearoom, then leads to stage left. Under the eaves of the tearoom hangs an old frame with Senkantei written on it. As the curtain rises, a maid is arranging several zabuton-cushions, on the decorative verandah. Another maid is preparing tea and cookies.

Soon, from stage right, Head Maid Kusano appears carrying a telescope and leading four female guests. The group is headed by Sueko, the wife of Marquis Daitokuji, and her daughter, Akiko. Following them are Noriko, the wife of army general Miyamura, and Sadako, the wife of Baron Sakazaki. Everyone is in formal Western dress.

KUSANO: Here, please make yourselves at home, ladies. My lady and the others will be joining you shortly.

SUEKO: You need not fuss about us. We can take care of ourselves.

NORIKO: May I borrow the telescope?

KUSANO: Please. *(She hands the telescope over to her and leaves stage right.)* *(From time to time, as the wind shifts, you hear distant military music from stage left.)*

NORIKO: *(Turning the telescope toward the left)* My, it's so pretty! All the feathers on their hats, fluttering in the wind.

SADAKO: Can you see your husband?

NORIKO: But there are so many hats. . . .

SADAKO: You know, it isn't as if there were a great many generals in the army.

NORIKO: Yes, I see him. Look at his mustache. He was applying a lot of brilliantine to it before he left this morning, and that worked: both ends of it are leaping to his ears. . . . He keeps looking toward us. *(She lowers her telescope and holds it to her chest.)* What shall I do if he finds out that I'm taking a peek at his parade from a spot like this?

SADAKO: Don't worry. There's no way he can see you. *(She takes the telescope and looks into it.)*

SUEKO: Can you see the master of this house?

SADAKO: I should give him a look, shouldn't I? After all, we are in his house. . . . My, what a terrible swirl of dust! The whole training ground is blanketed. . . . Now, the cloud of dust has receded. Where's the master of this house, Count Kageyama? Why doesn't he raise his hand as a signal?

SUEKO: I'm certain that he's in His Majesty's tent.

SADAKO: If he's in the tent, it's no good. Even those at the outer fringe are in full-dress uniform; all you see are their glittering chests, and their faces are hidden in the tent.

NORIKO: *(To Sueko)* Marquis Daitokuji doesn't go to parades, does he?

SUEKO: No, he's just *elegant* from head to toe and is terrified of horses, soldiers, and marches.

SADAKO: *(Looking into the telescope)* The cavalry march has started. Oh, how brave they look! I can clearly see the imperial banner in the front. *(The military music grows louder.)* There's that wind again, the dust has blanketed the whole thing. *(Handing the telescope to Akiko)* Why don't you take a look?

AKIKO: *(Apparently depressed all along, she refuses)* Oh, no, I don't have to, really.

SUEKO: She's her father's child. *(As if to protect her, she sits on the verandah alongside her. The other two continue to look into the telescope.)*

AKIKO: Isn't Lady Asako late?

SUEKO: She's deliberately late. She's extremely attentive. While these ladies are watching their husbands, she is purposely staying away. You know, every year, on the morning of the Emperor's birthday, we go to the court to congratulate His Majesty, and on our way home we come here. This is the only place where you can see the imperial review from a place much higher than His Majesty. Anyway, I can't help wondering why the Emperor's birthday is always so beautiful and balmy. The last florid day of autumn before the onset of winter . . . the fragrance of chrysanthemums . . . the lucid, dry morning air. . . . Look *(pointing to the audience)*. All the trees in this spacious garden, the sheen over the pond, the way the roofs of the main building spread out in a leisurely fashion. . . . And the shapely small pine tree on the islet in the pond. In every nook and corner, happiness seems to live, holding its breath, don't you think? *(Gently)* Your sad face does not become this view.

AKIKO: But, mother, isn't it the case that only a sad person is qualified to look at a beautiful landscape? Happy people don't need a landscape.

SUEKO: That would mean that the owner of this garden is not happy.

(Noriko and Sadako also walk to the tearoom and seat themselves on the verandah.)

NORIKO: Mrs. Kageyama did not go to the court to congratulate His Majesty this year, either, when wives accompanying their husbands is finally becoming a custom in Japan, too.

SADAKO: It would be even odder if she did not go to the ball at the Rokumeikan tonight. Count Kageyama himself is the host. Shall we all try to persuade her . . . ?

SUEKO: No, no. She'd never attend it. Though she doesn't look it, she's stubborn, and once she decides not to attend it, she will not do so.

NORIKO: But that would put the count in a difficult position. He loves socializing so much he practically runs the whole Rokumeikan himself, but his wife is so retiring.

SADAKO: *(In a whisper)* Where does her retiring nature come from? I'm afraid she's hesitant about showing herself in public. She was a famous geisha in Shimbashi, yes, but we don't see why she ought to be concerned about such a thing. Have we even once indicated to her by any gesture that we want to treat her differently from ourselves?

SUEKO: You shouldn't say that. But that isn't the only reason. I have confidence that I know her better than anyone else. Yes, one reason may be that she's from Shimbashi, but even in those days she was a specialist in matters of love and sex. But aren't we women all doctors in that field, more or less? Men are, as it were, engineers, and we are the ones who are responsible for theory and logic. . . . And she dislikes politics. She dislikes everything official. That's because an official place is where lies and falsities begin. Men's lying is all nurtured in the public world.

NORIKO: But isn't the geisha world a world of lies and calculations?

SUEKO: But that's where weak women tell lies only to protect themselves. She dislikes going to official places because there women, like men, learn to tell lies voluntarily.

SADAKO: Are you saying that we have become bigger liars than she?

SUEKO: I have. She's different. She always treasures the emotions her own skin feels. . . . Yes, her husband has tried very hard and countless times to bring her out to official functions, provided her with a dance teacher, and provided her with a French tailor. She must have many more evening dresses than I do tucked away in her closet. I can guarantee it. Her dancing is impeccable, and she looks elegant in Western dress. And yet, she stubbornly wears a kimono with a trailing skirt and never appears at any official function, no matter what it is.

SADAKO: In this new, wonderful age?

NORIKO: In this age where women are able to bask in the sun for the first time in hundreds of years?

SUEKO: No, but no one can criticize someone for her taste.

NORIKO: *(Looking toward stage right)* Here she comes; here she comes, walking up the path by the spring water.

AKIKO: She's finally coming.

SUEKO: *(To her daughter)* You understand? Be patient, until I bring it up.
(From stage right, the lady of the house and Count Kageyama's wife, Asako, appears, followed by Kusano. She's holding up the trailing end of her kimono, dressed as she is in completely palatial style.)

ASAKO: Welcome, everyone. I do not know how to apologize for having kept you waiting for such a long time.

SUEKO: No need for stiff formalities. We were just discussing if there was some way of inducing you to come to the ball at the Rokumeikan.

ASAKO: You must be joking. I am such an old-fashioned woman, I can't possibly go to such a fashionable place.

SADAKO: This garden is wonderful no matter when I look at it.

ASAKO: We don't take enough care of it. Incidentally, Mrs. Miyamura, have you seen your husband?

NORIKO: Yes, I could spot him easily because of his mustache.

ASAKO: His is certainly a magnificent mustache.

NORIKO: He's only fastidious about grooming his horses and his mustache, and he doesn't even try to look at me when I'm in a Western dress like this.

SADAKO: I must go now. I must be home before my husband returns from the parade.

NORIKO: Same here. I'm afraid I must be going. Thank you for having us.

ASAKO: I'll come with you to the gate.

SUEKO: I have something I'd like to discuss with you.

ASAKO: I see. . . . Come, Kusano, would you please have the maids escort the ladies? *(Kusano calls the maids out of a room in the tearoom and instructs them to accompany the ladies).* . . . I must excuse myself now. *(Noriko and Sadako leave toward stage left, bowing. To Sueko and her daughter)* Why don't we go inside? There I can listen to your story and be more relaxed. *(Kusano brings two chairs into the tearoom. Sueko and her daughter go up to the room and seat themselves. Asako seats herself on a* zabuton. *Kusano exits to a different room at an appropriate moment.)*

SUEKO: You handled the two of them splendidly. Even hypocrisy becomes something like a fragrant bouquet in your hands.

ASAKO: What a terrible thing to say! The only thing I do is give an appropriate bouquet to everyone.

SUEKO: Savage you! But I came here to ask your advice about my daughter because you are like that and I can count on you. I want my daughter to live the new age fully, live the kind of life I could not. In that sense her love affair is mine as well.

ASAKO: She's such an innocent child and you say she's in love?

SUEKO: She is. Both her parents are from aristocratic families, but like her ancestors who did not know what to do with their long sleeves, she loves radical things. True aristocratic blood is radical blood. Just as only the rich can despise money, so can we with a warehouse full of conventions despise conventions. An irresolute man like my husband can't be called an aristocrat.

ASAKO: You mean she's having a radical love affair, with her lovely face. Who is her lover? Could it be a blue-eyed foreigner. . .?

SUEKO: I like foreigners, but Akiko does not, do you? *(She looks into her daughter's face.)*

ASAKO: Did she fall in love with someone from the lower class?

SUEKO: No, he isn't a man from the lower class, but he's on the side of that class.

ASAKO: Don't tell me he's a remnant of the Liberal Party. . . .

SUEKO: He is a remnant of the Liberal Party, most likely.

ASAKO: *(Turning pale)* He is?

SUEKO: I understand why you are alarmed. Those remnants are the enemy of your husband; they are rumored to be trying to kill him.

ASAKO: They are!?

SUEKO: Come, Akiko, tell her everything. A woman in the coming age must be able to talk about herself clearly.

AKIKO: Well. . . . It was at the end of summer. Cholera was still raging, and father would not allow me to go out, but mother and I secretly slipped out to see Charine's circus horses.

SUEKO: *(To Asako)* Have you seen Charine's circus horses?

ASAKO: No, not yet.

SUEKO: You haven't? They are so wonderful.

AKIKO: Neither of us had gone out for quite a while, and the horses were wonderful, so we were excited.

SUEKO: The way those two horses danced under Charine's direction!

AKIKO: Their names were Fugal and Beaumiteau.

SUEKO: They danced to music. Bonnets with glittering stars on their heads, they were like two Pegasuses. I was sure wings were hidden under the flesh of those white horses' shoulders.

AKIKO: After a lion tamer's performance, there was the last performance of those horses. *(To her mother)* We came out of the tent in the Navy Field in Tsukiji, did we not? Above the sea a summer moon was hanging like a ringing gong.

SUEKO: It was a noisy moon.

AKIKO: That was because our hearts were disturbed. Then, mother, you noticed that you had dropped your French-imported handbag.

SUEKO: You are right. It had a diamond clasp that was a bit loose so I had taken off. . . .

AKIKO: Then he called out to you. In white ikat and hakama trousers.

SUEKO: I accepted the handbag he had brought. I offered to recompense him.

AKIKO: But he merely smiled, giving a glimpse of his white teeth, and shook his head.

ASAKO: So that young man became your lover.

SUEKO: Yes, he kept declining but we persuaded him to join us for lunch the following day. You might think that we behaved in an extremely light-headed manner, but he has something about him that is truly attractive. Well, how can I put it, if he were a woman, he would be someone like you.

ASAKO: You don't say. . . . And Akiko's friendship with him did not work out happily.

AKIKO: Last night he came to say farewell. He said we might not be able to see each other again in this world. . . . I repeatedly asked why, but he would not tell me. But I could see that he was doing something that might cost him his life.

ASAKO: How could you tell . . . ?

SUEKO: Because the remnants of the Liberal Party are making a lot of noise opposing the Rokumeikan.

ASAKO: So you found out he was one of them, did you?

SUEKO: His father is a famous one. The mere mention of his name terrifies people—the leader of the opposition group. Do you not know Kiyohara Einosuke?

ASAKO: *(Upset)* Did you say Kiyohara?

AKIKO: Because of a certain circumstance, he is not living with his father, but from his fierce temperament I know he is preparing to give up his life for his father.

ASAKO: What is his name?

SUEKO: Hisao is his name.

ASAKO: *(Alarmed)* Hisao. . . . I understand. So what is it that I can do? How can I rescue Akiko? Tell me. I'll do anything I can.

SUEKO: My wish is to end this terrible day without an incident so that tomorrow, with no one hurt, we may let this child and Hisao leave for some distant place. What I'd like you to do is this: for one thing, to rescue the happiness of these young people, and for another, for your own sake. . . .

ASAKO: For my own sake?

SUEKO: Yes, you have the power to rescue your husband. Hisao does not tell us anything, but rumor has it that the Liberal Party is aiming to assassinate your husband. If Hisao abandons his mission and decides to elope with Akiko, the danger to your husband may go away, too.

ASAKO: For my husband. . . . I think it's better to leave him out of this. I'd rather you say it is for Hisao and Akiko. Since you have decided to count on me in matters of love, I will do everything I can to open the passage of love for the two of them. For that I can muster courage. No matter how large a tree may be blocking their passage of love, I'll remove it for them, woman though I am. What did you plan to do, should he happen to die?

AKIKO: I planned to kill myself.

ASAKO: Those words alone give me confidence to do everything for you. Listen, Sueko, Hisao's job that might cost him his life, that's the kind of job that makes a man forget things like a woman once he makes up his mind—that is the kind of thing we women must shatter.

SUEKO: It certainly is. We women must work together to grab hold of the legs of a man ready to sprint forward blindly, to pull him back. Men get excited and destroy themselves. The only thing men should reasonably get excited about are women. Everything else is worthless. . . . So you are lending us a hand?

ASAKO: Yes, I am.

SUEKO: Thank you. I truly thank you. This is good news, isn't it, Akiko? Now let us have Hisao come here.

ASAKO: Is he here?

SUEKO: We managed to talk him into coming to your house. We thought that if we could have him meet you and see your gentleness, his heart, hardened with all his political thinking, will melt, and he will stop thinking only with his head and start thinking with his heart. *(She steps down to the garden, turns the telescope toward the audience, then hands it over to Asako.)* Can you see that? Someone moving in the kiosk by the pond? *(She takes out a fan.)* For a signal, I'm supposed to open and shut a fan in front of my chest. See, he's running up the stone steps breathlessly to come here. . . . *(To her daughter)* Come, we shouldn't be here when the two of them talk. The matter is in good hands now. Let's go home and wait for good news. We'll leave it to you, Asako. *(Kusano emerges from her room.)*

ASAKO: Don't worry about it, Akiko.

(Mother and daughter, led by Kusano, leave toward stage right. As they exit, Hisao enters from stage left. In blue ikat and hakama, he is dressed like a university student.)

HISAO: How do you do, ma'am? . . . Where are Mrs. Daitokuji and. . . ?

ASAKO: They left. They thought it would be better if the two of us talked alone.

HISAO: . . .They did, did they?

ASAKO: Come, be seated. Where shall we begin? Well . . . Akiko is beside herself about you. She says if something terrible happens to you, she will immediately follow you, killing herself.

HISAO: She does, does she. . . .

ASAKO: That's a lukewarm response, isn't it? Or are you indicating you don't like Akiko?

HISAO: No, ma'am.

ASAKO: I understand why you are wary of me. My husband is a minister, and your father loathes this cabinet. You are, as it were, in enemy headquarters.

HISAO: Don't talk about my father.

ASAKO: I see. . . . May I choose not to begin with trivial household matters as women are supposed to, but to begin by asking blunt questions as men are supposed to?

HISAO: You are free to ask any question.

ASAKO: I shall, then. What is it that you are attempting to do today, saying farewell to someone you love? *(Getting no response)* The fact that you do not respond means that it is not only a secret but also some spectacular, magnificent task you don't want other people to know in advance, does it not?

HISAO: Not at all. It's the sort of task someone shameless undertakes.

ASAKO: A man should not deprecate something he's going to do, betting his life on it. Regardless of what society at large may think of it, even if it is a crime from a legal point of view.

HISAO: I can tell you this. As you say, I am betting my life on it. I don't know if I will be able to look up at the sun tomorrow. But this is a meaningless act and it will merely add a small stain to history.

ASAKO: If that is the case, why do you feel you have to bet your life on it?

HISAO: I don't like ideals. I heartily dislike things like banners and magnificent shop signs. To show how silly those who die for ideals are, I am going to die for a mere personal thing, for a personal sentiment. But the act itself requires the same courage and presence of mind dying for an ideal does—no, it requires more of it. I think I have courage and presence of mind.

ASAKO: What is going to happen to Akiko?

HISAO: Please do not remind me of her.

ASAKO: What are you going to do? Just tell me. You must tell me. As if you were talking to your mother.

HISAO: This has nothing to do with you.

ASAKO: Still, I am after all the wife of Count Kageyama, whom you are aiming to kill today, assuming that is the case. *(Hisao, with a faint smile on his face, does not respond.)* So you are not going to tell me. *(She hesitates, then says determinedly)* . . . Suppose the wife of the person you are trying to kill is your mother, what do you do?

HISAO: I have nothing like a mother.

ASAKO: You don't? *(She reconsiders and hesitates to make the confession)* . . . Your father brought you up adding your mother's love to his.

HISAO: *(Clearly)* He did not.

ASAKO: No?

HISAO: He did not give an iota of thought to his family. He left everything in his household to the nurses he'd had from long ago. His wife died. Of the five brothers, I was the only one who was not his wife's child, but the child of someone unknown. So the old nurses treated me, only me, shabbily. I alone was brought up in the kitchen. My father doesn't know this. He is an idealist. The only thing he has to do is remain devoted to his ideal.

ASAKO: Well, I never suspected anything like that.

HISAO: Why should you? It's someone else's household. Anyway, as I grew up, I began to resent my father. He is an outstanding human being. An impeccable idealist. A figure like a leader of the French Revolution. A genuine liberal. And this idealist's home is totally dark and depressing, not something you can show to people. . . . It is natural that I should gradually have begun to harbor doubts about ideals. In time I began to be obsessed with the thought of putting my father's ideals in a ridiculous light. Last year I left my house. I began to associate with hooligans. . . . I can't tell you what has happened since. . . . I see you are crying. Why? You feel sorry for me. What can I do to keep you from feeling sorry for me? Shall I praise my father? . . . Yes, I have a mountain of words of praise for him, if you excluded my position, my life. Kiyohara Einosuke. He's a noble character. I have never once seen him behave in a despicable manner. He is utterly unconcerned about money; he's a man like a fireball when it comes to his ideal. A believer in Rousseau, a Japanese Jacobin, a man who doesn't give a damn about his life for liberty and equality, an idol for hot-blooded young men. When he dies, he will be deified in some new, smart-looking shrine.

ASAKO: I see now. So you are dying for your noble, coldhearted father.

HISAO: I leave it to your imagination.

ASAKO: The time has come to reveal my secret. Listen, I must reveal to you today a secret I have kept for more than twenty years, a secret that as a mere girl I decided not to tell anyone for the rest of my life.

HISAO: You are going to tell this to me, someone you've met for the first time?

ASAKO: Yes, to you, whom I have met for the first time, to you, who have grown up marvelously but who carry my sin in your dark face . . . you, who have the right to punish me in whatever way you like, to trample me under your feet. . . . Of course I could make an excuse for myself. As a young girl, I single-mindedly believed this, that when your father made the kind offer to take care of you, I, though I felt torn apart, decided that was best for your future, for your career. Separated from you—you weren't yet one year old—I cried and cried night after night, sometimes on the verge of deciding to kill myself. Still, when I thought of your future, I couldn't possibly make you a fatherless child.

HISAO: You are saying you are my mother. (*He thinks for a while.*) I can't believe in such a farcical story.

ASAKO: I understand why you don't. Ask me questions. Question me on various things. Then you will gradually see that I am not telling you a lie.

HISAO: I'll ask you then, assuming that you put your child in my father's custody and withdrew yourself, what happened to you after that?

ASAKO: I lived as a half-invalid for a long time.

HISAO: Then what happened?

ASAKO: I gradually resigned myself to it. . . . I was a geisha.

HISAO: Then what happened?

ASAKO: A cruel inquiry! But that's all right. You must ask me about anything. So, after that . . . *(Looking away)* I gradually forgot.

HISAO: Ah, you are honest. I can at least see that. And then, long afterward, you came here as a bride. *(After a pause, Asako nods in silence. Hisao becomes worked up despite himself.)* About the time you forgot about me, I began to grow up. My body became equipped with a heart, equipped with sorrows and anxieties. Listen to this. Ever since I became aware of things, I have not had a single day when I did not think of my mother, who was unknown to me. And you had completely forgotten about me. *(Catching himself)* All this is nonsensical. Duped by an unbelievable farce and getting so excited.

ASAKO: *(Quietly)* I know—that you have a small birthmark on the right side of your back shaped like a maple leaf, that you have a small, thin scar on your left kneecap. . . . One summer afternoon, after you fell asleep, I began to doze despite myself. Then you woke, crawled away, and stabbed your knee on a pair of scissors. The wound was big enough to require two stitches. . . . I was a careless mother. I am certain that I could not have brought you up to be such a magnificent young man.

HISAO: *(Worked up again but restraining his emotion)* That's enough! That's enough, I say. You know everything. Know everything. Unmistakably you are my mother. I guarantee it. All you need is my guaranty, isn't it? . . . I beg you to keep your mouth shut for a while. *(A long silence.)* . . . And did you love my father?

ASAKO: Yes, I was utterly in love with him. *(Silence. Suddenly, from stage left, there is a distant rumble of artillery being fired.)* What is it?

HISAO: That's the gun salute on the Emperor's birthday. The artillery of the imperial guards has begun to fire a hundred and one times. . . . And even now?

ASAKO: Yes?

HISAO: Are you still in love with my father?

ASAKO: About the time I forgot about being a mother, I became a woman once again. You must think it's all so shallow of me. Since about that time, every day, every month. . . .

(There is another roar of firing.)

HISAO: Yes?

ASAKO: . . . every month, every year, my longing for your father deep-
ened and I no longer could *not* think about him. Even after I came to
the Kageyama family, this did not change. I have no excuse for my husband, but I have never yearned for anyone but your father. And this
feeling became stronger after I stopped seeing him. . . .

(Another roar of artillery. —A silence.)

HISAO: The man I plan to kill tonight is not your husband.

ASAKO: Pardon?

HISAO: The man I plan to assassinate tonight is my father.

CURTAIN

ACT 2

*One o'clock on the afternoon of the same day. The stage set is exactly the same
as act 1. As the curtain rises, Asako and Kusano are standing, talking.*

KUSANO: Milady, shouldn't you check your watch once again?

ASAKO: *(She takes a small gold watch out of the sash, opens its lid, and takes a
look.)* It is one o'clock. He's still not here. No matter what happens, I
must have a talk with him before our lordship returns from the lunch-
eon meeting of the cabinet. Kusano, may I trust that you have done
everything without a hitch?

KUSANO: Yes, ma'am, I didn't miss a thing.

ASAKO: You gave all the proper instructions to the gatekeeper of the rear
gate, did you not?

KUSANO: Do not worry. *(She walks to the stage-right side of the teahouse and
makes a gesture suggesting that she is looking down.)* Milady, the gatekeeper
is waving a towel. He's finally come.

ASAKO: Would you return the signal? Quick!

*(Kusano waves a handkerchief. The two of them turn their backs to the audience
and take a good look for a while. They return to stage front.)*

ASAKO: He's coming! He's coming! Kusano, what a shameless thing I have
done—as if bringing in a paramour!

KUSANO: This is no time to be saying such a thing. You are on the verge
of saving the lives of three people: Mr. Kiyohara, Mr. Hisao, and Miss
Akiko.

ASAKO: But think of it, Kusano. I've been simply left imagining what
rumor has said, that as he grew older, he became even more magnificent. I've stayed home, without going out all these years and months, as
a means of avoiding running into him. Now, all of a sudden, I send a
messenger to summon him. No matter how he may have changed, no

matter how my feeling has remained unchanged, I can imagine how aged and ugly I'll look in his eyes.

KUSANO: You are so young and beautiful. . . .

ASAKO: Don't try to give me false comfort. Does he prefer Japanese-style clothes or is he dressed Western-style? He's as strongly opposed to this present cabinet as to the fusses made at the Rokumeikan, so I'm sure he dislikes Western suits. On the other hand, men's tastes, I must say, have nothing to do with their ideology or thought. If he dislikes Japanese-style clothes now, how can I see him in this kimono with a trailing hem? . . . Oh, my heart is pounding like a girl's. Let me quickly see the mirror again. Take a look, Kusano. Isn't my age more clearly etched on my face than usual because I am tense with the thought of telling such grave news? At my age, it is difficult to show sincerity and youthfulness at the same time, isn't it? Because, you see, you can't look young unless you work some trick and working a trick subtracts from the crucial thing, sincerity.

KUSANO: Rest assured, milady, that your great decision illuminates you from the inside like a morning sun, making your face youthfully taut, so you do not even have to put on rouge. . . . He's here. I hear the sound of his shoes coming up the stone steps.

ASAKO: Bring him here right away. And while I'm speaking with him, you must keep the telescope turned toward the main building to watch out for his lordship.

(Kiyohara, dressed in a suit, enters from behind the teahouse. Kusano announces his arrival and, as instructed, turns the telescope toward the main building.)

ASAKO: Come, come this way. In case something happens and you must leave quickly, be seated on the verandah.

KIYOHARA: I have not seen you for a long time.

ASAKO: You haven't changed. . . . You certainly have not changed at all. Your hair remains glossy black.

KIYOHARA: Did you expect to see a man bent down? If I have not aged, that is probably because of the government's repression. I have seen with my own eyes that in any country the repressed people are more youthful than the rulers. Still, I must say this theory can't explain your mysterious youthfulness.

ASAKO: That must be because yours is true youthfulness and mine false. But the way you make lighthearted jokes, you are exactly as you were twenty years ago. Why is it that words also come out of my mouth without any effort? I had expected to become tongue-tied once I saw you.

KIYOHARA: We must have been preparing ourselves so that we might be able to relive some hours of the past any moment. We meet, and from that instant the hours of the past begin. This makes us a little giddy, but once we let ourselves go we can carry ourselves forward with ease.

ASAKO: Do you think we can? Mysterious, the way we are now, I do not feel at all awkward; I feel liberated. As if the air had suddenly become easy to inhale. As if I had come out of a crowded, close room suddenly into a spacious field. . . . How is it that we can be so natural?

KIYOHARA: Is it not because you have been away from natural feelings for far too long?

ASAKO: That must be it. The idea that love is suffocating is a childish thought, isn't it? Look at this. I am meeting you for the first time in such a long while, but my hands aren't even trembling. On the contrary, they are far livelier than usual, they feel like wings.

KIYOHARA: *(Holding her hands)* Don't fly away on those wings. Even with you here, time flies away relentlessly. Let's talk quickly. To tell the truth, I myself had to meet you to apologize to you. It's about Hisao. . . .

ASAKO: Hisao!

KIYOHARA: Yes. I was an incompetent father. That's the only conclusion I can reach.

ASAKO: Hisao. . . .

KIYOHARA: Have you heard anything about him?

ASAKO: No, no, nothing.

KIYOHARA: He left us suddenly last year. I have absolutely no idea where he went. He did not leave a note or anything. I think he's alive. I hope he is, but I can't be definite about it. I did not have the time to look after my family, and I could not do anything for him. But if he decides to come back, I am ready to welcome him warmly, any time.

ASAKO: *(In deliberate astonishment)* You tell me all that about Hisao!

KIYOHARA: I must apologize to you. I am sorry for all this.

ASAKO: Please do not apologize to me. Now that you have told me, I shall do my best to locate him. But if we find him, what's important is your feeling. May I ask, Mr. Kiyohara, if you are going to continue to have a fatherly feeling for him?

KIYOHARA: Even now it hasn't changed. He's a single-minded good fellow. Compared with my other boys, he hasn't inherited my unpleasant side. Your virtues, along with my virtues, which are probably very few, make him up, and he has grown to be a young man so single-minded as to be vulnerable. I love him. I couldn't show him any favor, but my fatherly feeling was more inclined toward him than toward the other sons. In retrospect, I should not have hidden these feelings but brought them out more.

ASAKO: Things seldom work out the way you want. No, they don't. . . . But I am relieved to hear what you have told me. No, this is no time to be feeling relieved. If your feeling is as you say it is, here is something I must ask you to do, no matter what. There is no other way to save your fatherly feeling and heal Hisao's wounded heart. It may even be that this is the only way to save the two lives, yours and Hisao's.

KIYOHARA: You know something about Hisao.

ASAKO: No, I know nothing. Even if I did, please do not ask me about it now. Don't ask anything. Besides, your imminent danger has nothing to do with him.

KIYOHARA: My imminent danger?

ASAKO: I'll tell you straightforwardly. Your life will be in danger tonight.

KIYOHARA: Pardon?

ASAKO: You don't believe me. I went out of my way to ask you to come today, because I wanted to help you.

KIYOHARA: I am grateful for your sentiments, but I am a man who lives with danger. Danger is my daily routine. Even this talk with you is part of my dangerous life. I have lived through storms, and I feel suffocated in a breeze. Allow me to declaim a little. Only ferocious summers and stern winters become me. Balmy springlike weather such as this is no more than a poison for me. So even on a day like this, I must have a scorching summer and a freezing winter ready inside me. That's what freedom is all about. And I must awaken those who are dozing, duped by this spring-like weather. . . . That's what I think. I have never tried to save my life.

ASAKO: You are exactly what you used to be. You are the same as twenty years ago. You, who are always youthful!

KIYOHARA: Even as I have grown old, an incorrigible child continues to inhabit me.

ASAKO: You must treasure that child. Women love, and the masses love, that unblemished child in a fierce, magnificent man. Trusting that child, I'll tell you the rest. I know—that tonight, under your direction, the young zealots[1] among the remnants of the Liberal Party plan to break into the ball at the Rokumeikan with drawn swords. And you will park your hansom outside the fence of the Rokumeikan to direct the men who carry out the break-in. Is this not true?

KIYOHARA: *(In consternation)* How do you know this?

ASAKO: I am only telling you what I know.

KIYOHARA: You know. And you accuse me. For a woman, that is quite understandable. I suppose you want to tell me this: What on earth could such a dangerous harassment accomplish? Or to borrow your husband's manner of speech, I could put it this way: The government is pressing

---

1. The *sōshi:* Initially the fighters for liberty and civil rights who came into being in the mid-1880s; not long afterward, many of them came to be identified as chauvinistic fanatics not averse to resorting to intimidation and extortion for their private gain. Normally they had no professions and stayed with rich businessmen and politicians.

for treaty revisions for the future of Japan. For this purpose, we must show the foreign people a civilized and enlightened Japan that deserves treaty revisions. We must show them not the Japan of cholera and terrorism, but the balls at the Rokumeikan. In these circumstances, why should you bring in young zealots in white headbands brandishing drawn swords and show them once again a barbarous and primitive Japan? —This has become a cliché. It's just a humiliating excuse.

ASAKO: Why do you say that to me? I have never told you anything from my husband's position. You speak as if my husband were saying things through my mouth, as if this were all a trap set up by my husband. Your suspicions are too much. Such suspicions do not become you.

KIYOHARA: I know it—I know your true feeling. I went a bit too far in my indignation. Forgive me. But the fact that the information that no one is supposed to have has been detected suggests only that it came to you through your husband.

ASAKO: No, I swear. This did not come from my husband. I found it out myself, and I worried about your life, and decided to plead with you like this. Please abandon your plan tonight.

KIYOHARA: *(After a long silence)* It is known. . . . It's known. *(But he renews his resolve.)* . . . . I thank you for your good intentions. I regret that the plan has leaked out, but this is something I decided to do, so I'll carry it out. As for my life, I take enough precautions and you needn't worry. Your telling me that the plan has leaked out beforehand has been immeasurably helpful. Thank you. I am grateful.

ASAKO: Please abandon it. I plead with you. Abandon it!

KIYOHARA: You think this is all silly. For a lady that's understandable. But, listen, Asako.

ASAKO: Oh, you have called me by name for the first time.

KIYOHARA: But, listen. It is well known that you dislike politics. You are in the midst of evil government and evil diplomacy, so that is entirely natural. You know about the *Maria Luz* incident. In the Japan of the fifth year of Meiji there were such great instances of independent diplomacy. There were spectacular men of justice such as Ōe. Soejima, the minister of foreign affairs at the time, was also a great man, and the American legal counsel, P. Smith, worked for Japan's independent diplomacy. Everything went downhill as soon as the Satsuma and Chōshū factions started running the government. We went back to the age that submitted itself to the roaring commands of British minister Parkes. Who among the foreigners invited to the Rokumeikan do you think reassess and respect the civilized and enlightened Japan as the government hopes? All of them are laughing at us up their sleeves. They are sneering at us. They think ladies of nobility are the same as cheap dancing girls and regard their dances as monkey dances. The subservient smiles of ranking government officials and aristocratic ladies do not help treaty revisions at all, but simply intensify the foreigners' contempt. Listen to me, Asako. I know this because I have made a round of visits to foreign countries. Foreign people never respect you unless you have self-respect, unless you are a people with self-respect. The young zealots' break-in may be a silly thing, but if I manage to throw a cold blanket over the government and show the foreigners that there are Japanese with guts, I'll be satisfied. I have ordered them not to give even a scratch to the guests while brandishing their swords. Those young men may simply do a sword dance or two and withdraw with fanfare. That's all. . . . I don't expect anything more. The world at large is talking as if I were the boss of murderers, but that's no more than rootless rumor. If I am killed for doing such a thing, it certainly will be a dog's death, but people who carry forward my wishes will appear one after another. . . . You understand, don't you? Since I was young, I have never been able to put up with my own humiliation or any act that people voluntarily perform to humiliate themselves.

ASAKO: I think I understand what you are saying perfectly well. But I must repeat myself. Please abandon the plan. When a man does something just, a woman should not try to stop him. I know that well. Yet, I plead with you—like this. *(She places her hands on the verandah in a bowing posture.)* Please abandon the plan.

KIYOHARA: I cannot, not at this late hour. You never go to a ball. I may give some trouble to your husband, but not to you.

ASAKO: *(As if something occurred to her)* To a ball at the Rokumeikan . . . me?

KIYOHARA: They say you never attend official functions, no matter what. This has suited me perfectly. I knew you were different from the others after all.

ASAKO: Me, to a ball? . . . Mr. Kiyohara, suppose, suppose I break my own rule for the first time in my life and go to the ball, what would you do?

KIYOHARA: You, to the ball? That can't happen.

ASAKO: I say, suppose. Suppose I do, would you despise me?

KIYOHARA: That should not happen.

ASAKO: If I did, people would clap their hands and laugh. There would be no greater shame than that to me. But I would be getting what I deserve. To put it in a Western way, if I were to attend the ball that my husband is hosting, then the ball strictly would no longer be his, but mine— Asako's ball.

KIYOHARA: I should imagine so.

ASAKO: In that event, your men would be ruining not my husband's ball, but my ball. You would be damaging not my husband's honor, but my honor.

KIYOHARA: You've come up with a difficult question.

ASAKO: *(Coquettishly)* Or are you saying you wouldn't like me in Western dress?

KIYOHARA: I can't even imagine. You might look good, or. . . .

ASAKO: I might look like a monkey.

KIYOHARA: A beautiful monkey, no doubt.

ASAKO: Ludicrous, isn't it, Countess Monkey! But that will be all right with me. Tonight I'll be a monkey, as you say.

KIYOHARA: Asako.

ASAKO: Can you imagine what a bold gesture it will be, what kind of sacrifice it will be to me? A woman would rather die than destroy an assessment made of her, a reputation she has created for herself. I will destroy mine tonight, for you.

KIYOHARA: That will be unbearable. You are going to throw yourself into the whirlpool of politics. . . .

ASAKO: No, we are not talking about politics. We are talking about love. Do you understand? You must make a response in kind—not of politics, but of love.

KIYOHARA: What do you mean?

ASAKO: Just as innocent and poor lovers exchange heartfelt gifts, so do I give you a gift. You will have no use for it, but it comes at any rate from a sincere heart.

KIYOHARA: What is it?

ASAKO: My going to the ball tonight. If you love me, you must respond in some way.

KIYOHARA: It is a hard gift for me to accept.

ASAKO: I know. But this is a gift simply because I'd like to save your life. So if it touches your heart, please respond in kind.

KIYOHARA: I know what that response is supposed to be: my abandoning my plan tonight, my not going to the Rokumeikan. . . . But that I cannot do.

ASAKO: *(Falling on her knees and holding his knees)* Please, I beg you, please. If you love me at all.

KIYOHARA: Ah, you are trying to melt a man's work, a man's obligation. A man can't succumb like this. But succumbing is also. . . .

ASAKO: . . . something only a man can do. From a woman's viewpoint, no honor can be more appropriate for a man than this one.

KIYOHARA: *(Caressing Asako's hair)* Your hair . . . your black hair . . . this hair that the darkness of the night has dyed every night, making it darker, longer, and glossier over the last twenty years when I have been unable to see you. . . .

ASAKO: For this hair the night is always long, the daybreak never coming. When my hair turns completely white and when I cease to be a woman, the dawn will dye my white hair—the dawn that has no suffering or anxiety and has no fear that something will begin during the day.

KIYOHARA: Do you understand—the kind of terror that seizes a man when breaking an obligation is not a sorrow but, rather, a joy?

ASAKO: *(Rising to her feet and sitting close to Kiyohara)* So you have already broken your obligation.

KIYOHARA: You see it well. . . . I promise.

ASAKO: I also promise—to go to the ball tonight, in that shameless attire. And tonight's ball at the Rokumeikan will be mine.

KIYOHARA: I also promise—that I have canceled my plan tonight. My hansom will not go to the Rokumeikan.

ASAKO: I don't know how to thank you.

KIYOHARA: It's reciprocal, reciprocal. You must turn into a monkey, too.

ASAKO: This is wonderful, this is wonderful. To this woman's eyes, you at this moment are a dazzling man. *(Standing up ecstatically, she nips a large yellow chrysanthemum from the garden.)* I'll give you a medal. Women give medals that are not cold and dead with gold and jewelry. *(She puts the chrysanthemum into the buttonhole of Kiyohara's lapel.)* A live medal, a medal that intensifies its shine through frost every morning.

KIYOHARA: But this medal will wilt some day.

ASAKO: Trust me, this will last to the end of this day.

(Kusano, who has been invisible to stage right, enters hurriedly with the telescope in one hand.)

KUSANO: Milady! Milady!

ASAKO: What? *(Rises to her feet.)*

KUSANO: His lordship has returned. He's accompanying a guest, coming toward this place.

ASAKO: *(Handing a handkerchief over to Kusano)* Come, signal with this toward the rear gate in a way his lordship won't notice. *(Guiding Kiyohara protectively)* Quick, from the rear gate. *(She starts to take him to stage right, but turns back toward stage left)* It's better for you to go this way and turn around the back of the teahouse. *(Guiding him from stage left to the back of the room, she leaves. In a while, Kusano and Asako emerge from there, walk on stage right to its end, and hide themselves behind a tree in a way that leaves them clearly visible to the audience.)*

COUNT KAGEYAMA'S VOICE: *(From stage right)* That Senkan-tei is best. It's a good place to talk.

TOBITA TENKOTSU'S VOICE: *(From stage right)* Yes, sir.

(The two of them emerge and go into the teahouse.)

KAGEYAMA: Make yourself comfortable.

TOBITA: It's very kind of you, sir.

KAGEYAMA: As I was saying. . . . You see, Tobita, this is what I think. As-sassination normally refers to the killing by a malcontent element of an important figure of the majority party of the government or someone of the ruling class. It's nice that society at large also believes this. They think, without asking, that an assassin is a remnant of the Liberal Party. Thanks to this, every day I receive equal numbers of letters—those stating why my life must be taken and those sentimental ones saying that a prayer has been offered because of concerns for my life. This puts me in a dilemma, making me wonder if it's all right to die or if I should remain alive. Any-way, you may assume that the majority of people think my life is at risk.

TOBITA: Just as you say, sir.

KAGEYAMA: That is to say, it's highly unlikely that I plan an assassination. Furthermore, even if it comes to light that I did it, everyone would sim-ply assume that I did it in self-defense. Am I right?

TOBITA: Just as you say, sir.

KAGEYAMA: The government in power is always subject to criticism and attack, but criticism as it rises tends to become more and more uniform; it becomes criticism for criticism's sake, its sources becoming more and more immaterial. If Kiyohara Einosuke is killed, people will immediate-ly attack me. Even though no one thinks I killed him, they'll attack me. But that kind of attack will in fact be our friend. As the attack mounts, the clearer my innocence will become to them.

TOBITA: Just as you say, sir.

KAGEYAMA: This is because I am in a position to lament upon hearing Kiyo-hara's death. I'll say, "I have lost a great opponent." The assumption of course is that hatred and murderous intent are only with malcontent el-ements, not, ever, with the government. The opposition represents hu-manity, and the government hypocrisy. . . . I trust you understand this: I am killing Kiyohara not because of hatred or enmity. It's simply be-cause his barking day and night is a bit too loud. You want to kill a dog when its barking annoys you, don't you?

TOBITA: I always kill them. In my neighborhood there is not a single dog alive. Besides, my in-house university students[2] love dog meat and al-ways want it for their cooking pot.

(Behind the tree, the two women register shock.)

---

2. *Shosei:* University students who lived with reasonably well-to-do families; they were provided room and board for running errands and teaching the younger family members. *Shosei* were common until the early Shōwa era (1926–89), though the custom of keeping them evidently peaked around the end of the Meiji era. In earlier periods they were often *sōshi*.

ASAKO: Oh my, the assassination order came from his lordship. Kusano, hold me. How could I have imagined that my husband was the one who put the lives of my old lover and my son in danger! Where in the world is a woman forced to a realization like this?

KUSANO: I understand how you feel, milady, I really do.

TOBITA: I may be repeating myself too much, sir, but why didn't you give that assignment to me? I don't want to boast, but when it comes to the number of people killed since before the restoration, no one can beat me. Also, once I target somebody, I never miss. There isn't a single weapon I don't have experience with—not to mention sword, dagger, spear, I've even used matchlock and pistol. Like you, sir, though saying this may be inappropriate, I have never killed anyone from personal grudge. I have followed an order, in every case. Therefore, I can kill as easily as I deliver an entrusted thing to the designated party, and I don't feel any particular pity. I also love to see blood. I'd say that it's wasteful to normally wrap under the skin something that is prettier than maple leaves and blossoms. What refreshes my heart the most are the clear autumn sky and the color of blood. I'm puzzled why you didn't give this work to me. It would be good for my health, too.

KAGEYAMA: Here you go again. In a different case, I wouldn't have hesitated to turn to you. But this time we have the best assassin you could hope for. By using him, even if it were exposed, it wouldn't be a political assassination. A son kills his father. It's just a personal incident. Just a family incident, you see.

TOBITA: Just as you say, sir.

KAGEYAMA: Was it about a month ago that I met that young man, Hisao? He was staying with you for about half a year. I thought he had something tough about him. He lives a life of loathing.

TOBITA: Besides, he doesn't even try to hide that he's Kiyohara's son.

KAGEYAMA: He has a murderous flash in his eyes. This is something you rarely get. Compared with him, you are like a woman who gets excited with joy to see a Yūzen kimono—your eyes suggest a hobbylike delight at the sight of blood. Of course, I must say that's something to be valued, too.

TOBITA: It's very kind of you to say that, sir.

ASAKO: I had never imagined that his lordship used as a secret weapon a man who says such repugnant, cruel things. This spacious, curiously cold mansion, I now see, has long been a bloody nest of criminal acts. Kusano, I can no longer take it. I must go out and tell his lordship whatever has to be said.

KUSANO: Wait a little while, milady. You shouldn't hurry. You must hear adequately what is being said. You have chanced upon a once-in-a-lifetime opportunity.

ASAKO: You are right in what you say, Kusano. I'll try to restrain my disturbed heart for a while and listen to such scheming as would soil the ears. Ah, I feel as if my hands and feet were being bound in a horrible dream.

TOBITA: But, sir, what I have doubts about is the father-son relationship. You may hate your father a great deal, but can you carry that hatred to the end? Even the tip of the sword you've honed with hatred becomes blunt, I'm afraid, once you press it close to your father's face. I know I am being rude in saying this, sir, but I'm afraid you will not understand this because you have no children. You see, sir, your child is a very lovely thing to you. They say it wouldn't hurt even if you put your child in your eye—well, sir, that happens to be true.

KAGEYAMA: May I venture to suppose that you'd regard the blood of your child as lovely?

TOBITA: Well, sir, that's a wicked joke, sir. When you see your child crawling round, it's so cute you're tempted to put it in your mouth.

KAGEYAMA: Like the favorite sport of the university students you have around, you want to cook it in a pot.

TOBITA: Oh, no, no, no, your joke is sickening, if I may say so, sir. Besides, when my angelic child looks at me and gives me a blooming smile, that smile, that limpid color of his eyes—when I look at it, I can't imagine that even if we ended up as enemies in the future, he would ever turn a sword against me.

KAGEYAMA: You understand children's feelings very well, it seems.

TOBITA: Well, sir, I can thoroughly see through them.

KAGEYAMA: That's why I didn't give the work to you. You can kill only when you don't know the feelings of the man you're killing. To me, that wouldn't be enough. Even if the killing of Kiyohara were to be carried out on my order, I'd like to have complicated sentiments in between. Hisao's suffering, his hesitation—only when there were enough of such things and then if that bastard killed his father could I be satisfied. I love other people's suffering, though I don't necessarily *love* blood. I'd want a current of feelings between the one who kills and the one who gets killed—at least the sparks between them. What I'd like to give Kiyohara is not the honor of having been assassinated, but the irrecoverable humiliation of having been killed by his own son's hand.

TOBITA: Just as you say, sir.

KAGEYAMA: Besides, you can't say your comparison is appropriate, can you? Your child is the child you made between yourself and your wife. But Hisao, though he definitely is Kiyohara's son, has a mother whose *provenance* is utterly unknown. And that's why he suffered throughout his youth.

ASAKO: Even he, my lordship, doesn't know it—that Hisao is my son.

KUSANO: Milady, that is one secret you should keep to yourself. If his lordship knew it—just imagining that is terrifying. . . .

ASAKO: Whatever did you imagine just now?

KUSANO: Well, milady, I must say to you that his lordship, coldhearted though he may be, loves you dearly, from the bottom of his heart.

KAGEYAMA: And that's why I'm saying this. The love between blood relations turns into horrible hatred once it becomes twisted. The relationship between parent and child, between brothers, where there is no flow of understanding, becomes more distant than the one between strangers. I do understand Hisao's hatred of his father, understand it very well indeed. Politics is the ability to understand the hatreds of people who are strangers to you. You see, it is to take advantage of the hundreds of thousands and millions of cogs of hatred that turn this world round, and then to try to move it. . . . Let's see, for example, look at those chrysanthemums. Luxuriant yellow petals piling one upon another, they are gently swaying in the breeze. Now, do you think that they are the end result of the gardener's meticulous caring and love? If you do, you can't be a politician. A politician would understand these chrysanthemums this way: these are the flowering of the gardener's hatred. The gardener's discontent over his poor wages, which leads to his hatred of his master, that is to say, me—that kind of hatred of which the gardener himself is not aware has congealed and magnificently translated into that blooming. Every flower-raiser smells of vengeance. The same is true of painters, writers, and artists. What they create are large chrysanthemums raised by the hatreds of the powerless.

TOBITA: Just as you say, sir.

KAGEYAMA: Have you read the silly novel called Setchūbai, by Suehiro Tetchō?[3] No, no, this is no time to talk about novels. I trust all the preparations and details are in place for tonight.

TOBITA: I have talked to Hisao about everything, sir, and nothing is amiss. Her Highness the imperial princess and her entourage are expected to come to the ball at the Rokumeikan at ten-thirty this evening. Kiyohara and his bunch don't want their actions to affect members of the imperial court. They are expected to break in before ten. About that time, Kiyohara is supposed to park his hansom outside the fence of the Rokumeikan to use it as his command post and observe the developments. When Kiyohara's men break in, leaving his cab unguarded, Hisao will attack him out of the darkness. That's the plan, sir.

(During this conversation, Asako, who wants to come from behind the tree, struggles with Kusano, who tries to restrain her. In the end she comes out, crosses the

---

3. A critic and politician (1849–96) who took part in the movement to promote liberty and civil rights in early Meiji.

*small bridge hung over the rivulet, and stands in front of her husband without em-
barrassment. And as Tobita finishes his words. . . .)*

ASAKO: Sir, that information is wrong. There will be no break-in tonight.

TOBITA: Oh, milady.

KAGEYAMA: *(Skillfully hiding his surprise, and politely)* Lo and behold, we
have a rare guest joining us.

ASAKO: Yes, I have been eavesdropping.

KAGEYAMA: This is something I wouldn't have expected. So you have
begun to take an interest in politics, have you? If that is the case, I'd be
your guide in politics.

ASAKO: But the kind of politics I just heard discussed is of the most despicable kind. Since it was the first I heard. . . .

KAGEYAMA: You are right, you are right. You happened to see the sewage
of politics before anything else. From now on, I will show you the
kitchen, the dining room, and the guest room as chance arises. . . . Now,
with much confidence, you have just now conveyed to us some fascinating information, have you not?

ASAKO: Well, I do not know if it is fascinating to you, sir.

KAGEYAMA: There's no need to tease me.

ASAKO: I said the break-in at the ball tonight has been abandoned.

KAGEYAMA: I see. I don't know where the information comes from, but
do you have a reliable source?

ASAKO: I can't tell you. But I can invoke all the deities of heaven and earth
for my words. There will be no break-in tonight.

KAGEYAMA: Invoking the deities of heaven and earth is something you
have never done. You can only invoke yourself. You can only invoke
your glossy black hair.

ASAKO: Now I can expect noble and beautiful words on politics.

KAGEYAMA: Tobita, you may excuse yourself now. *(Tobita diffidently bows
and leaves toward stage right. At the same time Kusano retires into a room in the
teahouse.)* Come, let's hear your political theory. Let's find out definitely where that fascinating information of yours comes from. *(He smiles as
he says this.)*

ASAKO: A surprise. You smile gently as you always do, as if you were
making some joke. *(Sensuously)* You must remember that you are the
person whose horrible secret has just been divulged to his eavesdropping wife.

KAGEYAMA: From early on, you've known that nothing surprises me.

ASAKO: I have, but I'd have expected you to react at least like a child discovered in hide-and-seek.

KAGEYAMA: Men are proud of their ability to remain calm, but women
seem not to like it.

ASAKO: We think it lovable when a man who is normally imperturbable becomes perturbed. . . .

KAGEYAMA: But I know—that no matter what secret you may have, you will simply put it in your feminine box never to bring it out to a public place. I'd be happy to take this opportunity to reveal all the political secrets to you.

ASAKO: I'm glad you trust me.

KAGEYAMA: So may I assume that your eavesdropping was of an innocent kind?

ASAKO: I am no longer young enough to be innocent. But I wouldn't mind your thinking that way.

KAGEYAMA: You must be angry about something. I wonder if there was something in my talk with Tobita that made you angry.

ASAKO: (To forestall her husband's further probing, she says with deliberate cheerfulness) Talk of murdering someone may scare a woman, but it won't make her angry. A woman becomes angry only when she's betrayed in love or out of jealousy.

KAGEYAMA: You are saying the discovery that your husband was a murderer is nothing to be angry about.

ASAKO: You are right, sir.

KAGEYAMA: Oh, you are such a broad-minded person. An understanding, tolerant character. I might not necessarily be able to say that you are a warm-hearted person—a good-natured person isn't my type, you see. . . . Well, now, how about dealing with the main subject? Where did you hear the rumor that the break-in tonight has been abandoned?

ASAKO: It's not rumor; it's fact.

KAGEYAMA: Normally, we wouldn't call fact something that has yet to happen.

ASAKO: Then you are saying the break-in tonight is also mere rumor.

KAGEYAMA: You got me there. . . . Yes. . . . Come, say it. Tell me any thoughts you may have.

ASAKO: When you compare the two rumors and compare the two persons who have brought these rumors to you, you will see which is closer to fact. One of them is Tobita, and the other me.

KAGEYAMA: I am not saying I don't believe you, but Tobita is a professional in that field, and you are, as it were, an amateur.

ASAKO: Which do you accept—something a professional says to protect his job or something your wife, amateur though she may be, tells you by invoking all the deities of heaven and earth?

KAGEYAMA: (Thinking for a while with eyes closed) Hmm. . . . All right. I believe you, not him. This is a husband's duty, you see. . . . Hmm, hmm, still, all this means that you have casually discarded your retiring habit of

all these years, giving me political advice for the first time. May I take it
that from now on you will cooperate with me in politics?

ASAKO: You have plenty of people who cooperate with you, don't you?

KAGEYAMA: Who are they?

ASAKO: All those beautiful ladies who gather at the Rokumeikan.

KAGEYAMA: Today is full of surprises. You are saying you are jealous?

ASAKO: What will you do if you see that my jealousy has become so bad I
am scheming something that will truly perturb you?

KAGEYAMA: You are not planning to assassinate me, are you?

ASAKO: No. Something wonderful. I am scheming something that will
give you a lot of trouble.

KAGEYAMA: Tell me. Tell me.

ASAKO: I am going to go to the ball at the Rokumeikan tonight.

KAGEYAMA: What?

ASAKO: *(She rises to her feet and begins to dance.)* I'll wear a décolletage that
you've had made for me, try the steps you have taught me, and shock
everybody tonight. Like this, sir, I'll wonderfully dance the waltz and
polka and make those supercilious ladies blanch. The ball at the
Rokumeikan tonight won't be a ball but my geisha debut, which I once
had in Shimbashi. I can dance. *I* can dance. You see, just like this. Besides, when it comes to handling gentlemen, I'm far more experienced
than the run-of-the-mill lady, am I not?

KAGEYAMA: Come, now, don't forget that you are now a legitimate aristocratic lady.

ASAKO: All the other ladies may have high purposes, for Japan, for politics,
when they sally forth to the Rokumeikan, but all I want is to show how
sensuous a woman can be. That opportunity has finally arrived. My
feigned timidity all these years has been just for tonight.

KAGEYAMA: Well, well, you are a far more elaborate conspirator than I am.
So how about the break-in. . . ?

ASAKO: I am going to the ball. I will not allow any zealots to enter the place.

KAGEYAMA: So that is the source of your information.

ASAKO: It is a magnificent source.

KAGEYAMA: *(With a bitter smile)* You must have some logic.

ASAKO: A woman doesn't need anything like logic. I tell you now. *(In a
declarative tone)* Tonight I shall go to the ball. And there will be no break-
in by any toughs. Should there be a break-in, I'd never see you alive.
(They glare at each other. A long silence.)

KAGEYAMA: I see. . . . So, what is it you want me to do?

ASAKO: Free the university student named Hisao from that horrible assignment right away and put him in my custody.

KAGEYAMA: If there is going to be no break-in as you say, Hisao tonight will have nothing to do. But what does a university student have to do with you. . . ?

ASAKO: Marchioness Daitokuji asked me. The student is her daughter's lover.

KAGEYAMA: *(After thinking with eyes closed)* All right. I agree. I'll put him in your custody on condition that there will be no break-in tonight as you say.

ASAKO: I thank you very much. This takes care of everything. . . . Oh, thanks to you, this Emperor's birthday is going to end peacefully—in clear springlike weather, with the fragrance of chrysanthemums wafting quietly through the air.

KAGEYAMA: Yes . . . peacefully.

ASAKO: I detest the smell of gunpowder.

KAGEYAMA: This is just the smoke from the gun salute in the parade ground.

ASAKO: There will be fireworks in the evening. . . . Let us hope that all the powder prepared for today will explode only for celebration!

KAGEYAMA: *(Still thinking about something)* It will. Today is a felicitous day.

ASAKO: Let us hope that all the red throughout today will be confined to the rising sun of the national flag and the wines for the banquet!

KAGEYAMA: *(Looking away)* I don't like blood, either.

ASAKO: This bright mild sunlight must not betray human beings.

KAGEYAMA: Rest assured. I should have chosen a different day. On a bright, balmy day like this, nothing can happen.

(From stage right, a maid runs in.)

MAID: Milady, Mrs. Daitokuji has arrived.

ASAKO: I see. Would you ask her to wait? I'll be there right away.

KAGEYAMA: Yes. I'll join you soon.

ASAKO: Before you, sir, then. Excuse me.

(She exits to stage right, with the maid walking in front of her. Kusano, who had emerged during the conversation, hurriedly tries to follow Asako, but Asako exits without noticing it. Kageyama, standing at stage center, blocks Kusano. She steps to the right, and he steps to the right; she steps to the left, and he steps to the left, blocking her way. Each time she bows in her attempt to get away, but fails.)

KAGEYAMA: You are loyal to her ladyship, aren't you? . . . Very loyal. . . . She always praises you. . . . Very loyal. . . .

(He suddenly grabs her, holds her tightly, and kisses the astonished woman violently.)

KUSANO: Sir. . . . Sir. . . .

CURTAIN

ACT 3

Four o'clock on the afternoon of the same day. Before sunset.

The second floor of the Rokumeikan. To stage right, the banisters of a large staircase from the first floor are visible. At the center is an exit to the balcony. From the balcony, too, you can go down to the front garden. To its left, in front of the wall, is a buffet table loaded with drinks and appetizers. To stage left, there is a tall entrance decorated with a raised sumptuous drapery, suggesting a large ballroom beyond it. Further to the left, there is the suggestion of another staircase leading to the first floor. Chairs are placed here and there.

As the curtain rises, the door to the balcony at the center is open, and Akiko in her décolletage and Hisao in his suit are leaning against the balustrade.

The evening glow is in the sky.

AKIKO: The sun is setting.

HISAO: A wonderful evening glow, isn't it? The forest of Hibiya looks as if it were set on fire.

AKIKO: Why doesn't anyone try to dance in this evening glow? They dance only late at night, in man-made light, to man-made music, on the man-made floor. . . .

HISAO: I'm sure it is because this evening glow is too large, too roaring a kind of music. In this kind of music, your feet would become too intimidated to dance. It would become suffocating and you wouldn't be able to laugh.

AKIKO: You say that because you look pained but you don't want me to worry about it. Why do you still feel sorry? I no longer feel any worry; I can breathe so comfortably that I would dance in this evening glow. Besides, you look so nice in your suit. Truly nice. We owe all this to Mrs. Kageyama.

HISAO: She ordered me to wear something like this and come to the ball tonight. She told me never to leave her side. She's still worried, I think, that I might do something terrible if I went out of her sight for a moment.

AKIKO: You talk as if you didn't like it! She's our savior, isn't she? You agreed, did you not, to take a long trip with me once this night is over, because she persuaded you not to do your work tonight? I'm sorry. I'm selfish in being overjoyed with things that are going my way. But please don't feel bad. Because I think my joy, my happiness, is also your happiness. . . . I'm glad you decided not to do it. No, I wouldn't say it was for me. It was because Mrs. Kageyama skillfully, sincerely, and with all her gentleness, dissuaded you. As if she were your mother.

HISAO: *(Startled)* My mother? . . . . No, that isn't the case. It's just that, how shall I put it, I succumbed to her simple, unadorned personality.

AKIKO: You are right. Everyone succumbs to her. You succumb, but with a pleasant feeling. . . .

HISAO: Yes. With her egoism and all, but everything so pleasant.

AKIKO: Again you are speaking ill of the person who saved you. A bad boy!

HISAO: To make up for being quiet as she tells me to, I can, can't I, speak ill of her a little. When I speak ill of her, I'm actually praising her. She has lived her life as she pleases. Moreover, no one can blame her for that. Suppose she were a bird. Suddenly she spreads her pretty wings, flies in the window to your table, perches on the rim of your soup plate, and begins to sing—everyone will be enchanted to hear her song and won't try to stop her rude behavior.

AKIKO: Yes, she's like that.

HISAO: And that same bird—let's see, suppose she lays an egg. She does that in someone else's nest. The fledgling will grow up in a nasty environment. But she won't be blamed for that. Why? Because the young bird will begin to console himself with the song she sings throughout the forest. And despite himself he will gradually begin to pray that no note of sadness will enter her song, that her song will remain a cheerful love song, never aging.

AKIKO: Listening to you, I begin to feel jealous of her.

HISAO: Jealous. . . . You don't know her well.

AKIKO: What a thing to say! You met her today, for the first time. . . . But *I* shouldn't speak ill of her. You, in any case, because of her, have returned from the world of terrifying work to the world of the gentle love of women. *(Fingering Hisao's jacket buttons)* Now I'm going to sew each of these buttons to my kimono with an invisible thread. Think of me as that large tent for Charine's circus horses under the starry sky, where we met for the first time. The top of that tent was sewn into the starry sky with an invisible thread, and that is why the tent did not collapse to the ground. . . . These buttons on your chest are the stars, and I am the tent that is finally tied to them and can now withstand the wind. . . . If you go away from me, the tent will collapse to the ground . . . and will die.

HISAO: But, listen, suppose . . . suppose the sky is clouded, what would you do?

AKIKO: No matter how clouded the sky, I'll do everything I can to find a star.

(Hisao holds her in his arms and kisses her for a long time.)

(Then the voice of Daitokuji Sueko is heard as she is climbing up the staircase to stage right.)

SUEKO: *(Only her voice)* Wonderful, wonderful! It looks so nice on you! Oh, please keep standing there! *(She comes up to the top of the staircase in décolletage and speaks toward the lower part of the staircase)* Yes, there, lean on the railings and look up at me. Like a picture, Asako, you are like a Western picture!

ASAKO: *(Coming up to the top of the staircase, in a décolletage)* It is so hard to climb up a staircase in a dress like this! No, it isn't that my feet get tangled. I'm used to that because of the kimono with trailing hems that I wear. Climbing up a staircase in a dress like this, I feel naked.

SUEKO: You are bold to say that. I like you because of that. I do. But you are such a wicked person! By saying you liked neither Western dress nor dance, you had deceived us. In reality, you look so nice. Tonight you will outshine everybody else, making us pale. We may be used to wearing décolletage, but we have shown ourselves so often that we can't startle all the guests as you will.

ASAKO: Akiko, your mother is such a flatterer that I am embarrassed. You must help me.

SUEKO: So you have arrived before us.

AKIKO: We are supposed to be here four hours before the ball starts to help.

HISAO: Is there anything I can do?

ASAKO: Thank you. This is my first time here and there are a host of things I do not understand. You must help me in everything. *(Clapping her hands)* Please, would you start decorating the place.

(From stage left the headwaiter enters and instructs the waiters to bring in potted chrysanthemums and other things. During the following conversations, a carpenter and others also appear to do things like putting up decorations on the pillar and hanging a bunting and, on the wall at stage left, a purple drapery with a white chrysanthemum crest dyed in it. Things like stepladders and step stools may also be brought in.)

SUEKO: I hope the two of you thanked Lady Asako adequately. Everything has worked out the way it has, thanks to her. All the past trouble has been eliminated, and you have the happiness you wished to have.

ASAKO: You shouldn't talk about the future. You shouldn't talk about the fancy dinner until you finish eating the whole thing. Because, you see, the happiness of these young people, your happiness, Sueko, and also my happiness—all this depends on our trust in other people.

SUEKO: When trusted by someone like you, one can only respond in kind.

ASAKO: I do not rate myself that highly. But it certainly is true that you can count on time better than human beings. No matter how trusting they may be. . . . You see, Sueko, for mutual trust between two people to deepen takes a great deal of time.

HISAO: There is also a lost time, and a long time, that was forgotten.

ASAKO: I am talking about time in the future. Young people shouldn't think about time in the past. *(To the one putting up the drapery)* Would you move the drapery a little to the right? Yes, so you can show the imperial crest clearly.

AKIKO: May the ball tonight run its course peacefully, and quickly!

SUEKO: It's all right, Akiko, it's all right. We may be anxious, but if we are, it's probably no more than the joyful expectation we have before a ball begins. Before a ball, my heart beats like a little girl's, every time. Especially tonight, as this is a special ball in which Lady Asako is appearing for the first time. I have to be at my best, too. Besides, this Rokumeikan, though it was built for dazzling work, is a weird building that somehow makes you feel restless.

ASAKO: *(Calling out to a boy carrying potted chrysanthemums)* Let me see those chrysanthemums. Well, I think we want a pot at the bottom of the staircase. Would you take that one downstairs? . . . . And, headwaiter *(She claps her hands to get his attention)*, would you tell them it's about time to light up the lamps?

(Waiters light the gaslights. The chandelier at the center of the ceiling is also lit.)

HISAO: Lights that never go out are tasteless, aren't they?

SUEKO: You talk like an old man.

HISAO: The fire in those gaslights is burning up every second, isn't it? But it looks continuous as if it weren't ever going out.

(Two groups of foreign musicians come up the staircase, each carrying his instrument. One group is German; the other, French. The conductor of each group kisses the hand that Asako stretches out, bowing exaggeratedly; each then kisses the hands of Sueko and Akiko.)

ASAKO: *(Summons the headwaiter)* This is good timing. Offer these gentlemen drinks in the hall and make them feel comfortable for the rehearsal. And *(to Hisao and Akiko)* I've found something you can help us with. Would you select music for tonight with these gentlemen? Waltzes, polkas, mazurkas, and lancers as well. *(The young couple agree and, with the headwaiter, lead the musicians to the hall at stage left.)* I'm concerned about the decorations at the entrance. *(To Sueko)* Would you mind coming with me? Have you seen the large fan, six by nine feet, covered by green cedar leaves, with the letters *welcome* raised in white chrysanthemums?

SUEKO: No, not yet.

ASAKO: I'd like you to see it. And I'd like you to tell me what you think of it. *(Going down the staircase)* . . . By the way I wonder what happened to Kusano. She should be here by now. . . *(The two of them leave.)*

(As they leave, Count Kageyama comes up the staircase at the back to stage left and enters. Kusano follows him. The people busy with decorations courtsey in silence.)

KAGEYAMA: A surprise, indeed. Asako is utterly calm, as if she'd done this kind of thing a hundred times. It's as if she'd been training for this.

Women are good deceivers. The Asako who was stiff with Japanese tastes until now, and the Asako of this evening—which is the real thing? I can't believe my eyes.

KUSANO: No one can deceive people as skillfully and as beautifully as milady. *(She offers a chair to Kageyama, who sits down.)*

KAGEYAMA: *(Extending his hand behind him and holding Kusano's hand)* Kusano. . . .

KUSANO: *(Hurriedly pulling her hand away)* Milord, everyone is looking at us.

KAGEYAMA: What do you mean by everyone? All these men here are my underlings. Down to the last craftsman, none of them will ever reveal a secret about me. Isn't that right, Yamamoto? *(The headwaiter bows.)* Kawata? *(One of the waiters bows.)* Konishi? *(Another waiter bows.)* Matsui? *(One of the craftsmen bows. Kageyama continues to call out to each of the rest of the people on stage and each, in turn, bows toward him conspiratorially before resuming work. Then, there is an intermittent sound of music from the ballroom at stage left, suggesting that the musicians have started rehearsal.)* . . . Good timing. Because of this intermittent sound of the musicians rehearsing, no one can hear what you say.

KUSANO: Milord, may I understand that you were truthful in the promise you made a few minutes back?

KAGEYAMA: You know the saying, don't you, "The demon and the deity never do anything nefarious." I'd like to think I showed you all the sincerity I have. I said I'd find an appropriate house for you, I'd provide money for your parents and brothers, so that you might live comfortably for the rest of your life. If you wish to have any other thing, you ought to tell me.

KUSANO: Most people will think it a risky business to try to live the rest of one's life lying comfortably on a bed of betrayal, but I don't. Because, sir, I have watched milady's relaxed way of life from close quarters.

KAGEYAMA: You are talking about Kiyohara. When you told me about it, I thought it was a likely story.

KUSANO: You hid your jealousy well.

KAGEYAMA: The sole pleasure of my life is to hide my emotions.

KUSANO: *(At this juncture one of the craftsmen starts noisily hammering a nail. Kusano covers her eyes.)* Oh, no, this noise! This noise! The noise of hammering a nail! —No matter how I try, my betrayal would never be like milady's calm betrayal. I was born a trustworthy servant after all. I dare say you have to have a much nobler genealogy than a loyalist needs to be a good betrayer.

KAGEYAMA: As you know perfectly well, Asako was a geisha. You mustn't be thinking of such silly things endlessly. . . . Well, now, thanks to you, I have the overall picture, but there's one thing I still don't get. Why is Asako so protective of Hisao? I understand why she's protective of Kiyohara, but why Hisao. . . ? Isn't it odd that she's so keen on Hisao just because Daitokuji's daughter likes him?

KUSANO: Well, I don't know . . . it's all up to milady.

KAGEYAMA: Is she in love with that young man? He's a ninny, but he does have a face that attracts women. He doesn't have what's crucial, a man's strength, but he's got what provokes women old enough to begin to feel protective of someone. The beauty of a man at that age can still be translated into the beauty of a woman. I remember seeing a popular geisha who looked like him, someone who looked like him. . . . *(Suddenly realizing what's what, he says in a terrifyingly overbearing tone)* Hey, Kusano. You know something you haven't told me.

KUSANO: *(Scared stiff by his looks)* Yes, sir. . . . He's milady's son.

KAGEYAMA: Who's the father?

KUSANO: You can guess, sir.

KAGEYAMA: Kiyohara?

KUSANO: . . . yes, sir.

KAGEYAMA: *(Controlling his fury)* I see. . . . So she has schemed to take advantage of her husband to salvage all her past.

(Conversation midway on the staircase is heard.)

ASAKO: *(Voice only)* I can hear the music already. Would you like to go listen to them rehearse?

SUEKO: *(Voice only)* I'd like to rest a while longer. Please go ahead.

KUSANO: The ladies are coming. I can't be here. I'll see you later, sir. *(Hurriedly exits to stage left.)*

ASAKO: *(Enters)* Isn't Kusano here?

KAGEYAMA: No, I haven't seen her.

ASAKO: *(To the headwaiter)* Haven't you seen Kusano? *(The headwaiter respectfully shakes his head. She turns to the other waiters.)* How about you? *(They shake their heads.)* What happened to her? Things don't work well without her.

KAGEYAMA: A woman like that, who's worked only in a Japanese setting won't be of much use in a place like this.

ASAKO: Milord, have you been drinking already?

KAGEYAMA: Not yet. Why?

ASAKO: You normally look sallow, but now you look ruddy and your eyes are gleaming.

KAGEYAMA: Well, that may be because for the first time I am going to act driven by an emotion.

ASAKO: How terrifying! But making an exception from time to time should be pleasurable, too, I imagine.

KAGEYAMA: Right. Finding a rarely seen self is good for my body, too. After all, the self I see remains all year-round like a framed portrait painting, with no signs of making any move.

ASAKO: So that portrait is going to walk out of its frame.

KAGEYAMA: Yes. And the one who's most surprised by this is, above all, myself.

ASAKO: This is a strange day when all the immobile portraits on the wall have suddenly begun to move. Look at me. This ridiculous hoop under my skirt. I feel as if my legs came out wearing a large bell. When you wear a kimono, gentle silk constantly clings to your legs, but today all I have around them is a shifty wind.

KAGEYAMA: *(Coldly)* But you look nice. Very nice. And no matter what you wear, even when you attend a ball for the first time, you never change a bit, you never move. You remain what you have been all these years.

ASAKO: *(Becoming uneasy for the first time)* That means, I suppose, I won't be able to move as you move along. You are saying I will not be able to play the role of hostess tonight, are you not?

KAGEYAMA: Not at all. I did not mean to say anything like that. You are the hostess, so you can stay in one spot, without moving. And I, being your pitiable husband, can only scurry around.

ASAKO: My, I have never heard you talk like that. If I have done something wrong or something obtrusive, would you tell me now? To be told of such things after our guests begin to arrive would be painful.

KAGEYAMA: How can you do anything wrong? Or anything obtrusive? You are attentive in every way.

ASAKO: *(At a loss, she assumes coquetry.)* You are not nice, milord. You make fun of me like that, so I, dressed in such an embarrassing way, may feel even more awkward; you are scheming to tease me, aren't you? All right then, though I don't like it, I'll try to do my best to make myself presentable.

KAGEYAMA: Mysterious. As I look at you. . . .

ASAKO: Pardon?

KAGEYAMA: Your person doesn't seem to suggest a smidgen of compunction.

ASAKO: I have transmogrified myself, haven't I?

KAGEYAMA: There is in this world no monster more horrible than our trust.

ASAKO: That is your usual self.

KAGEYAMA: Come, let me hold your arm Western style.

(He holds out his arm. Asako puts her hand on it. At that moment a photographer comes up at stage left.)

PHOTOGRAPHER: I see, perfect timing. Allow me, sir, to take a commemorative photograph. Stay in that posture. I'm afraid that the other people have to go.

ASAKO: Would you start decorating the ballroom? This place looks fine now. *(All except Count and Countess Kageyama and the photographer exit stage left. A photograph is taken. Sueko, who has come up the staircase at stage right, watches.)*

PHOTOGRAPHER: Thank you, sir. I'll make sure to deliver this the day after tomorrow.

SUEKO: Both of you look nice. Together, you are magnificent.

KAGEYAMA: How are you? *(He gives her a light bow; then walks to stage left and says to the photographer in a manner inaudible to Asako and Sueko)* Get Tobita. Tell him to come here without being noticed by these ladies. *(The photographer exits.)*

ASAKO: *(As Kageyama walks to stage left, she walks to stage right and speaks to Sueko. The following exchange between the two women occurs at the same time as Kageyama's preceding instructions.)* Stay with me for the rest of this evening. Somehow I don't feel like talking to my husband tonight.

SUEKO: All right. Let's go to the ballroom. *(The two of them bow to Kageyama and exit toward the ballroom at stage left. As they exit, Tobita enters from stage left.)*

TOBITA: *(Looking around)* Are you all right, sir?

KAGEYAMA: Yes. They have just left. Listen, I have something I'd like you to do.

TOBITA: At your service, sir.

KAGEYAMA: There will be a break-in of those zealots tonight, and Kiyohara will direct them. That's the information you gave me.

TOBITA: Nothing is more accurate than that, sir.

KAGEYAMA: I know. Yes, the information is accurate. Accurate, yes, but the situation has changed. They have abandoned their break-in tonight. So Kiyohara won't be here, either.

TOBITA: Impossible, sir.

KAGEYAMA: I am saying this and I am right. The situation has changed. I often talk about the essence of politics. Do you know what that is?

TOBITA: Pardon me, sir?

KAGEYAMA: The essence of politics is this. Listen. There is no truth in politics. Politics knows that there is no truth in it. So politics is required to make a counterfeit of truth.

TOBITA: . . . Yes, sir.

KAGEYAMA: Tonight, the situation you described to me will not happen. That situation no longer exists. But when a certain situation ceases to exist, we must create another like it. That's what politics is all about. That's the essence of politics. You understand?

TOBITA: Just as you say, sir.

KAGEYAMA: Tonight there has to be a break-in by zealots. White headbands must flutter around their necks and their gleaming swords must flash under the dazzling lights of the chandeliers. Kiyohara must stop his hansom outside the fence. The cab must be crouched under the starry sky of early winter like an embodiment of dark scheming. I make history. The government of the day makes history. No one can change that. . . . So, Tobita, what do you have to do?

TOBITA: What has to happen tonight is that the zealots will break in and Kiyohara will come, right, sir?

KAGEYAMA: Right.

TOBITA: You have an idea about how to make Kiyohara come here, right, sir?

KAGEYAMA: *(Smiling)* Right.

TOBITA: I am only responsible for the zealots, right, sir?

KAGEYAMA: Exactly.

TOBITA: Leave it to me, sir. White headbands and white sashes can be arranged immediately. We have plenty of swords ready. As for the crucial players, we have plenty of young men in my house killing time. . . . So, how many should we have, sir?

KAGEYAMA: About twenty should be adequate.

TOBITA: The timing remains the same, sir?

KAGEYAMA: Yes. Don't worry about the police guards; I'll give them proper instructions. They'll put up some resistance but will let the men pass—the hot-blooded young men of our dear Liberal Party.

TOBITA: I think I have understood everything, sir.

KAGEYAMA: But you must keep one thing in mind. There will be absolutely no blood spilled within the gate of the Rokumeikan. Blood must be spilled outside it—outside the fence, in the darkness of a November night; it must be spilled secretly.

TOBITA: Holding a woman in your arms or seeing blood, it's preferable to do it in the dark.

KAGEYAMA: You may excuse yourself now. Once you start talking about blood, you never stop. Go, now, and begin your preparations as soon as you can.

TOBITA: Yes, sir.

(In trying to exit to stage left, Tobita bumps into Kusano, who entered earlier and has been standing quietly. Tobita exits.)

KUSANO: *(Staying where she is, at stage left)* Milord, and what is my part? The part for this female spy?

(The exchange between the two that follows is conducted with neither looking at the other, Kusano facing the audience and Kageyama pacing back and forth.)

KAGEYAMA: Later, you will go to Kiyohara at the time I tell you.

KUSANO: To Kiyohara?

KAGEYAMA: Right. Kiyohara trusts you because of what you did this morning. You will be going as Asako's messenger again. Use the same *jinrikisha* that you used this morning.

KUSANO: What is the purpose, sir?

KAGEYAMA: You will be going as Asako's trusted maid. Tobita's fake zealots will break in around ten o'clock. You will pretend that their break-in occurred around nine-thirty and hurry to Kiyohara with the news, so that he will arrive outside the gate just a little past ten. And you say this to Kiyohara: "Your men broke in against your orders, sir. Milady is furious. You must come right away to stop them."

KUSANO: "Your men broke in against your orders, sir. Milady is furious. You must come right away to stop them."

KAGEYAMA: Right. As for Kiyohara's whereabouts around that time, you needn't worry; I'll have it checked out. The only thing you have to do is to look harried and convey the emergency to him.

KUSANO: I understand, sir. *(Glancing at Kageyama for the first time)* Milord. . . .

KAGEYAMA: What is it?

KUSANO: Am I still beautiful?

KAGEYAMA: Yes, what? . . . You? Beautiful. Yes, *very* beautiful. *(So saying, he walks up to her with a near sneer and puts his hand on Kusano's shoulder. Kusano evades it and hurriedly walks away into the darkness to stage left. Kageyama remains standing at the same spot, thinking.)*

(Hisao and Akiko emerge from the ballroom at stage left, hand in hand.)

AKIKO: We still have time. Would you like to take a walk for a while?

HISAO: It's cold outside. You'll catch a cold with your pretty shoulders bare like that.

AKIKO: I feel hot on the shoulders—the shawls are too hot to me.

HISAO: *(Looking out)* It's dusk, but the leafless treetops remain bright. The trees become their brightest at this time of year, though the ground is dark, covered with dead leaves.

AKIKO: I wonder why those trees have shed their leaves so early. There's no need to hurry to be leafless, is there?

HISAO: Perhaps they wanted to become bright, feel refreshed.

AKIKO: You talk in such a way as to throw a wet blanket on me when I have finally begun to feel excited and happy. Lovers shouldn't be talking like this.

HISAO: Do you want fake cheerfulness from me?

AKIKO: No, I'm sorry I made a mistake. I'd rather you act as you feel. Because sooner or later I am going to see your true face, a cheerful face, after we start out on our trip tomorrow, in some distant land we'll be traveling to.

HISAO: Starting out on a trip tomorrow. . . . Your mother was saying something like that, wasn't she? We are to go to Yokohama by the train that leaves Shimbashi at 8:45 in the morning; then we'll wait for a couple of days in Yokohama. In the meantime, she will run around to get tickets for us to go to Europe either via the United States or Hong Kong by express boat and deliver them to us.

AKIKO: We are supposed to spend some time in some strange foreign country until we get permission from my father to marry.

HISAO: Once, for a while, I was obsessed with the thought of going on a trip.

AKIKO: Do you no longer want to go on a trip?

HISAO: Well, you see, the trip I had in mind became more and more beautiful, more and more fantastic. I mean, it became a trip that did not require trains and ships. Once, in this country, which is filled with falsities, I thought of a country beyond the seas, which is peaceful and orderly, always laden with shiny fruits, the sun always shining, then trains and ships became just too slow. The way it should be, the moment I think of such a country, that moment, I must be in that country. That moment, the fragrance of the fruits I am imagining must become real; the sunlight I am dreaming must begin to pour all over me. . . . Otherwise, it would be too late.

AKIKO: Outside there is no fragrance of fruit, no sunlight. The only thing here is the turnaround for the horse carriages with white gravel standing out in the twilight. There are no fireworks yet. I never thought that the dusk before the ball could be so hushed. . . . But don't you think that if we walk on those pebbles where the chilly evening winds blow, we alone will attract the sunlight, we alone will have a waft of the fragrance of fruits? Come, let's go out for a walk.

(She is ready to open the door to the balcony. Hisao is still hesitant.)

HISAO: . . . Well.

KAGEYAMA: *(Coming out, he calls out)* Hisao.

HISAO: *(He turns around, surprised.)* Sir?

KAGEYAMA: I have to have a talk with you. Take a walk later.

AKIKO: *(Ignoring him)* Come, let's go out for a walk.

KAGEYAMA: *I* have to have a talk with him.

AKIKO: *(To Hisao)* Talk later.

KAGEYAMA: If you insist, you, lady, can take a walk by yourself.

AKIKO: How. . . !

KAGEYAMA: You are polite to ladies, aren't you, Hisao? That habit becomes you perfectly. You are the kind of fellow who can play any role.

HISAO: *(Offended)* Is that what you wanted to talk about with me, sir?

KAGEYAMA: No, I am somewhat disappointed, that's all. I thought you were a little better than just chasing skirts.

HISAO: I regret you misunderstood me.

KAGEYAMA: Go to some mirror and look closely at your face that has gotten so lax, so cowardly. Look at what the face of a scared young man looks like. You'll never be satisfied with your face reflected in the mirror.

AKIKO: I know this gentleman's face very well, sir. Judgment of men's faces should be left to women. I wouldn't be associating with him if he did not look gallant.

HISAO: Akiko. . . .

KAGEYAMA: You once saw a phantom and are now looking at him through that phantom. Yes, Hisao was gallant until this morning. I would even say he embodied a noble feeling. Hatred made him tense; the frost that formed in the morning made him taut, but it all melted away. Young lady, your friend was a solid man until this morning, but now he's just a woman. You are in love with a woman.

HISAO: (Controlling his anger) I am doing this after I have given it adequate thought. No matter what you might say, I won't be bothered by it.

KAGEYAMA: You don't look unbothered to me. Anyway I'm glad you've at least retained the toughness of mind to get angry. You have neither courage nor guts, but you still have some embers left to get angry like this. You better treasure that. It may serve some purpose one of these days . . . when a crack forms between your forced relationship with this young lady and you find out what a woman is like.

AKIKO: You! (She covers her face and bursts out weeping.)

HISAO: You may insult me, but why should you insult her?

KAGEYAMA: I see I went too far. Forgive me, young lady. Besides, I did not mean to insult Hisao, either. Listen, young men are pitiful beings. They swing back and forth between fiery action and ashen despondency, dissatisfied with both. They think they can do anything, then they think they can't do anything. Meanwhile, they manage to be terribly good at filling their stomachs and having a good sleep. Within this day you reversed yourself from one extreme to the other—without being aware of the contradiction you made.

HISAO: There's no contradiction.

KAGEYAMA: Being unaware of one's contradiction is also a youth's characteristic. Think about it. Thanks to someone's sweet persuasion, you have decided there will be no break-in tonight. You have also decided that, therefore, the man you were aiming to kill won't appear, either.

HISAO: I haven't decided; I believe it. It's the trustworthy testimony of a trustworthy person.

KAGEYAMA: You believe it? I see. I didn't expect to hear that from you, a man who professes not to believe anything. Well then, let me ask you this. You may believe in that trustworthy testimony of a trustworthy person. But where is the source of that testimony? The testimony that the man in question will not appear can only be made by the man himself. Do you believe the man whom you are aiming to kill?

HISAO: No, I regret this, but I don't.

KAGEYAMA: Is he an outstanding, noble character?

HISAO: Neither outstanding nor noble. *(Angrily)* That's why I am aiming to kill him. You know that.

KAGEYAMA: If that is the case, why did you decide to believe so light-headedly that he will not appear tonight?

(Hisao is unable to respond.)

KAGEYAMA: Come, why do you think this is worth believing?

HISAO: *(Furious)* You are trying to force me to betray some trusted person.

KAGEYAMA: You are talking more and more strangely. From the outset you did not believe in anything, you said, but you are now talking about trust and betrayal. What's going on here?

AKIKO: *(Clinging to Kageyama)* I pray of you. Please do not torture him like this.

KAGEYAMA: I am not torturing him. I am simply asking logical questions. And I am trying to salvage your lover from a miserable chaos so that he may act a little more logically. Hisao, isn't this true?—that you are forcing yourself to believe he'll not appear tonight because you have been overcome by cowardice and you are now praying, "May he not appear tonight! May everything proceed in peace, uneventfully, as a pretty occasion!"

HISAO: *(Abruptly)* I am not a coward!

KAGEYAMA: Yes, sir, that's all I wanted to hear. You are what I thought you were. You are after all a young man with some strong points. *(Taking out a pistol from an inside pocket)* Come, you better carry this.

AKIKO: *(Preventing Hisao from taking it)* No, you must not accept anything like that.

KAGEYAMA: Young lady, keep your mouth shut and allow him to accept this. Nothing hurts a man's pride worse than a woman's interference in a situation like this.

HISAO: *(To himself)* Is he after all. . . ?

KAGEYAMA: Is he after all? Yes, he may be appearing after all. You are in any case supposed not to believe him. The doubt you have now makes your reasoning logical. It makes you a rational man. Come, this pistol proves it.

(Hisao accepts it in stunned silence.)

AKIKO: Hisao, you must not, you must not do such a dangerous thing.

KAGEYAMA: Don't worry. It is no more than proof that he has made his reasoning logical. It is no more than an instrument that salvages him

from chaos and brings him back to logic. Young lady, I'll tell you this—
that a weapon is the most powerful instrument that gives a man logic.
That's all.

HISAO: *(Putting the pistol in an inside pocket)* Don't worry, Akiko. Thanks to
this pistol, I can feel calm.

*(There is a good deal of noise at the staircase on stage right. Enter Noriko, the
wife of General Miyamura, and Sadako, the wife of Baron Sakazaki, both in décolletage. They greet Kageyama with noisy gaiety.)*

NORIKO: So you are here before us. Your wife looks so magnificent in
Western dress that you feel excited, I dare say.

SADAKO: There is a great deal of talk everywhere because Asako is appearing at tonight's ball in décolletage. We wanted to see her so much
we came before our husbands.

KAGEYAMA: She is with Mrs. Daitokuji, in the ballroom.

NORIKO: *(To Sadako)* Let's go now. We can be great gossips by seeing her
before everyone else in Tokyo.

*(The two of them hurry into the ballroom to stage left. Their loud surprise is
heard. A rehearsal for a waltz begins. Kageyama, Hisao, and Akiko stand in silence. In due time, Asako enters surrounded by the merrily babbling Noriko,
Sadako, and Sueko.)*

SADAKO: She's so magnificent. So beautiful.

NORIKO: Compared with yourself in a kimono, you look younger by ten
years.

SADAKO: And you look so nice. You look as if you had never worn anything but Western dress.

SUEKO: You are an evil person, don't you think? You are wearing it for
the first time but do it far better than those of us who are supposed to
be used to it.

NORIKO: Your husband must be very proud. *(To Kageyama)* You have
never looked forward to a ball as much as you do tonight, have you?

SADAKO: When you wear that dress, it flows down your body like water.
I'm jealous. My water gets sidetracked by stones and rocks.

ASAKO: If you treat me like that, I will feel like a rare animal brought back
from a strange land.

KAGEYAMA: *(Merrily)* You are all here now, so let us have a toast. *(Clapping his hands)* Bring some wine!

*(The waltz continues. A waiter carrying a tray loaded with wine enters from the
ballroom and has each person take a glass. When there is about to be a toast,
Asako drops her glass by mistake.)*

KAGEYAMA: You are nervous—very unlike you.

ASAKO: It is fortunate that this was just a glass. *(The waiter quickly gives her
another glass.)* We can replace it.

KAGEYAMA: Yes, there are things we can't replace.

SUEKO: *(To Kageyama)* Say something for the toast.

KAGEYAMA: This is after all the Emperor's birthday. Shall I say, "May His Holy Majesty live forever"?

SUEKO: The way you say that, it sounds like mockery.

KAGEYAMA: Well, then. . . . Let's see, for nothing . . . toast!

(All raise their glasses.)

CURTAIN

ACT 4

Past nine that evening. The stage props are the same as in act 3. The decorations are now all in place, there is a hubbub among the many guests, and waiters are weaving through them.

Count and Countess Kageyama stand at the top of the staircase to stage right, receiving guests. At stage front stand Baron and Baroness Sakazaki and heavily bemedaled army general Miyamura in uniform and his wife, each holding a glass. The general has a magnificent Kaiser mustache.

MIYAMURA: Phooey! A soldier can never feel comfortable in a place like this. Above all, he must not feel comfortable. He delights in galloping through a battlefield, but not in a feminine meeting of girls and women. *(While saying this, he stares at one of the ladies.)* . . . A man can't switch his concern from one thing to another so skillfully. Waiter, give me another. *(To the lady he was staring at)* Excuse me, ma'am, what is that pretty liquor you are drinking? No, I just wanted to know its name. Waiter, may I have the same thing?

NORIKO: I'm sorry, you look bored.

(She continues her chatting with Sadako.)

MIYAMURA: No, it's beyond bored. To me, sword and horse and swirls of dust are most congenial. *(Turning his attention to another lady.)* Excuse me, ma'am, where did you acquire that fan? No, I just wanted to know. I'd like to buy something similar for my wife. *(He begins to chat with her.)*

SAKAZAKI: *(Trying to join the conversation between his wife and Noriko)* Now, you see, that issue is. . . .

SADAKO: Is there anything I can do for you?

SAKAZAKI: Not really. *(Crestfallen.)*

(Sadako resumes chattering with Noriko.)

SAKAZAKI: You see, that's what I've been saying. When it comes to. . . .

SADAKO: Is there anything I can do for you?

SAKAZAKI: Not really. *(Crestfallen.)*

(A loud and clear announcement from the staircase at stage right.)

VOICE: Ladies and gentlemen, His Excellency Prime Minister Itō Hirobumi and his wife.

(The couple come up. Itō shakes hands with Kageyama and kisses Mrs. Kageyama's hand. The kiss lasts very long.)

ITŌ: These balls are enjoyable, aren't they? We are planning to throw one ourselves, early next year—a masquerade. My wife thought of it. Right, Umeko?

UMEKO: We expect both of you to come.

KAGEYAMA: We'll be very honored to, ma'am. Everyone's waiting for you in the ballroom. *(Mr. and Mrs. Itō walk to the ballroom in a leisurely manner, returning everyone's greetings, and exit.)* The special train from Yokohama was supposed to arrive at Shimbashi at nine, was it not?

ASAKO: It will bring most of our foreign guests.

KAGEYAMA: It's about time they arrived.

VOICE: Ladies and gentlemen, His Excellency Vice Admiral Hamilton, of the Royal Navy of Great Britain, and his officers.

ASAKO: So here we have the first group.

(The vice admiral and each of the officers shake hands with Kageyama, kiss Asako's hand, and leave to the ballroom at stage left.)

VOICE: Ladies and gentlemen, His Excellency Minister of the Army Ōyama Iwao and his wife.

(Ōyama in uniform comes up, greets Kageyama and Asako bluntly, and bumps into Miyamura.)

ŌYAMA: Here you are, Miyamura, what a place to find you!

MIYAMURA: Dancing isn't your cup of tea, either, I take it.

ŌYAMA: Embarrassed to say this, but in our household, wife commands and husband follows is the rule. My wife is taking dance lessons in our house, see. *(Meanwhile, Mrs. Miyamura and Mrs. Ōyama are chatting. Ōyama lowers his voice.)* . . . Well, let me say this, Mrs. Kageyama is far prettier than rumor has it, isn't she? If Lord Itō starts paying attention to her, there'll be trouble.

MIYAMURA: Lord Itō is shrewd. He didn't show it when he spoke to her a few minutes back, but he must be aiming to dance with her.

(Ōyama and his wife, along with Miyamura and his wife, go into the ballroom.)

VOICE: Ladies and gentlemen, His Excellency Ambassador Ch'én, of Ch'ing, and his entourage.

(Enter the ambassador and his entourage, each dressed in florid Chinese dress with gold and silver embroidery, with drooping whiskers and a pigtail. After greeting Mr. and Mrs. Kageyama in Chinese style, they exit into the ballroom.)

(Suddenly, a quadrille starts and there is applause.)

KAGEYAMA: The dance has started.

ASAKO: We must join them.

(Several foreign and Japanese couples come up the staircase as a continuous group and, exchanging greetings with Mr. and Mrs. Kageyama, exit into the ballroom. For a while the stage is empty. Soon, to the tune of a quadrille enters one end of a row of dancers from stage left. It includes Daitokuji Sueko, Akiko, and Hisao. For a while dancers swirl around on stage, one couple after another. In time they all disappear to stage left, leaving the stage empty. The music continues. . . . From the staircase at stage right, the headwaiter hurries up, evidently upset, his hair mussed. He turns round, looks downward, and runs into the ballroom at stage left. In no time he returns with Asako. Kageyama quietly follows them and stops at the entrance to the ballroom.)

ASAKO: What did you say? Zealots . . . will be coming upstairs? No, this can't, this can't happen.

HEADWAITER: Downstairs everyone is running around trying to escape them. They are brandishing drawn swords, threatening them, laughing. They are destroying the decorations.

ASAKO: This can't, this can't happen.

HEADWAITER: While you are saying that, ma'am, they are coming up to the second floor.

(From the bottom of the staircase at stage right rise clattering noises of people running about and screams and laughter.)

ASAKO: *(Determinedly)* Leave this to me. Our guests should not become aware of this. That's your responsibility. Tell the waiters to prevent our guests from coming out into this room, that they must wait on them in the ballroom. Do you understand? *(Screams and barbarous laughter.)*

HEADWAITER: Yes, ma'am.

(As he exits into the ballroom at stage left, the headwaiter stops as if to learn of Kageyama's wishes. Kageyama scolds him with his eyes and dismisses him. As soon as the headwaiter exits, enter Hisao, Sueko, and Akiko. Asako determinedly walks to the staircase at stage right. Hisao, Sueko, and Akiko watch her together. There are noises of people coming up the staircase and a hubbub.)

ASAKO: *(Standing at the top of the staircase and staring down)* You can't come up here. You can't take another step this way.

(Kageyama signals at the staircase in the back at stage right to summon Tobita. Tobita and Kageyama stand together at the end of stage right.)

ASAKO: Look at yourselves! Do you think I'm scared of you? I'm not afraid of drawn swords. Step back, step back fast!

HISAO: *(Furious)* He betrayed me after all. It was a lie after all. He did not only betray me, but my mother as well. I'll show him what I can do!

AKIKO: Hisao! Hisao!

HISAO: Coward! See what I can do!

(Disengaging himself from the two women, he opens the door to the balcony and runs outside. Akiko clings to Sueko, trembling.)

ASAKO: So you are determined to come up here. All right, then. You must kill me first. Kill me.

KAGEYAMA: *(In a whisper to Tobita)* What are you doing! Get them to go away, quick! *(Tobita gives a stiff bow and hurries out down the back staircase.)*

ASAKO: Cowards all! You are brandishing swords and can't even kill a single woman? If you really want to come up here, kill me. Come up here and kill me!

(In a moment there is the suggestion that the men with drawn swords retreat and go away. Finally, Asako turns around and walks toward stage left. Kageyama, along with Sueko and Akiko, hurries to welcome her. Asako clings to Kageyama.)

ASAKO: *(Almost falling down)* They finally retreated. . . . They finally left us.

SUEKO: You were magnificent. Magnificent. You put your life at risk to protect this ball.

KAGEYAMA: The promise was not kept after all.

ASAKO: Just as you said. Everything turned out as you predicted. *(Suddenly)* Where's Hisao? Where *is* Hisao? *(Sueko and Akiko lower their eyes.)* Hisao? Come, where is he?

(Two shots are heard from outside.)

ASAKO: Oh! *(She falls onto Kageyama's chest.)*

(The quadrille music rises again and, despite the waiters' trying to stop them, dancers enter from stage left, swirl around the stage, and in time exit to stage left like an ebbing tide. Again there are only the Kageyamas, Sueko, and her daughter left on stage. A figure appears on the balcony.)

ASAKO: Hisao! You. . . .

(But it is Kiyohara who appears. In a frock coat and with a chrysanthemum in a button hole as in act 2, he looks distraught. He enters and remains standing in stunned silence. This takes the four people by surprise.)

ASAKO: You are alive. *(She shows a flash of joy but is instantly overcome with anxiety.)* But what happened to Hisao?

KIYOHARA: Hisao . . . is dead.

AKIKO: Oh no! *(She puts her face onto Sueko's chest and cries.)*

ASAKO: *(Furious)* I did not expect you to be like this. You broke your promise. What a coward. Hisao died because of that. You betrayed me and Hisao, mother and son, for your own disgraceful survival.

SUEKO: So, Hisao was your. . . .

ASAKO: You intended to deceive me from the beginning. You made a promise you did not intend to keep. For the first time in twenty years I see it. You do not deserve love. You are a vile person. A coward. Such a medal does not become you. *(She snatches the chrysanthemum from his lapel hole, throws it down, and tramples on it.)* I have a better idea. *(She picks up the chrysanthemum.)* Now it becomes you. This trampled upon, dirty chrysanthemum is your medal. Come, take this and go away. And live forever after, disgracefully. I shall not see you again.

(Kiyohara takes the chrysanthemum and puts it in his pocket. The music stops for intermission, and a couple of guests are about to come out. Kageyama gives a quiet order to the waiters, who skillfully lead the guests to the exit. Tobita appears from the back staircase at stage left and stands by Kageyama.)

KIYOHARA: Let me have my say. I was climbing down from my hansom, when somebody in hiding shot at me. The bullet missed and hit the ceiling of my carriage. At once I shot back for self-protection. It appeared to hit a fatal spot, for the man fell. Under the street lamp I saw his face for the first time. It was Hisao.

Tobita: *(Excited)* You should have left it to me. To me.

(Tobita takes out a pistol and aims at Kiyohara. Kageyama stops him with his hand and makes him put his pistol away.)

KIYOHARA: *(Taking the chrysanthemum out of his pocket and playing with it)* . . . Hisao breathed his last breath in my arms. When I saw his expression, I had an intuition. I understood everything. Don't you see? Hisao did not attempt to kill me. He wanted to be killed by me. That was his revenge.

ASAKO: What?

KIYOHARA: At such close range you can't miss someone. Don't you understand? He deliberately missed me to be killed by me. By his father whom he hated. By his unworthy father who never returned his love. . . . I saw it—that because he did not get anything fatherly from me, he wanted my own bullet at the end. He schemed to give me a sorrow that would last for the rest of my life. He plotted to force me not to forget him morning and night.

TOBITA: *(In a whisper)* Sir, you misjudged that rat.

KAGEYAMA: *(In a whisper)* Right. I misjudged him.

ASAKO: And Hisao. . . .

KIYOHARA: Kageyama, you killed your political enemy magnificently. More magnificently than you could ever have imagined. I'm finished now. My ideals, the government I dreamed about, are all finished. Unless some kind person kills me, I'll continue to live uselessly, but in fact you won't be able to describe me as alive. I have been killed by something larger than a bullet. I will no longer get in your way. Ideals have failed. Government has failed. You carried out your orders far more faithfully than you had imagined. You should build a grave for him. . . . Asako, your husband's success will continue to grow. This is certain as long as the sun rises in the east in the morning. But there's one thing I must make clear to you.

ASAKO: I seem to have said something terribly wrong to you. When I should have grieved with you hand in hand, I seem to have cursed you. I just. . . .

KIYOHARA: That's all right. But one thing I must make clear. Those zealots who came here were not my men.

ASAKO: What?

KIYOHARA: Those men were not the remnants of the Liberal Party. They were fake. Your husband made some young men disguise themselves as mine to draw me out.

ASAKO: (Turning to her husband for the first time) So you!

KIYOHARA: That's all I wanted you to know. I keep my promises. Good-bye, now. I'll never see you again.

ASAKO: Wait!

AKIKO: Mother, I no longer have the strength to live.

SUEKO: Akiko. . . . Akiko. . . .

ASAKO: Wait!

(Kiyohara exits by the staircase at stage right. At the same time Tobita exits by the back staircase at stage left with a conspiratorial air.)

ASAKO: (To Akiko, determinedly) Akiko, you can't say any such weak-hearted thing. You must by all means try to live. Let me say something cruel. Hisao did not die for you. So it would be useless for you to follow him in death. Am I not correct, Sueko?

SUEKO: You have said a good thing. It will be the best medicine for Akiko. (After glancing at Kageyama, to Asako) I can imagine how you feel. It all started with my request.

ASAKO: You shouldn't say that.

SUEKO: When you have made up your mind, please come to my place, any time. Consider ours your home. Staying in Kageyama's household can only make you unhappy.

ASAKO: I am grateful for your offer. Please be careful.

SUEKO: Do remain strong. We will go to see Hisao, though he is dead. (She exits by the back staircase at stage left, following her daughter as if to protect her.) (Kageyama and Asako glare at each and remain silent for a while.)

ASAKO: (Trying to maintain a calm tone) I have been thinking about what you have done today. Politics . . . politics . . . politics. . . . Everything is no more than politics for you. In these circumstances, I don't have to bother to blame you.

KAGEYAMA: Politics, politics, politics, you say. But suppose I asserted to you clearly that what I have done has to do with the matter of love, what would you do? Can't we say that this incident was caused by love? . . . I . . . was jealous.

ASAKO: *(Contemptuously)* You certainly were!

KAGEYAMA: Listen to me. I was jealous of that indescribable trust that exists between you and Kiyohara. I was jealous of that transparent, unstated trust that doesn't allow for anybody else. You were separated for such a long time, but you could trust each other. Was there even a fragment of that kind of trust between us?

ASAKO: There wasn't. But that is because you disliked such a thing and I went along.

KAGEYAMA: It is an absurd thing. Human beings can't make pledges or trust each other unconditionally as Kiyohara and you have done. That can't be possible. That sort of thing should never exist in our human world.

ASAKO: Don't you mean in the political world?

KAGEYAMA: In the human world I have in mind. Nevertheless, I was jealous of what should not be. This is only too human, is it not? Kiyohara and you, like magicians, wove a mysterious fabric out of transparent thread. You wore it—then through its magical power, the cold rules of the human world were hidden, and in its place, an absurdly rosy world, a fairy-tale world where people can trust one another, a world that kids call ideal, began to open up. I can't stand things like that. In this Hisao was like me, but in the end he was just a kid. He blatantly betrayed me and helped you and Kiyohara in your fairy tale of trust from behind the scene.

ASAKO: This trust will not be broken.

KAGEYAMA: It may not be broken, but Kiyohara is one of the living dead. He will not even give you a glance.

ASAKO: I have been listening to you calmly. You said this was caused by love. Would you please explain to me how you can deceive yourself like that?

KAGEYAMA: I am saying that I did all this for you. Yes, I schemed and plotted. But the central point was to destroy for you the fairy tale that trust between human beings can be achieved. Everything was supposed to work out according to plan. If Hisao had killed Kiyohara, you would have believed for the rest of your life that those zealots were the real thing. You will say this is a deceit. But a deceit makes human beings wiser than a fairy tale.

ASAKO: You put on the show of fake zealots to trap him.

KAGEYAMA: Why should we need a fancy procession like that to trap him? I could have just told him that his men broke in.

ASAKO: So you are saying those barbarous dances with drawn swords were simply designed to entertain me.

KAGEYAMA: Yes, of course. Think about it. For what else did we need them? I arranged the show for you only. My bashful, timid love for you made me do it.

ASAKO: *(Gradually losing control over her excitement)* No, you did it to provoke Hisao.

KAGEYAMA: It was his business that he got carried away. And he betrayed me and did what he wanted to do.

ASAKO: You lie! Who gave him the pistol?

KAGEYAMA: Everything was caused by my jealousy.

ASAKO: No, enough of that soiling everything!

KAGEYAMA: Soiling, you say? I am cleansing things. I am cleansing what you regard as politics with love.

ASAKO: Please do not talk about love and human beings any more. Those words are unclean. When they come out of your mouth, they become repellent. You are clean as ice only when you totally isolate yourself from human emotions. Please do not bring in love and humane feelings with your *sticky* hands. This is unlike you. Be yourself again and stop concerning yourself with nonpolitical things such as affairs of the heart. As Kiyohara said, you are a successful politician. You can do anything as you see fit. What else do you want? Love? That is ridiculous. The heart? Isn't that laughable? They are the things powerless people hold dear. You shouldn't want to have the cheap toy that a beggar's child treasures.

KAGEYAMA: You do not understand me at all.

ASAKO: I do. I will tell you. For you, the only thing that happened tonight is that a nameless young man died. It does not mean anything to you. Compared with a revolution or a war, it is a trivial thing. You'll forget it tomorrow.

KAGEYAMA: Now your heart is talking. In the flowing tide of anger and grief, your heart is talking. You think you are the only person equipped with a heart.

ASAKO: You are looking at an honest me for the first time since our marriage.

KAGEYAMA: You are saying this marriage was all political to you.

ASAKO: Let me say yes. We deserved each other. Truly deserved each other. . . . But good things don't last long. I am leaving you tonight.

KAGEYAMA: I see, but where do you plan to go?

ASAKO: I'll go to Kiyohara.

KAGEYAMA: It will be great fun to be married to a dead person.

ASAKO: I can do it all right. Marriage to a dead person. . . . There is no woman more used to it or more experienced in it than I am, is there?

(A waltz starts in a grand fashion.)

KAGEYAMA: Oh, my, here's another dance.

ASAKO: A mother dances in mourning for her son's death, you see.

KAGEYAMA: Right. With a smile.

ASAKO: I can easily put on a fake smile so long as I know this is the last time I do it. *(Weeping)* I can do it easily. As long as I know this comes to an end in a brief while.

KAGEYAMA: Her Highness the imperial princess and her entourage will be here shortly.

ASAKO: Let us welcome them pleasantly.

KAGEYAMA: Look. The people old enough to know better are slowly coming toward us, feeling bitter about the absurdity of it all, dancing. Rokumeikan. These deceptions are what slowly make the Japanese wiser, you see.

ASAKO: We have to put up with it only a while longer. Fake smiles and fake balls won't last that long.

KAGEYAMA: We must hide our true feelings. We must dupe them—the foreigners, the whole world.

ASAKO: Nowhere in the rest of the world should such a faked, shameless waltz exist.

KAGEYAMA: Still, I'll continue to dance it for the rest of my life.

ASAKO: That's exactly like you, milord. That's exactly your true self.

(Groups of dancers enter from stage left and spread all over the stage. Kageyama and Asako bow to each other, hold hands, and join the dance. The dance continues for a while. Then there is a pause in the music. At this point Mr. and Mrs. Kageyama are at stage center. Suddenly, there is a gunshot in the distance.)

ASAKO: Listen, I heard a pistol shot.

KAGEYAMA: You just think you did. Or it was fireworks. Yes, it was the fireworks they failed to shoot off in celebration.

(The pause lasts from "Listen, I heard a pistol shot" to "Or it was fireworks." During it, everyone stays still. Then the waltz resumes and as the lively dancing continues. . . .)

CURTAIN

BACKSTAGE ESSAYS

A brief history of Japan's modern theater should help in understanding "A Small Scar on the Left Kneecap," one of the two backstage essays that follow. I will also introduce some of the actors and actresses and explain several of Mishima's references.

Japanese popular theater was dominated by kabuki until the late nineteenth century. Shimpa, "New School" or "New Style," was the first movement that tried to outgrow it by dealing with contemporary issues. It began with plays featuring *sōshi,* fighters for liberty and civil rights, that Sudō Sadanori (1867–1907) started in Osaka in 1888. Kawakami Otojirō (1864–1911), a prominent figure in the "liberty and civil rights" movement, pushed the theatrical approach further. In the early twentieth century, Shimamura Hōgetsu (1871–1918), Osanai Kaoru (1881–1928), and the kabuki actor Ichikawa Sadanji II (1880–1940) started Shingeki, "New Theater," specifically to oppose Kyūgeki, "Old Theater"— the standard term for kabuki, in which Shimamura and others may have included Shimpa. Shingeki stressed realism through the staging of works of writers such as Chekhov and Gorky. J. Thomas Rimer's book *Toward a Modern Japanese Theatre: Kishida Kunio* (Princeton University Press, 1974) is a detailed study of this movement. The Bungaku-za (Literary Theatre), founded in 1937, is the most prominent theater group in the Shingeki movement.

Of the players Mishima mentions, Sugimura Haruko (1909–97) was, by popular consensus, one of the three greatest actresses in postwar Japan, the two others being Mizutani Yaeko and Yamada Isuzu. She became a founding member of the Bungaku-za and remained active both on stage and in film until her death. (In Kurosawa Akira's movie *Red Beard,* she plays the spiky proprietress of a brothel.) Mishima wrote *The Rokumeikan* for her, but in 1963 when he wrote another play at the request of the Bungaku-za, *Yorokobi no Koto* (The joyful koto), the theater company turned it down for ideological reasons, a move that prompted Mishima to part company with the group. As a result, it became impossible for the Bungaku-za and therefore Sugimura to stage *The Rokumeikan* again. In 1995 while on her company's tour in Kyūshū, Sugimura was offered the Order of Cultural Merits, but she turned it down. She explained that an award was something she could strive for but an order wasn't. By then she had received many awards.

Nakamura Nobuo (1908–91), another founding member of the Bungaku-za, quit the theater company over the fracas about *Yorokobi no Koto.* Thereafter, he moved through several theater groups until he founded, along with Akutagawa Hiroshi and Kishida Kyōko, the company En (Circle) in 1975. A representative actor of Shingeki, he played Count Kageyama Hisatoshi in *The Rokumeikan.*

As for Tanaka Chikao (1905–95), *Toward a Modern Japanese Theatre* says he "began his career as a young playwright under Kishida [Kunio], and a number of his important postwar works, many of which owe their mystic and poetic qualities to his study of the modern French theatre, were first produced by the Literary Theatre. In dramas like *Maria no kubi (The Head of the Madonna)* and *Chidori (Plover),* both written in 1959, Tanaka can lay claim to being the finest serious literary playwright in Japan during the period."

Hankechi (Handkerchief) is a story Akutagawa Ryūnosuke (1892–1927) wrote in 1916. It describes a Western-educated Japanese professor living in Tokyo with his American wife. He is an exponent of classical Japanese virtues to the West. While reading J. A. Strindberg's *Dramaturgie* one summer afternoon, he is visited by the mother of one of his students who has come to tell him of her son's recent death. While reminiscing about her son, she maintains a dignified mien, even a faint smile. But the professor, by accident, finds that her hands under the table are "violently trembling and, trembling, perhaps in an attempt to forcibly restrain the fierce movement of her emotions, gripping the handkerchief laid on her lap tightly as if to tear it apart."

Impressed by another concrete example of classical Japanese conduct, he tells his American wife about it. Yet when he picks up *Dramaturgie* after the mother leaves, the first paragraph that catches his eye describes an acting technique developed by one Frau Heiberg in which she tears her handkerchief apart while smiling, confounding the professor.

The model of the professor is said to be Nitobe Inazō (1862–1933), who was married to a Quaker and was famous for his book *Bushidō: The Soul of Japan,* published in the United States in 1899. In the German translation of Strindberg's book that the professor is supposed to be reading, the word that corresponds to *kata,* "pattern," is *Manier.* Strindberg characterized Heiberg's technique as *Mätzchen* (*Akutagawa Ryūnosuke Zenshū, I,* Chikuma Shobō, 1985, pp. 159–73). My friend Doris Bargen tells me that *Manier* means "affectation" and *Mätzchen* something like "antics performed to increase one's self-importance."

The Teahouse of the August Moon is John Patrick's Pulitzer Prize–winning play, adapted from Vern J. Sneider's novel—"a whimsical comedy fantasy about the foolishness of the American military bureaucracy's attempts to impose American ideas on occupied countries—in this case Okinawa," according to Pauline Kael (*5001 Nights at the Movies,* Henry Holt, 1991, p. 745). In the play Americans try to build a teahouse to please the natives. The play was produced on Broadway in 1953, and the MGM movie version, with Marlon Brando, came out in 1956.

Mishima wrote these essays during the first production of *The Rokumeikan.* They were then published under the overall title of *Gakuya de kakareta Engeki-ron* (Essays on theater written backstage) in the January 1957 issue of *Bungei Shinchō* (New tides in literary arts).

A SMALL SCAR ON THE LEFT KNEECAP

During a rehearsal of *The Rokumeikan,* a question came up in the scene where Asako, played by Sugimura Haruko, while talking to Hisao, a son whom she hadn't seen for twenty years, reveals their mother-son relationship by saying, "I know . . . that you have a small, thin scar on your left kneecap. . . . One summer afternoon, after you fell asleep, I began to doze despite myself. Then you woke, crawled away, and stabbed your knee on a pair of scissors." At first, Mr. Nakatani Noboru, playing Hisao, just listened intently to these words of Asako—without even turning his eyes toward his knee, let alone touching it with his hand. This was natural to the acting of Shingeki.

But Mr. Nakamura Nobuo, while watching this, at one point said, "The previous generation Ganjirō[1] would have made a big deal of this." He then showed a highly dramatic reaction: looking startled, he stiffened his body, put his hand on his knee, and exaggeratedly let it slide until it touched the floor. Our consensus was that Mr. Nakatani didn't have to go as far as putting his hand to the knee but he could at least glance at it. Since then he has done so—when absorbed in his role, even putting his hand on the knee without really meaning to.

This minor issue in truth points to the essence of the so-called Shingeki acting. First of all, in Shingeki there is rarely a scene where a mother reveals her identify to her son—absolutely no melodramatic story line exists where a mother brings up a scar on her son's knee as proof of their relationship. This

---

1. Probably the kabuki actor Nakamura Ganjirō I (1860–1935).

means that in normal circumstances there is no room for an issue such as this to pop up. It just happens that my work presented this difficult question. In Mr. Tanaka Chikao's play *Sabu-chan to Rie* (Sabu-chan and Rie), Rie's words are made to overflow with a histrionic quality. But what these words demand on stage is above all a satiric effect. In Shingeki there is no play with words and a story line like those of mine that have no satire in them, though in kabuki there are a countless number.

This naturally raises the question of the genre of acting. One answer is to say: "In Shingeki you get into everything through emotion; in Kyūgeki you do so through *kata*.[2] So, there is nothing wrong about something producing a conventional 'pattern' as long as you get into it through emotion." Needless to say, this is a correct argument. But even though it is, it does not at all touch on the question of patterns in acting that any drama demands and that resolutely exist even in Shingeki.

I think Shingeki has neglected this question too much. Not only during the Rokumeikan era but during the era of our own past there were what may be called patterns of psychology. Whether you began your salutation by referring to weather or by mentioning good fortune, misfortune, disaster, or happiness, everything began with a pattern and the daily psychology itself was satisfied with patterns. Today such things survive only in the pleasure quarters[3] and in the society of entertainers.[4] During those ages, in those societies, when something unexpected, even a tragedy, occurred, a pattern quickly enveloped your emotion, and expression through a pattern itself became a consolation for it. The word "sentimentalism" came out of the popularity of the eighteenth-century English literary work *A Sentimental Journey*—a popularity that reached such a point that today it is said that sentimentality is needed to attract the ordinary people in England just as cynicism is in France. The tears of the Japanese are also unmistakably a similar pattern of emotion. Akutagawa Ryūnosuke's short story *Hankechi* is an excellent study of this question.

Now you might say that the acting technique of Shingeki was born when modern life destroyed society's conventional stereotypes of emotions. For example, for shedding tears nō has one pattern called *shioru,* but modern life has added countless nuances to it, adding personal coloration or so-called individualism. Stage Character A's expression of sorrow must necessarily be different from Stage Character B's expression of sorrow. Just as emotional reactions are countless, so are their expressions. There is no such thing as emotional expres-

---

2. *Kata:* A set gesture or movement; also, style, mannerism.

3. Not long after Mishima wrote this, legalized prostitution ceased to exist.

4. *Geinin:* Performers in traditional entertainment arts, such as *rakugo* narrators and *taikomochi.* This sentence is an exaggeration; prescribed or traditional "patterns" are still common in epistolary salutations and other circumstances.

sion that is common to both A and B. The technique of psychological acting was thus born.

Shingeki was founded where the acting techniques of kabuki and Shimpa end. In the acting of kabuki and Shimpa, which you enter through patterns, the patterns themselves were born of emotional stereotypes of the society in which the audience lived, and because the audience sympathized with the drama through sympathy with those patterns, the actor had only to satisfy those patterns, although to make up for this he was unable to move the audience with anything that went beyond the existing emotional stereotypes. As a result, the drama could not develop its motifs beyond a certain point, unable as it was to separate itself from the tastes and daily emotions of the audience. It was not only because kabuki and Shimpa were commercial theater, but also because such characteristics of acting suited commercial theater.

Shingeki shouldn't be like that. This is as it should be, and the actor who plays Asako's son should in no circumstances visibly stiffen or let his hand slide off his knee. But the main problem lies beyond this. What adjusts and controls the exchange of emotions between stage and audience should be, in Shingeki, not the patterns in acting but the writing style of the play. What awakens the audience, what calls the audience out of the existing daily emotions in which it sleeps, should indeed be the *style* of the play; for you can say that the audience of Shingeki comes to see a drama not to seek familiarity in acting patterns but to be awakened from sleep.

But without certain common denominators, or where any such common denominators have been outgrown, you can't really be sure that the stage can expect to awaken the audience. This was clearly shown by the nonplussed faces of the audience in the first production in Japan of *The Teahouse of the August Moon* in which long speeches were delivered in English. What was missing was no less than the common denominator of language. In Shingeki, whether the play is one purely based on speeches or not, the audience and the stage are united in language, which is to say, Japanese, naturally, in place of patterns. And there the language itself is a pattern.

A play as a Japanese literary work creates, on top of the common denominator of the Japanese language, a whole range of variations of linguistic patterns, which, in the style of writing, emerge as unfixed, fresh patterns. Thus a play without style can only engender the familiarity of existing quotidian emotions between audience and stage. Style as a pattern becomes necessary to eliminate that familiarity. In a strict definition, a play without style is merely nonsensical.

My conclusion, therefore, is that Shingeki's acting techniques depend on a grasp of the style of writing of the play, as well as the ability to digest the play and understand its meaning. "The small scar on the kneecap" is a question that a style has raised, but the answer to it lies only in the style. That is what I, the writer of the play, thought.

THE PSYCHOLOGY OF A WALK-ON ROLE ON THE STAGE

Every day I go to Daiichi Seimei Hall and, drenched by taunts inside and outside the curtain, appear on stage in the walk-on role of a carpenter. By doing this I fulfill my wish of all these many years to appear in the world of a play I myself have written and to live it. But the unexpected harvest is that by continuing to do this I have come to see the curious shape of the stage as seen with the eyes of someone playing an important role.

The people who play the main and other important roles are constantly driven by the lines they have to say and the gestures they have to make and are tired from, as it were, their rushed lives. In contrast, to a walk-on whose only job during his appearance of three to four minutes is to provide someone with an occasion to say his lines, twice, and who doesn't say a word himself and, mostly with his back turned to the audience, is allowed to while away his time by making some meaningless, arbitrary gestures, the stage can be looked at like a party he is not invited to, with, let's say, a certain kind of wicked pleasure.

For some time now I've been heaping criticism on the bad manners of Japan's operatic choruses, but now that I appear in a role like a chorus, I can see the cause of the unspeakable badness of their manners. The drama rushes by you. You are linked to it with only two tiny knots, only two cues.

The drama on the stage may look like a comprehensive whole to the audience, and it should look that way. But to the actors it is like an invisible monster that moves blindly in a certain direction while sucking them into the maelstrom it has created, stopping here and there along the way. Speeches cross over there, cross over here. The drama thrashes about, constantly changing its focus, assaults various people, at times flies away beyond the background of the stage, or else leaps in through the window. The actor's personal continuity is merely a fiction that would immediately collapse if a desperate effort were made to maintain it.

Yes, I said "the actor's personal continuity." What ultimately guarantees that continuity, the actor himself believes, is the psychological, sensuous continuity that he reconstructs intelligently, but in fact it is nothing but the continuity of his *body* that is his externally identified being. It is precisely in that fact that characteristics of acting techniques lie—this is what I wrote a while ago in a small book called *Shōsetsuka no Kyūka* (A novelist's holiday).[5]

5. A collection of essays on a wide range of subjects written in the form of a diary from June 24 to August 4, 1955, and published that same year. In the entry for July 9, he attempts to answer the question, What in the world is an actor? One answer he is "tempted" to give: "The actor as an artist is a kind of human being whose inside and outside are precisely reversed, a truly *naked, visible* spirit." *Shōsetsuka no Kyūka* (Shinchō Sha, 1982), pp. 37–39.

Now, because a walk-on can't do any obtrusive acting, he has excess energy; he does not take on enough of a portion of the drama to fill his inner self and charge it. Thus those who appear on the stage take on the drama with a range of differences, from the main actor who is completely recharged by the drama to walk-ons who scarcely are. If we are to compare a drama to a landscape painting, the main actor is the foreground and the walk-ons are the background. If you become a figure in the painting and walk deeply in its woods, you will find that the background is a landscape that has the same density as the foreground. By skillfully expressing this continuousness a drama can increase its depth and suggest and symbolize even the figures outside the drama. That is, a walk-on is where he comes into contact with his life (of course, the life of the character he plays), and the spot where he stands is the last spot where the landscape suggests the world, where the drama suggests life. As a result, he also has the right to watch the drama from the standpoint of life. This becomes all the more clear when you think of the role of the audience in a drama-within-a-drama.

The walk-ons have a glimpse, from outside, of a drama in which they ought to take part in their roles. The drama now wildly embraces the actress who is playing the main role. Ah, this is the moment to watch. It's as though a disaster has struck. But we must coolly stay outside the pale of the drama and must never extend our helping hands. We walk-ons are thus completely exempted from ethical obligations. What is it like if it's in real life? Before your eyes, a child falls into a river. He's about to drown. The socially enforceable ethical idea pushes us onlookers, arouses in us the anxiety that we must play the role of child-rescuers. We cannot wait leisurely for someone who "plays the role of rescuing a child" to leap in from the outside zone.

What are the moments when life intervenes with the stage? They occur when the actor momentarily goes blank, delivers his lines in the wrong order, or forgets his cue. These are the moments when "a hole forms on the stage," as they say.[6] The audience detects them with enormous acuity. For example, suppose an actor is saying his words by placing them on his psychological waves as he is expected to but then delivers a line woodenly. It may be the critical moment when he has managed to rescue from oblivion the line he was about to forget. But the audience senses it quickly. This is because from that small "hole" the wind of real life instantly blows in, not of the life being acted out on stage; because the bemusement of the actor who has just rescued the line is the bemusement of actual life. Thus the "hole" that forms on the stage is a kind of life accident. When that happens, another actor must plug it with

6. *Butai ni ana ga aku.* My Broadway actor friend George Lytle says the expression for forgetting a line is "to go up" on a line, but he wonders if this is applicable here.

the kind of instant response required in real life, with the kind of ability to meet any crisis with an appropriate response on the spot. And that actor, the rescuer, must smoothly effect this emergency response within the constraints of the cool dramatic psychology on the stage, which is separated from the psychology of real life.

In the eyes of the audience the stage is like a guest room. The audience becomes conscious of time only when bored. But to the actors the stage is time. On the stage time flows smoothly. Like a school of minnows in a stream, it circles, comes up close, changes direction in unison, and moves on without slackening—before the walk-ons' eyes.

Yet we walk-ons remain calm. "We have no need to wet our feet by putting them in such a cold stream."

THE DECLINE AND FALL OF THE SUZAKU

Suzaku-ke no Metsubō (The decline and fall of the Suzaku) deals, at least on the face of it, with one of Mishima's recurrent themes: the decline of the Meiji aristocracy. To endow the play with appropriate atmosphere, Mishima chose the family name Suzaku, which readily evokes ancient, aristocratic Kyoto: it is the name of one of its great boulevards, the name of the imperial detached palace built during the reign of Emperor Saga (786–842), and the name of an emperor (sixty-first: 923–52). In his literary biography of Mishima, Okuno Tateo suggests that the Suzaku is modeled after the blue-blooded family the Saionji (*Mishima Yukio Densetsu*, Shinchōsha, 1993, p. 277).

The time Mishima chose for the play is also something that concerned him greatly: Japan's defeat in the Second World War, a cultural and social divide that vanquished, Mishima thought, whatever was noble and sublime in Japanese society.

In the play, both Suzaku Tsunehiro and his fiancée (almost), Matsunaga Ritsuko, are made to attend the Peers' School, which was established in 1877 exclusively for the children of aristocrats. It is assumed that members of the Suzaku family refer to the Emperor as *o-kami,* "our lord," rather than the more standard or, shall we say, plebeian *heika,* "his majesty," because of their sense of proximity to the Emperor. (Prince Takamatsu, for one, referred to his older brother, Hirohito, in the same way.) Similarly, for the atmosphere of a ranking aristocrat's household, the servant O-Rei is made to refer to Tsunetaka, the head of the house, as *tonosama,* "milord," and his son Tsunehiro as *wakasama,* "(young) master."

The island (name not given—"deliberately," according to Mishima) to which Tsunehiro is sent to "die"—as the Japanese would have it—may well be modeled on Iwo Jima, which saw thirty-six days of battle after it was subjected to seventy-four consecutive days of naval bombardment and aerial bombing. The U.S. attempt to subdue the island killed all but a thousand of the 21,000 Japanese defenders.

In his afterword to *The Decline and Fall of the Suzaku,* Mishima explained that the Euripidean drama in the subtitle is *The Madness of Heracles* (rather than *The Children of Heracles*). That drama begins with the tyrant Lycus about to kill Heracles' foster father Amphitryon, his wife Megara, and his children while Heracles is away on a long expedition in the underworld. Megara prays, and Heracles miraculously returns. He kills Lycus, but at Hera's command, Mania takes possession of Heracles, who, in a fit of madness, slays his wife and children. He is about to kill Amphitryon also, but Athena intervenes. Regaining his sanity, he is aggrieved to discover what he has done and decides to kill himself. But Theseus, whom he has rescued in the underworld, dissuades him, and Heracles agrees to live, in grief.

Mishima adds: "The theme of this play is an existential analysis of the spirit of *shōshō hikkin.* That is, the axis of the drama lies in the way perfectly passive loyalty evolves, unbeknownst to the person, into fealty as a kind of identification. What corresponds to Heracles' madness is *kochū* as madness or else fidelity as destruction." The term *shōshō hikkin* means something akin to "keeping a deferential distance after receiving an imperial summons" and *kochū,* "solitary loyalty"—to wit, remaining steadfastly loyal when there are no other sympathizers with the cause. Both were common patriotic phrases during the war.

In this play, and elsewhere, Mishima at times resorts to fanciful—or, as one reader put it, "surrealistic"—descriptions, as when Suzaku Tsunehiro, contemplating the South Pacific where the Imperial Japanese Navy was being destroyed in one battle after another, is made to say: "I feel as if my cheekbones were being slapped with a bag packed with the placer gold of despair and glory." There is no way of translating such descriptions into more *natural*-sounding sentences, whatever that may mean.

Mishima completed *The Decline and Fall of the Suzaku* at the end of July 1967. It was printed in the October issue of the monthly *Bungei* (Literary art) and staged in October of the same year, with Matsuura Takeo directing. Muramatsu Eiko, who played Matsunaga Ritsuko, was an actress Mishima chose to nurture.

THE DECLINE AND FALL OF THE SUZAKU

Based on Euripides' Heracles

TSUNEHIRO, played by Nakayama Jin, and RITSUKO, played by Muramatsu Eiko. Kinokuniya Hall, October 1967. *Courtesy of Waseda University's Tsubouchi Memorial Theatre Museum. By permission of Gekidan NLT.*

Time: Spring, autumn, summer, and winter in one or two years before and after the end of the war

Place: Count Suzaku's mansion

Persons:
Suzaku Tsunetaka
Suzaku Tsunehiro
O-Rei
Matsunaga Ritsuko
Shishido Mitsuyasu

ACT 1: SPRING

To stage right is the room attached to the Suzaku mansion's nineteenth-century-style greenhouse. To stage left, upstage, at the top of the stone steps is a Benzai-ten[1] shrine. Between the two is a three-way intersection in a garden, one path leading to the shrine, one to the entrance to the greenhouse, and one to an over-look with a view of the sea. As the curtain rises, O-Rei is offering prayers in front of the torii, with Ritsuko, dressed in the uniform of the Peers' School for Women and seated in a chair in the greenhouse, watching her through the glass.

Prayers finished, O-Rei climbs up the steps, opens the door of the shrine, takes out something large wrapped in paper, and holding it up reverentially, steps back.

O-Rei returns to the greenhouse room, places the wrapped object on the table before Ritsuko, unwraps it, and spreads out for her a gorgeous court lady's dress known as jūni hitoe *and a ceremonial "cedar fan."*

RITSUKO: Is this it? This is the first time I've seen it. So this is the *jūni hitoe* Lady Akiko wore for her wedding? And the cedar fan, too. . . . She must have been quite beautiful.

O-REI: Beautiful, young, and she died in no time. Just as a splendid spring day darkens in a hurrying evening wind.

RITSUKO: Did you see her in her splendor that day?

O-REI: Yes, I did, from a great distance.

RITSUKO: I only saw her in photographs.

O-REI: It was, after all, two years before you were born.

---

1. Sarasvati in Sanskrit. A goddess of music, oratory, happy wisdom, longevity, freedom from harm, and victory. Along with Kichijōten (Sri-mahadevi in Sanskrit), Benzaiten is one of the two most revered goddesses originating in India, though in Japan the two are often mixed up and regarded as the same. She is one of "the Seven Deities of Luck." Benten is an abbreviated, more familiar name for Benzaiten.

RITSUKO: After marrying into this Suzaku family she lived for only one year. As soon as Master Hiro was born. . . .

O-REI: Yes. You see, the master of the Suzaku is not supposed to take a bride.

RITSUKO: No?

O-REI: I seem to end up telling you things no one else will tell you. Look at their genealogy closely. Of the thirty-seven generations of this family, only five, including our present count, have had wives. And with all the five, their wives passed away immediately. What do you think of that?

RITSUKO: But in this day and age. . . .

O-REI: There is no difference between past and present. I am told that all this derives from the family's guardian deity, the shrine over there. The Suzaku was originally a biwa[2] house. In Meiji they moved the shrine from their Kyoto mansion, where it had stood since ancient days, to Tokyo, and they call the deity Princess Tsukubu-suma, but her original form is Lady Benten, of Chikubu Island,[3] a beautiful goddess with a biwa in her arms. Because she prefers watery places, the previous master, through divining, selected this high spot overlooking the sea just beyond to build this mansion.

RITSUKO: But Lady Benten is the guardian deity of the Suzaku, is she not?

O-REI: Both guardian deity and goddess. She is a beautiful, young goddess.

RITSUKO: Then why is it . . . ?

O-REI: Don't you see? This goddess is very jealous.

(During this conversation, Tsunehiro enters from stage right dressed in the uniform of the Senior Grades of the Peers' School. He stops briefly in front of the Benten shrine, offers prayers, seems to become suspicious about the fact that the door of the shrine is open, and eavesdrops outside the greenhouse.)

TSUNEHIRO: *(Entering the greenhouse cheerfully)* So O-Rei has finally started it.

RITSUKO: Oh, how are you? Did you come in from the garden?

TSUNEHIRO: Because it's convenient for eavesdropping. She finally started it. I was wondering when she might start frightening Ritsuko. Going so far as to bring out Mother's *jūni hitoe* and cedar fan. . . . And I know what she would say in the end—that the masters of the Suzaku have all been married not to women, but to Lady Benten.

---

2. A lutelike instrument with four or five strings.

3. A heavily wooded island with a circumference of about 1.2 miles in the northern part of Lake Biwa. The nō drama *Chikubu-shima* describes the virtues of the resident deity of this island. It is one of the locations for the Five Bentens, the other four being the Amanogawa (river), of Yamato; Enoshima (island), of Sagami; Miyajima (island), of Aki; and Kinkazan (island), of Rikuzen.

RITSUKO: *(Striving to be cheerful)* We haven't got that far yet.

TSUNEHIRO: Then she plans to administer the coup de grâce. You better not mind whatever this ghoulish old woman says. *(To O-Rei)* Come now, fold that *juni hitoe* quickly and take it back to the shrine. What are you going to do if Father sees that you've carelessly taken out Mother's important mementos?

O-REI: The count hasn't come home for two days now.

TSUNEHIRO: Because two nights ago he had an assignment to stay overnight with His Majesty. Not only that. He must have something that keeps him busy at the court. But in the first place, who gave you permission to bring out Mother's. . . .

RITSUKO: *(Trying to ease the tension)* I was the one who asked O-Rei. I have always admired your mother in those beautiful photographs and wanted to see her *juni hitoe* at least once.

(Ritsuko and Tsunehiro ignore O-Rei while she silently folds the dress, takes it back to the shrine, offers prayers, and returns.)

RITSUKO: How have you been doing at school?

TSUNEHIRO: Nothing but drills. What's turned the school all into drills is that arrogant SOB Prime Minister Tabuchi's intervention. I am a platoon leader. I don't have to carry a gun, though, and that makes it easier to bear.

RITSUKO: Did you come here as soon as school was over today?

TSUNEHIRO: You didn't wait that long, did you?

RITSUKO: No, . . . but I'd like to know more, about how beautiful Lady Benten is, what she looks like.

TSUNEHIRO: Adorned with various necklaces, loops, and earrings, topped with a jeweled crown, our Lady Benten is smiling, holding a beautifully inlaid biwa in her arms, like a regular human being. As the sound of music she plays pours into her face, a lake, just as the moonlight does, her smiles appear like glistening ripples. All this is the divine effect of music. Water is music. There she rules it. The human body is made of water. Therefore she rules it and turns it into music. Blood is made of water. Therefore she rules it and blood turns into music.

RITSUKO: You are saying the Suzaku's bloodline is music and you, Hiro, yourself are music.

TSUNEHIRO: Count Suzaku's house itself is music. Therefore, it must end one of these days. Is there music that does not end?

RITSUKO: If she is a goddess with that much beauty, with that much power, she should turn into music not only the sea we can see immediately from her shrine over there, but also every corner of the Pacific that is contiguous to the bay. She should at once turn into music the battling sea, the ominous sea that is raging with pain and fear, where Japan's warships are

sunk one after another, where southern islands are bloodied and abandoned one after another. If the battling sea were suddenly filled with
music just as with ice, both enemy and friend could only stop and smile,
I would suppose.

TSUNEHIRO: We never know what a god desires from us. But this is an
age when men die. You needn't allow yourself to be taken in by O-
Rei's scare tactics. In an age like this women seldom die.

RITSUKO: *(Uneasily)* I don't want you to say something like that.
(O-Rei returns.)

O-REI: I have done what you told me to, sir.

TSUNEHIRO: Good. . . . Come, there's no need for us to rot indoors on
such a warm, bright spring afternoon. Let's go out into the garden and
look at the sea.

RITSUKO: Yes. *(She hesitates. Suddenly)* I have decided to learn the biwa.

TSUNEHIRO: You surprise me. Not me. I have never even touched the
one in this house.

RITSUKO: How about your father?

TSUNEHIRO: He certainly was good at it once upon a time. But now I
don't know. First of all, if he keeps busy with our lord like this, he won't
have time to teach you the biwa.

O-REI: You must do the biwa yourself, sir.

TSUNEHIRO: Are you telling me to carry a gun in one hand and play the
biwa with the other?

O-REI: But you must learn to play it from the master while you can. The
Suzaku is above all a biwa house, you know.

TSUNEHIRO: Father, you see, is someone who considers our lord the most
important. In a peaceful time our lord might express his wish to listen to
the biwa we have inherited from generation to generation in this family. If that were to happen, Father might teach me in earnest, and the two
of us, father and son, might successfully perform in our lord's presence.
But we are at war now. Father has abandoned the biwa in a desperate
attempt to protect our lord all by himself. Above all, from Prime Minister Tabuchi's dictatorial conduct.

O-REI: Yesterday I saw an itinerant merchant I'd never seen before loiter-
ing near the rear gate. I think, sir, that Mr. Tabuchi is sending *kempei*[4]
in plainclothes to check each visitor to this place.

TSUNEHIRO: I'm also followed. This guy talks to me in a streetcar about
innocuous nothings, but obviously he's trying to find out about Father's
movements from me, his son. All our boarding students have been taken

---

4. Japan's military police whose duties, during the 1930s and 1940s, went far beyond
the normal boundaries of military affairs, turning them into an all-powerful secret police.

to be soldiers. Even our butler,[5] despite his age, was taken as a private second class. Father was so dependent upon him; I hear he was immediately sent to the front. I hear Tabuchi is saying he'll root out all the men of the Suzaku family. . . . All this means that Father is a powerful opponent he can't push around.

RITSUKO: Let's forget unpleasant things for now and go out into the garden to look at the sea. The sea is quiet.

TSUNEHIRO: But far in the distance where you can't see, plenty of blood is being shed today, too.

RITSUKO: As red as the setting sun.

TSUNEHIRO: Right. We still have some time before the sunset.

(The two of them go out into the garden. O-Rei puts things in order. The two young people sit down on the overlook, their backs toward the audience.)

RITSUKO: I wonder what's going to happen to Japan?

TSUNEHIRO: To us, is what you are asking, no?

RITSUKO: The two are the same.

TSUNEHIRO: Yes, you are right. The same thing.

RITSUKO: When our country's right arm hurts . . .

TSUNEHIRO: . . . so does our own right arm. And when our country's skirts, spread resplendently to the end of the sea, are ripped apart . . .

RITSUKO: . . . so are we ripped apart.

TSUNEHIRO: And the screams of the silk being ripped apart . . .

RITSUKO: . . . reach us from beyond the sea. . . . Is it possible that Japan will lose?

TSUNEHIRO: That means that the world will turn into night. It means that the most elegant thing in the world will be trampled under muddy feet. We can't allow that to happen.

RITSUKO: Are you saying. . . .

TSUNEHIRO: The sea is drawing me. I don't know why. The sea wind that's rushing up to us is impregnated with despair and glory. With my face exposed to the wind coming up from the sea like this, I feel as if my cheekbones were being slapped with a bag packed with the placer gold of despair and glory. Why and when did the sea begin to accuse me?

I once told you. Until the middle grades I used to love to see steamship freighters in newspaper advertisements and dream about things. All the names of the ports of call were written in Chinese characters: "New Felicitous Wave" for Singapore, "Waves-Like-These Bay" for the Persian Gulf, "Semi-Consecutive Mountains" for Alexandria. . . . I was proud that I was able to read all those odd characters. Freighters and the mideastern moonlit night and the evening calm of the Persian

---

5. The original for this word is *Sandayū*.

Gulf that is as heavy as the long-haired carpet—that was all the longing I had for the sea. The sea used to be that gentle. When did it begin to slap me on the cheeks; when did it begin to accuse me?

I know. It is since the time when the sea, having loaded the table-cloth spread like blue waves with golden tableware of death and despair and glory, and having made himself ready, began to approach me from the other side, in stately composure, waiting for me to be seated. The table has mountains of coral just drawn up from the tides, it is adorned with tropical cumuli. A golden compote with an imperial crest has a load of tropical fruits of various colors. And the moment I put one of them in my mouth, that will be death. The sea is denouncing me for being so hungry and yet so unwilling to take my seat at the table. The sea knows my terrible hunger better than anyone else, probably even better than you.

RITSUKO: All the women know; they know that no woman can appease a man in that hunger.

TSUNEHIRO: Perhaps Lady Benten, only that Princess Tsukubu-suma. . . .

RITSUKO: I haven't offered prayers yet. Let's go there. And let us pray to the goddess that she maintain a firm hold on Hiro. No matter what may become of me.

(At this moment a bell rings at stage right to announce the arrival of a guest. The sound of the bell does not reach the two young people outside. O-Rei exits stage right and, in a while, reappears, following Shishido Mitsuyasu.)

O-REI: Do I understand you did not come home with the master?

MITSUYASU: I decided to take leave a step before my brother, so I might tell Tsunehiro of his papa's wonderful exploits as soon as possible. I want to tell him before a newspaper, before the radio. Where is he?

O-REI: He is in the garden. I'll bring him, though he is with Miss Ritsuko.

MITSUYASU: That's all right. She's like his fiancée now. Also, O-Rei, you may stay here and listen to what I have to say. Now that the Suzaku family has been reduced to such a few people, we must add you to our number.

O-REI: I am too lowly for that.

MITSUYASU: What are you saying? I've been treating you as a family member for a long time, haven't I? *(O-Rei makes a move to leave the room.)* Wait, you must also be prepared to see that my brother gets adequate rest when he returns. He has been working for two days and nights without almost any sleep.

O-REI: I understand, sir. *(Outside)* Mr. Shishido is here to visit you.

TSUNEHIRO: Uncle. . . . What business could it be?

O-REI: He says it's urgent business.

(The three of them move inside.)

MITSUYASU: Come, be seated here. My brother, as you know, is old-fashioned, and he's not the kind of person who comes home and boastfully chats about what has happened in the court. Knowing that, I have hurried home before him. I wanted to bring the news to you faster than the radio.

TSUNEHIRO: What happened?

MITSUYASU: Glad tidings. Tabuchi has lost his position.

TSUNEHIRO: Yes?

MITSUYASU: And my brother, all alone, did all the necessary work to drive him up against the wall.

TSUNEHIRO: You mean, sir, that Tabuchi is abandoning his cabinet?

MITSUYASU: He is. In no time bells for selling extras will be ringing throughout the city. No matter who succeeds him, he can't possibly be worse than Tabuchi. With this we may have a glimmer of hope for the war.

TSUNEHIRO: But how could Father do so much?

MITSUYASU: I can only say that powerless, quiet man, because of his devotion to our lord, was suddenly endowed with the strength of a thousand men. He has smashed the usurper's palace with Herculean strength.

With our lord's tacit instructions, he talked to this man, he talked to that man. When the outcome was set, the chief of the naval staff, in particular, held my hands and shed tears of joy. It may already be too late, he said, but Japan might still be saved. This is all thanks to Grand Chamberlain Suzaku, said he, who, despite his look, is gentle-hearted, and he shed tears. Finally, just about an hour ago, that arrogant prime minister begged our lord to allow him to resign. Our lord accepted his resignation. The imperial command will go to the moderate General Uesugi. When that happens, my ritualistic work at the Bureau of Rites will simply mean reverentially standing by, my heart hiding the joy after the dark clouds have cleared.

TSUNEHIRO: So Father did so much, a man who never takes any initiative, a man who is quiescence itself.

MITSUYASU: He did. He will come back here soon. You must pretend you haven't heard anything from me; otherwise, I'll be in trouble. No one dislikes as much as he does someone stepping in for him or telling on someone else. All you need to do is to say kind words for his hard work and give him adequate rest.

O-REI: So suspicious *kempei* in plainclothes will no longer loiter around this mansion.

MITSUYASU: No. And Japan will brighten up a little. This will boost the morale for fighting and help tighten into a single force the people's feelings about to be shattered into smithereens.

O-REI: Oh, if only the war ended before doing any harm to our young master! If only he could move on to university, then find a peaceful job in a world where the war is all over! *(She cries.)* That is my only wish.

TSUNEHIRO: That is a small, cowardly, pitiful wish. O-Rei does not understand honor and pride.

MITSUYASU: Come, don't be so hard. Let O-Rei say whatever she wants to say. In fact, there are times when the silly words of women who don't give a damn about appearances are accepted as justice by the society. *(The bell rings. All rise to their feet. O-Rei exits. In due time, enters Tsunetaka, followed by her.)*

TSUNETAKA: Oh, so all of you are here. Let me relax a bit. O-Rei, check the bathwater, would you?

O-REI: Yes, master.

(O-Rei exits. Everyone sits down. Silence for a while.)

MITSUYASU: So, when you say "relax," you mean holding your back straight against the chair, not even crossing your legs, while seated like that. I've been seeing this all these years, but it still surprises me. And this, right after working hard for two days and nights.

TSUNETAKA: Don't make fun of me. I can't possibly be something other than myself.

(Enters O-Rei.)

O-REI: The water is just right, sir. You may bathe whenever you wish.

TSUNETAKA: I see. O-Rei, you should stay here, too. I have something I wanted to say when everyone is here.

MITSUYASU: I already told them. . . .

TSUNETAKA: You weren't adopted by the Shishido family to learn to be a big mouth, were you? The previous Viscount Shishido was such an orator, as you know.

MITSUYASU: I didn't expect you to be sarcastic.

TSUNETAKA: Because I am now relaxed to the core of my heart. What I wanted to tell you is none other than this. For the last couple of days I have behaved in a manner truly inappropriate for a chamberlain. I have created a turmoil around our lord. I cannot tell you what the matter was about, but I finished what was to be done for the moment. So I requested leave from our lord. He did not give permission on the spot, but as someone who behaved outside the boundary of his role, and as a warning to those who will succeed me, I think I must take leave by all means. Assume that I am no longer a chamberlain as of today. From tomorrow on I shall take the liberty not to report to work.

TSUNEHIRO: Father. . . .

MITSUYASU: That goes against logic no matter how you put it. You have accomplished an admirable deed. There's no reason. . . .

TSUNETAKA: Stop jabbering, Mitsuyasu. From now on I shall serve our lord from this house, from a distance. It is indeed excruciating for me to stay away from him, but I shall lead the rest of my life modestly, enjoying the scent of the chrysanthemum in the distance. However far our lord may be, I dare say his heart is linked to mine. . . . Come, O-Rei, I'll always be home from now on. The first thing to do is to take a bath.

O-REI: Yes, milord.

(Exits Tsunetaka. So does O-Rei, following him.)

(The rest remain silent.)

MITSUYASU: That was shocking. My brother makes up his mind in a direction opposite that of normal people. Ordinarily, one might not allow oneself to count on a reward from our lord, but certainly one would use his greater trust to redouble one's efforts, wouldn't one? Didn't he give himself to this great task day and night for that alone? His sudden departure will mean trouble to our lord, not to him. Does this decision of his mean he's thinking of throwing himself into a dangerous situation where he could use his loyalty in a more clear-cut manner? That worries me. As always, he doesn't tell us anything, but. . . . *(He looks at his watch.)* No, this is no good. It's time to go back to the court. Listen, if you see any worrisome symptom in my brother, let me know at once. *(The three of them rise to their feet.)* No, stay where you are. No need to see me off.

TSUNEHIRO: Good-bye, Uncle.

RITSUKO: Good-bye.

MITSUYASU: Yes, good-bye.

(He departs hurriedly.)

TSUNEHIRO: To serve our lord in the true sense of the word, one must distance oneself from him. One must serve him from a distance. That is what Father means. . . . Ritsuko, I didn't tell you this yet, but today, at school, I completed the application for the navy's student reserve.

RITSUKO: You did?

TSUNEHIRO: The school guarantees that I'll be accepted. You see, I'll soon be a naval officer.

RITSUKO: Hiro!

TSUNEHIRO: You shouldn't look so sad.

RITSUKO: You are going away to a distant place.

TSUNEHIRO: Look after my father, would you? There are many things O-Rei, alone, can't take care of. Besides, Father is going to be home all the time from now on. You'll have ample time to learn the biwa from him. . . . Right, we must make an air raid shelter for this house that's a little better than what we have; *(looking around)* all the glass of this room won't last a minute in an air raid.

RITSUKO: You are going away to a distant place. . . . And have you already gotten permission for that from your father?

TSUNEHIRO: No, not yet.

(Enters Tsunetaka with O-Rei following him.)

TSUNETAKA: That was a wonderful bath. At a time like this, it cannot be easy to have the bath ready for the master when you don't know when he may be home. I owe all this to you.

O-REI: I don't deserve such kind words, sir.

RITSUKO: Mr. Suzaku. . . .

TSUNEHIRO: I'll tell him.

TSUNETAKA: What is it?

TSUNEHIRO: Today I applied for the navy's student reserve. Would you give me permission, sir?

(O-Rei, startled, stops.)

TSUNETAKA: You did? *(Silence. He seats himself in a chair. He gives a quiet, composed smile.)* . . . You did. You may go.

TSUNEHIRO: So you give me permission.

TSUNETAKA: Yes.

RITSUKO: Mr. Suzaku. . . .

TSUNETAKA: *(Ignoring Ritsuko)* It's natural that the members of the Suzaku family should serve our lord, each in his own way. It's a good thing that men of the Suzaku family should fight. So few of our ancestors actually fought.

(All fall silent. Soon there is the sound of a bell selling an extra.)

O-REI: Sounds like an extra. I'll go get . . .

(She rises to her feet.)

TSUNETAKA: No need for that. I know. There's no need to buy an extra. . . . Look, spring is coming to an end like this. It may seem to be coming to an end as if nothing is happening, but any spring day prepares a great deal of young leaves and at the same time stores a great deal of decay. Look at the garden. Cherry blossoms have been scattered, while pink azaleas and flame azaleas are beginning to bloom. For all the briny winds, nature stubbornly protects its own law.

. . . I have never discussed matters related to His Majesty in this household, but today I will make an exception and tell you the reasons I requested leave from him. For the last several days I was engaged in a once-in-a-lifetime task, which I think I managed to pull off. I fought and fought in a way none of our ancestors ever did. I dedicated my entire body and soul to a cause that I think met our lord's wishes. It was done. Something no one thought possible was accomplished.

. . . I went to our lord and reported the outcome. There should be no mystery if I had expected to see joy in our lord's eyes as he listened to my report. Yet, though he did not say a word, and only I know this, for a brief second I spotted sadness in our lord's eyes.

. . . Do you understand? That is why I requested leave. Through his mind our lord told me, "Do nothing, just do not do anything. . . ." And I felt at once what he meant. I did so on account of the blood of the Suzaku that has lasted for thirty-seven generations. There is something our lord sees through. It was then I firmly made up my mind not to do anything further.

TSUNEHIRO: You mean. . . .

TSUNETAKA: No, you must fight. Fight for our lord, for the honor of the Suzaku. Ours is not a military house, but someone must fight. You are young, you have strength. What else could you do but fight? And I. . . . *(Silence)*

O-REI: Yes?

TSUNETAKA: Would you close the curtain over there? The westerly sun is too harsh on me.

CURTAIN

ACT 2: AUTUMN

Same as in act 1. All the glass is sealed with cross-shaped paper cutouts and covered with dark blackout curtains. Night; insects are chirping. For a while after curtain rise, stage is empty. From stage right, laughter of several people.

TSUNETAKA: *(Voice)* Come, let's get together here. *(Enters)* Let us have after-dinner coffee where we can hear insects chirp.

(Led by Tsunehiro in an ensign's uniform, enter Ritsuko, Mitsuyasu, and O-Rei.)
O-Rei, feel free to join us, too.

O-REI: I have to do the dishes.

TSUNETAKA: You can do the dishes any time. Take your seat there and be with us to relax after dinner. Feel free.

O-REI: Thank you, sir.
(She takes her seat at one end of the room.)

MITSUYASU: So the training is that tough. I'd never make it. I'd heard about the "spirit stick," but you say they hit you right on the buttocks with it.

TSUNEHIRO: It gets right into your brain. But now that I've been commissioned, I'm the lord and master. At the place of assignment, I'll pass as a legitimate ensign, as you see, anywhere, though brand-new. I'll behave as if I were born an ensign.

MITSUYASU: And tonight you are leaving here and heading to the place of assignment tomorrow morning. They certainly keep you under pressure, don't they? Where are you going to be assigned?

TSUNEHIRO: You can't trick me like that. You ask that question with such deliberate casualness. You've already asked the same thing three times. I am cautious now and won't carelessly let it out. Rest assured. It's a certain place in Japan, the safest spot you can imagine. I should be able to be back again during a furlough.

MITSUYASU: I hope you are right. . . . The war situation is so bad, you know.

TSUNEHIRO: I'm more concerned about this house. Can't you make a more solid air raid shelter? Can't Father evacuate soon? He has no office work to tend to.

RITSUKO: He won't listen, though we've urged him to. The Karuizawa[1] house says they'll gladly welcome him.

MITSUYASU: You are indeed giving us a lot of trouble. Now that Tsunehiro has been commissioned, you should take this opportunity and evacuate. That will be reassuring to your son, too.

TSUNETAKA: While our lord remains in Tokyo, I cannot possibly move to a safer place. To experience daily at least one-hundredth of the danger that falls on his jeweled body, that's what true service means. I am serving him by doing nothing, by enduring it, making no move.

MITSUYASU: There's nothing we can do about that kind of unrebuttable talk. Still, as Tsunehiro says, you should at least do something about the air raid shelter. . . .

TSUNETAKA: About that, you see *(pointing toward stage right)*, it's right there, under the floor of the dining room. That is adequate, isn't it?

TSUNEHIRO: Not adequate at all. If the dining room goes up in flames, that will be the end of the story. You must make something bigger, with concrete. . . .

TSUNETAKA: We don't have the material. It's too much trouble to ask people. You know, no matter where he is, a human being will be killed when he will be killed; he won't when he won't. At this late date you just don't put up unseemly struggle.

RITSUKO: There is no use speaking to him. Hiro, we have nothing we can do except to pray to Lady Benten that she protect this entire family. I was hoping to offer prayers with you, Hiro, when you returned. To pray

---

1. A summer resort northwest of Tokyo, it is on the outskirts of Mount Asano, in Nagano. Initially a favorite resort place for foreign missionaries, it was taken over by rich people.

for your father's safety and for your safety. *(Rising to her feet)* Would you come with me?

TSUNEHIRO: Go on ahead. I have a little bit to talk about with Father. I'll be with you right away.

O-REI: I'll come with you. These days there are even dogs running wild, and just going out in the garden can be dangerous at night.

(Ritsuko and O-Rei go out into the garden and walk up to the shrine.)

TSUNEHIRO: *(Making sure that the two are gone)* Please don't tell Ritsu. I thought I'd at least tell you, Father, my real place of assignment. But this is a military secret. I cannot say it aloud.

(He writes on the table with his fingers.)

MITSUYASU: That island! Tsunehiro, going there is the same as getting killed.

TSUNEHIRO: Please don't tell Ritsu.

(He hurries out to the garden. He offers prayers at the shrine side by side with Ritsuko. O-Rei steps back and returns to the room. Insects chirp. Tsunetaka and Mitsuyasu remain silent. Sensing a strange tension, she tries to say something but holds back and exits stage right. At stage left, after finishing their prayers, Tsunehiro and Ritsuko exit to the garden at stage left.)

MITSUYASU: And so.

TSUNETAKA: Hmmm.

MITSUYASU: We must do something about this. If we leave the matter as it is, the Suzaku will have no one to carry the family forward. . . . Here's something that has occurred to me just now. When you smashed the Tabuchi cabinet, Mr. Akiyama held my hands with tears of joy. I'll do anything to return this favor, he said firmly; ask me to do anything. As he is, he is such a straightforward, honest man. We can believe his promise. At the time he was chief of the naval staff but in the new cabinet he is minister of the navy. . . . Listen, I've heard about a couple of cases like this, and I'm not saying I'll be asking Mr. Akiyama to do something he can't do. I'll ask him to reassign Tsunehiro to some place within Japan. And this is urgent, too. You should even go to see him at his house tonight, if possible.

(Tsunetaka does not respond.)

MITSUYASU: I know it would be difficult for you to do that. The best thing of course would be for you, his parent, to make a direct appeal, but your personality won't allow that to happen. If it is all right with you, I will go there in your behalf. . . .

(Tsunetaka maintains his silence.)

MITSUYASU: This is no time to keep quiet. Whether or not you save your son's life will determine whether or not the bloodline of the Suzaku will continue; this is that critical moment. I understand how you feel. You are one person who cannot kneel before someone and make a plea. I have no choice but to make this my own job, not so much for you, my brother, as for the nephew I love, for the Suzaku family. The matter is very simple. Switching a fresh ensign's place of assignment from this to that spot won't affect the war situation a bit. Just one word, and the minister of the navy will understand everything and at once move Tsunehiro to a safe place. I know he will.

(At this moment O-Rei enters the room with a coffee tray. Evidently sensing something is awry, she steps back and eavesdrops. The two men do not notice her presence.)

And we must take care of this now, tonight, before tomorrow morning. Once Tsunehiro leaves for his place of assignment, it will be too late. Once there, it would take time to find a new place for him, and in no time that island will fall into the hands of the enemy. When that happens, Tsunehiro will be killed.

(Tsunetaka keeps his silence.)

MITSUYASU: Is it your intention to kill Tsunehiro? As it stands now, he is sure to be killed, so if you, his father, just sit back and do nothing, it's the same as killing him, your son. Are you deranged?

(Tsunetaka remains silent.)

MITSUYASU: You are deranged. I began to sense something frightening about your mind when you stubbornly submitted your letter of resignation even though our lord was so distressed by it and tried so very hard to stop you. Your retirement despite our lord's wishes was, as it were, disloyalty, was it not? Since that time you've been losing whatever humanity you had. Like a white tree-pillar stripped of its bark you just sit like that, your back straight, neatly, keeping yourself, and yourself alone, clean.

(Tsunetaka does not say a word.)

MITSUYASU: What is it that makes you keep quiet when your own brother is calling you mad? You are a quiet madman. You are a small, clear, deranged lake in the midst of a mountain no one visits. Only the bird that flies over you knows that the lake is deranged. And only he knows why all the birds have perished in the forest that surrounds the lake. . . . You are annoyed by all the human beings that are alive, are you not? Even your own son. Above all, this harassing, chatterbox brother of yours, why don't you kill him. Come on, why don't you kill him with those cold, white hands of yours?

(Tsunetaka is still silent.)

MITSUYASU: So you are not giving me permission, no matter what. You are not going to say Yes, no matter what. I see. I can regard the fact that you keep quiet as a sign of tacit understanding. Well then, with your tacit understanding, I will go to Mr. Akiyama now. *(He rises to his feet.)*

TSUNETAKA: Wait.

MITSUYASU: What do you mean?

TSUNETAKA: You cannot go. You cannot do anything like that.

MITSUYASU: But. . . .

TSUNETAKA: I am not at all angry. I am grateful to you for the way you feel. Come, sit down.

(Mitsuyasu reluctantly sits down.)

It's my turn to beg you. Please do not go to the minister. If you did anything like that, that would destroy everything. It would destroy not only me but also Tsunehiro's pride, the Suzaku house itself. You might say the secret would be kept. Yes, the secret might be kept in the society at large. But I would know. You would know. The minister of the navy would know. The small wound of this knowledge would grow day by day, and in time a large, rotten wound would begin to sing. Compared with that, Tsunehiro's life wouldn't count. Our lord says, "Go." Our lord says, "Give up your life." When he does that, you just go and give up your life. It is evident that my son is determined to do just that.

MITSUYASU: So you are saying I cannot do it.

TSUNETAKA: No, that is one thing you cannot do, Mitsuyasu.

(The two fall silent. O-Rei hurries forward from stage right, kneels on the floor, and kowtows.)

O-REI: Please, I beg you. This is the one plea I must make in my whole life. Please save the young master's life. Milord, I beg you, like this, with my hands on the floor. I know, I know, sir, that I am acting above and beyond my state. I know, but please, please. Milord, please do let Mr. Shishido do what he wants to do. I pray to you, my hands joined.

(She cries. Tsunetaka and Mitsuyasu remain silent for a while.)

TSUNETAKA: O-Rei, you must understand. There are things we can do and things we cannot do.

O-REI: *(Furious)* That is why I am making this plea, because it is something you can do. If Mr. Shishido goes tonight in your behalf, you can pretend ignorance. If you dislike it so much to bow and ask someone to do something for you, you don't need, milord, to say even a word of gratitude to Mr. Akiyama, isn't that right, sir? In return for this favor, I'd be happy to go to Mr. Akiyama's house and work for him for free the rest of my life. Just to keep yourself clean, you do not have to go as far as sacrificing the young master, do you, sir?

MITSUYASU: O-Rei, you are going too far.

O-REI: What about you, milord, sir?

TSUNETAKA: *(Remains silent for a while)* I cannot do that.

O-REI: You cannot. All right, then.

(She dashes out as if deranged, looks around, and hurries out stage left.)

TSUNETAKA: I have never seen her in such a state.

MITSUYASU: It's quite understandable. This is not something you can get out of by simply scolding her.

TSUNETAKA: It appears the moon is up. The garden has grown light. Because of the blackout these days the moon and stars have become closer to us. Likewise, we human beings have come closer to our destinies.

MITSUYASU: We've already lost this war, you know.

TSUNETAKA: Don't say that in Tsunehiro's presence.

MITSUYASU: Everybody knows this, it's just that no one says it. I'd say it's just like a family secret.

TSUNETAKA: I am simply thinking day and night what might become of our lord when that happens. His eyes said, "Don't do anything, just don't do anything." My heart heard these words as if he uttered them, one by one, clearly. His heart still flows through my heart just as clear water flows under a boulder. There cannot possibly be any mistake in what my mind's ear heard. You see, I was his classmate since he was such a small, lovely boy. . . . "Don't do anything, just don't do anything. . . ." That is to say, he meant, "Just let yourself be destroyed," did he not?

(Startled, Mitsuyasu looks his brother in the face. At stage left enters O-Rei forcibly bringing the young couple. She says breathlessly.)

O-REI: Do you understand, master? The only thing you have to do is just to say, "I'll do whatever Uncle wants me to do." Don't say anything else. Please leave the rest to me. . . . Those words sum up everything I've done in bringing you up. Please do not ask any question. . . . If you pity me, you just say those words and go. Do you understand?

(Tsunehiro and Ritsuko look at each other, confused, but he nods. O-Rei leads them into the room.)

O-REI: *(To Tsunehiro)* So, now, please say them.

TSUNEHIRO: *(Awkwardly)* I'll do whatever Uncle wants me to do.

(Tsunetaka and Mitsuyasu try to say something, but O-Rei restrains them desperately yet feigning cheerfulness.)

O-REI: So, everyone, this is it. Please do not say anything. The master himself said it, and that settles it all. This settles it all, doesn't it? Oh no, don't say anything. I beg you. Please, I beg you. This has settled everything, so please leave everything the way it is, please do not touch this matter, until the master takes his leave. Now, I'll bring some tea.

(All in awkward silence. Tsunetaka suddenly rises to his feet and heads toward stage right.)

TSUNEHIRO: *(Jumping up)* Father!

TSUNETAKA: What is it?

TSUNEHIRO: What is this all about?

TSUNETAKA: You say you'll do whatever your uncle tells you to. Ask your uncle.

O-REI: Milord!

TSUNEHIRO: *(Stopping Tsunetaka who has made another move to leave, he says to Mitsuyasu)* Uncle! What is this all about? What in the world is this all about?

O-REI: Mr. Shishido! . . . Mr. Shishido!

(Mitsuyasu says nothing.)

TSUNEHIRO: Why don't you answer me? This is terrible. This is after all the night before I leave this house for the war, but all of you have contrived such a depressing joke.

RITSUKO: Mr. Shishido, please, do respond to Hiro.

O-REI: Miss Ritsuko, that won't do!

TSUNEHIRO: Father, what on earth is this farce about?

TSUNETAKA: *(Returning)* You mean you didn't. . . .

O-REI: *(Trembling)* Oh, no! Milord!

TSUNETAKA: You don't know anything?

O-REI: Yes, he knows everything. He's faking ignorance. You are, aren't you, master? I told you all, didn't I? If you feel any pity for me. . . .

TSUNETAKA: Tsunehiro, answer me like a man.

TSUNEHIRO: Well, I. . . .

O-REI: Don't say that!

TSUNEHIRO: Well, I was asked by O-Rei just a minute ago to say only, "I'll do whatever Uncle wants me to do," when I come back here. She didn't give me any explanation. *(Looking at each person's face)* . . . What is this? Something important?

TSUNETAKA: So you didn't know. O-Rei overheard what Mitsuyasu had to say and wanted you to follow his wishes. I mean . . .

O-REI: Oh no!

TSUNEHIRO: What is it? Please tell me now.

TSUNETAKA: Mitsuyasu proposed that he go to the minister of the navy tonight and ask that your place of assignment be changed from the dangerous place to some place safe in Japan.

TSUNEHIRO: That's cowardly. . . . Uncle, is that true?

(Mitsuyasu nods in silence. O-Rei, thoroughly beaten, is crying, facing the wall.)

TSUNEHIRO: And, Father, you certainly. . . .

TSUNETAKA: Did I agree to it, you ask.

TSUNEHIRO: Yes, sir.

TSUNETAKA: I did not. I told him he could not do anything like that.

TSUNEHIRO: Thank you very much, sir. You definitely said that to him, sir?

TSUNETAKA: Yes, I did. And O-Rei. . . .

RITSUKO: *(Hurrying to the side of Mitsuyasu)* Mr. Shishido. You know where Hiro is going to be sent. Where is it? Tell me. Where is it?
(Mitsuyasu whispers in her ear the name of the island.)
What? That island! Why didn't you. . . . *(Suddenly holding Tsunehiro in her arms)* Why didn't you tell me? That is the most dangerous island, the enemy's biggest target, and yet you lied to me, saying you are assigned to some place in Japan.

TSUNEHIRO: *(Ignoring her)* Father. So what about O-Rei?

TSUNETAKA: I understand how she feels. She threw herself down on the floor and pleaded with me to give consent.

TSUNEHIRO: Why is it? Why is it that you understand how she feels? She tried to trample upon my courage on the eve of my departure, wound the pride of the Suzaku house, and envelope my future with the most cowardly notoriety. Hers was such a wrongheaded sentiment of love. How can you say that is understandable?

TSUNETAKA: I only said I understand how she feels.

TSUNEHIRO: Why are you running away, Father? Why can't you be good enough to face up honestly to my honest anger, your son leaving for the battlefield tomorrow? Are you intimating that I have inside me the smallest fragment of O-Rei's cowardly sentiment?

MITSUYASU: Come now, Tsunehiro. You don't throw yourself in all directions like that. All of us here are worried about your future, each after his own fashion.

TSUNEHIRO: Uncle, do keep quiet, please. You are the one who used the term "protecting the Suzaku house" in the basest meaning and tried to smear the pure mind of a young man heading to a place of death with the mud of worldly vulgarity.

TSUNETAKA: I understand your fury well. But I declined your uncle's offer and you are grateful that I did. I can't think of anything that makes the Suzaku house shine more brightly than this tacit understanding between us. You are the first man from this house who is going to take up a sword to serve our lord. You are the man who proves that this long, long, pliant braided cord of silk that has been our family line was in fact the strapping cord attached to the golden scabbard. You are the gallant, rightful son of the Suzaku. Am I running away? We are the same in that neither you nor I can run away from this proud lookout tower. However exposed we may be to the enemy's eyes, however severely attacked we may be with arrows, we have no place to flee to.

TSUNEHIRO: I understand your thinking well. Now I can go to the battle zone without any worry. I will be at the forefront of those who protect our country, and I will throw myself proudly into the most dangerous battlefield. And O-Rei.

(O-Rei turns to look Tsunehiro straight in the eye.)

O-REI: So in the end you do not listen to my plea, master. If only you had said those words and left. . . . If you had, everything would have worked out fine.

TSUNEHIRO: *(Getting one step closer to her)* You have trapped me.

O-REI: Trapped you?

TSUNEHIRO: A cowardly trap. You tried to embarrass me by trapping me. I know. When I said those words you told me to say without knowing anything, everyone fell silent, and then Father stood up. When I stopped him, he said, "You say you'll do whatever your uncle tells you to. Ask your uncle." . . . Those words of Father's. At the time I did not understand what they meant. Later I understood, but now that I understand it, I'm left with a troublesome thought. And you are the one who created it.

O-REI: What are you saying? Master, I just wanted to save your life.

TSUNEHIRO: *(Severely)* Don't say that. Now I understand what was in Father's mind during that brief moment between the time he stood up silently and the time he said those words. It was me, an abominably ugly, base, despicable, timid me. I can't bear the thought that such a false image of me lodged in Father's mind even if it was only for a second or two. It was you who created and gave birth to such an image of me.

O-REI: *(Struck with fear)* I did?

TSUNEHIRO: That's why I say you trapped me. Whatever your motive, whatever your love, you created such a base doll of me with your eyes, your mouth, your breasts, your body, your blood, your flesh. That's what I can't bear. If there's something that prevents me from leaving this world with a clear conscience, it's this bitterness.

O-REI: Master. . . .

MITSUYASU: Don't torture O-Rei like that. You are excited. The words you utter in your excitement will become seeds of regret later. We all understand what you want to say. You have said enough.

TSUNEHIRO: How many times do I have to ask you? I just asked you to keep quiet. . . . O-Rei, I plan to torment you as much as I please. I'll leave to you all the ugly words I can leave to this world. You plotted to pull me down from the height of the pride of the Suzaku house. You planned to make out of me an ordinary, and by ordinary I mean as ordinary as you, fearful, loving, gentle-hearted, non-wave-making, timid, hardworking young man. Didn't you? This has been clearly revealed tonight. And then your grief, your sorrow, your full-bodied love set up a trap. A young, quick-moving, prideful animal was almost trapped but brilliantly got away from it. He escaped and ran away from this base trap cleverly hidden with the mud of love, which has no use but to soil the shoes polished with honor and glory—hidden with the mud and humus of love. Now I can depart. Listen, O-Rei, chances are I'll never see you again. Tonight I part *not* with Father. Father and I are linked with a solid bond of pride, and no matter where I go, this bond will not be severed. What will be severed is my bond with you. What I am parting with is you. I am parting with your self-conceit of love, your opprobrium of honor, your unbearable baseness.

(While he says these words, O-Rei continues to cry quietly.)

O-REI: Master. . . .

TSUNEHIRO: Stop calling me that. Your voice annoys me. Your voice will stay in my ear, become an obstacle to my honor, become a troublesome thought.

O-REI: *(Half to herself)* Where in the world is a mother who must be cursed so by her own son?

(With these words, all are chilled into silence. O-Rei herself notices this and clams up. A long silence.)

TSUNETAKA: *(With his eyes closed)* O-Rei, that is no good. You cannot say that. . . . Those are the words you cannot ever say in the Suzaku house. Everyone here knows it, but no one says it. There's no one who is surprised to hear it. But the moment you say it, the pillar of this house receives an invisible scar and the mirror of this house becomes clouded. . . . Listen, O-Rei, this is a happy night for celebrating the rightful heir of the Suzaku family going to war. You must restrain yourself no matter what he might say to you.

O-REI: *(Silent for a while)* I am terribly sorry. I shall be careful from now on.

TSUNETAKA: That's good. Tsunehiro, I understand how you feel, but you better keep quiet now. Tonight wasn't supposed to be a night of sorrow and tears. It was supposed to be an evening of honorable parting and brave joy. Let us revive the joyful conversation and noisy laughter from dinner. It is my hope that the hearts of those of us gathered here will become one, so that Tsunehiro may depart with that one heart stored in his body. The gallantry of going to battle on a quiet autumn night, bathed in the moonlight, our ancestors knew how to play that on the biwa, how to transmit it later to generations as music. That way the Suzaku family can be complete. O-Rei, bring out the brandy set aside for just this kind of occasion. Everyone, take your own glass. Let us toast to Tsunehiro's departure.

(All take their seats. O-Rei brings the bottle and glasses. All raise their glasses.)

RITSUKO: Mr. Suzaku.

TSUNETAKA: What is it, Ritsuko?

RITSUKO: Would you please use your office to make this a toast not only for Hiro's going to battle, but also for another celebration?

TSUNETAKA: What do you mean?

TSUNEHIRO: *(Lifting his face, startled)* Ritsu.

RITSUKO: Actually, this is not something a woman should be proposing, but would you make this a toast for the wedding of Tsunehiro and me?

O-REI: *(Alarmed, terrified)* Miss Ritsuko!

MITSUYASU: Oh, that is a good idea. Nowadays we don't know what might happen tomorrow. We knew you were fond of each other, but we had refrained from saying it ourselves, though in our hearts we had given blessings to your relationship, of which we had approved. That is a good idea. Well now, let us raise our glasses. . . .

TSUNEHIRO: Wait, please, Uncle. I haven't given my consent yet. Don't be carried away by Ritsu's temporary excitement. You are a fully grown-up person. Please don't say anything so unthinking. I am fond of her, and I believe we are fond of each other. But I am going to that island. With that in mind, I had myself refrained from proposing this, if nothing else. But now, without even thinking of a young woman's future, you are rashly making it a matter for a toast.

TSUNETAKA: Tsunehiro is right in what he says. I have no objection whatsoever to these two people getting together. The way they look, their ages, their family status all match, and I know Ritsuko will make a superlative bride, and I have loved her like my own daughter. But that is different from what we are talking about. This is something we can announce publicly when everything has calmed down and all the social conditions have become right.

RITSUKO: Yes, do you believe that the day will come when everything calms down and all social conditions have become right?

(Tsunetaka says nothing.)

RITSUKO: You don't believe it, do you? You know, don't you, that this is the only time we have for this.

TSUNEHIRO: Ritsu, look me firmly in the eye. We are fond of each other. We are hopelessly in love with each other. You can tell this by looking into my eyes. . . . But I have not made the proposal. A marriage can't take place unless the man makes the proposal first. You remember how in the *Kojiki*[2] Izanagi-no-mikoto and Izanami-no-mikoto turned around the heavenly column and called to each other. As it turned out, first the

---

2. Or *Record of Ancient Matters,* a semimythological account of Japanese history compiled in 712.

female deity called out, "Oh, behold, what a beautiful man!" and then
the male deity called out, "Oh, behold, what a beautiful woman!" Because the female deity called out first, an ominous thing happened. . . .[3]
Now I cannot bear the thought of allowing myself to succumb to my
heart and make the proposal and hurt you for the rest of your life. Because that would simply be my egoism.

MITSUYASU: Come now, there's no need for you all to be mulish about it,
is there? As my brother said a while ago, what's important is to send
Tsunehiro off with joy and blessings, with smiles on our faces. Now. . . .

RITSUKO: That "now" is sliding down.

MITSUYASU: That's why *now*, why we must treasure that *now*. . . .

RITSUKO: The *now* you are talking about and the *now* I am talking about
are different.

MITSUYASU: You must hear me out. The glasses we have just raised we
should turn into glasses for a provisional celebration. What do you think,
Tsunetaka? A provisional celebration is all right, isn't it? With you, too,
Tsunehiro?

RITSUKO: You say "provisional"?

MITSUYASU: Right.

RITSUKO: I wouldn't like it if it were "provisional." I wouldn't like it unless it was formal, a wedding you can't backtrack on even once.

TSUNEHIRO: Ritsu!

RITSUKO: Unless I became here, right now, a formal, true bride, whom
everyone recognizes as such, not a provisional bride. I wouldn't like it
unless I could call Hiro my husband and Mr. Suzaku Father. I'd like you
to raise your glasses to that celebration.

TSUNEHIRO: *(Firmly)* Ritsu, I will not permit it.

RITSUKO: You don't have to permit it. I decide this matter. Please raise
your celebratory glasses. Come, everyone, say, "Toast." Say, "Congratulations!" . . . So, none of you is willing to do it. I'll do it myself. *(She
rises to her feet and raises her glass)* Congratulations! Suzaku Tsunehiro and
Matsunaga Ritsuko have been married tonight. *(She downs the whole
glass; then laughs)* We, Tsunehiro and Ritsuko, swear that he, Tsunehiro, will call her, Ritsuko, his wife and she, Ritsuko, will call him,
Tsunehiro, her husband forever and ever, that we will be harmonious
and helpful to each other, and that we will love each other as long as
we live. *(She laughs)* I can do the whole thing by myself, from our own

---

3. As the *Kojiki* tells the story, "after each made his utterance, the male deity Izanagi
said to his wife, 'It's no good for a woman to speak first.' Nevertheless, they had intercourse in their bedroom, and the child she gave birth to was a leech child. They put this
child in a reed boat and let it flow away."

pledge to congratulatory speeches. I'll do the whole thing all by myself. *(She falters.)*

TSUNETAKA: *(Holding her up)* Steady. Come, steady. This is because you've gulped down liquor you aren't used to.

RITSUKO: *(Supporting herself against his knees)* Father. . . .

TSUNETAKA: I understand, Ritsuko. We all live in an illusion. Illusion has gradually permeated reality, and we live in a world where we can't even be certain of tomorrow. If just a moment ahead is illusory, we can call even this moment illusory. You become a formal bride in illusion. I approve of that. There will be no one to blame you. Come, let us all raise our glasses for the illusion of Ritsuko.

RITSUKO: No, I am not an illusion. It would do no good unless we had a formal wedding ceremony now, right here.

TSUNETAKA: *(Gently)* Here you go again. . . .

RITSUKO: This is necessary for the Suzaku family.

TSUNETAKA: For the Suzaku family, you say?

RITSUKO: *(Calmly)* Yes, it is. Did you know that until today I've been coming to the shrine in your garden every day to offer prayers? Most of the time I just offer prayers and go home, without saying hello to you, so O-Rei is the only person who knows this. Since Hiro joined the student reserve, I haven't missed a single day. . . .

TSUNETAKA: No, I didn't know that.

RITSUKO: I have prayed for only one thing. Only for Hiro's safety. For a prayer you need a pledge, and I chose the most painful pledge: that if you return Hiro safely, if you protect his body to the end, I'll give up marrying him. . . . Because, you see, the young, beautiful goddess of the shrine wants to marry Hiro. Because she firmly assumes that she is his bride. I thought that she would gladly accept the kind of pledge I made and protect Hiro's body.

. . . But tonight I saw it clearly: that all my daily prayers and my pledge were for naught. Why, praying like that, though my pledge might have been painful, was after all praying for both Hiro's safety and my own safety. The Lady Benten of the Suzaku family never kills a woman who doesn't marry the master of this house. In each generation such a woman lived long enough to hand down progeny for the Suzaku house. *(She looks at O-Rei. O-Rei looks away.)*

. . . Tonight I saw it. Hiro is going to a dangerous battlefield. To save Hiro, the goddess wants a sacrifice. So I had to change my pledge and become his formal bride tonight, so that I may stand in for him. Unless I do this, the bloodline of the Suzaku family will die out; if I do this, then when Hiro returns safely someday, he can produce his heir through some other woman whom he does not call his wife.

(Tsunetaka, alarmed, pulls Ritsuko away.)

Just as you did. . . . Yes, the goddess lets men live. They are her valuable husbands. All I have to do is to become a young bride of the Suzaku family who dies immediately, whose brief life is like a spring day that ends lost in an evening breeze, a young bride who fades away like gossamer. Just like your wife, who was so beautiful. This is the only way to save Hiro's life.

(All fall into dark silence. Some time elapses.)

TSUNEHIRO: *(Looking at his watch)* Now I must go.

TSUNETAKA: So you must.

MITSUYASU: Take care of yourself, Tsunehiro.

O-REI: Please stay well.

(Tsunehiro puts on his dagger and navy cap and salutes.)

TSUNEHIRO: Farewell.

TSUNETAKA: So you leave through the garden. Ritsuko, you better walk him to the gate. It's very dewy. Get her a shawl.

RITSUKO: I'm all right, sir.

TSUNETAKA: The moon is bright. There should be no problem coming back.
(Tsunetaka, Mitsuyasu, and O-Rei walk to the exit in the garden. Tsunehiro and Ritsuko walk to stage left, where Tsunehiro salutes once again and exits, urging Ritsuko on. Tsunetaka, Mitsuyasu, and O-Rei go back to the room and take their seats, dazed. Insects chirp.)

TSUNETAKA: . . . He's gone now.

MITSUYASU: . . . He has.

O-REI: Bathed in the autumn moonlight, they were truly a beautiful bridegroom and bride. The new bridegroom and bride of the Suzaku family . . .

TSUNETAKA: *(Slowly lifting his smiling face)* have melted away in the moonlight.

CURTAIN

ACT 3: SUMMER

In the garden at stage left, Tsunetaka, in a straw hat, a shirt, and knickerbockers, is pulling weeds. In the greenhouse at stage right, O-Rei in silk mompe[1] *sits on a couch, her legs sloppily thrust forward. She rolls a cigarette from rationed tobac-*

1. During the war, "because of fabric shortages, women sewed new clothing out of scraps of old. Turning necessity into virtue, some fashion-minded women and girls took pains in the design of their *yarikuri shitate* patchwork garments. By 1943 there was no longer enough fabric in the country to fulfill rations. Baggy trousers called *mompe* became women's daily dress [which was] worn over a shirt or an old kimono." Liza Dalby, *Kimono: Fashioning Culture* (Yale University Press, 1993). The *mompe* was also adopted for greater mobility and convenience to deal with the dangers of air raids and such.

co and smokes. The windowpanes of the greenhouse are still sealed with cross-shaped paper but the window is open wide. The conversation between Tsunetaka and O-Rei is conducted through the window.

TSUNETAKA: *(Resting his weeding hand)* O-Rei, would you give me a cigarette?

O-REI: Want me to roll another one?

TSUNETAKA: Yes. If you could, I'd like you to roll the next one with paste. With your spit, it falls apart in no time.

O-REI: There's nothing like paste. Why don't you use your own spit?

TSUNETAKA: Don't you see my hands are soiled?

O-REI: If they are, why don't you wash them.

(Silence.)

TSUNETAKA: All right then, give me tobacco and paper. I'll do it myself.

O-REI: I feel lazy. I feel so worn-out I don't want to move. You understand. You eat things not worth speaking of, yet are full of such energy, aren't you? At your age, in this sunlight, weeding. . . . You see, don't you, people with a lot of sexual drive can be energetic in doing anything. . . . I don't even have enough strength to move my own body.

TSUNETAKA: . . . Just give me tobacco.

O-REI: Why not come and get it?

TSUNETAKA: *(In a low voice)* O-Rei.

O-REI: *(Very languidly she puts paper and tobacco on a newspaper, rises to her feet, and walks to the window)* For what reason, for what purpose, do I have to serve up such kindnesses to him? If I were his wife, I wouldn't be able to help it, but I'm not even his wife. . . . Nowadays we get such terrible air raids, things like servants have all disappeared. What am I after all? I'm not supposed to exist, but I do. I must be my own ghost. The ghost of a servant who used to be here.

TSUNETAKA: *(Putting out his hand outside the window)* Be quick. . . .

O-REI: Quick, you say, but I won't be. *(Moving the paper wrapper out of Tsunetaka's hands)* There is something I want you to give me—in exchange for this.

TSUNETAKA: What is it?

O-REI: You know. I don't have to tell you. You have something you are hiding, don't you?

TSUNETAKA: What in the world . . . is that?

O-REI: It's the telegram.

(Silence.)

O-REI: Out with it. It must be in the pocket of your knickerbockers or something.

TSUNETAKA: A telegram it is, but, no, it's trivial business. Matsunaga, in Karuizawa, urges us to evacuate and join them as soon as possible. He's told me this a number of times, but I didn't respond to the invitation, so he finally took the ostentatious step of sending a telegram. I'm grateful that he's concerned about us, but this is unnecessary interference. How can I remove myself to a safer place while our lord does not move out of Tokyo?

O-REI: As long as you keep lying to me, I won't give you the tobacco.

TSUNETAKA: *(With false gaiety)* You seem so delighted to tease me. You must have gotten the wrong idea that I had a telegram from a woman or something.

O-REI: I'll give you the tobacco in exchange for the telegram. Nowadays we must barter everything.

TSUNETAKA: A telegram. . . . There was nothing like that that came to me. You must have misunderstood something.

O-REI: No, I heard it clearly. Even lying on that rattan couch all day, I hear what I hear. In this house where I've lived forever, no matter what the sound may be—that sound just now in the dining room is of the dry cracking of the mahogany tableware cabinet, that sound just now is of the steam moving through the steam pipes on the second floor, that noise just now of someone climbing the staircase is of the master, that noise just now is of the wind hitting the louvered door in the guest room. . . . I've been able to tell what each such sound was. How could I not be able to tell when a telegram arrived? Now stop trying to talk yourself out of it, and show me the telegram. Otherwise I'll never give you the tobacco.

(Tsunetaka does not say a word.)

O-REI: So I was right on target, wasn't I? Or if you hate the idea of bartering things so much, you better give up on tobacco, even tobacco as tasteless as this rationed stuff. . . . You, milord, don't even allow me to get tobacco on the black market. . . . Well, if you are dying for this wretched rationed tobacco, be quick and show me the telegram.

TSUNETAKA: Don't be so childish. I didn't want to show it to you in the first place because of you.

O-REI: Compassion for me!

TSUNETAKA: I don't need the tobacco.

(He goes back to weeding. O-Rei remains standing, as in shock.)

TSUNETAKA: *(Weeding, as if talking to himself)* What tough grass! Nowadays it's difficult even to slake our hunger, and yet grasses and trees continue to grow so luxuriously. They say, "Grass and tree have no heart," and they are right. The turning of seasons is felt with greater certainty than usual, and the green appears far more furious, far darker than it usually does. Just weeding it is such a pain. What is all this lively green trying to rebel against? What makes all the grasses and trees vainly luxuriate so?

When people die and houses burn down, the only thing that prospers and flourishes and survives is the green of grass and tree, and the evening flow of the sky.

O-REI: *(Leaning against the window, as if talking to herself)* Compassion for me! It's too late. . . . It's already a month. This is something that was settled a month ago. . . . That island fell into the enemy's hand, the people on the island were "all shattered like jewels"[2]; the newspapers and the radio told us a month ago. Only mad people could have hopes after that. He knows all this. . . . Ah, the day I heard the island fell into the enemy's hand, the bones and marrow within me that are invisible from outside shattered. After that it became impossible for me to do anything except just lie on the rattan couch to nurse my shattered bones and flesh. My personality changed, everybody said, and I thought so, too. I feel languid all day, just raising a hand is too much trouble. . . . Out of too much sorrow? People say that. Sorrow may be consoled, but how can consolation reach someone who has gone way beyond sorrow. . . ? Only mad people can have hopes. . . . And yet he tries to show compassion for me. He tries to do that because he imagines that some hope remains in me and wants to use *that* to stir his own hope. But there should be no mystery if he had hope. He is a mad man after all. . . . But with today's telegram even his hope died. A madman is weeding. He is plucking the weeds in his head. . . . By not showing the telegram, which is a public notice of "killed in battle," he is trying to convince himself that *that* did not happen. . . . I cannot tolerate this. . . . *(She turns toward stage left at the window)* Come, I'll give you the tobacco.

(She throws the newspaper-wrapped tobacco. Tsunetaka takes a telegram out of his pocket and hands it over to her through the window. She accepts it with her face turned away. She opens it.)

O-REI: Ensign Suzaku Tsunehiro has been promoted by special decree to the rank of second lieutenant on account of his honorable death in battle. . . . What's this! Such an ostentatious telegram at this late date!

(She walks to the side of the rattan couch, lights the telegram, and burns it. Then she lies down on the rattan couch and, apparently dazed, toys with the ashes. In a while she puts them in her mouth and starts to cry. . . . At stage left, Tsunetaka, puffing on a cigarette, pricks up his ears, noticing her crying. O-Rei stops crying. Lying on her back, dazed, she's looking into midair. . . . Soon Tsunetaka washes his hands, enters the room, and stands by her, looking down at her.)

---

2. *Gyokusai*, total defeat or destruction of a large military unit: one of the euphemisms used with an increasing frequency as the military situation became hopeless. In addition to the Japanese military doctrine that frowned upon surrender or retreat, the overextension of the fronts often made it impossible to execute retreat or evacuation.

TSUNETAKA: What did you do with the telegram?

(O-Rei does not respond.)

TSUNETAKA: The telegram, what did you do with it?

O-REI: *(Expressionlessly)* I burned it.

TSUNETAKA: You did. . . . That was all right.

(He starts slowly to stage right. O-Rei stands up with ferocious speed and grabs Tsunetaka's shirt.)

O-REI: You killed him! It was you who killed him! It was you who killed him!

TSUNETAKA: *(He brushes her off and reluctantly returns.)* I've heard you say that many times now. For the past month you have tortured me by saying the same thing every day. . . . That's why I did not want to show you the telegram.

O-REI: The official telegram came today, didn't it? So from today on I can officially call you a killer.

TSUNETAKA: Are you saying because the telegram came there's now something new?

O-REI: Yes, there is something new. Something new that I haven't said before.

TSUNETAKA: Is there something you haven't said before? Is there anything your tongue hasn't said yet, your tongue which is incomparably more persistent than the tongue of flame that day after day assaults us from the sky with air raids?

O-REI: About my child.

TSUNETAKA: Say "master."

O-REI: No, in what I have to say today he must be my child. Not about the master.

TSUNETAKA: O-Rei, I will gladly overlook, pretend not to hear, when you, out of sheer sorrow, forget your manners, go beyond your bounds. But Tsunehiro is now a heroic spirit.[3] You cannot lose your modest ways in relation to a heroic spirit.

O-REI: It is not about a heroic spirit. What I want to talk about is my child.

TSUNETAKA: If you want to talk, if it soothes your heart to any extent, go ahead and talk. But be careful with your words. Tsunehiro is no longer even my son. Because he gave up his life for our lord, he is now a deity.[4]

O-REI: Thanks to the fact that you killed him, he became a deity.

---

3. *Eirei:* name given to someone killed in battle.

4. It was held that a soldier killed in battle after distinguished exploits would turn into a deity, *kami,* hence "military deity," *gunshin.* Some say the first military officer accorded the title of *gunshin* in modern times was Commander Hirose Takeo (1868–1904), who during the Russo-Japanese War was hit by an artillery shell while searching for a subordinate in a sinking ship. During the Second World War the title became ordinary.

TSUNETAKA: O-Rei!

O-REI: You, with your own hands, let my child climb high into the sky like a kite, then cut the string. As a result, he became a deity. You took care of that, and drew the borderline between my child and yourself, between deity and human. You no longer have to worry that he will give you trouble. Because he has become a remote deity the same color as the blue of the sky. But in my case it is different. While he was alive, he was a master. I am base but I bet everything and called my child master. . . . It's different now. The moment my child died, he dropped headlong from the height of the blue sky and came back here *(she taps her belly)*, here into this bloody womb once again. Returned to be enveloped in my base, warm blood and flesh and enjoy a peaceful sleep where painful honor and glory would not trouble him. Now, once again, I feel all of him here. The way he looks at you, the way he smiles, his firm hands and feet inside here.

TSUNETAKA: I've heard that a number of times, heard that a number of times, O-Rei.

O-REI: That's why you must listen to *my child*.

TSUNETAKA: I am listening.

O-REI: I cannot forget it, that autumn night of parting. It was a good moonlit night.

TSUNETAKA: The moon shone into all of us who were here, to the bottom of each heart.

O-REI: My child cursed me. In the presence of other people, using all the words he knew.

TSUNETAKA: That was a different form of farewell, for you, his mother. . . . I knew. His curse was in fact directed to me. It must have been an indescribable feeling. . . . Listen, he died without saying a word, not a word of complaint to me, his father. But at that very juncture of parting, his resentment against me exploded for not having allowed him to call the mother who gave birth to him "mother." On the surface, his words were curses to you, but the other side of his words was resentment against me. That was clear to me while I listened. All the curses that came out of his mouth were all directed to me, and all the appeals and sorrows he could not say were directed to you. You must understand that. You must love him for the reverse side of those words of parting.

O-REI: Is that all; is that all you have to say?

TSUNETAKA: That is all.

O-REI: What self-serving, what shallow thinking! Are you saying that was the human truth you grasped in that scene? You are self-centered in everything; you turn yourself into a tragic father; you divine other people's feelings as you please; you construct a sublime tragedy in which you are at the center. That's how you always do things. You can never step into the depths of other people's feelings; you look at everything in this world through a brocaded wrapper. Your life is like a gift on a ceremonial tray that is presented to our lord covered with a brocaded wrapper of purple silk that, after he has given it a glance, is immediately handed over to someone.

TSUNETAKA: I heard that, too. You mouthed the same metaphor yesterday.

O-REI: So I will say something new. That night, before you all, he cursed me so because of terror.

TSUNETAKA: Terror?

O-REI: Yes, he was terrified. When he was a child, he was timid.

TSUNETAKA: That isn't true.

O-REI: He and I knew you didn't want to think that, and we hid it from you. Yes, that was a conspiracy through which we communicated with each other. Though a child, he knew you hated timidity. It was easy to hide it from you. You were too preoccupied with our lord to tell day from night. . . . Once, when he was a little boy, at school, a friend of his grabbed his pencil case, ran off, and threw it out of the window on the third floor. I was there with him to look after him, so I saw everything from beginning to end. The pencil case had dropped on the concrete floor below, and the Mont Blanc fountain pen he treasured was broken in it. It was something you had bought especially for him.

TSUNETAKA: Yes, I remember.

O-REI: He looked sad as he squatted down, picked up the broken fountain pen, and looked at it on his palm. The flesh of his white thighs exposed from his shorts was trembling. Because a treasure for him had broken. And right next to him stood the strong perpetrator, a rascal, with a derisive smile on his face. He didn't even hit him, didn't even look at the bad friend's face, but just gripped his little palm dyed blue with the blue ink of the broken fountain pen and walked away in silence. When I said to him, Let's keep this a secret from Father, he smiled for the first time. And when we went home, he told you that he had broken the fountain pen because he had dropped the pencil case from the station platform.

TSUNETAKA: I remember. And I immediately bought him a replacement.

O-REI: This is not the only story like that. He was timid and prone to terror. He was ashamed of it and hid it. And I always provided protection, helped him to hide it.

TSUNETAKA: But he was different after he grew up, wasn't he?

O-REI: A man doesn't change that much. A man is most honest when he is a child, and he begins to lie after he has learned to hide something. But after he grew up, I can tell you, he gradually learned to ascribe his shame to me. Timidity, terror, cowardice—for all the characteristics he wanted to hide, he blamed my bloodline, and courage, boldness, honor—all the characteristics he wanted to be proud of he began to be convinced came from the bloodline of the Suzaku family. No, I think he persisted in believing that, he forced himself to believe that. Thanks to his admirable father's education, he thought he'd be influenced by his courageous, bold and intrepid, righteous and strong father. He thought he'd be influenced by the ancestors who never once wielded a sword, but for generation after generation wore long-sleeve robes, with light makeup, and yet were quite admirable as far as their words are concerned.

TSUNETAKA: It was partly your sin, wasn't it, that you led him to think that, your sin that you protected him in his weakness in everything and spoiled him.

O-REI: As heir to the Suzaku family, he ended up forcing himself to do things that were hard in order to turn away from his weaknesses and timidity. Concubines' children are quite common among those of higher station, but he felt that inferiority more than anybody and he was tied to me all the more for it. Those curses of his were to hide his own terror, to falsify his unwillingness to die, to sever himself from his mother's baseness at the very juncture of parting because if he showed the smallest bit of his attachment to life, it would be apparent that such an attachment derived from my base bloodline, to force himself to die as heir of the honorable Suzaku family—they were the curse words that he desperately told to himself. It is not that he had courage, but that he had the need to prove his courage no matter what. It is not that he was influenced by your courage, but that he was influenced by the same need you have.

TSUNETAKA: How is it that you understand his feelings like that, from one end to the other?

O-REI: I am his mother. He did not want to die. But you. . . .

TSUNETAKA: No one wants to die on his own.

O-REI: He had another fear that was much stronger than his fear of death, the fear that if he acted cowardly, it was because he was my son. Because of that fear, he deliberately pretended to plunge into death himself. And you helped him and ended up truly killing him.

TSUNETAKA: Are you saying he was unhappy?

O-REI: Is there anything more unhappy than this in this world? Such a beautiful child, so young, on the most painful battlefield, he had to die in the most painful way.

TSUNETAKA: But he must have had pride. He must have had honor that fulfilled him.

O-REI: "Must have had," you say. As if you ascertained it with your own eyes.

TSUNETAKA: Our lord issued the command, "Go." Our lord issued the command, "Die." He must have felt the joy that he had done what he was told to.

O-REI: Forget about our lord's command. It was something that could be done by simply rewriting a word in a document on a desk. He must have understood that.

TSUNETAKA: Tsunehiro probably knew that his small death was utterly useless, that even if tens of thousands of deaths were piled up, there was no way of re-forming the raging wave that had already crashed.[5] But he also knew that living during a reign like this and dying in a reign like this, he was being molded into a large golden ring that was already being closed up to become a molecule in the ring that would brilliantly and eternally turn round and round through history, to become a molecule in a rainbow of sorrow he spanned with his own body. . . . No matter how hard the battle situation might have been, Tsunehiro must have died fulfilled as a man.

O-REI: As if you had been right on the spot. You, who could not have known the smallest fraction of the pain my son felt as his flesh was torn.

TSUNETAKA: There's something called pride that transcends agony. For example, a tree is linked to the ground. That is agony. That is pain. But the white cloud that touches the treetop belongs to the blue sky. We always see both the beautiful layer of cloud and the tree in a single picture, do we not?

O-REI: Always see. You just look at it. Even the last moments of your own son you only see as if you were looking at a painting.

TSUNETAKA: It was Tsunehiro himself who had hoped to merge into a single picture. He knew that that and nothing else is the purpose of living in this world. He was an admirable fellow who knew it at his young age. What came to his mind's eye in his agony of death was that picture of honor adorned with the chrysanthemum crest.[6] At one point his agony disappeared and he was invited into that picture.

O-REI: It is as if you were overjoyed to have lost your son. For the past month I've been suspicious about this and have been reading your face.

TSUNETAKA: I feel as if I've been able to go one step closer to His Majesty's heart since I lost my son. I dare say I feel I came to understand more clearly the true sorrow in the depth of my lord's heart, which I had been unable to surmise before. If you are to speak of joy, this could be my joy.

O-REI: The lord you speak of has not lost a single one of his children.

5. "Reforming the raging wave" etc. is a phrase from Han Yu (768–824).
6. The imperial crest.

TSUNETAKA: Be quiet! That's disrespectful.

(O-Rei says nothing.)

TSUNETAKA: You say that once more and I'll have no mercy.

O-REI: You'll kill me? It's not enough to kill your son, you must kill his mother, too? . . . You madman.

TSUNETAKA: You are wrong to think that you could join your son if I killed you. O-Rei, you have fallen into living hell out of sheer sorrow. You have lost sight of the distinction between what is noble and what is base, between what is beautiful and what is ugly, between honor and shame.

O-REI: You are right that this is living hell. There is no food; the house is in disrepair; the garden is full of weeds; sometimes flames descend from heaven and burn up places; and you are here.

TSUNETAKA: To your eyes, this must be hell. But my heart is much closer now to my lord and is in touch day and night with that large sorrow he never discloses to his subjects. In comparison, the sorrow of a father who has lost his son is insignificant. I wouldn't call it joy, but I am in luck, as long as I feel clearly on my cheek the wing of His Majesty's deep sorrow as he preens it from time to time. . . . But when I think of what might happen to him when we are finally defeated. . . .

O-REI: If that is the case, why don't you go to work in the court so that you may work on various schemes to end the war in a way that will keep your lord safe? With that ferocity with which you drove Prime Minister Tabuchi out.

TSUNETAKA: That they in the court are working to end the war in some way, without telling the military, has reached me. But I will not do anything.

O-REI: Don't you mind that Japan may be ruined?

TSUNETAKA: I told you before. This is His Majesty's command. He did not say it in words, but he did so with his eyes: "Do nothing, just do not do anything. . . ."

(At this juncture a preliminary air defense warning sounds in several successive bursts.)

O-REI: A preliminary air raid warning. It's such a rare thing in daylight.

TSUNETAKA: We can't say it will turn into an air raid alarm. Nowadays we even have erroneous warnings.

O-REI: Shall I turn on the radio?

TSUNETAKA: That shouldn't be necessary.

O-REI: Isn't it strange? No matter how bad an argument we are having, the moment the warning sounds, I feel as though both of us are sucked together into that sound, like insects that are sucked into a large test tube. Whatever we may be arguing about comes to naught.

TSUNETAKA: You no longer bring together the bags to be taken out at the sounding of the warning.

O-REI: What sort of treasure is left in this house? There's nothing I'd like to take to the next world left here.

TSUNETAKA: And yet you dash into the air raid shelter.

O-REI: That is to be expected, isn't it? I am the timid mother of a timid son. *(Silence.)*

O-REI: To celebrate his promotion to second lieutenant, how about our presenting him with a gift?

TSUNETAKA: Presenting what?

O-REI: A while back you said his fulsome curses on the eve of his parting were in fact directed at you, that his resentment against you exploded for not having allowed him to call the mother who gave birth to him Mother.

TSUNETAKA: I did.

O-REI: *(Cheerfully)* Well then, the least we can do for the repose of his soul is for us to formally be married.

TSUNETAKA: O-Rei . . . what in the world. . . .

O-REI: Why, you look surprised. What is there to be surprised about? For a couple who are common-law husband and wife to get officially registered, this is something that happens often in this society, doesn't it? It's just that we are doing it belatedly.

TSUNETAKA: For these twenty years you have never once committed such a discourtesy. How dare you say such a thing to me.

O-REI: Marry me—that's all I'm saying.

TSUNETAKA: Think of your status.

O-REI: My status? Well, what sign of status does the Suzaku house have now? Does it have an automobile, a driver, and a butler? Do you have lots and lots of servants and maidservants? Does it have so much rice we can never finish eating, so much wine we can never finish drinking? See, there's nothing. All this house has are you and me. And I am in fact your wife. We are starved; we scavenge for food, and, like beggars, sleep in the air raid shelter holding each other.

TSUNETAKA: A person's worth cannot be measured by material possessions, still less his honor.

O-REI: Where is the sign of honor? The center of the imperial capital has turned into a sea of fire; all the mansions have turned to ashes except for the fireplace chimneys; medals have been burned; full-dress uniforms have burned up. Those paulownia flowers brocaded with gold lace that adorned the breasts of those uniforms have turned to ashes. The feathers for the military caps, the sashes for staff officers have turned to ashes. . . . This country has no more time left to laugh at us.

TSUNETAKA: Don't be silly. In the first place you took on that role, know-ing fully well that you were helping avoid Lady Benten's curse.

O-REI: I have survived long enough not to be afraid of Lady Benten. Once upon a time, when I was prim and pretty, I would have made the ex-cuse of being content to be in a position like this for fear of Lady Ben-ten. For twenty years since then, I've been waiting to grow gradually ugly. It's all right now; I've waited long enough. *(Sticking her face out)* What do you think? These wrinkles? The wrinkles I've chiseled into my face carefully year after year, looking forward to this day? Look. My old-ness and ugliness turn away Lady Benten's jealousy, and I, a woman you no longer need to fear will bear children, will make a good example as the first long-living bride of the Suzaku family? What do you think? This gray hair? The gray hair that scintillates in the sunlight as it hovers around the bride's head like gossamer? I am the very bride that your an-cestors, along with the young, beautiful Lady Benten, have eagerly wait-ed for generation after generation, for two thousand years. A bride whom Lady Benten is willing to bless with longevity and happy virtues, to whom no one objects, who is so old and ugly that even a passerby looks away, such is the bride most appropriate to you and your family. Now you understand. I understood it from the start. That's why for twenty years I put up with it; I endured it, waiting until I became ugly, body and soul. You were all mistaken. The bride the Suzaku family sought was not a happy, young, beautiful, and *feeble* woman who dies right away. The bride the Suzaku family wanted was a grief-filled, old, *tough* woman who had already given birth to a child and lost that child. . . . Come, let's get married at once. With a mere preliminary warning the ward office should be willing to do the clerical work. Go at once and include me in your family registry. When it comes to the an-cestral bureau,[7] you can have them confirm it after the fact, the way things are nowadays.

TSUNETAKA: Are you serious? . . . We have what we call order in our society.

O-REI: Go out in the garden, climb the mound, and look around. Every-where you look is a burned-out field. Do you call that order?

TSUNETAKA: Things may burn and lose their forms, but you can't burn your heart. Order is in your heart. Tsunehiro died for the sake of the beautiful, invisible order.

---

7. A tentative translation of *Sōchitsu-ryō,* an office within the Ministry of the Imperial Household that handled matters related to the imperial family, imperial conferences, no-bility, Korean nobility, peerage, and people with court ranks. The office was abolished after the war as the ministry *(shō)* was downgraded to an agency *(chō).*

O-REI: For the sake of the order that prohibits a son from calling his mother Mother?

TSUNETAKA: It is the order that you from the start agreed to and cooperated with. It is also the order of that beautiful goddess in the shrine of the garden who has guarded us every day, all day, for two thousand years. It is the order of the exquisite sound of the biwa. It is the order that the tunes of the biwa have always made as its sound spread, wherever the Suzaku family lived, be it a lake, a river, a sea, the uncertain wavering of water. Japan may become nothing but a burned-out field, but the quiet, cold music of the lake will keep holding us tight in its embrace.

O-REI: Hold us tight in its embrace, suffocate us, and kill us. And once again you lend your hand to the murder. First, your young, beautiful wife, the second one is your young, healthy son, and the third. . . .

TSUNETAKA: Who is going to kill you? You may kill someone, but you are an unlikely woman to be killed.

O-REI: You are afraid of being killed by me if we are married, aren't you? When you don't have any assets to speak of.

TSUNETAKA: Obey the order quietly, O-Rei. You were determined to do that for a long time, were you not? As our lord says, we shall do nothing, do not do anything, and quietly die away. There is no road left for the members of the Suzaku house to take.

O-REI: I am not a "member of the Suzaku house" yet. If you want to use me as you please, want to force me to obey that order, include me in your family registry at once. This is the only way to save my son from the shame and humiliation that gripped him up to the very moment of parting, the only way to cleanse his soul.

TSUNETAKA: What are you saying? His soul is already cleansed. His spirit is already high in the shining sky. You can no longer touch him.

O-REI: For his sake we must be married at once. We won't be around long either. In the next world the three of us, parents and son, will live in harmony and in peace, untroubled by anything.

TSUNETAKA: We never had anything that troubled us. You created the trouble.

O-REI: *(Extending her hand)* Come, marry me.

TSUNETAKA: That I cannot do.

O-REI: Cannot? Cannot just include me in your family registry? What on earth are you trying to protect? Protect the burned-out field all around you?

TSUNETAKA: There is only one thing I protect. It is something that can't possibly concern you.

O-REI: I can no longer bear it, can no longer take it.

TSUNETAKA: *(With gentleness)* You must bear it a while longer. Just a while longer. Soon death will visit us.

O-REI: At least while we are alive. . . .

TSUNETAKA: We must not sully the fact of being alive.

O-REI: Oh, just for one day. . . .

TSUNETAKA: You mustn't say such a despicable thing. You recognize that order in your heart. Not only recognize, but revere it. That is precisely why you want that one day.

O-REI: I am a base woman after all. Just as my child agonized all his life.

TSUNETAKA: He didn't agonize at all. He was the embodiment of the honor and glory of the Suzaku house.

O-REI: Marry me. This was my child's wish.

TSUNETAKA: That cannot be done.

O-REI: So you are . . . truly . . . truly rejecting this out of hand.

TSUNETAKA: I am.

O-REI: As always, you say just one thing, with your impassive, mannerly way, just one thing, "I cannot do it."

TSUNETAKA: Right. . . . I cannot do it.

(The two glare at each other. An air raid alarm sounds out in successive interruptions.)

O-REI: An air raid alarm. We've got it after all. I'm really worried about the air raid shelter under the floor of the dining room. But that's the only place we have to hide ourselves.

TSUNETAKA: There's no point in complaining. Come, quick.

O-REI: *(About to go stage right, she notices Tsunetaka following her and bursts out into loud laughter.)* You are coming, too? My, it's so funny. My, it's so funny. You who propose to do nothing and quietly die away going to an air raid shelter with a suspicious woman you haven't even put in your family registry. After all, you hold your life dear. . . . You ought to stay here, leaving yourself to what you call the order that is a quiet, large lake, in a wool-gathering, dreamy state. That would be far safer. You see, that order only protects you, but not me, a stranger. Do stay here. Your going into the air raid shelter with me *(Shrieking with laughter)*, look at yourself in the mirror. It's ludicrous. Truly ludicrous. . . . Don't come! Don't come with me! You should be burned to death, all by yourself.

(She turns round and exits stage right. Following the noise of the trapdoor to the air raid shelter being shut, there is a distant rumbling of bombers. Left alone, Tsunetaka sits in a chair, then rises to his feet. He goes out into the garden. He stands before the shrine, his back turned to the audience. The rumbling comes

closer. Tsunetaka looks up at the sky. Suddenly he flings himself on the staircase to the Benten shrine. The rumbling comes even closer. With the piercing, shrieking metallic noise of a bomb falling, the

CURTAIN

is cut. As the curtain falls down, the bomb explodes.)

ACT 4: WINTER

At stage right the room in the greenhouse, burned down, is now a pile of rubble. Among the standing trees seared black, the Benten shrine at stage left is the only thing untouched by fire. Where the greenhouse room used to be is a low-slung shelter, with a door made of a sheet of burned galvanized iron attached to it like a lid. The overlook downstage is now conspicuous, with the cloudy winter sky spreading behind it.

At curtain rise, the stage is empty. Soon the door to the shelter is lifted and Tsunetaka in a crumpled overcoat and a muffler around his neck emerges and starts picking up pieces of wood. When this is done he lights the pieces of wood gathered in one spot, takes his gloves off, and warms himself. Enter Mitsuyasu from stage right carrying a large bundle.

MITSUYASU: Hello. . . .

TSUNETAKA: Oh, Mitsuyasu.

MITSUYASU: I haven't come to see you for quite a while, but I see, just as I had expected, you are still living like this. It's four months since the war ended, you know.

(Tsunetaka says nothing.)

MITSUYASU: Christmas is coming soon, so I've brought a small bit of food for you, though I hesitate to call it a Christmas present.

TSUNETAKA: That's kind of you.

MITSUYASU: Shall I take it into the shelter?

TSUNETAKA: Yes, that would help.

MITSUYASU: *(Carrying the bundle into the shelter and speaking from inside it)* When you leave, you had better hide at least your food somewhere. You never know when someone might steal it.

TSUNETAKA: *(To Mitsuyasu who has come out)* You speak of leaving but I have no business to take care of. There are some people other than you who bring me food from time to time. I hadn't expected the bit of compassion I showed long ago to come back in such a form. . . . Well, I won't starve if I reduce the amount I eat. The water is there *(pointing stage left),* trickling out of the tap water pipe in the kitchen twenty-four hours a day. I rinse my mouth with it; I wash the plates I've salvaged with it. A man can live somehow if he puts his mind to it.

MITSUYASU: I can keep whatever valuables you may have.

TSUNETAKA: Valuables, well, all I have are the suit His Majesty gave me and five memorial tablets. Three are old ones, those of Father, Mother, and Akiko; two are new, one of Tsunehiro and . . . one memorial tablet of O-Rei. I keep all of them in that shrine. A mixture of Shintoism and Buddhism as in the past,[1] yes, but I don't expect the Shinto deity to criticize me for this. I watch the shrine all day, right up close, so there's no chance for a thief to get to it. It may be that for me, the last man of the Suzaku house, to die as guardian of the goddess of the biwa is most fitting.

MITSUYASU: *(Looking at the shrine)* Mysterious, isn't it, that that shrine alone was unscathed. . . . You can never tell when you will have luck, when you won't. O-Rei, who was in the air raid shelter, was hit directly by a bomb and killed, while you, who deliberately stayed outside, clinging to a readily flammable shrine, came away unhurt. But what I don't understand is, why didn't you go into the air raid shelter in the midst of a bombing, offering prayers instead? Did you have something terribly important you had to offer prayers to? . . . To tell you the truth, my saying something like this may put you off, but this story is pretty well known among our acquaintances. Just the other day, someone said, "The count in those days was having a bit of a nervous breakdown. That's why he wouldn't go into the air raid shelter but ran outside, thereby saving his life."

TSUNETAKA: As always, you say whatever comes into your head. Yes, I may have been deranged. In the midst of that derangement, my son died, my wife died.

MITSUYASU: You call O-Rei your wife. . . .

TSUNETAKA: Now that she's dead, I'll call her my wife. She was a woman who deserved pity. . . . But if I was deranged, what kind of madness was it? Was it my own madness? Or was it madness I received from a great distance, by His Majesty's wishes? Even if I were mad, that madness had something that shone brightly, that was revelatory, at its center. At the core of that madness was sincerity as transparent as a crystal. The blessing I had from it was that loss was not a loss, that even losing my only son made me feel I gained something larger. My wings may have been cut, but being a bird was my madness, and on account of that madness I flew with airy lightness. . . . What about now? You may say I've become normal. I don't know. *I* cannot possibly tell whether I am still mad or have become normal. The one thing I can tell is that at the center of

---

1. The shrine is Shinto in origin, and the preparation of memorial tablets for the dead *(ihai)* is Buddhist. The amalgamation of the indigenous and foreign religions started early.

this normalcy there is no sincerity, that even though this normalcy is splendidly equipped with wings, it never flies. Just like an ugly ostrich. I don't know about me, but you have all become ostriches. . . . I can only remain just as I am, managing my nest in a terribly dirty hole, divining my past madness, lying in a quiet, do-nothing bed, while I wait for the second coming of the madness. . . . Aside from all that, have you been to the court recently?

MITSUYASU: Yes. His Majesty asked me about you.

TSUNETAKA: Why didn't you tell me that first?

MITSUYASU: Is Suzaku doing all right, is all His Majesty said, sir.

TSUNETAKA: He did. *(He sheds tears.)* . . . Our lord is aggrieved. He is carrying all the sorrows of the land on his shoulders. It is at a moment like that I am tempted to rush to his side, but it is precisely at a moment like that there must be someone who stays even further away and worries about him.

MITSUYASU: I do not know what dreadful thing is going to happen to the imperial house.

TSUNETAKA: The lord had expected for a long time that such a day would come. That day has come as it should. I have known this since I was given leave.

MITSUYASU: *(Changing the subject)* Today I came to seek advice from you. Prince Daigo recently started a company to sell antiques to Westerners and asked me to be its chief executive officer, and I agreed. He said that in order to collect objects of various historical importance all the executives had to be members of the nobility, so I mentioned your name, and he said to ask you by all means, and that was a command to me. Would you please join us as an executive?

TSUNETAKA: You came to make such a request?

MITSUYASU: Yes, please do say yes. I'd be in trouble if you didn't, with the prince pressing me. If you become an executive, I think I can manage to find a house for you. Besides, as your younger brother I can't stand leaving you in this sort of constrained way of life any more.

TSUNETAKA: You are embarrassed about it, you are saying.

MITSUYASU: That's not the only reason.

TSUNETAKA: I'm grateful for your kind thoughts, but I must decline. Tell the prince not to feel bad about this.

MITSUYASU: Why do you decline?

TSUNETAKA: That is something I cannot do.

MITSUYASU: Why can't you?

TSUNETAKA: I myself do not understand why I cannot. Probably because my madness is not adequately healed yet. Well, you may ascribe any reason you wish to this. I have nothing left to do in my life, except to serve

His Majesty from a great distance, doing nothing. People will say I am just being lazy. But this, in its own way, is fearful, mind-wrenching work that requires forbearance, that requires gigantic strength, that deprives you of sleep with the fear that the fire before the divine altar might be extinguished, that packs your life with invisible procedures twenty-four hours a day. Of course, there is assistance from those behind the scene. There is also help from those numerous pure souls who perished. But I am the only one who is alive. I am shouldering all the work you can do only if you are alive. That is to say, the painful work that requires the hand that is alive and can still move not to move for someone.

MITSUYASU: You are as stubborn as ever, aren't you? When the times have already changed and everything has turned inside out like a glove.

TSUNETAKA: It may simply be that the photo negative turned positive, that the picture remains the same.

MITSUYASU: You do not say yes to this request, no matter what?

TSUNETAKA: I cannot do what I cannot.

MITSUYASU: That's a heartless response. Can't you at least reserve your response for a couple of weeks?

TSUNETAKA: I cannot.

MITSUYASU: Well then, for now I must excuse myself. I have other people I have to ask to be executives.

TSUNETAKA: When you feel like it, come to chat with me once again.

MITSUYASU: Yes, thank you. (He starts to leave, offers prayers toward the Benten shrine, then turns around again.) You must go out to town from time to time and expand your knowledge of what's going on. Japanese women are walking about arm in arm with Western soldiers as if the whole world were theirs. The black market is all the rage, and Tokyo is full of vulgar vigor of a kind you have never seen before. One of these days I'd like to accompany you there.

TSUNETAKA: You would. . . . Well, stay well.

MITSUYASU: Stay well.

(He leaves. Tsunetaka, leaving the fire, paces around the burned-out place. He then walks up to the overlook downstage and sits down at a spot where he can look down at the sea.)

TSUNETAKA: (Monologue) Layers and layers of clouds cover the sea. It seems we'll be having snow.

The sea and clouds have melted into the suffering of a single color, making the white bottoms of the foreign ships anchored offshore look like the white, brilliant teeth gnashed out of pain. Japanese ships are nowhere in sight. All Japanese ships have been sunk.

The sea Tsunehiro longed for was not this kind of sea. I just pray that the sea at the moment of his death was blue. For his sake, the sea glistened bright and blue, and it was there that fiery columns of honor rose, the abundance of youthful blood dyeing the semitropical sea like the scarlet coral visible in the water. I pray that the sea surrounding that island was clear, without a speck of cloud, on Tsunehiro's last day. I'd like to think that he chose a death like the scarlet strapping cord of the golden sword that generations of the Suzaku family never used.

Why, you ask? Because with that, Japan was defeated, was destroyed. Because everything that is old, elegant, pure, and gallant was destroyed. An empire that was once sublime and glorious was destroyed. An incomparably beautiful fabric woven with the most sensuous warps and the bravest wefts was, through the torments of blood and fire, defiled, trampled upon, and finally reduced to ashes. No one, ever again in history, will be able to weave such a splendid fabric.

Ah, milord, noble, exalted, revealing, divine lord, now you too are about to be defiled by the aliens' muddy boots. For the sake of your people, you are willingly going to bear the unbearable shame. Because of what karma have we, two classmates, survived in a country that has been completely burned up? I know. I was born in order to serve in the role of supporting him, from a distance, doing nothing, in his sorrow, his relentlessly increasing sorrow, his suffering, his relentlessly increasing suffering. This country, which was once the Country of Fresh Rice Ears, the Country of the Rising Sun, has now become a country of tears. Milord is the fountain of tears for this country. On a distant, mossy mountaintop his tears flow endlessly—I was to be a single pipe, far down at the edge of the mountain skirt, to connect that fountain to the river.

Ah, I can vividly feel his suffering, the dripping of his tears on my bear-bamboo body. Tsunehiro. Come back. If not in your flesh, then listen with your spiritual ear to the suppressed sound of the faint dripping of his tears that are conveyed to your father's eyes.

Everything is gone. Great, illustrious power, honor, pride, and the great aim that enables a man to be a man has been lost. The best of this country, like burned trees, withered black, crumbled, and died out.
(The snow starts to fall.)
The snow has started.
(He receives the snow with both hands.)
How immaculate and cold. The snow is a power that pacifies all, but that is because it makes everybody tremble uniformly. The snow resembles the goddess. Resembles the cold, beautiful, proud, and cruel goddess. Because of the goddess' cold jealousy, brilliant summer days have been erased.
(The snow falls harder. From inside the Benten shrine comes the sound of a biwa being played.)

The sound of a biwa . . .

This can't be true. . . . That . . . That certainly is the oldest tune that has been handed down in the Suzaku house, of the greatest historical importance. That is one of the three secret tunes that Fujiwara no Sadatoshi learned to play, during Shōwa,[2] while he was in T'ang for seven years, which legend says Yang Kuei-fei[3] composed and is called "Yang Chên Ts'ao." How can this be possible. . . .

(The snow falls even harder. The door of the Benten shrine opens, and a woman in jūni hitoe *emerges, holding a cedar fan against her face.)*

Oh! You, Akiko. . . .

(The woman, holding the fan against her face, walks down the staircase. Tsuneta-ka runs up to her.)

Akiko! Akiko! Have you been resurrected? You died twenty years ago.

(The woman moves her fan away. It is Ritsuko.)

RITSUKO: It's me, Ritsuko, Mr. Suzaku.

TSUNETAKA: Oh, Ritsuko. That's a bad practical joke. But I have never seen you so beautiful, so terrifyingly beautiful before.

RITSUKO: Because you see me with eyes of remembrance. You, who saw the real bride of the Suzaku house, a fleeting illusion who died young, you alone can tell whether I am qualified or not. Am I?

TSUNETAKA: You are the real bride of the Suzaku house. This is unbelievable—that the bride of our house has revived in the midst of this burned-out field, in the midst of this country that has been destroyed.

RITSUKO: I was waiting for a long time for you to say that. When I was playing the "Yang Chên Ts'ao" tune in the shrine, I for the first time believed strongly that you would say that. Because by wearing Aunt Akiko's wedding dress I could go through your remembrances to be Hiro's bride.

TSUNETAKA: And when you are dressed like that, you can meet the dead Hiro.

RITSUKO: Yes, but by having a husband who died young, the bride of the Suzaku house has become immortal. Now, the long-lasting jealousy has been brushed aside, and the goddess' world has arrived. The goddess, tormented by her jealousy for a long, long time, realized that it was useless to kill her rivals in love and, tired out by her own jealousy, has finally gained peace of mind by killing the very person with whom she was in love. The goddess having lived through such sorrow, for the first

2. An era that began in 834 and ended in 848. The Fujiwara is the most important aristocratic family, but there is no one of historical importance with the name of Sadatoshi.

3. The great beauty and consort of Emperor Huang Tsung (685–762). Yang's ability to enamor the Emperor was such that she is reputed to have become the primary cause of his ruination. Born in 719, she was killed by a soldier during an uprising in 756.

time a world has arrived where she will never be jealous again, her heart bright. This new goddess, the new bride of the Suzaku house, has appeared to destroy you, the one still yearning for the goddess of the past. Are you not afraid?

TSUNETAKA: Why should I be afraid? You are beautiful. You are beautiful. You are the unexpected, last evening glow of the Suzaku house.

RITSUKO: Now you call me the bride.

TSUNETAKA: Yes. . . . You are beautiful. I had thought that the beauty of this country had all been destroyed.

RITSUKO: Now you call me the bride. Why did you not do it that time— that bright moonlit evening, the night of parting with Hiro?

TSUNETAKA: I was doing that from a distance. From behind you as the two of you melted into the moonlight.

RITSUKO: It did not reach my ear. Nor Hiro's. . . . That is, it was the same as if you did not. You were like that for quite a while. You may have done something a little. But it was the same as doing nothing. Why? Tell me why.

TSUNETAKA: . . . You . . . are beautiful.

RITSUKO: You did not do anything. You just kept holding back. You did not offer help even when it was needed, you just kept watching as you might someone passing by. Why? Tell me why?

(Tsunetaka does not respond.)

RITSUKO: You allowed Hiro to be killed. And probably allowed the person not called your wife to be killed. Yourself doing nothing. If you had killed someone with your own hands, you might have also saved someone with your own hands. But for the sake of a "sincerity" you dreamed of, you let everything destroy itself—including the person who was most important to me, who could never be replaced, thereby depriving me of him. Why? Why?

(Tsunetaka does not respond.)

RITSUKO: You enveloped your son, your wife, your son's fiancée equally in your own illusion. Now the bride of the Suzaku house will strike you with revived strength. The goddess of jealousy who once loved you has now raised a sword of vengeance. An invisible sword is pressing down on your head. Give me a firm reply. Why did you try to destroy so many people?

(Tsunetaka does not respond.)

RITSUKO: No, it is not that you tried to destroy them. You had no such will. You had no will. Without moving a finger, you just waited for your own destruction. Yet someone different stood in, each time, for that destruction. Why, each such person had a will. Hiro, O-Rei, and I. And you alone have survived. What is the secret?

(Tsunetaka does not respond.)

RITSUKO: Look at my face steadily, and give me a steady reply, Mr. Suzaku. You deprived me of the person I loved. You let loose a flame through his heart, making him neglect me, filling him with longings for death. What is the secret of that terrifying seduction? Where did you get hold of that secret? Where?

(Tsunetaka does not respond.)

RITSUKO: The cavern of your hollow heart gradually swallowed people up, while you let on that doing nothing was a passion; you made incomparable coldness "sincerity"; and you have survived by linking night to day, day to night. And you made the thirty-seven generations of the Suzaku family stall in your own body, damming up all the flow of people's gentle feelings. Everyone was destroyed thanks to you. Why are you the only one who remains undestroyed?

(Tsunetaka does not respond.)

RITSUKO: I am the bride of the Suzaku house who will never die. Because the bride has become the goddess and the goddess the bride. Because I am a resurrected, new goddess who has bathed in the waterfall of sorrow. But Mr. Suzaku . . . you are the last man of the Suzaku family. When you die, the Suzaku house will die out forever. After that, all that is needed is an immortal bride by the water making a strong, sensuous sound on the biwa. I've come here to urge you. As Hiro's bride, and as your own resurrected bride, I've come to urge you. Why is it that you, who should have been the first to die, are still alive like that, surviving? Why?

(Tsunetaka does not respond.)

RITSUKO: Die. Destroy yourself! Destroy yourself right now, on this spot!

TSUNETAKA: *(Raising his face, he looks at Ritsuko carefully. —Silence)* How could I possibly destroy myself? I destroyed myself long, long ago.

CURTAIN

MY FRIEND HITLER

In one note on the play Mishima said he was inspired to write *Waga Tomo Hitler* (My friend Hitler) because of the assassination of Ernst Roehm as described in Alan Bullock's *Hitler: A Study in Tyranny,* published in London in 1952—the first biography of the dictator to use the captured German documents produced at Nuremberg. Roehm was one of the victims in a series of assassinations, from June 30 to early July 1934, that were carried out under orders from Adolf Hitler, then reich chancellor of Germany.

Roehm became chief of staff of the SA (Storm Detachment—the paramilitary apparatus of the Nazi Party) in January 1931 and by 1934 had increased the number of storm troopers sixty times, to nearly 4 million. But despite the spectacular rise in number, the feeling that the SA had already fulfilled its "revolutionary mission" was growing, and this, coupled with Roehm's moves to legitimatize it by absorbing the regular army, the Reichswehr, had created a political crisis for Hitler by early 1934. In the first half of the year Hitler made various maneuvers to alleviate the situation.

Another character in the play, Gregor Strasser, was the Nazi Party's Socialist theoretician and national organization leader. In that double capacity he was the second most powerful man in the party until he suddenly quit in December 1932. He was killed along with Roehm. At the time he had been back at his pharmaceutical business for a while and apparently had no political affiliations.

My Friend Hitler deals with two other historical figures—Hitler, of course, and the industrialist Gustav Krupp—and covers late June and early July 1934. But if there was any connection between Roehm and Strasser, it was probably no more than a rumor circulated by Hitler's agents to justify their assassinations, and though Krupp openly supported Hitler, their relationship as depicted in the play may be more symbolic than factual. Mishima himself has noted that Strasser seems to have been a hard-drinking, outgoing man, rather than the kind of scheming "callow intellectual" presented here.

Why Hitler? Mishima was asked, engaged as he was in ostensibly nationalistic political activity. He was fascinated by Hitler as a political genius, he said, but writing about him had little to do with such things. The purpose of the writing of *My Friend Hitler* lay elsewhere. Technically, he meant this play, the four characters of which are all male, as the mirror image of another of his plays, *Sado Kōshaku Fujin* (Madame de Sade; translated by Donald Keene; staged by Ingmar Bergman, among others), the six characters of which are all female. In the two plays, he said, he wanted to refute the popular criticism, "He can't portray men," "He can't portray women," adding that he wanted to convey, through Roehm, "the impossibility of eroticism" as suggested by Georges Bataille, just as he had in *Madame de Sade.*

In translating this play I have consulted portions of Hitler's speeches quoted in translation in English biographies, but I am by no means certain that this has helped bring the flavor of German by way of Japanese into English. Indeed, after this translation was done, I was amused to read an anecdote about William Faulkner while he was working in Hollywood. As Ian Hamilton tells it in *Writers in Hollywood, 1915–1951* (Harper and Row, 1990, p. 209), he once agreed to help the director Howard Hawks on *Land of the Pharaohs:* "Puzzling over the question of 'how a pharaoh talks,' Faulkner asked Hawks: 'Is it all right if I write him like a Kentucky colonel?' Hawks told him to go ahead, it didn't really matter, since the whole thing would surely be rewritten on the set." Though apparently for different reasons, in his stage version of *Madame de Sade,* Bergman is said to have omitted a great many lines.

My Friend Hitler was completed on October 13, 1968, published in book form in December of the same year, and first produced on stage from January 18 to 31, 1969. In one production Mishima played Hitler.

MY FRIEND HITLER

ROEHM *(standing),* played by Katsube Nobuyuki, and KRUPP *(seated),* played by
Nakamura Nobuo. Kinokuniya Hall, January 1969. *Courtesy of Waseda University's
Tsubouchi Memorial Theatre Museum. By permission of Gekidan NLT.*

Time: June 1934

Place: The Berlin chancellery

Characters:
  Adolf Hitler
  Ernst Roehm
  Gregor Strasser
  Gustav Krupp

ACT 1

The great hall of the Berlin chancellery. Balcony at upstage. Hitler, in a morning coat, stands on the balcony facing upstage, giving a speech. Cheers from the crowd at intervals. To Hitler's right, Roehm in SA uniform, and to his left, Strasser in civilian suit; their backs to the audience like Hitler, both men stand, waiting.

Hitler's speech and cheers begin before the curtain rise and continue as the curtain rises.

ADOLPH HITLER: Think, my fellow Germans, how our fatherland has now put the time of humiliation behind and begun to go forward, step by step, toward a time of new independence and construction. Remember eighteen years ago, the year 1916, toward the end of the World War. At that time I, a courageous soldier, was wounded and was in a garrison hospital in Berlitz,[1] but there I was boiling mad. The germs that corrupted the souls of German people after the war were already germinating then. In the garrison hospital serious soldiers were laughed at, and a man who had deliberately wounded his hand on barbed wire and was sent there boasted of his cowardice—not only boasted but asserted that his act was far more courageous than the death of a courageous, gallant soldier. What do you think, my fellow Germans? Postwar decadence had already shown its signs on the home front during the war. All those perversions of values after the war, cowards' pacifism, democracy far more putrid than an asshole, the conspiracies of Jews who exulted in the defeat of the fatherland, Communists' despicable plots—all of them had manifested themselves in those days. Ah, what voluminous tears were shed by the corpses of the noble heroes of the battlefield brought in by

---

1. An anonymous reader has pointed out: "Mishima's mistake. Hitler was in the military hospital at Pasewalk in 1918, where he was treated for the effect of a British mustard gas attack rather than a wound. And he invariably referred to himself as 'an ordinary soldier' in his speeches."

the Valkyries to golden Valhalla once they were awakened by the spirit and surveyed this condition of our fatherland, Germany! What a clamor of lamentations arose from the coffered ceiling made of shields and the chairs made of armor, illuminated by the flames on the table. . . . But now all that is finished. All the grounds for falsity, defeatism, and filth have been cleansed. Since I assumed the chancellorship in January of last year, the gods have entrusted my cabinet with true loyalty to our country and with a mission. With the loathsome Reichstag arson, the Communist Party dug its own grave. Our Reichstag no longer has that clique of swine, the Communist Party. It no longer has that gathering of unpatriotic bastards, the Social Democratic Party. It no longer has that nest of opportunists, the Catholic Center Party. It now has only the inheritor of the fatherland's brilliant tradition, the bearer of the powerful future Germany, our *Nationalsozialistische Deutsche Arbeiter Partei!*

(Midway through the speech, the aged Gustav Krupp enters with a walking stick, stops and listens for a moment, yawns, proceeds to stage center, and, facing the audience, sits on the couch left of center; for a while he makes conspicuously bored gestures. Soon he signals to Roehm, but Roehm does not turn around. Finally, Roehm turns, notices Krupp's signals, and, hesitant because of Hitler, comes downstage; he begins to talk to Krupp just when Hitler finishes saying "Arbeiter Partei." Amid cheers, Hitler's speech continues, but as soon as the conversation between Krupp and Roehm starts, his voice becomes inaudible, with only his gestures continuing.)

ERNST ROEHM: So here you are again, to meddle with Adolf's speech.

GUSTAV KRUPP: His speeches have more meaning when you listen behind him rather than in front. A good prima donna's song reaches backstage. Since the old days I've played the role of waiting in the wings, you see, with a bouquet pressed to my chest.

ROEHM: You've brought such a bouquet today too, I suppose?

KRUPP: Yes, indeed, a bouquet of iron. Herr Roehm, you think capitalists are a dime a dozen and treat them all as "reactionary," but at least my Krupp Works has moved in accordance with iron's will, iron's heart, you see, the dream shaped by iron, which its president's personal wishes can't budge. Do you think iron has enjoyed being made into motion picture cameras, cash registers, pots and pans, as it has been at our firm since the war? Do you think that, all its dreams shattered, iron has been content, being at the mercy of feckless children, women, and petty dealers? The Krupps must let iron fulfill its own dreams at all cost.

ROEHM: So, go ahead and let it.

KRUPP: You are a soldier, so you can be that simple about things.

ROEHM: Yes, sir, I am a soldier. But I am not one of those smug Reichswehr men who snooze their time away behind medals and fat bellies.

Mine is a live army, an army of young, violent, fearless, truly honorable and heroic wild men, who drink like fish and eat like wolves, kick in show windows if the mood is right, and don't mind shedding blood on behalf of downtrodden people.

KRUPP: I understand that's the slogan of your Storm Detachment.

ROEHM: And my dream, the dream of this chief of staff of the Storm Detachment—is for such an army to become the core of the Reichswehr and to kick out those diabetic generals. . . . And then comes this damned talk that the SA's mission is over and all that. . . .

KRUPP: Whoever says such a thing?

ROEHM: Adolf does. . . . No, Adolf can't possibly think that. Somebody has made him say that. . . .

(At this point Hitler's speech begins to be heard again, while conversation between Krupp and Roehm, though it continues, becomes inaudible.)

HITLER: For all this, my fellow Germans, a revolution can't last forever; we can't let it go on and on and destroy our national economy. We can't bring the age of starvation, inflation, and ruination upon Germany again. That would be just what our enemies want. Now a brilliant age of construction has begun. We must channel the flood of revolution that broke the dam into a safe waterway called "progress." Our slogan doesn't tell us to be mere *vandals* like fools or madmen. It tells us to realize our God-inspired, correct ideas, wisely, carefully, step by step. Only they are true Socialists who believe that no ideal is higher than the prosperity of the fatherland, and who really understand the words of our great national anthem, "Deutschland, Deutschland, uber Alles." My fellow Germans, now is the time for all of us to become a single body, raise the iron hammer rather than a rifle, and struggle onward for the reconstruction of a glorious, great Germany!

(At this point Hitler's voice becomes inaudible, and conversation downstage becomes audible.)

KRUPP: Now's the hammer's turn, he says. The grievances of the Essen industrialists who are saying, "Hitler's leading us to destruction," seem to have reached the ears of this fellow.

ROEHM: But Adolf is a good fellow. Since he began putting on a black tie and a morning coat, he's become an unbearable dandy, but he still has his old good points. He's strong on friendship.

KRUPP: If he's strong on friendship, why was he so slow in making you minister?

ROEHM: He had his own ideas for me. He took hold of power all right, but for a time he was completely shackled and couldn't do a thing. Until he finally welcomed me as minister, he had to fight all by himself, laying the groundwork.

The one to blame is Goering. That medal-maniac! The only medal he earned on his own is the Bull of Merits of the Prussian army. When he got the rank of marshal from the president last summer, he was ecstatic, and now he talks like the spokesman of the Reichswehr. He's the one who threw a wet blanket between my SA and the Reichswehr. And he's so, so despicable. He declared that the SA was no longer needed and had to be disbanded. How could anyone do that? Just completely ignore me, who lead the 3-million-man SA, ten times bigger than the Reichswehr. . . . I, who have increased them from ten thousand when I agreed to be commander to the present 3 million in a matter of only a few years. . . .

KRUPP: Herr Roehm, no one can drive you out of your nest. Your SA uniform is your eagle feathers. Pluck the feathers and you'll no longer be able to live. I would say, though, the best eagle is a stuffed one.

ROEHM: I agree with you; I'm a born soldier. I sleep better in this *(tugging at his uniform)* than in pajamas. The uniform has become part of my flesh. From my childhood I thought of only one thing, I wanted to be only one thing and that was to be a soldier. So I—just think about it, how I felt mutilated when I quit the army ten years ago. But now I know very well that we are sure to be defeated in the next war if we leave it to the Reichswehr, which has no revolutionary spirit, and to those army men, who are still manipulated by the Prussian generals.

KRUPP: Don't get so cross—after all, you've made your own dream army, the great family of 3 million men called the Storm Detachment.

ROEHM: And those same 3 million are treated as parasites.

KRUPP: Calm down. You'll soon have better luck.

ROEHM: Herr Krupp, you've been brought up in silk shirts since childhood and don't know how refreshing and beautiful an army is.

KRUPP: True, I don't, but my iron does. Iron, melting in the flames of a blast furnace, dreams of cold nights in the barracks.

ROEHM: The army is paradise for men. The brass-colored morning sun that filters through the trees is itself the brilliance of the bugle that tells of the wake-up time. It's only in the army that men's faces become beautiful. The blond heads of the young men who line up for morning roll call stand out in the morning sun, and the glint of their steely blue eyes is charged with the destructive power accumulated through the night. Young animal pride and holiness fill their thick chests thrust out against the morning wind. Their polished guns and boots tell of the fresh thirst of awakened steel and blood. Every single young man knows that the heroic pledge of death alone entitles him to demand beauty and opulence, willful destruction and pleasure.

During the day soldiers metamorphose into nature through camouflage, and they become trees that spout fire, become bushes that kill.

And at night, how violently, with what brusque gentleness, the barracks welcome each one, covered in sweat and mud! The young men whose cheeks still radiate, like the evening glow, the destruction they wreaked during the day, reaffirm in the smell of grease and leather, as they clean their equipment, the barbarous lyricism that has seeped into their flesh, the sensations of the dark blue hordes of minerals and beasts that hold this world together at its base. As they pull the coarse army blankets up to their chins and close their eyes, the gentle taps—those smooth metal fingers—caress them quietly, wistfully, over the eyelids lined with long eyelashes, and put them to sleep.

The army life, where all the special male qualities reveal themselves and all manliness comes forward, is, precisely because of it, laden with a gentleness like that of sweet, lustrous oysters within their shells. These sweet souls, the souls that have pledged to live and die together, are the festoons that link the warriors, despite their outward sternness. I'm sure you know that stag beetles can live on honey alone.

KRUPP: And so, tell me, what is the mission of your SA?

ROEHM: A revolution. A revolution that renews itself eternally. The SA is, as it were, a dredge, which is used to grab up the mud of the sea bottom with a gigantic, powerful crane and make that bottom deeper and deeper, so that ships far larger than those we have now may pass there.

KRUPP: You mean to grab up corpses along with the mud.

ROEHM: Occasionally, live human beings too, yes. Herr Krupp, you realize that we are reluctantly putting our powerful iron arm into this immoral, corrupt, reactionary, lazy, internationalist, most abominable mud. Until we dredge every bit of all this, we'll never be able to stop.

KRUPP: So that larger ships may pass. . . .

(They fall silent. Cheers fill their silence.)

KRUPP: I now well understand that what is more important than anything else to you is an army such as you envision. . . . But I wonder if Hitler thinks the same way.

ROEHM: In those days of battles, in Munich, he was my unmistakable war buddy. Look at him. He has become a bit too much of a dandy, but he's still my war buddy.

(Roehm stands up as if pulled by a string, returns to Hitler's left, and waits with his back to the audience.)

HITLER: And so, my fellow Germans, the great struggle of the German people has entered a new stage. The threat of the Reds has already been eradicated, and our tractors have begun rolling into flat, open fields. Our immediate task in this new stage is education. Education to nurture German people fit for a new, great Germany. We no longer need any of the anemic, eternally pettifogging professors. We no longer need any of the intellectuals too powerless to lift a gun but who love themselves dearly and raise hysterical pacifist screams, who can't remember where they left their balls. We no longer need any of the unpatriotic teachers who impart defeatist ideas to our boys, who deny and distort the history of our fatherland. The teacher who educates Germany's young men to enable them to fly through the sky on white horses as gallantly, as beautifully, as Wotan, is the German teacher. Is that not the case, my fellow Germans? Each one of you who have awakened has the mission to become a teacher and educate those several million people who have not yet truly become members of our party. Only when this is achieved will our National Socialist revolution have a monolithic foundation.

(During this part of Hitler's speech, Krupp first looks bored, then signals to Strasser, until the latter notices it and comes to Krupp's side. Strasser begins as Hitler finishes saying, "monolithic foundation.")

GREGOR STRASSER: What can I do for you, Herr Krupp?

KRUPP: Well, I am terribly puzzled to see you and Herr Roehm, who are like cat and dog to each other, standing to Hitler's left and right as you used to.

STRASSER: I'm puzzled, too. Hitler, who didn't allow me to come near him for a long time, suddenly summoned me, and here I am, awkwardly face-to-face with Roehm, apparently summoned in the same way. Moreover, in his usual style, Hitler keeps us waiting just like this during his interminable speech, leaving all the business to the end. And I'm sure his business, which is the main thing, will be taken care of in a few minutes. I don't know what it's about, though.

KRUPP: Looks like a lot of trouble for you. Come, what do you suppose it is about, Herr Strasser?

STRASSER: It's probably about breaking cleanly with reactionary capitalists like yourself.

KRUPP: It's very kind of you to say that. Everyone calls me dirty names simply because he needs me. Already two years ago, is it, it was because we were relieved that Hitler broke with you, that we saved Dr. Schacht's face and underwrote the Nazis' enormous debt. I think it is because of this that the Nazis are what they are today. Business calls you the creator of bad luck. We can't let a man who knows nothing but how to incite laborers meddle with a nation's economy, you understand.

STRASSER: But don't you ever feel that we're nearing my kind of age once again? Our party is facing "the danger of piled-up eggs."[2] The year 1932 may reappear and allow me to deal out much better cards.

2. This is an old Chinese expression.

KRUPP: There's some logic in what you say. And I well understand what you want to say. But leave it unsaid. People of the Krupp family become deaf as need be.

STRASSER: My ideas haven't changed a bit since I was discharged, married, and worked as a chemist in Landshut. My hand is always the same, and what changes it, I'd say, is whether Hitler wants to use it or not. Herr Krupp, you know, you are a gun-maker, and I am a chemist. Whether you put a bullet in somebody's belly or save his life, it's all up to your business inclinations. The only thing is that the medicines I sell are superbly effective and revive people who are about to die, but I wouldn't deny they have some side effects. Your rights to heavy industry and large real estate can only be absorbed by the government in light of the aims of our National Socialism. If possible, we'd like you to put on workmen's overalls—I'm quite sure you'd look wonderful in them—and spend as much time as you like puffing a good cigar, learning how to operate at least one machine tool.

KRUPP: The members of your party drive to a villa in a Mercedes-Benz caravan, while I stoop to fiddle with a machine tool, that's what you mean.

STRASSER: Hitler's very reluctant to agree with me, but yes, Herr Krupp, that's exactly what Germany desires. Selfless service to the nation, not lip service but decisive actions. You should lead the way—returning the war profits to the country, opening your cellar to entertain the people, opening up the hunting grounds that are nothing but British imitations, and drinking genuine milk from the German meadows instead of champagne.

KRUPP: Milk would make me sick.

STRASSER: Roehm said the same sort of thing. Frittering away his life playing soldier at his age, he's nurturing youths who can do nothing but drink. What would happen to the future of Germany? Also, Roehm drinks like that because he is a "man among men."

KRUPP: And you are a milk lover and Socialist who risks his life for a healthy future. My, my, I don't want to live long!

HITLER: . . . . let us advance to the future, arm in arm. And I want you to follow me. I guarantee that I will be your leader and spearhead, remove one by one the obstacles that lie ahead of you, and clear the dangerous minefields at the risk of my own life, so that the steps of your powerful march forward won't be disturbed for a single second. Long live Germany! Long live Germany!

(Strasser is already back at Hitler's left. The crowd's cheers and "Heil Hitlers" continue for some time. Krupp reluctantly rises to his feet. Hitler faces the audience and, still visibly excited, wipes his sweat with a handkerchief.)

KRUPP: *(He walks upstage, holding out his hand to shake hands)* Now, that was excellent. That was excellent, Adolf. A wonderful speech.

HITLER: How was the crowd's response?

KRUPP: I can't imagine a more enthusiastic reaction.

HITLER: That shows you weren't looking. *(To Roehm)* Ernst, what did you think?

ROEHM: There could have been no better response, I think.

HITLER: Didn't you see the woman in a yellow suit, who was standing on the eastern corner of the plaza under the street light? In the middle of my speech, and at the most important point, she just turned around and left. I'm sure she wore a suit of that color, stood at such a conspicuous spot, and left, all on purpose, so that I'd notice her. She's a Jewess. She's got to be. *(While talking, Hitler sits on the couch with Krupp. Roehm and Strasser remain standing, apart from each other.)*

The more I look, the gloomier I find this building, this damned chancellery. I just can't believe that I so much wanted it to be my residence. . . . Well now, Herr Krupp, I'm glad you've come to visit me, but today, as you see, I have two old friends I asked to come. May I see you after I've talked to them? Would you mind waiting until then in the antechamber?

KRUPP: As you wish, Chancellor. The only thing is, don't forget that I'm an old man and have little time left.

(So saying, Krupp rises to his feet and looks equally at Roehm and Strasser.)

HITLER: You're first, Ernst; you stay.

(Krupp and Strasser leave. Roehm joyfully walks up to Hitler and shakes hands with him anew.)

ROEHM: That was good, Adolf, a beautiful, powerful speech. You are after all an artist.

HITLER: An artist but not a soldier—that's what you want to say, isn't it?

ROEHM: Exactly, God wrote out the roles for us—Adolf the artist, Ernst the soldier.

HITLER: Are your men in good spirits?

ROEHM: That's up to you, Adolf.

HITLER: We'll talk about that later. Anyway, these days I don't have enough time for a tête-à-tête with anyone except my cabinet, but no matter when I look at you, you are healthy, youthful, and full of energy. Is it that you, like Wotan, have someone who feeds you honeyed water?. . . . I asked you to come because I wanted to get away from my bothersome government duties and have a talk about the old days with an old friend, the one I can be truly open with.

ROEHM: That means the twenties again. Ten years ago, the age of our myths, our struggles.

HITLER: When I first met you in Munich, I instinctively knew, here was my comrade. Captain Ernst Roehm, on the staff of the Regional Command of the Munich Army—before I knew it, I clicked my heels and saluted. *(He salutes.)*

ROEHM: *(Feeling good)* Private First Class Hitler, I'm going to teach you everything—how important the backing of the military is for building a party, how necessary the organizational ability of the military is for organizing a party, how effective the knowledge of tactics is for party campaigns. From this moment on I will commit my life, my being, to you. . . . That was what I swore in my heart. And that is exactly what I did. I put the military on your side, bought you a newspaper with the army's secret fund, put together a corps of volunteers and reservists through the power of the army, taught you the ABCs of military tactics, and shoulder to shoulder with you, dashed into the storms of that age of deceit and betrayal.

HITLER: Ernst, you always were courageous.

ROEHM: And we sometimes overdid it.

HITLER: You still do.

ROEHM: *(Pretending not to have heard)* Wasn't it fun when we storm troopers beat up the Reds at the Hofbraeuhaus meeting in November 1921? The Reds ended up smearing their flaccid pale faces with the color of their flags.

HITLER: And the thing about the boot, about that Adorst the Mouse.

ROEHM: That's right, the boot, I remember. I came out of the brawl and suddenly realized that I was quite all right but my boot had suffered an honorable wound on my behalf.

HITLER: It had a big hole in the toe and the sole had half peeled off, opening a big mouth.

ROEHM: I wanted to take it to a cobbler at once, but you, Adolf, objected.

HITLER: That's because I believed there was nothing better than the SA chief of staff's boot bearing battle wounds for commemorating our mythical struggle and for raising the troopers' morale. So you acquired a new pair of boots, and I put the respectfully polished boot on top of the bookcase in my office for decoration.

ROEHM: Who the hell put the cheese in it?

HITLER: Well, the culprit still remains unknown. Again, it's got to be a Jew, I'm sure.

ROEHM: Somebody put cheese in it. So one night I visited you in your office, and there was this mysterious nibbling going on somewhere. And I discovered this mouse, who stuck his nose out of the hole of the boot.

HITLER: You got furious and tried to kill it.

ROEHM: It was you who stopped me.

HITLER: Yes, aside from the thing about cheese, the courageous mouse that slipped into your historic boot somehow struck me as auspicious.

ROEHM: Then you started to supply him with cheese every night.

HITLER: He gradually became used to us. When you and I talked alone late into the night, he would invariably show up, in the end coming near us without fear. So it became necessary for us to give him a name.

ROEHM: One night I went in and he showed up. He had this green ribbon around his neck. I looked, and it had "Ernst" on it. Didn't I get furious? *(Roehm and Hitler look at each other and laugh.)* But I pretended not to notice anything, and the next night it was you. . . .

HITLER: This time it was I who got furious. You see, the mouse had a red ribbon tied around its neck, and there was "Adolf" written on it. *(Both laugh.)* We fell upon each other. Until ten years ago . . . yes, till then we were so young that we fought with each other, grappling barracks-style, just like that. . . . Of course I was no match for you in brawn. In the end I came up with a compromise. After that night the mouse began wearing a white ribbon around his neck and was called "Adorst," wasn't he?

ROEHM: Adorst the Mouse. He doesn't show up even in Grimm's fairy tales.

HITLER: He was quite a droll mouse.

ROEHM: I wonder what he did after that.

HITLER: He gradually stopped showing up.

ROEHM: Did he die?

HITLER: He probably did. *(Sings) In death, let's be together.*

ROEHM: *(Sings) Let's fight together.*

HITLER: *(Sings) With gun in hand*

ROEHM: *(Sings) In battlefield*

HITLER: *(Sings) Poppies in bloom*

ROEHM: *(Sings) Blazing our chests.* . . . We often sang this in those days, didn't we? It was a sentimental song. Music and lyrics by Adolf Hitler. You no longer allow the party members to sing such a song, do you?

HITLER: Don't make fun of me. When I was a student in Vienna, I once even tried to compose a musical drama.

ROEHM: You mean "Wieland the Smith." What did you do with the score?

HITLER: In the spring I often went alone to the Vienna Woods for a walk. Once I went as far as the Semmering Pass in the Alps. I let the score fly in the wind from the pass. It scattered and descended slowly into the Alpine valleys where patches of snow remained. The sheets that fell on the snow became indistinguishable from it, and those that fell on the green of spring grass looked like edelweisses. . . . Ernst, the more I think about it, the more it seems I should have become an artist.

ROEHM: That would make our story more plausible, Adolf. Ernst the soldier, Adolf the artist—that way we should be able to go hand in hand.

HITLER: Do you think we could still do it now?

ROEHM: We can still do it.

HITLER: I wonder. . . . In any case, I should have become an artist. I should have, like the great Wagner, firmly gripped this caldron called the world by the handles of nothingness and death, and like a good chef, put all the representative men of the world and their emotions on a skillet, and roasted them over the eternal flames of the giant Solt. I would have had a much easier time that way and gotten a much more comfortable reputation. I've become chancellor all right, but they whisper about my lowly birth, my lack of education, and so forth behind my back. . . . And so, Ernst the soldier, I'd like you to remember what you used to carefully tell me when you were captain.

ROEHM: What?

HITLER: You said the same thing just now, "how important the backing of the military is for building a party."

ROEHM: And so?

HITLER: And so I'd like you to remember what you used to say in the past.

ROEHM: Things are different now from the past.

HITLER: No, political rules never change.

ROEHM: Let me say this, then. As you say, now and the past may be the same, to be sure. Military backing may be necessary. Except in the past that was genuinely for the party, now it's just for you to become the next president. President Hindenburg is dying. It's doubtful he'll make it through the summer.

HITLER: Don't say that, Ernst. You sound like my political enemy. As my comrade, can't you put it more considerately?

ROEHM: I'll put it considerately then. I agree that it's a good idea for you to step into the shoes of Field Marshall Hindenburg. I'll help you to the best of my ability—yes, with the backing of the new army of 3 million storm troopers.

HITLER: That's why. . . .

ROEHM: Wait. I would oppose you if you stepped into the shoes of the corrupt and the reactionary. I would oppose you if you betrayed the new Germany we ourselves have remodeled and were content to be on top of those puppet capitalists and Junkers, those conservative, senile politicians and senile generals, those incompetent officers of aristocratic stock who dared snub me in the Officers' Club, those pretentious white-gloved Prussian army bastards who never once thought about revolution or the people, those paunchy bourgeois belching beer and potatoes from the morning on, those manicured eunuchs called bureaucrats—I would oppose you if you buttered up those guys and busied yourself in political antics to become president. I'd be absolutely opposed. I would stop it even if I had to use force.

HITLER: Ernst!

ROEHM: Listen. I want you to become president. I truly want you to. But that's after we have worked together and cleaned this rotten ground of garbage. Don't give a damn for the Reichswehr. We shouldn't be afraid of that gilded scarecrow who threatens you with words but has nothing inside his uniform. Germany has only one revolutionary army, and that's my 3-million-man Storm Detachment. . . . I tell you, Adolf. After the great cleanup, we will cover the Berlin plaza with snow-white carpets and crown you as president. Don't forget, our revolution isn't over yet. After our next revolution, Germany will truly revive, and with Hakenkreuz flags fluttering in the morning breeze, Wotan's country rid of every shred of corruption and decrepit ugliness, resurrected and youthful, a country, a community of warriors who are strong, their oak-solid arms locked, beautiful and manly, will be established. You'll be leader of that country. To be leader of that country is, Adolf, your brilliant destiny. For that I would even give my life.

HITLER: Thank you, Ernst, I now understand your feelings well. I no longer can doubt your passionate sincerity.

ROEHM: So don't deal with the Reichswehr.

HITLER: You mean, the Reichswehr without you wouldn't be worth a dime.

ROEHM: Correct. You have the SA behind you.

HITLER: But I can't deny the fact that the Reichswehr is right there, can I?

ROEHM: I gave up on them a long time ago.

HITLER: You may have given up on them, but you can't deny the fact that they are there.

ROEHM: If you can call an army without a revolutionary spirit an army.

HITLER: As long as they rattle sabers, they are an army, are they not?

ROEHM: Don't forget, Adolf, I taught you everything military.

HITLER: Come, come, don't get angry, Ernst. You surely haven't forgotten how much I have done for your SA as comrade, as war buddy. You are the one who's destroyed whatever I did, every single time. . . . Come, come, listen. Your desire was, from the beginning, to incorporate the SA into the Reichswehr and make it its core. That would make the German army a national revolutionary army for the first time—that was your belief. That's it exactly, isn't it?

ROEHM: That's it exactly. But the old-fogy Reichswehr. . . .

HITLER: No, you had your own problems. What can you say about the disgusting things the SA did during the last two years? No wonder the

Reichswehr was put off. You made hideouts in basements and ware-houses; you tortured, kidnapped, demanded ransoms—I've even heard the story that in some districts troopers took their rivals in love affairs into basements, tied them up on the wall, and cut them up.

ROEHM: That lasted only a while. It's just that the young men wanted to mimic what secret police do. I've kept them in check and there's been nothing like that since.

HITLER: All right, let's say it lasted only a while. But, Ernst, if you allow me to be frank about it, wouldn't you say your SA is an enormous army of nostalgia?

ROEHM: What do you mean by that?

HITLER: Can you say that your 3 million soldiers are a solid political group? Wouldn't you say their sole pleasure is playing soldiers? Ernst, it's all right for you to be nostalgic about the good old army. But you shouldn't let so many young men be poisoned and carried away. The SA is dreaming not of a future war but of a past one. It's a re-creation of the beautiful friendship in the war we lost and memories of the old war bud-dies you horsed around with at the supply base. At the slightest excuse you start an old-fashioned exercise, even on the silly Flag Day you pa-rade in uniform, and you never fail to go on to a beer hall and make sure to smash a hundred windowpanes, then, after off-key military songs and interminable horseplay, the men on duty go around picking up their dead-drunk buddies. I've heard that the SA's rule is not to give a damn about lights out but to stay up all night acting rowdy. I've heard that your men swagger about so obnoxiously that serious-minded citizens are completely put off, and as soon as they spot one of your men in the dis-tance, they quickly hide their daughters.

ROEHM: *(With some bitterness)* Don't judge the forest from a tree.

HITLER: Let's make a concession and say all that is all right. But when it comes to the SA, you go out of your way to make the world impossible for it. I have done everything I could to defend it against the Reichswehr and against Goering, who is snotty because of the Reichswehr's backing. The law I passed last February after you joined my cabinet, which would give storm troopers wounded during political campaigns the same pen-sions as the soldiers wounded during the war—the effort I made to pass it, you know because you were right there and saw it. But what did you do? Immediately you did an awkward thing. At the worst time you pro-posed that the SA be used as the basis of rearmament and that a special minister be appointed to direct a national army that includes irregular troops. And of course, you meant to get that post. As a result Defense Minister General von Blomberg went over to your enemies and the whole Reichswehr stiffened. I hastened to veto your proposal, but it was too late then. You became decisively suspect in the Reichswehr's eyes. And that's what you chose to do. The Reichswehr thinks of you as the man plotting to take over the army and redo the revolution.

ROEHM: They aren't all that blind.

HITLER: It's no joke, Ernst. We're now up against the wall. I've been handed this statement by Defense Minister von Blomberg. You can regard it as representing the Reichswehr's consensus or as the Prussian National Army's tradition beginning to roar at last.

(Hitler takes a piece of paper out of his pocket and shows it to Roehm.)

ROEHM: *(He reads)* "His Excellency, Adolf Hitler, Chancellor of Germany, Dear Herr Chancellor: We hereby respectfully request that either the government's own power be employed to immediately relieve the current political tension or the president be asked to declare martial law and government power be transferred to the Reichswehr. . . ."

HITLER: They're asking that I choose one or the other.

ROEHM: Either of the two. . . .

HITLER: Yes. And immediately. . . .

ROEHM: It's a threat, blackmail. Such courage in the army . . .

HITLER: Is unthinkable, that's what you want to say. I'd like to believe that myself. But even if they don't have courage, they have this antiquated Prussian pride. They've come too far to turn back.

(They remain silent for a long time.)

ROEHM: *(Suddenly he rises to his feet and embraces Hitler)* Adolf, make up your mind. This is the moment of decision for us National Socialists, too. No compromise will do. If you compromise, the movement we've staked our lives on will be defiled forever. . . . Adolf, let's start from the beginning, let's go back to the drawing board. I'm with you. See, I am with you, Adolf.

HITLER: *(Stunned)* Yes, you are. You are with me. . . . .

ROEHM: *(He forces Hitler to his feet and pulls him around the room)* We'll do our revolution once again. We'll recover the youthful power of our Munich days. Otherwise, what can we say to the souls of our comrades who shed blood? The people are ours. The young men are ours. I'll show you; I'll defeat the old-fogy claptrap authority in a day. Besides, Adolf, we still have 6 million people out of work in Germany. Their complaints and dissatisfactions are ours. *(Pulling Hitler out to the balcony)* Look, look. Young but spiritless men are sitting vacantly on the benches all over the plaza. That's how we were once, how we found ourselves when we were thrown out of the war into starvation and inflation. We ourselves know very well that youth, poverty, lethargy were kindling that caught fire easily. Let's put fire to that miserable kindling now. It will burst into flame. It will burn all over Germany. And it will become the holy flame of Solt.

HITLER: *(Trying not to look out the balcony and stepping downstage)* No, Ernst, don't tempt me. Don't tempt me. Don't pour that sweet, benumbing liqueur into me once again.

ROEHM: It's up to you, Adolf.

HITLER: *(He finally frees himself from Roehm, sits on the couch, and speaks without looking at Roehm, who is standing behind him.)* You're forgetting something. You're forgetting one important lesson that you shouldn't forget. You can't make an enemy of the Reichswehr. What happened in 1923? I pleaded with General von Lossow, but he refused to provide me with weapons. Both the military and the police declared that they would shoot at us as soon as they saw any disturbing move on our side. In the meantime, we had already issued an emergency call to our twenty thousand storm troopers. We had to stand back; we couldn't do a thing while we watched the Reds march down the Munich boulevard. The weapons you had stolen from the barracks were absolutely useless in the face of a general's order that the weapons be returned. We surrendered. . . . This is what I'd like you to think about, Ernst. I'll think about it carefully tonight myself. Let me see you again tomorrow morning for breakfast and tell you my thoughts. . . . Will you tell Strasser in the waiting room to come here?

(Roehm exits. Hitler meditates. Strasser enters.)

STRASSER: Herr Chancellor.

HITLER: Oh, I haven't seen you for so long. Would you come over here?

STRASSER: Yes, sir.

HITLER: I've asked you to come simply because I wanted to renew our old friendship and because I wanted to borrow some of the wisdom you've developed during your long seclusion.

STRASSER: You know perfectly well, Herr Chancellor, that I have no new wisdom. I'm merely repeating like a parrot our old ideals, the ideals that we've now lost.

HITLER: We've now lost?

STRASSER: Haven't we? Where are the party slogans? Where is the anti-capitalism, the destruction of Prussia, and the autonomous parliaments of the Fascist front that were to replace the Reichstag? Everything remains the same.

HITLER: So?

STRASSER: And so I've said everything remains the same. Those who are weeping are still workers' children. Not a single thing has changed.

HITLER: And so, don't you have any wisdom for improving the situation?

STRASSER: Wisdom . . . I have none. I only have ideals, at least in myself.

HITLER: What about the means of realizing your ideals?

STRASSER: Have I come here to be tested, at my age?

HITLER: Well, but the unions under your influence are still reciting the same ideals as yours. My minister of the economy and foreign trade, Dr. Schmitt, doesn't know what to do about that. He complains that he can't tell the leftists of our party from the Reds.

STRASSER: The Reichswehr doesn't seem to think so.

HITLER: My, it doesn't? . . . You say the Reichswehr, but you mean somebody like the outdated von Schleicher.

STRASSER: Not necessarily. I meant the Reichswehr in general.

HITLER: You're terribly knowledgeable about them.

STRASSER: The military is a double-edged sword. They might help realize the long-neglected party slogans.

HITLER: Herr Strasser, will you stop talking as if you had something stuck between your teeth?

STRASSER: A hope can't but take opaque expression.

HITLER: You mean, you have a hope.

STRASSER: Yes.

HITLER: You have some information.

STRASSER: I know about Defense Minister von Blomberg's statement, if that's what you mean.

HITLER: *(Surprised)* That's an excellent information network you've got.

STRASSER: If martial law were declared. . . .

HITLER: I wouldn't allow such a thing.

STRASSER: I'm saying if it *were.* Where do you think the army would go for political advice? To the dying president or to you?

HITLER: To be honest, neither.

STRASSER: What would you do if they came to me?

HITLER: I'd say that's some conceit.

STRASSER: It may be conceit, but how about making preparations for it, just in case?

HITLER: What kind of preparations?

STRASSER: You must think about it—if you intend to become president with the Reichswehr's backing.

HITLER: You're saying you can get in the way.

STRASSER: I haven't gone that far.

HITLER: I had the absolutely wrong idea. I'd thought you were genuine. That a Socialist should align himself with the military, of all things!

STRASSER: I don't mind what you think. But what is certain is that the party, if things continue like this, will splinter into nothing. You have no choice but to do something about it.

HITLER: So what is that something?

STRASSER: It's to return to the spirit of the party slogans. It's to definitely stand on the side of the workers and to advance National Socialism.

HITLER: You're going round and round in circles.

STRASSER: In any case, it's your decision, Herr Chancellor.

HITLER: Thank you for your good advice.

STRASSER: You are most welcome.

HITLER: Would you come again, for breakfast tomorrow morning? I'll work out some good measures by then and tell you about them.

STRASSER: I'll see you then, tomorrow morning.

(Strasser exits. Hitler, left alone, walks about irritably. He goes to the balcony and, back turned to the audience, falls into deep thought. Soon, Krupp enters.)

KRUPP: Are you free now?

HITLER: Yes, Herr Krupp.

KRUPP: It appears the rain has started.

HITLER: It isn't much of a rain. It's odd. It invariably rains after I give a speech.

KRUPP: Your speech calls forth the clouds, I suppose.

HITLER: As soon as the rain darkened the plaza, people disappeared from every bench. What a tasteless, vacant plaza. Not a single soul left. I can't believe that until a moment ago crowds filled it, heating the whole place with roaring cheers and applause. A plaza after a speech is like the blank drowsing of a madman after spasms. Human beings endlessly hurt other human beings. Every cloak of power has seams through which fleas get in. Herr Krupp, isn't there power like unbattered white armor,[3] which no one can possibly damage?

KRUPP: If such a thing doesn't exist, why not make one yourself?

HITLER: Would you be my tailor?

KRUPP: I must take your measurements first.

(He steps back and makes the gesture of taking measurements with his stick.)

HITLER: What do you think?

KRUPP: I regret to say, but you still don't exactly measure up.

HITLER: Do I need some more training?

KRUPP: A tailor is very cautious, Adolf. If he can't expect to get paid, he can't just go ahead and make a suit. He may be dying to make a suit for his customer, but he won't get any artistic satisfaction if the customer doesn't have the right proportions. And he won't feel good unless his customer feels happy in what he has made. He wants him to feel relaxed, comfortable in it, as if unaware of having it on. . . . I don't want to give

---

3. Here, apparently with tongue in cheek, Mishima commits an improbable cross-cultural anachronism. What Hitler refers to, in the original, is the *horo*, a cloth bag, sometimes with a basket in it, that a mounted Japanese warrior used to carry on his back to protect himself from arrows. The original says: *nuime mo hokorobi mo nai, shiroi horo*, "seamless, unfrazzled white *horo*."

you a tight vest, because it's different from putting a straitjacket on a madman.

HITLER: If I were a madman. . . .

KRUPP: *(Gently putting his hand on Hitler's shoulder)* I've had that experience myself many times before. When you reach the moment when you can't possibly stand it, no, you can't even comprehend it, unless you think you're a madman. . . .

HITLER: When I reach such a moment?

KRUPP: You should think that all the others, except you, are madmen.

HITLER: I seem to have reached exactly that sort of critical moment— though I am at least chancellor of a nation.

KRUPP: Before rain I always have rheumatic pain, but today I had no such premonitions.

HITLER: Herr Krupp, would you mind making me a tight vest for a mad- man, in which, arms constricted, I won't be able to hurt other people but at the same time I won't be hurt by others. . . ?

KRUPP: *(Shaking his head as he walks away)* You aren't up to it, Adolf; you aren't up to it yet. . . .

CURTAIN

ACT 2

Next morning. Same place. At stage center is a breakfast table prepared for three. Hitler and Roehm have just finished eating; their plates are empty. Seated to the left and right of the table, they are having coffee, smoking. The table must be wheeled, for it is to be drawn off stage later. Through the open doors to the bal- cony, a clear morning sky is visible and there's sunlight coming in.

HITLER: It's a nice morning. It's just like the old days. . . . To put off all the meddlesome attendants and share coffee and cigarettes with you—I wouldn't mind having breakfast this way at least once a month.

ROEHM: The other cabinet members would get very jealous. Well now, Adolf, you are going to be busy today. Before we part, I'd like to con- firm our points of agreement once again.

HITLER: Not agreements, orders, Ernst.

ROEHM: For the contents of those orders, you've got my prior under- standing. We've operated that way since the old days, haven't we?

HITLER: The form doesn't matter, really. I give you an order: you put your 3 million storm troopers on leave for the next full month, that is, till the last day of July. During the leave, the troopers will be forbidden to wear uniforms, demonstrate, or take part in military exercises. You will issue a statement on this. . . . In short, that's all.

ROEHM: Will the president be dead by the end of July according to plan?

HITLER: He's on the brink of death, Ernst. Even if the best of peerless German medicine were employed, it would be impossible to extend his life until August.

ROEHM: All right, we'll have a political truce till then. . . . I thought about it a lot last night, but as you say, your wisdom, in this case, will be the only way to get through this storm. The trick of keeping us quiet until you become president should work as a temporary windbreak against the furious Prussian generals. Even I am willing to compromise that much.

HITLER: Thanks. You are my friend, after all.

ROEHM: The timing is good, too. Liberated from their tensions during the summer, our wild men will recover their energy in their hometowns and get ready for the harsh training of this coming fall—that isn't bad at all. If the army doesn't see uniformed troopers or their parades for a while, they'll feel relieved, if temporarily, and marvel at your leadership, while the citizens will truly learn how helpless they are through the summer and eagerly wait for the SA's return to the battlefront.

HITLER: That's exactly what will happen. For now, the point is to cool the bloated soufflé for a while, to cool the iron that's gotten too hot for a while. Once I become president, it'll be easy to arrange to put the entire army in your charge. All you have to do is put up with it till then, so I want you to bear the unbearable with me. We may look like a resplendent chancellor and cabinet member, but in that we share indescribable problems, we are back to the time of hard struggle of 1923. But if you view it not as a painful burden borne alone but as a burden carried by you and your true friend, the sweat that comes will acquire the luster of courage. Ernst, I have never needed to count on you so much as I do now. If we can get through this now, together. . . .

ROEHM: I know it, Adolf.

HITLER: Thanks, Roehm.

ROEHM: One thing is, though, that if I give them a long leave abruptly, my men will surely be disquieted. There's got to be some kind of acceptable reason. . . .

HITLER: Wait. I've thought about that myself. Well, now . . . how about your becoming ill. . . ?

ROEHM: *(Beginning to laugh)* Me? me, getting ill? *(Slapping on his chest and arms)* This eternally young body of steel that has had nothing to do with medicine and doctors ever since it dropped into this world—this body of Captain Roehm getting ill?

HITLER: I'm saying. . . .

ROEHM: Who'd ever believe such a thing? The only thing that can hurt me is a bullet. Or rather, when the steel of my body happens to betray me and attract into it the small iron lump of my comrade's—yes, when iron and iron, to be intimate, draw together and kiss, that's the only time I'll fall. Even then, I'll not breathe my last breath in bed.

HITLER: Yes, courageous Ernst, you've become minister but you aren't the kind of man who dies in bed. But, whatever the case, feign illness and make an announcement to that effect along with your statement. Promise that as soon as you recover after a few months' treatment you will discipline the SA into an even more elite army.

ROEHM: But who would believe that?

HITLER: Simply because it's unbelievable, all your men will believe it. That is, that there must be some compelling reason behind this.

ROEHM: There's some truth to what you say. And I. . . .

HITLER: How about going to Wiessee? Put up at one of the pensions there and have a good time.

ROEHM: *(Dreamily)* Wiessee. . . . Pleasure is waiting for me there. Pleasure appropriate for a hero. *(After falling silent and thinking for a while)* Good. I'll issue my statement this afternoon and leave for Wiessee by evening. I'll have kicked all the guests out of the Pension Hanselbauer by then.

HITLER: Good idea, Ernst. And the content of your statement. . . .

ROEHM: Wait. Let's do it when I finish this coffee. *(Thinking aloud)* "On the first of August, when its vacation ends, the Storm Detachment, which will have recovered its energy, will respond with ever-increasing proficiency to the honorable task that our German people and our fatherland expect. . . ."

HITLER: *(Discouraged)* Is that how you'll open your statement?

ROEHM: Yes. And my peroration will go like this: "The Storm Detachment remains now, as in the past, the destiny of Germany." What do you think?

HITLER: Well, it sounds all right.

ROEHM: I can't do a thing unless you approve of it, you know.

HITLER: I have approved.

ROEHM: You understand what I mean, Adolf. I am chief of staff of a 3-million-man army.

HITLER: I do understand, Ernst.

ROEHM: That's a friend. . . . Incidentally, isn't Strasser terrible? Not showing up at the breakfast the chancellor invited him to. . . . Though, come to think of it, that was all the better for me. After all, I hadn't had breakfast alone with the chancellor for a long time.

HITLER: That shows what he's worth. As soon as he sees that he can't get anything out of threatening me, he goes back to his den and starts busily spinning a web or else he tries to mend his complicated nets of conspiracy. We really shouldn't get in the way of such a busy hermit's life.

ROEHM: If he tries to get in our way as we crown you as president, I won't tolerate it. It would be a cinch to dispose of a pettifogger like that. If the workers made any noise, my SA would shut them up. I hope he didn't hint about that possibility to you yesterday, or did he?

HITLER: No, he didn't.

ROEHM: If he shows any such sign, tell me at once. It will be a cinch to get rid of him.

HITLER: Thanks, Ernst. I'll tell you if that happens. Now. . . . *(He rises.)*

ROEHM: Come, my friend, don't worry. Go back to your government duties. A host of administrative work appropriate neither to a soldier nor to an artist is waiting for you. All the aged goats who have survived on documents are craning their necks, awaiting the food you give them. You spend your days daubing everything with your signature. The muscles of your sword-brandishing arm are forgotten. What is authority? What is power? It's been reduced to the movements of the thin, slender muscles of pale fingers for signing.

HITLER: Don't tell me the rest. I know what you're going to say.

ROEHM: That's why, my friend, I am going to say it. Don't forget that your power lies not in the movements of your fingertips but in the powerful arm muscles of the young men who watch with yearning every single move you make at a distance and who are determined to sacrifice their lives for you at a moment's notice. When you get lost deep in the forest of administrative structure, the only thing you can rely on is the muscles that bulge alertly with dawn-colored veins—they will help you cut down the branches and fight your way clear at last. Whatever age may come, the basic substance of power is the muscles of young men. Don't forget that. Don't forget at least that you have a friend who hoards such muscles for you alone and will use them for you alone.

HITLER: *(Putting out his hand for handshake)* I will never forget, Ernst.

ROEHM: I won't forget either, Adolf.

(They look each other in the eye.)

HITLER: Now I must go.

ROEHM: We don't have to wait for Strasser any longer, do we? Though it would be fun to shovel this cold food in his pursed-up mouth. . . .

HITLER: Let's call in the waiters and get rid of it.

ROEHM: No, I'll show you my muscle power. I'll show you the power of the giant that Skirmir followed, joining Thor's group, carrying a bag of food.

HITLER: My, weren't you supposed to be Siegfried?

ROEHM: Look how the giant moves. *(He pushes the table.)*

HITLER: Well, well, a minister of state bothering to put the meal away!

ROEHM: That's the wrong way of thinking, Adolf, that's the wrong way of thinking.

(Merrily pushing the table, Roehm exits stage right. Hitler watches him until he exits, and starts to walk to stage left, when Krupp emerges from the balcony.)

KRUPP: Adolf. . . .

HITLER: Good morning, Herr Krupp.

KRUPP: Good morning. It's a refreshing, beautiful day. I was forced to perform an act unfit for my age and was sunbathing on the balcony, but I killed two birds with one stone, so to speak, for it pleased my knees—look at my foul-tempered knees, they're happiness itself this morning. *(He walks around proudly without using his stick.)*

HITLER: That's very good, Herr Krupp.

KRUPP: And besides, nothing is more rejuvenating than to peek into a room through a crack in the window. At my age I no longer have the energy to track down my wife's affairs, but that's because jealousy, like white wine, makes me drunk and utterly lazy. . . . While I was performing the act of hiding myself on the balcony as you told me to and listening to your conversation, I felt as if you were actors hired to rejuvenate me. How things turn solemn and romantic if you see and listen to them in secrecy—it's rather surprising.

HITLER: In other words, you're saying ours was a liars' histrionic conversation.

KRUPP: No, you were sincerity itself. Herr Roehm's sincerity was double yours. The nobility of your sincere hearts was, shall I say, almost jarring.

HITLER: That's exactly what I wanted to show you, Herr Krupp. I wanted you to see, because you are suspicious, how political sincerity is possible when no third party is around. Roehm hadn't intended to compromise but did. That the military will accept what we do . . . at least *I* don't believe it, no, I'll never believe it . . . but I hope they will.

KRUPP: I, too, at least *hope* they will. I haven't much time left to live and I can afford irresponsible hopes. But then why is it, Adolf, why, the moment Roehm proudly exited with the table, you put on an indescribably gloomy expression as if you'd aged ten years in a moment?

HITLER: *(Caught off guard)* You are a very conceited physiognomist.

KRUPP: I put my hopes not in your conversation but in that gloomy expression of yours when left alone. Does that make it easier to understand?

HITLER: Herr Krupp . . .

KRUPP: Let's put it this way, Adolf. A storm came. It was bound to come. Mountains were shrouded with fog, the large, open meadow darkened. The sheep uneasily bleated, and the shepherd frantically ran about to drive them toward the barn. . . . Then you—well, you couldn't feel you were the gigantic storm itself, but instead you felt more like the confused shepherd. And you plotted a compromise with Roehm. With a sheep, that is.

HITLER: Roehm, a sheep? He would be furious to hear that.

KRUPP: Maybe not a sheep, but his ideas are of the kind that belong to a flock, aren't they? What flashed across your dark brow after you parted with Roehm was neither of a sheep nor of a shepherd, but the storm that would bathe mountain peaks in purple lightning, shake the world, and shoot electricity through the living souls of human beings, reducing them to a handful of black ashes in an instant. You probably didn't feel that way yourself.

HITLER: At that moment I was afraid. I was confused. I was sad. That's all.

KRUPP: Even a chancellor doesn't have to be ashamed of having human emotions. Except, if you expand the fluctuations of human emotions infinitely, they will become nature's and, eventually, providence. In history, only a very, very few people have managed this.

HITLER: In human history, you mean.

KRUPP: I don't know about gods. But iron . . . iron, Adolf, goes through this every day and night in the blast furnace. By going through the storm of three-thousand-degree flames, the iron ore turns into pig iron. This becomes something different.

HITLER: I'll give careful thought to what you said, Herr Krupp.

(Krupp and Hitler exit stage left. A while later, Roehm enters from stage right as if fleeing. Then Strasser enters as if in pursuit.)

ROEHM: Why do you follow me like that? You can tell from my face that I don't want to speak to you.

STRASSER: I know that. Not only us, but the whole world is saying it: Roehm's the right, Strasser the left. They're like cat and dog. If they come across each other in public, they rudely avert their eyes. They look as if a word spoken would bounce back as a curse. . . . I know all that. You don't have to tell me that. That's why, that's why we must talk to each other, now.

ROEHM: You were late for the chancellor's breakfast meeting. He's already back at work. Why don't you go to him to apologize?

STRASSER: The matter has already gone beyond such court protocol, Herr Roehm.

ROEHM: Do whatever you like, then.

STRASSER: I'll do whatever I like. *(He sits in a chair at stage right; to Roehm)* Why don't you take a seat too?

ROEHM: I'll do whatever I like. *(He remains on his feet and walks irritably about while he speaks.)*

STRASSER: *(He laughs)* We're like kids quarreling. . . . Don't be so upset with everything. You aren't satisfied with the chancellor, are you? You are completely disappointed with the way he is now, aren't you?

ROEHM: There's no need for you to speculate on my emotions. Adolf and I are old friends. You may be an old party member, but you're at best a mere acquaintance.

STRASSER: But there's no doubt that you are disillusioned with the way he is now.

ROEHM: What makes you say that?

STRASSER: Because, in truth, I was disillusioned myself. I was very dissatisfied. Hitler as chancellor, Hitler ironbound by antiquated, tattered dragons. . . . I was very disappointed with that.

But now my outlook is changing somewhat. Especially since I met him yesterday, my point of view has been changing. Now, I am neither disappointed nor disillusioned. Hitler is doing quite well.

ROEHM: *(Interest aroused a little)* Is that the reason you skipped breakfast today?

STRASSER: The reason for that is different. I thought I wouldn't like it at all if I were poisoned at the breakfast I was so kindly invited to.

ROEHM: A silly joke, that. . . . *(Getting involved in the talk despite himself)* Your view, that is, that Adolf is doing quite well—is that in view of mankind itself or the era. . . .

STRASSER: Both, I'd say. Hitler is facing a new age, one never experienced before. In it there should naturally be a new attitude that never existed before. Whether or not we demand it from him, the circumstances where he can't help taking it as his own problem are pressing upon us day by day. I wouldn't dare say that he's taking care of himself well, but it's clear that he recognizes the situation better than anybody else. That's what I meant when I said he's doing well.

ROEHM: It's as if you're celebrating this "new age"—when it's such a dead-end, depressing age. At worst you are a revolutionary . . .

STRASSER: The revolution's already finished.

ROEHM: I know it, Herr Strasser, that's why this time we must . . .

STRASSER: You're talking about the future. You aren't talking about a new revolution that you would start today. You, who at least have agreed to a political truce. . . .

ROEHM: How did you know that?

STRASSER: I knew it. I did no eavesdropping, but my politically trained ear heard it in the distance. The question is *now*. Now. . . . That the revolution is finished, even you can't avoid conceding that.

ROEHM: *(Reluctantly)* That is true.

STRASSER: The revolution is finished. You have become a minister, Hitler chancellor, and as for me, I have gone into seclusion. Each has gotten what he deserved.

The signs for all this have long existed. It's strange that no one should have thought of the day when the revolution would be over. *(A pigeon coos on the balcony.)*

Look, a pigeon's cooing. I've got some Melba toast I filched from the breakfast table left in the hall. Thought I'd give it to the pigeons. *(Gropes in his pocket)* I'm sure I put it in here. . . . Oh I see, it's all crumbs. *(He rises to his feet, walks to the balcony, and scatters the crumbs. Roehm leaves the balcony and sits in the chair at stage left.)* The pigeons are happily eating the crumbs. Beautiful sunlight. A revolutionary morning is nothing like this. I never expected a morning like this, with no smell of blood anywhere.

(Strasser talks, with his back leaning against the railing of the balcony, from time to time throwing crumbs to the pigeons.)

This shouldn't have happened. But one day it began, slowly. The revolutionary pigeons flew back and forth through the flying bullets with important messages attached to their feet. Their fat white chests could be splattered with blood any moment. Look at them now. They're foraging for crumbs, just like that, grumbling solemnly.

The locomotive smoke covering the elevated railway no longer smells of gun smoke but of a backyard fire. Walk under the window where a brightly colored rug is being dusted, and all that falls on you is cigarette ashes and the mud from the shoes, not powdered, dry blood. A clock strikes. The clock no longer points to the definite, critical moment, but just marks flowing time, and gold watches, silver watches, and marble clocks—all the timepieces that were once solid have turned to liquid. The wine in the shopping basket on the arm of a woman turning a street corner sparkled like a jewel when it was used as a stimulant for those wounded in the revolution. It has now turned a brick color.

The pot that once swallowed a stray bullet put out blue flowers, but it puts out only insipid pansies now that the fertilizing bullet is gone. The same is true of songs. For songs have lost the quality of sharp, clear screams. The distant blue sky that was reflected in the eyes of the dead was once a phantom of transformation, but now the blue sky has been shattered into smithereens in the water of the washtub. Every cigarette has lost that sweet, piercing taste of an unbearable separation.

Nature, human beings, all phenomena have lost that piercing power, that penetrating power and, like the water and air, merely slide past our skin. Our delicate, sharp, lacelike nervous system has turned into something loose, worn and coarse.

Then a different smell begins to assault us. The smell of putrefaction familiar from a distant past—that peculiar smell of a decomposing game bird that a hunting dog neglected in dead leaves—a smell that vaguely muddies the stripes of sunlight in the forest. Everywhere, this smell of putrefaction begins to numb the sensations of our fingertips, as if we were lepers. Our fingers, which once showed directions as alertly as fire road signs in the dark, are now used only to sign checks and pry open women's bodies. Apostasy, apostasy, invisible, transparent daily apostasy—Herr Roehm, you too must have experienced all these sensations.

The stringed instrument no longer makes a true tremolo; the flag no longer waves as sinuously as a panther; the coffeepot no longer shows its noble boiling fury; the holes on the wall that were once loopholes suffer from cataracts; political leaflets that were once stained with blood now advertise sales; socks no longer acquire the wet smell of a beast on the run; the stars have ceased to be compasses, and poems to be code words—now that this is where we are. . . . Herr Roehm, the revolution is all finished.

The revolution was the age of white, cruel, but unsullied teeth, the age of sets of white teeth that all young men flash both when they smile and when they get angry. The age of white, sparkling teeth. But next came the age of gums. The red gums soon turn purple and start rotting. . . .

ROEHM: That's enough. If I hear any more of that, my ears will rot, my heart will rot. Herr Strasser, what are you trying to tell me?

STRASSER: We must have another revolution—I know you think that. I myself think that we must have another revolution. The two of us have plenty of things to talk about, don't we?

ROEHM: But our methods our different. So are our ends.

STRASSER: Like the mirror images, your right is my left, but my right is your left. If we shattered the mirror, we might become one and the same.

ROEHM: So that's what you want to discuss with me, is it? Interesting. Please have a seat there.

STRASSER: Your permission, finally. (He sits in the chair at stage right.)

ROEHM: Let me make one warning. It is that I have never in the past, never in the present, and will never in the future agree to your Communist way of doing things, your way of agitating unionized workers so that they can't distinguish between loyalty to Germany and loyalty to the Soviet Union. If this is understood, I can hear your story.

STRASSER: Come on, don't be so stiff. You, a minister, talk like someone in a youth corps. You said, "If this is understood." I'd say, "Aside from that." It's a matter of a totally different dimension.

ROEHM: What do you mean?

STRASSER: What do you think of old Krupp? What do you think of that iron dealer like Reineke Fox? You know, he follows Hitler as the shadow follows the body. . . .

ROEHM: Honestly, I don't like that old man, either.

STRASSER: Like or dislike, do you think he believes Hitler?

ROEHM: Well.

STRASSER: I can't possibly think he does. He has come from the Essen industrial region to sound out the marriage between the Hitler administration and Essen. He has come to see if the prospective bridegroom is fit to be a lifelong companion. I judge that he hasn't reached a conclusion yet. I say this because Essen, the daughter of iron, though extremely good-looking, failed in her former marriage—that is, in the European war. For this second marriage, her go-between can't be too cautious.

ROEHM: But last year, during the first election after Hitler came to power, Krupp, as Schacht says, made the 3-million-mark campaign contribution with all the others, didn't he?

STRASSER: That was the beginning of his sounding-out efforts. But he's still sounding it out. The recent political crisis has prompted the Essen industrialists to make some warning signs. Krupp hasn't decided which side to take. He won't, for the next two or three days especially.

ROEHM: For the next two or three days especially . . .

STRASSER: Right. The National Socialist Party was about to fall apart because of you.

ROEHM: You were trying to pull it apart yourself. But we've already come through the crisis. If Adolf becomes president, then a truly refreshing morning sun will shine.

STRASSER: Do you really believe it?

ROEHM: I believe in Adolf. When he becomes president, the dreams that my beloved SA has had for so long will be fulfilled.

STRASSER: Do you really believe it?

ROEHM: *(Somewhat disturbed)* Naturally.

STRASSER: What have you paid for that?

ROEHM: Concession. Compromise. Following Adolf's orders. We storm troopers will be on leave until the end of July, during that time we won't wear our uniforms, engage in demonstrations or exercises, and I, so full of beans, will be ill. . . . If this is all it takes, even I can pull off the trick.

STRASSER: Do you think that's all that's needed to take care of everything?

ROEHM: It will work, at least as a stopgap measure. Until Adolf becomes president.

STRASSER: Do you think the army will be duped by such a cheap trick? If Hitler believes that, then he's a big fool. If you believe that, you're an outright lunatic.

ROEHM: What? What did you say?

STRASSER: I'm saying either Hitler is a fool or you are a lunatic. I'm not saying that Hitler is a fool *and* you are a lunatic. You know what I'm trying to say.

ROEHM: A despicable man. I see you're trying to break us up—Adolf and me.

(They remain silent for a while.)

STRASSER: Let's stop talking about Hitler. Let's talk about your SA. You are anxious to install the SA that you've nurtured by your own hand at the core of the Reichswehr. Right?

ROEHM: You don't have to ask me that.

STRASSER: What would you do if you could do it by a certain method?

ROEHM: *(Brightening up despite himself)* I could! . . . No, the moment Adolf becomes president. . . .

STRASSER: That's just a promise.

ROEHM: Don't you ever speak ill of my friend.

STRASSER: Let me go back a step. Will he definitely become president?

ROEHM: He will.

STRASSER: I said "definitely."

ROEHM: Definitely?

STRASSER: Yes. The army is quite stubborn. Unless you disband your SA, Hitler will definitely not become president. The one who is blocking him in his ambition is nobody else but you, Herr Roehm. And at the same time you're staking your dreams on his becoming president. Isn't that acting like a spoiled child?

ROEHM: *(Suppressing anger)* What's that "certain method" of yours?

STRASSER: General von Schleicher.

ROEHM: You mean that senile army man.

STRASSER: He alone holds the key to making you and me shake hands. That's because he alone can persuade Defense Minister von Blomberg, who gave Hitler the ultimatum.

ROEHM: In other words . . .

STRASSER: Yes. "Without Hitler." Don't forget. The army's ultimatum to Hitler that he declare martial law was addressed to him, not to you.

ROEHM: Without Hitler! Humph! That's enough to expose your plot. You get together with the army, first cutting me off from Adolf, and then with the army you take care of us separately. So you think I will let you do that? We are one in body and spirit.

STRASSER: Doesn't Hitler know better than anybody else that nothing works unless that one-in-body-and-spirit business is sliced apart? Why is it that that one-in-body-and-spirit business is going to live separately, with tears no doubt, during the summer?

ROEHM: How many times do I have to tell you it's just a temporary political gesture?

STRASSER: All right. I give up trying to persuade you. Just like the person
who, having looked at the sun, sees its yellow afterimage in everything,
you can't look at the world without seeing the image of Hitler.

Well. . . . I have an idea. I'm going to think out loud. I'd like you to
listen calmly. If you hear nothing worthwhile, that's one thing, but if
there's anything in what I say, try to remember it.

Herr Roehm, this is a simple matter. It's a cooperative revolutionary
plan for you and me. Now, at this moment, you and I lock our arms,
and you, with the force of your SA, drive Hitler out of the National Socialist Party and become party leader yourself. Schleicher persuades von
Blumberg to reconcile with you now that you've separated from Hitler.
What the Prussian army fears is, in fact, the unity between you and
Hitler. Meanwhile, I carry out Socialist policies with the backing of your
armed forces; we have von Papen as president temporarily; and he ap-
points me chancellor and you commander in chief of the Reichswehr.
There's no need to worry about money. If you and I join arms right here
and now, from that moment on there's no more need to worry about
money.

ROEHM: Why is that?

STRASSER: Krupp will change sides and come to us.

(They fall silent.)

ROEHM: . . . All right, I understand. I understand what you are trying to
say. At the same time, you too understand—that I am not, for a single
moment, tempted by any plan to betray Adolf.

STRASSER: Thank you for listening calmly, Herr Roehm. But I'm not finished with my talk yet. Even I don't expect you to come around so easily to a plan such as I am describing now. And yet, Herr Roehm, unless
you and I join arms and drive Hitler out now, and unless we unite our
forces and achieve a blitzkrieg revolution . . . if we don't do that . . . if
we miss this opportunity now . . . what do you think will happen? Now,
wait. Think carefully before answering that.

ROEHM: Nothing will happen, Herr Strasser. The world will remain the
same. Adolf and I will remain friends so dedicated to each other that neither would mind the other's chopping off his head, and you will remain
a base swindler, Krupp a merchant of death—each in his own role, living according to the movement of the earth.

STRASSER: Will that really be the case? Come, think harder about it. What
will happen?

ROEHM: Nothing will happen.

STRASSER: Are you sure?

ROEHM: Yes. . . . Well then, what do you think will happen?

STRASSER: . . . Death.

ROEHM: Whose?

STRASSER: Yours and mine.

(They fall silent.)

ROEHM: *(He bursts out laughing)* What an imagination you have! Death? Your death and my death? Have you been taken in by an astrologer or something? Come to think of it, everything you've said strikes me as raving nonsense. Your plan for revolution is clumsy. While jeering at me for taking the army lightly, you take it even more lightly.

STRASSER: I know it is a clumsy plan. But in this case a clumsy plan is better than doing nothing. I am at any rate breathlessly trying to run away from my enemy and jump on the horse you're racing. If you halt the horse, that'll be the end of both you and me. And yet you are carelessly trying to halt it. I can no longer just watch. I accuse you of stupidity in not perceiving the danger, because I'd like to save my own life, too. At this point there's nothing we can do but forget everything, ride the horse together and whip it on. Should we manage to get over the hill on the horizon, the dawn of revolution would break upon us. . . . Try to understand this, Herr Roehm. I am trying to stake everything on your 3-million-man Storm Detachment, your revolutionary army.

ROEHM: You stake everything on my SA and then use it for betrayal.

STRASSER: No, that's not it. Riding your horse, your revolutionary army, is the only escape route left for both of us. Hitler is obviously no longer betting on your SA.

ROEHM: *(Uneasily)* He is. . . .

STRASSER: He's betting on the pursuer. Can't you see that, Herr Roehm?

ROEHM: And so what? Join hands with a traitor—is that what you're saying?

STRASSER: All right, suppose you are right and I am the traitor. But the matter is urgent. Unless we unite now and face up to Hitler . . .

ROEHM: What will happen? Death?

STRASSER: Yes, . . . death.

(Roehm laughs loudly. Strasser falls silent. At his silence Roehm's laughter stops suddenly.)

ROEHM: What kind of death. . . ? Struck by thunder? Or is the Midgard serpent going to rise from the bottom of the ocean where he's been hiding, and though you manage to shatter his head with your hammer, you're overcome by his venom? Or like the courageous Tyr, the last god who survived the twilight of the gods, am I going to be bitten to death by Garm, the dog of hell?

STRASSER: That sort of death would be nice. But, Herr Roehm, even if we assume that you are a hero, you may not necessarily meet a heroic death.

ROEHM: *(Cheerfully)* Then, die of an illness?

STRASSER: You're already suffering from an illness, as I said before. You're suffering from the illness called trust.

ROEHM: Am I to be assassinated or executed?

STRASSER: Probably both. Do you think you can put up with torture?

ROEHM: *(Mockingly)* Who's going to treat you so badly, worrywart, cowardly you? Tell me. Are you afraid to tell me the name of the man? Do you think saying the name will bring down a curse?

STRASSER: Adolf Hitler.

(They fall silent.)

ROEHM: Let me ask you one thing: Do you intend to interfere with our installation of Adolf as president at any cost?

STRASSER: If I could. If I could do that, Germany would be saved. I said that to Hitler yesterday at the risk of ruining his mood.

ROEHM: Just as I thought. If that's true, as I promised Adolf, I must take your life.

STRASSER: I'll give it to you any time. But there are two conditions for that. For you to kill me, first, I must be alive at that time. Second, you must be alive.

ROEHM: You mean we'll be killed by Adolf before then.

STRASSER: It's simple logic. If you and I join hands, we'll save our lives and at the same time carry out our revolution. If we don't, I'll be killed sooner or later by Hitler or by you—either way, it's the same to me. If possible, I'd like you to kill me. Since I've talked to you today, I'm beginning to like you.

ROEHM: You're going to be killed either way—what an unlucky fellow you are. But why can't Adolf kill us if I join hands with you? He has his own SS Guard detachment.

STRASSER: You and I uniting means that your SA won't be disarmed. Hitler's SS in the face of your SA would be like a praying mantis in the face of a chariot.

ROEHM: What about the army?

STRASSER: The army never gets involved in assassinations. They don't like to stain their white gloves. . . . Besides, Herr Roehm, if we join hands, the biggest obstacle to Hitler's killing us will appear.

ROEHM: What's that?

STRASSER: Krupp. He'll come to our side. Hitler would never, never make an enemy of the Essen industry, even if he had to lose power.

ROEHM: Hmmm. Do you think so? In any case, that has nothing to do with me.

STRASSER: Nothing to do with you?

ROEHM: Does it? It's impossible that Adolf should kill me.

STRASSER: *(Dumbfounded)* Herr Roehm, you . . .

ROEHM: Listen to me carefully, weak-nerved Herr Strasser. Your brain is disturbed and you are babbling all sorts of nonsensical things. All this comes from fear. I wouldn't say for now that there's no reason for that fear. There may be some solid reason. But don't pass your disease on to others. You are free to be killed, but what does that have to do with me? If Adolf is going to be the killer, listen, you may be killed but I won't. I can tell you that definitely.

STRASSER: Why?

ROEHM: Because Adolf is my friend.

STRASSER: Stupid. . . .

ROEHM: Listen, it is, yes, possible that you'll be killed. As a matter of fact, if your obstruction becomes too much to take, I will do it without Adolf's asking. . . . I must say, though, the idea that the two of us will be killed—it's a delusion or else a threat. Can you think that I, Captain Roehm, would be duped by such a childish threat—I, a man of many battles?

If it's a delusion, you are already insane. You are not in the least different from those who insist that the earth is a flat piece of paper, who run into a police station saying radio waves will kill them, and who run around saying men live on the moon. You better go to a hospital at once. You have lost the ability to see and judge reality—or rather the condition that makes reality possible—without prejudice.

STRASSER: What is the condition?

ROEHM: Trust in humanity.

STRASSER: What? What did you say?

ROEHM: Trust in humanity. Friendship, comradeship, military brotherhood, and other such noble, manly, divine qualities. Without them, reality would collapse. And so would government. Adolf and I are connected at the root, which makes reality possible. You with your despicable head wouldn't understand this.

The earth's crust on which we live is hard, yes. There are forests; there are valleys; and it is covered with rocks. But if you go under the green-covered ground, the temperature goes up, and you get to the core of the earth, where the hot magma is boiling. This magma is the source of all power and spirit, this red-hot formless matter is the flame within that gives form to everything. The alabaster-like, white, beautiful human body is beautiful only when it shares the flame inside and when that flame can be discerned from outside. Herr Strasser, this magma is the power source that moves the world, endows warriors with courage, urges them to actions that lead to death, fills the hearts of youth with yearnings for glory, and boils the blood of all who fight gallantly. Adolf and I are connected not in any form on the earth. Human beings as forms are separate entities that part with one another, that betray one another. We are connected in formless matter at the base of the earth, the magma where everything melts.

Do you know the story about Adorst the Mouse?

STRASSER: Good God, it's a mouse's turn. Do I at this point have to hear the story of a mouse?

ROEHM: If you don't want to, I won't tell it. Adorst the Mouse was a single mouse. There never were two mice.

STRASSER: Herr Roehm, your story is certainly beautiful. No matter how much you dislike me, I seem to like you more and more. But yours is a boy's idea. It's the idea of boys who like to play war in the woods, exchanging whistle signals, being taken prisoner, and pretending to be killed. As long as you're involved in politics, you can't allow such ideas to rule you; otherwise you'll be in big trouble.

ROEHM: I'm a soldier, not a politician.

STRASSER: Do you mean to remain loyal even to one who's wishy-washy?

ROEHM: Who is wishy-washy? Being human, we may at times waver. We may change our minds. I don't know about the others, but Adolf is my friend.

STRASSER: I'll tell you something. Adolf is your friend. That's quite good. And you—well, you are blind.

ROEHM: Beg your pardon?

STRASSER: Looking at Hitler's eyes yesterday, even somebody who knows nothing would have immediately guessed his murderous intent.

ROEHM: That's because you saw him through tinted glasses of delusion. Well yes, he confronted me with a difficult question yesterday. But he also delighted in reminiscing about the old days. The same is true of this morning. I've never eaten such an enjoyable breakfast as I did this morning. It had the real taste of a breakfast that simple, manly, German war buddies enjoy together. . . . Adolf's eyes, did you say? Since you mention it, they were somewhat bloodshot, but that's because he's too busy with his government work to get enough sleep.

STRASSER: You are blind. . . . I see everyone's murderous intent at once. I've learned the trick in my long political life. Yesterday Hitler had eyes much darker than I'd ever seen them before. Didn't you see those eyes, Herr Roehm? The color of the callused, dark blue waves in the winter Baltic Sea. The color of the eye that says "Nein" to every human emotion. That's the kind of eye that kills. . . . I do not necessarily think that Hitler is an extraordinarily evil man. The thing is that he is solidly entrapped in the machine of necessity. As he hopes, no, even if he doesn't, he must become president. The machine's already geared in that direction. The machine has begun to move, and the army has begun to constrict him. Cogs turn. The tightening continues. If tightened any further, Hitler will suffocate. If I were him—yes, as you see, I can't even kill a bug, but, this is what Hitler's thinking, I would have no choice but to kill the two of us, Roehm and Strasser.

ROEHM: You're merely jabbering away the outline of a horror story that you've written in your cowardly mind. Let's sum it up. If we don't do anything, both of us will be killed. If we drive Hitler out and carry out a revolution hand in hand, not only will we save our lives but also we can take over the world. Is that it? Let me give my conclusion. Even if I were going to be killed, I couldn't take part in any action to betray Hitler. That's my conclusion. . . . There's nothing further to talk about, is there?

STRASSER: *(A silence)* All right, Herr Roehm, I understand how you feel . . . . But listen to me a little longer. This time *I* will compromise. I can't bear it, but there's no other way of avoiding the worst situation. . . . The idea is this. Let's forget about "without Hitler." Let's bring him in on our side.

ROEHM: *(Beginning to laugh)* Bringing to your side someone who's going to kill you? I see, you can get that bad when your brain is disturbed.

STRASSER: Listen anyway. We join hands and support Hitler from the left and right wing. While I work on the army to break up its forces, your SA carries out the revolution and installs Hitler as president. But every one of his powers will be shared by you and me—we'll make him the nation's supreme symbol, noble but powerless.

ROEHM: A robot, that is.

STRASSER: Yes. That can be done if we join hands now. I'll be in charge of government, you the military, and Hitler the honor. This you can do. Your friendship and loyalty will remain in history as beautiful as they are now. . . . For that, Herr Roehm, I must tell you, since this is going to be for Hitler in the end, you must bear the temporary stigma of a rebel and rise with your SA today, immediately. Don't ever allow it to be disarmed.

ROEHM: Now you urge me to rebel, Herr Strasser. Out of an itinerant merchant's trunk jumps one unexpected fake item after another. *(Coldly)* Let me make this clear. I have never once gone against Adolf's orders. I shall never go against his orders in the future either. I'll tell you the reasons. First, I am a soldier. Second, I read in advance every one of his orders to me. His orders are, as it were, a friend's orders. . . . Don't you think it's wonderful . . . ? It isn't so much obeying as manly consent.

STRASSER: *(In despair)* No matter what I say, you don't see it. If you don't, you are doomed.

ROEHM: Enough advice from a double-dealer. I don't want to join hands with a sullied man. That's all.

STRASSER: No matter what happens?

ROEHM: Sure, no matter what happens.

(They fall silent.)

STRASSER: I see. You call me a double-dealer, and I don't want to talk any more. But if we part company as we do, you will die and so will I. That is clear. You will be killed by your friend, Hitler. You may be a little luckier than I am.

ROEHM: That's stupid. How could Adolf kill me?

STRASSER: *(Aside)* What a foolhardy . . .

ROEHM: There are *many* instances of an idea, which, once settled in a sickly brain, has uprooted beautiful human relationships. But Hitler would never kill Roehm. History will prove that—if it's a history of human beings. . . . Herr Strasser, you are ill.

STRASSER: So are you, Herr Roehm.

ROEHM: Let's, both of us, rest quietly during the summer.

STRASSER: There'll be no more time for resting.

ROEHM: Follow the example of Hindenburg who persists in living with one leg in a coffin.

STRASSER: *(He rises to his feet weakly, changes his mind, and seized by passion, clings to Roehm's knees)* Herr Roehm, I beg you. Help me. You're the only one who can help me. . . . Helping me will save your life. Don't pass up this moment; we'll never have it again in our lifetime. You are the only one. You are the only one who can do it.

ROEHM: *(Pushing him off coldly)* If you want to die, go ahead and die. You are free to be killed. I'll be glad to kill you here, if you like.

STRASSER: Yes, please. Kill me. I'll feel much better if you kill me right here. Your foolhardiness killing me has some saving grace that a terrifying dark wisdom killing me doesn't have. In any case, we're going to see each other soon in hell. Draw your gun and shoot me.

ROEHM: I regret to say this, but I haven't received an order yet.

STRASSER: An order?

ROEHM: Adolf Hitler's order.

STRASSER: It would be quite a show to see you obey the order that you yourself be killed.

ROEHM: Idiot. Shall I smash your front teeth so you can't talk?

STRASSER: Hitler will kill you. That's as definite as the sunrise from the east.

ROEHM: How dare you go on talking?

STRASSER: How your disbelief comes from such foolhardy trust—I do not understand.

ROEHM: I'm going now. I don't have any more time for a psychotic. I'm going to enjoy the summer in Wiessee. At the lakeside pension I don't have to suffer any of your kind of pitiful intellectuals; the days of rest will begin for merry, violent, godlike warriors with blond hair and blue eyes,

each as gallant and as beautiful as Balder. Adolf's orders will be faithfully carried out. *(Starts off to stage right.)*

STRASSER: Wait. I have one piece of advice to give you. I do this because
I've come to like you. You will please take it as advice I give because I
care for you. *(Roehm moves off, ignoring him)* Herr Roehm, if you're going
to Wiessee, at least take your staff bodyguard with you, just to be on the
safe side. I'm telling you. It's for your own good.

ROEHM: *(He turns around at the door at stage right and sneers)* To a man the
storm troopers are my subordinates. I have no need for your instructions
in deploying them.

*(Roehm puts on his military hat, clicks the heels of his boots, makes a deliberate-
ly reverential salute, turns about, and exits.)*

*(Strasser, stunned, collapses into his chair. He pulls himself together, totters to
his feet, and also exits stage right.)*

*(From stage left, Hitler enters with white gloves in his hands. He walks about
irritably, agonizing, goes out on the balcony and thinks, apparently unable to make
up his mind. Finally he loudly shuts the doors to the balcony with both hands.
He walks straight to the apron center and makes signals toward the audience with
his white gloves.)*

*(There is a sense that from the right side of the orchestra enters Marshall Go-
ering and from the left Chief of the SS Himmler.)*

HITLER: *(Toward the right side of the orchestra)* Marshal Goering. *(Toward the
left side of the orchestra)* Herr Himmler. . . . I am going to take a trip now.
Concerning the matter we've discussed, I shall send top secret instructions from wherever I am. As soon as you receive them, I want you to
act swiftly and decisively, in absolute secrecy. You will do it thoroughly, without a bit of hesitation, without a bit of leniency. Will you please
start making preparations at once?

*(Hitler nods to the two men as if to dismiss them. He turns back to stage cen-
ter and remains standing with his back to the audience.)*

CURTAIN

ACT 3

*Midnight on June 30, 1934—that is, several days after act 2. Same place. The
chandelier shines brightly.*

*From stage right enters Krupp, as usual with a walking stick. He sits on a chair
and waits.*

*Soon, from stage left, enters Hitler in military uniform. He looks pale and
emaciated, eyes dull.*

KRUPP *(standing)*, played by Nakamura Nobuo, and HITLER *(seated)*, played by Murakami Fuyuki. *Courtesy of Waseda University's Tsubouchi Memorial Theatre Museum. By permission of Gekidan NLT.*

KRUPP: Oh, welcome home. I'd heard that you returned from your trip last night, but I'm surprised at this abrupt summons.

HITLER: I'm sorry to have kept you waiting, Herr Krupp. Excuse me for the way I look. I've been in this emergency situation since I returned, and I must look presentable at least in what I wear.

KRUPP: What a face you have, Adolf. You've had no sleep, have you?

HITLER: I've asked you to come so late at night because I don't want to spend a sleepless night alone—would this explanation win your forgiveness?

KRUPP: I'm glad that you depend upon me. Besides, because of this strange wet weather my knees ache, and like you, I want someone to talk to through a sleepless night.

HITLER: That's very convenient.

    (They fall silent.)

KRUPP: You've finally done it.

HITLER: Yes. It was a step I had to take.

KRUPP: Both of them.

HITLER: Yes, both of them.

KRUPP: Aside from them, all the SA leaders were taken care of. The residents in the neighborhood of the Lichterfelde Cadet Academy where they were executed couldn't sleep from Saturday night to Sunday because of incessant gunshots—or so I hear. I've heard as many as four hundred people. Is that true?

HITLER: *(He counts with his fingers nervously, exaggeratedly; fails and goes over it, many times)* It is . . . three hundred and eighty. . . . So far that's about it.

KRUPP: I must say that's a generous treat. The army must be delighted. But how are you going to persuade the people? The city's buzzing with rumors.

HITLER: I'll give a speech to the Reichstag in a while. The number of those executed. . . . *(He counts with his fingers again, morbidly, nervously).* . . . It is at the most seventy or eighty—that's what I will announce.

KRUPP: You mean to put in your speech the charges against Herr Roehm and the charges against Herr Strasser in a most persuasive manner, I imagine.

HITLER: Yes, I do. As for Roehm, first his corruption was quite something. . . .

KRUPP: There must be many who won't care to hear that.

HITLER: Second, his terrible biases in personnel management. . . .

KRUPP: I thought that wasn't Roehm's alone, but the National Socialist Party's specialty.

HITLER: Third, his disgraceful conduct, and at that, extremely revolting, extremely abnormal . . .

KRUPP: That, too, was, to put it in Roehm's way, nothing but raising stag beetles on honey, wasn't it?

HITLER: But what is more unforgivable than anything else is that Roehm plotted to revolt. If I expose this, all the German people must approve of the step I took.

KRUPP: Strangely, in most cases, plots to revolt are exposed after the plotters are dead. In such dangerous things I'd rather get caught while I'm alive.

HITLER: *(Becoming furious, he shouts)* What are you trying to say, sir, for God's sake!

KRUPP: Adolf, you're irritated. No matter what an old man like me says, you shouldn't shout like that.

HITLER: I'll listen calmly. No matter how painful the things you may say, I'd rather you not walk away from me.

KRUPP: Blood has been shed. On a night like this, it is much more healing to be immersed in memories of blood than to seek consolation in liquor and women. I'm saying this out of my own long experience, and you can count on it. Adolf, you are tired. And so it may be necessary to supply your ears with a lot more of the shed blood—before the blood seeps into the floor and is lost in the color of the wooden tiles. . . . Fortunately, I have a great deal of information that may be more accurate than yours. The more power you have, the more isolated from accurate information you'll become.

HITLER: You're saying whatever pops into your head.

KRUPP: Strasser was arrested at noon, Saturday, here in Berlin. He wasn't even given time to eat lunch but was rushed to the prison on Prinz-Albrecht-Strasse and executed. Of course, there was no such thing as a trial, but there's no information, either on whether or not he ate his lunch after he was arraigned. This troubles me a great deal. I'd be sorry for him if he was killed on an empty stomach. About the same time, at General von Schleicher's villa, the doorbell rang, the general went to the door and was shot down on the spot; Frau von Schleicher was also shot to death. Your SS was quite busy. They had to make similar respectful individual calls, while at the same time they had to put together execution squads here, there, and everywhere. They had too many clients.

HITLER: I wonder how Strasser died? Do you have detailed information on that, such as the Reds' papers might?

KRUPP: Unfortunately, I don't. I suspect that he died calmly, with much more composure than you might expect. A man like that, who's born not exactly hot-blooded, dies like a vegetable—all the more so on an empty stomach. He was an intelligent fellow. Perhaps you should have given him poison, like Socrates.

HITLER: *(Furious)* He's the one I should have torn to shreds. *(He rises to his feet and begins to speak oratorically)* That gloomy hypocrite, while putting on the face of a friend of the working class, conspired with the old foxes of the army to plot the overthrow of my administration—a Jewish internationalist, a parasite in a lion's mane for new Germany, a despicable schemer, who was, for all this, essentially no more than a callow intellectual who all his life held on to the sort of ideas put forth in the editorials of student papers. I am investigating further and may even turn up evidence that he was communicating with Moscow.

KRUPP: That was a terrible thing to do, if true. He, too, died without being able to convince himself of the reality that the revolution was finished. And Roehm. . . .

HITLER: Oh, about his moment of death, I've heard that he completely lost his composure. But to the very end he never once uttered a bad word about me but instead kept screaming, "This is Goering's plot!"

KRUPP: He was quite a spirited fellow. He was pulled out of his warm bed in the pension in Wiessee, taken to Munich along with Heines and others, and shot at Stadelheim Prison, the same place that he was thrown in after the Munich putsch ten years ago. I must say death by shooting was most appropriate for him. . . . He lost his composure?

HITLER: That's what I've heard. Regrettably.

KRUPP: An unexpected thing happened, and he couldn't help it.

HITLER: You talk as if Roehm were innocent. *(Becoming furious)* Roehm was guilty. He was guilty. All the evidence that he plotted a revolt is in. He was guilty in every point. Herr Krupp, you shouldn't look away from his crimes. Well yes, he felt friendship for me, unaware that that itself was a crime. Furthermore, he expected friendship from me, unaware that that was a worse crime. . . . He was always dreaming of the past. He even compared himself to mythological figures. He loved playing soldier better than anything else; he loved sleeping in a tattered army blanket under the starry sky. Though holding a ministerial post, he always tried to lure me into such dreams. That was a crime. . . . He flattered himself that no one else was more manly, sturdy, and gallant than he. That was a crime. . . . He knew only how to give orders. Even in the sentiment that he called loyalty, there always was some suggestion of an odor of something burned. That was a crime.

KRUPP: Yes, nothing would be better as a memorial tribute to our time than to enumerate his crimes in detail tonight, as you're doing, under the humid night sky of a Berlin summer.

HITLER: Roehm said at least one thing that struck the right chord. He used to say, Ernst is a soldier; Adolf is an artist. Each time he said it I was angry, but as I think about it now, the word "artist" that he used with some pity begins to have far greater dimensions than his simple mind could have imagined. He had only dreams but no imagination, so he didn't notice that he was going to be killed, and he couldn't be completely cruel to others. His ears understood only army brass band music; he should have listened to Wagner more, as I do. He failed to grasp beauty, because he made no effort to do what is indispensable in creating beauty on this earth, that is, to know the root of the beauty one perceives. Didn't you once tell me that it all depends on whether or not you can feel yourself as a storm? That is to *know* why you are a storm, to know why you are so angry, why you are so dark, why you are so furious with so much wind and rain trapped inside you, why you are so great. That is not enough. Why you work so much destruction, try to fell giant rotten trees while making wheat fields fertile, to revive as with God's lightning the faces of the young men emaciated by the Jews' neon signs, and to make all the German people taste a tragic sentiment through and through. . . . That is my destiny.

KRUPP: Will the storm come? The night sky is dark and gloomy, without a single star *(walking out to the balcony)* and clouds pile up like countless corpses. The night air isn't good for my knees, but this room is thick with the smell of blood. *(From the balcony)* Adolf, are the executions still going on?

HITLER: They should be still going on.

KRUPP: I can't hear them from here. Which way is the Lichterfelde Cadet Academy?

HITLER: *(Joining Krupp and pointing to right from the balcony)* That way. *(When he says it, he loses heart and returns to his chair.)* They're working on all the little guys now.

KRUPP: Those guns are all my company's. For those who are shot, it should be a lot easier to be shot with the best-performing guns in the world, the guns of Krupp Works. For the guns, too, they are shooting the real human flesh to their satisfaction for the first time in a long while. They should be able to sleep, satisfied, on their oak gun racks, like the soldiers who've been to brothels on leave for the first time in a long time. I envy those who can sleep.

HITLER: *(To himself)* Ernst is a soldier; Adolf is an artist. . . . Better rephrase it this way: Ernst was a soldier, and Adolf will become an artist.

KRUPP: *(From the balcony)* Did you say something, Adolf?

HITLER: No, nothing.

KRUPP: Will you please come here again?

HITLER: Roehm's finally dead, and now you are giving me orders?

KRUPP: *(Startled by what is implied by Hitler's words, he drops his stick on the floor)* Oh!

HITLER: *(In his seat)* What's the matter?

KRUPP: You've seen it. I've dropped my stick on the floor.

HITLER: Are you telling me to pick it up?

KRUPP: I'm not telling you to pick it up. . . . *(He becomes obsequious despite himself)* but if I try to pick it up myself, my knees . . . if I bend them too much, they hurt shockingly.

HITLER: *(In his seat)* I'm coming now.

(Krupp remains standing, supporting himself with his hand against the door to the balcony, waiting.)

HITLER: *(He hunches his back and sings gloomily)*

> In death, let's be together
> Let's fight together
> With gun in hand
> In battlefield
> Poppies in bloom
> Blazing our chests

(He utters a low cruel gloomy chuckle.)

KRUPP: *(Almost screaming)* Adolf!

HITLER: *(As if awakened, he rises to his feet lightheartedly)* My, my forgive me, sir. *(He picks up the stick from the floor and hands it to Krupp with deliberate reverence.)* Do they hurt terribly, Herr Krupp?

KRUPP: No. Thank you. Thanks. It's all right now.

HITLER: *(Gently holding his arm)* You must be careful. . . . By the way, didn't you call me before? I was thinking a bit. . . . What was it that you wanted me to do?

KRUPP: It was . . . it was, well, I wonder what it was.

HITLER: You'll remember it later. Come, it's not good for your health. Let's go back to the room.

KRUPP: *(Coming into the room)* Oh, I remember, Adolf. Let's go to the balcony. And I'd like you to listen to them there.

HITLER: To what?

KRUPP: To the gunshots.

HITLER: From here you can't possibly hear. . . .

KRUPP: *(Passionately)* You think that. You think that. But they're the executions that you ordered. They must reach your ears. I'd like you to do your best concentrating and listening and hear the sound of the executions inside the high, inhuman walls of the Cadet Academy.

HITLER: You can't ask me to do such an impossibility. First of all, I myself may be shot any time, so I prefer not to go out on the balcony late at night. . . . *(Reluctantly going out on the balcony)* All I hear is the distant roar of wheels on the Stadtbahn and the infrequent honks of automobiles. Unter den Linden has dark tree shadows cast across it under the starless sky.

KRUPP: It's impossible that you can't hear them. They are the gunshots that you ordered.

HITLER: Herr Krupp, there's logic in what you say. It is impossible that the sound of the dynamo that moves this bloody night shouldn't reach my ears.

KRUPP: It is, Adolf. You must hear the sound, drown in it, drum up every gory fantasy possible, revive, and heal. There's no other way to recover yourself. That's the only medicine that can cure your insomnia.

HITLER: *(Eyes brightening)* I see, Herr Krupp. Now I'm beginning to hear them faintly. A volley of fire. . . . Though one or two shots have missed their timing. . . . They are an untrained firing squad hurriedly put together and they can't help it.

KRUPP: Can you hear them, Adolf, the gunshots that tear into the uniformed chests of the SA noncommissioned officers?

HITLER: I can hear them. They're being wasteful; they should put them up in a row and shoot them all, but they're doing it one by one. I can hear them. . . . Another volley. . . . Ready your guns! Fire! Fire! . . . Fire! . . .

I can see it vividly now. A blindfolded face suddenly turns away, arches back. A man's jaw, turned up, bathed red in the blood that spurted from his mouth. Then as abruptly as a shot bird, he drops his head on his chest and dies. . . . Look at them, we've put all of them in SA uniforms. That's because they put on their uniforms against my orders and attempted a revolt—that alone readily constitutes a crime. . . . The SA uniform that Roehm loved to put on to show off—about four hundred of those have red, splintering holes bored in their chests and, like target dolls, tumble into the holes dug under them. . . .

Fire! . . . Fire! . . . Fire! . . . Those young, sturdy rascals who could swagger about simply because Roehm was with them. Those fellows who counted only on their brawn—their youth has ended with this. . . . It's all over now. Their soldier games, the honor and heroism they gave lip service to, their blatant parades on every Flag Day, rowdy songs in beer halls, their antiquated roguish affectations, nostalgia, and sentimental military brotherhood are all over. . . . It's all over now. The revolution they were dreaming of is over too. . . . Because the SS bullets have made a lot of holes in their gold-laced chests that were full of childish dreams of revolution. . . . Now, all the revolution games are over.

KRUPP: All the revolution games. . . . There'll be no more men dreaming of a revolution again. Now that the revolution has been smothered to death, the entire army supports you. For the first time you are qualified to become president legitimately, for all the world. This is the way it should be.

HITLER: *(He returns to the room with Krupp and offers him a seat)* Those gunshots are, Herr Krupp, the last gunshots of Germans shooting Germans. . . . Everything has been taken care of now.

KRUPP: *(He sits comfortably in a chair)* I should say. We can now leave everything to you without any worry. Adolf, you did well. You cut down the left and, as you turned the sword back, cut down the right.

HITLER: *(He walks to stage center)* Yes, government must take the middle road.

CURTAIN

THE TERRACE OF THE LEPER KING

Jayavarman VII, the protagonist of *Raiō no Terasu* (The terrace of the leper king), was a legendary conqueror and unifier of Cambodia, who built Angkor Thom, a vast network of highways, and 102 hospitals. The stupendous construction projects he imposed upon his subjects, along with the large number of people and the great quantities of provisions required to maintain them, evidently exhausted Cambodia. The kingdom declined quickly after Jayavarman VII's rule and entered its "dark age," which lasted five centuries. The irony is that Jayavarman VII undertook all such work to express his faith in Avalokitesvara, the bodhisattva of compassion revered for his (or her) ability to save people in distress.

Jayavarman VII is thought to have been born sometime between 1120 and 1125, crowned himself king in 1181, and lived perhaps until 1219. This means he ascended the throne when he was somewhere between fifty-six and sixty-one, and lived well into his nineties. In Mishima's play, however, Jayavarman VII is presented as a youthful king, and events that are likely to have taken nearly forty years are telescoped into only a few. The play appears to have a few other matters contrary to history, although it also seems to incorporate a number of things written about Cambodia at the time and before.

In any case, the years before Jayavarman VII's royal ascension and the years after 1201, when he is known to have sent an emissary to the court of China, remain largely unknown. Indeed, the lack after 1201 of stele inscriptions, which were the principal recorders of events in Cambodia during that period, along with the construction of so many hospitals, is said to be partly responsible for the rumor that the king was afflicted with leprosy. In one note to this play

Mishima said that the idea of linking something "noble and glorious" to leprosy, as exemplified in a *conte cruel* by Villiers de L'Isle-Adam, "Duke of Portland," is "a predilection found in late Romanticism."

Mishima said he was inspired to write this play the moment he saw the statue of the "leper king" in Angkor Thom. However, in his *Angkor: An Introduction* (Oxford University Press, 1963), George Coede reproduces a photograph of the statue that Mishima talked about and says: "The so-called 'Leper King' was probably a god of death, who once held a staff in his right hand. This popular appellation is due solely to his lichen-covered body which gives the appearance of leprosy. Jayavarman VII may have suffered from leprosy, but this statue is not a presentation of him." (The information given here on Cambodia and Jayavarman VII derives from Coede's book and *A History of Cambodia,* by David P. Chandler, Westview Press, 1983.)

In this play Mishima puts what he imagines to be the upper-class speech of the Edo period (1603–1868) into the mouths of Cambodian aristocrats of the twelfth century. Whether this can be brought across in modern English is a big question.

The play was completed and produced in July 1969, with Jayavarman VII played by Kitaōji Kin'ya, an actor Mishima admired.

THE TERRACE OF THE LEPER KING

A Play in Three Acts

SECOND QUEEN RĀJENDRADEVĪ, played by Muramatsu Eiko, and JAYAVARMAN VII, played by Kitaōji Kin'ya. Teikoku Gekijō (Imperial Theatre), July 1969. *Courtesy of Muramatsu Eiko. By permission of Gekidan Kumo and Kitaōji Kin'ya.*

Time: The End of the Twelfth Century

Place:
Act 1, Scene 1: A Forest Near Angkor
    Scene 2: A Banquet in the Royal Palace
Act 2, Scene 1: The Construction Site of the Bayon
    Scene 2: The First Queen's Living Quarters
    Scene 3: Within the Snake God's Tower
Act 3, Scene 1: Terrace Overlooking the Bayon
    Scene 2: The Bayon

Characters:
Jayavarman VII
Queen Mother Chūdāmani
First Queen Indradevī
Second Queen Rājendradevī
Prime Minister Sūryabhatta
Mason (later Head Builder) Keo-Fa
Young Village Woman Khnūm
Chinese Ambassador Liu Ma-fu
His Wife
Astrologer Kralāpanji
Old Head Builder Kansa
Bas-Relief Carver Pandān
Painter Narāy
Tile Maker Paron
Gold-Leaf Craftsman Sa-uy
Exorcist Thayak
Messenger Soldier
Villagers A, B, C, D, E
Boys A, B, C
Leprous Beggar
Father
Boy Elephant Driver
Prison Guard
Prisoners
Soldiers
Maids
Palanquin-carrying Slaves
Musicians

Royal Dancers
Village Wedding Dancers

ACT 1
SCENE 1

A forest not far from Angkor, Cambodia; visible beyond is the Great Pilgrimage Road. Hemp palms, sugar palms, coco palms, betel palms, wild bananas, mango trees grow in profusion. Swamp at stage left.

At curtain rise, Boy A is squatting facing the swamp; Boy B is perched in the crotch of a tree; and Boy C, at stage right, is collecting sap from a sugar palm into a bottle.

Calls of jungle birds. Afternoon.

BOY C: *(To Boy B)* Hey, can't you see them yet?

BOY B: *(Eating a banana)* Not yet. Can't see a thing on the road.

BOY A: Shhhhhh!

(Silence for a while)

BOY C: *(To Boy B)* Can't you see them yet?

BOY B: Not yet. All I see is the thunderheads.

BOY C: They're so late.

BOY A: Shhhhhh!

(Boy C takes the bottle to stage left and stares at Boy A. When Boy A looks up at him, he licks the sap from his bottle ostentatiously.)

BOY A: Let me lick it, too.

BOY C: No way. Didn't we promise we'd exchange one kingfisher and a bottle of palm sap?

BOY A: Shhh! He's coming! Look at that decoy female in the cage, see it?

(He points at a cage hidden among the reeds.)

BOY C: You're right. The male bird is getting close.

BOY A: *(Holding up a net with one hand)* There!

(He catches a kingfisher.)

BOY A: *(Showing the kingfisher)* See this? You can sell the feathers of this fellow to a Chinese merchant for a lot of money.

BOY C: *(Holding up his bottle)* You can sell this for a lot of money, too, to the sugar-making man! *(Obviously finding it hard to part with his bottle, he takes another lick and gives it to Boy A.)*

BOY A: *(Looking up at Boy B)* Is it still all right? They aren't coming yet, are they?

BOY C: *(To Boy B)* You still can't see anything, can you?

BOY B: No, not a thing.

BOY A: I'll run home and leave these.

BOY C: Me, too.

(Boy A picks up his cage with a decoy in it, his net, and the bottle, and exits on the hanamichi[1] *at stage right, along with Boy C, who is carrying his kingfisher carefully.)*

(From the hanamichi at stage left enters Young Mason Keo-Fa, rowing a boat carved from a single log, carrying Young Village Woman Khnŭm.)

MASON: *(He stops his boat at the shore and calls to Boy B up in the tree.)* Hey, do you see anything?

BOY B: Not yet. All I can see is the thunderheads.

MASON: We made it then. Let's wait here.

(He takes the woman's hand and helps her off the boat.)

YOUNG WOMAN: Is it true that you go blind if you see the King in person?

MASON: That's the sort of nonsense the old people blabber about, Khnŭm. I hear that the King extends his compassion to high and low alike, and that the mere touch of his hand cures anybody of any illness immediately.

YOUNG WOMAN: Have you ever actually seen the King?

MASON: No, I haven't. He's been away on his military campaigns as long as anyone can remember. Today he's returning victoriously, but I myself have never left this place.

YOUNG WOMAN: They say the King is young, beautiful, and strong, and there isn't a single man in the whole world who doesn't look inferior when he's present.

MASON: *(A little put out)* Well, there may be some who don't.

YOUNG WOMAN: You are different, Keo-Fa. Any Cambodian girl would pick you over such a godlike being, of course.

MASON: *(Embarrassed)* Well, anyway, I revere our King though I've never seen him. He's almost my age, but while I've been wasting my youth on the repair and rebuilding of the palace ravaged by the Chams, he went on an expedition in pursuit of those barbarians who trampled upon this country and conquered the nest of their evils, the lair of their madness, the kingdom of Champa. At the same time, people say he is compassionate and deeply devoted to Buddhism, that he venerates Bodhisattva Avalokitesvara, that he himself is Bodhisattva Avalokitesvara incarnate. . . .

YOUNG WOMAN: My aunt told me once that the Bodhisattva gives birth to several thousand heavenly singers from one of his pores and several million people of wisdom through another pore. What large pores he

---

1. The runway unique to the kabuki stage. Originating in the short staircase attached to the front side of the nō stage (at first used for the actor to receive his costume from a noble in the audience; today merely decorative), it is said to have taken its current shape in the first half of the eighteenth century.

must have! I'm sure that each of his pores is as large as a tunnel. I'd rather that the pores are like yours, so small you can hardly see them.

MASON: *(Looking toward stage right)* Shhh! The Head Builder and others are coming. They'll pester us if they see us together. You better hide somewhere. . . . *(Looking up and seeing Boy B)* Oh, here's a good boy. Would you hide her up among those leaves?

BOY B: You bet.

(He extends his hand. After pushing her up, the Mason stands, looking innocent.)

(From stage right enter a group of people led by an old head mason: an old exorcist and a lively bunch of artisans such as a bas-relief carver, painter, tile maker, and gold-leaf craftsman.)

HEAD BUILDER: Well now, before long our victorious army will be marching home. This is the best place to welcome our King. He won't be able to see us lowly people, while we can, through the leaves, admire him and his procession marching up the Avenue of Pilgrimage. *(Noticing the Mason)* Oh, Keo-Fa, there you are.

MASON: I was waiting for you, Head Builder.

HEAD BUILDER: I bet you've been teasing a young girl again. Come over here and help serve some wine to your senior disciples. Gather up some bananas, will you? We'll eat them while drinking. We ought to be in a jolly mood to watch a triumphal procession, right? *(The Mason walks around gathering up some bananas.)* . . . Now, my dear Exorcist, what would you say is the best spot for us to have a little banquet?

(The Exorcist takes out of his chest a white cloth with zodiacal signs written on it, arranges on the ground several banana leaves, each carrying a number, and tries to determine the best spot. He changes his place a couple of times, each time followed by the whole group. In the end he stops at stage center.)

EXORCIST: This is it. On this spot we won't be bothered by the tree spirits or the water spirits.

(The whole group sits down in a circle.)

BAS-RELIEF CARVER: Aren't we lucky, Head Builder? When our King returns victoriously with great reparations and countless prisoners of war, we will no longer have to do all that repair and rebuilding work. Instead, we'll have one great project after another to show off our skills. I'll have a chance to make bas-reliefs no less detailed than those at Angkor Wat— of elephants, monkeys, dancers. . . .

PAINTER: I'll make one sketch after another, compare them, and devise ways of creating colors that will be more beautiful than the feathers of the parrots, more dazzling than the peacocks, under this strong sunlight. . . .

TILE MAKER: But to shelter all that from the great rain that falls every day during the monsoon, we need roofs. Roofs that arch like a dancer's back, roofs that bulge like a dancer's breasts—I'll be the one to bake the tiles to make those roofs. . . .

GOLD-LEAF CRAFTSMAN: But you see, to make everything that's been made and built look solemn and imposing, even from far away—to make the buildings, of course, but also the towers, their columns, and the exposed Buddhas as well stand out sharply from the green of the surrounding forests, you need my skill to apply gold leaf. . . .

BAS-RELIEF CARVER: Hey, young man, what about you?

MASON: *(After hesitating for some time)* I . . . I would like to make something noble and beautiful, something that people will venerate, which will make them fall on their knees and shed tears for a thousand years after it's been made.

BAS-RELIEF CARVER: You would, eh!?

(Everyone jeers at him.)

HEAD BUILDER: All right, all right. Let him say whatever stupid thing he wants to. But don't you all forget this. We are mere craftsmen. We shouldn't waste too much care on our work. All we have to do is dazzle our benefactors with our craftsmanship and get lots of money for it. A king's head is full of all sorts of crazy ideas. Outrageous evil deeds and outstanding virtuous deeds, like the floods of the Mekong, flow out of the river called the King, and they sometimes drown the people, sometimes fatten the cultivated lands. We might mimic a king, but we are all tiny streams that dry up in no time. To compare ourselves to gods, to try desperately to touch that burning azure sky with our fingers, or to aspire to something of unworldly beauty—none of that is our job. Remember this well. Grab as much money as you can, but try to get away with as much slapdash work as you can. Leave all the hard, painful work to the slaves and prisoners of war we're going to have plenty of.

MASON: But. . . .

HEAD BUILDER: What do you mean by "but"? Keep your mouth shut, you runny-nosed rascal! That "but" is what's wrong with you. Blow your nose into that "but" and throw it away.

(Everybody laughs.)

YOUNG WOMAN: I see it! *(She stands up on the branch.)*

BOY B: I see it!

YOUNG WOMAN: I finally see it—dust rising!

(Everybody rises to his feet.)

MASON: *(Unthinkingly, to the woman)* Be careful! You might fall!

YOUNG WOMAN: I'm all right. I'm holding a branch tightly, you see?

HEAD BUILDER: Just as I thought, you rascal! Making fun of me!

(He grabs at the Mason. Everyone tries to stop him. But all calm down as they become spellbound by the pleasingly clear voice of the Young Woman in the tree.)

YOUNG WOMAN: Look at that. Until a few moments ago all we could see at the far end of Pilgrimage Road was the green jungle and clouds, but now a smoky yellow swirl rises up like a dragon—because there's dust. It must be the dust swirled up by the elephants in the procession. . . . The clear blue sky is suddenly hazed over, and the dust comes nearer and nearer, little by little. . . . Something like sesame seeds are scattered around it—I wonder what they are. They look like birds. . . . Are they vultures? They aren't as big as vultures. I see, they're flocks of crows startled by the procession and fleeing this way. . . . Something glistened first, which now looks like a pin-cushion, glittering out of the clouds of dust and under the sun—it's rows of spears, spears! . . . And what looks like the flames of red candles are banners, I'm sure of it.

(From the hanamichi at stage right, with Boys A and C leading the way, enter Village Men and Women A, B, C, D, and E, running.)

BOY A: Hurry up, you won't make it!

BOY C: Hurry, hurry!

VILLAGER A: Wait, you don't have to be in such a hurry.

(All of them come on stage.)

BOY A: *(To Boy B on the tree)* Have they come yet? Do you see them?

BOY B: They've already come but they haven't come yet. I see them but don't see them yet.

BOY C: Let's go.

(Boys A and C, in their excitement, try to wriggle their way among the craftsmen who are standing upstage with their backs turned to the audience.)

VILLAGER A: Look at that. Children are always like that. If you remain on your feet from so early on, you'll end up exhausted. *(She squats down.)*

VILLAGER B: We sure ought to celebrate our King returning from his victorious campaigns. It's a pity, though, that he's coming back to such a mess.

VILLAGER C: Do you mean the Prime Minister?

VILLAGER B: Not only that.

VILLAGER D: Do you mean the Queen Mother?

VILLAGER B: Not only that.

VILLAGER E: Do you mean the two queens?

VILLAGER B: Not only that.

VILLAGER A: No, but our King won't mind any of that. He's so young, so beautiful, so strong, and he's got all the blessings he can get in this world. *(At this point crows fly noisily overhead.)*

VILLAGER C: Look, crows.

(All the villagers and artisans look up. From stage right enters a tottering figure, a Leprous Beggar. People are startled to see him. He does some begging, but everyone refuses him. He leaves on the hanamichi at stage right.)

HEAD BUILDER: What was that?

BAS-RELIEF CARVER: A beggar with leprosy.

PAINTER: We've seen a couple of them in the village lately.

GOLD-LEAF CRAFTSMAN: Where in the world are they from?

TILE MAKER: Oh, my! Oh, my!

YOUNG WOMAN: Don't you hear? Don't you hear it? The first sounds of the military band?

MASON: *(Listening)* That's right. Conch-shells. Drums. Cymbals!

(Their backs turned to the audience, all of them wait eagerly.)

YOUNG WOMAN: I see them now. A great many golden umbrellas, red umbrellas. . . . How beautiful they are! The first rank of golden-armored soldiers marching right in front of the King's elephant. They hold up their golden shields. . . . It's as if a giant golden pangolin is approaching us. . . . Listen to those footsteps. If the elephants' footsteps are like thunder, the soldiers' are like a squall. Their breastplates flash like lightning. They shine like that each time they look to right and left to see the woods and fields of their hometown, which they haven't seen for so long. And the King . . .

(As the music becomes louder, the Young Woman's voice is drowned out. She and Boy B climb down the tree and stand close to the Mason.)

(In the space upstage a procession of bandsmen and spearmen in dazzling gold solemnly march past from left to right.)

(On the back of a white elephant, whose tusks are encased in gold, is the royal seat with a parasol that has gold painted on white. A lion skin drapes the seat. The young King is standing on it, a commanding figure in his golden military uniform. Riding the elephant's neck is a black boy in a golden robe.)

(When they see the King, the villagers and others all fall on their knees and bow. Only the Mason stands up.)

MASON: Long live the King! Long live the King!

(The elephant stops. The King scoops up some gold coins and throws them toward the people. The people vie to pick them up. They hold up the coins.)

ALL: Long live the King! Long live the King!

(They shout. Starting to move forward again, the elephant raises its trunk high.)

SCENE 2

The Great Hall of the Royal Palace. Several golden chairs. The throne at stage center is empty. To its left is seated the First Queen; to its right, the Second Queen. The divan toward stage left, the Queen Mother's seat, is also empty. The place is loaded with decanters and cups, and assortments of banquet foods, including colorful fruits. Slaves stand erect at strategic places, and musicians are waiting for a signal to begin; so are dancers at stage left and right. The First Queen and the Second Queen do not directly communicate with each other. Maid A, who stands to the right of the First Queen, and Maid B, who stands to the left of the Second Queen, convey the words of each mistress to the other. A monkey, deer, and tigress are part of the props.

Upstage the Cambodian night sky and forest. The moon hangs in the center of the sky.

FIRST QUEEN: Musicians, strike up when our King enters. The important thing is the first tune. Ready yourselves. This is the banquet for His Majesty's triumphant return. If you strike a wrong note, I'll have you all beheaded on the spot. . . . Dancers, wait until Her Majesty, the Queen Mother, enters. She prefers to do the clapping herself as the signal for you dancers to begin dancing. Where is the Prime Minister? *(No one responds.)* Where is the Prime Minister? *(Everyone remains unresponsive.)* I, the First Queen, am asking the Second Queen. Where is the Prime Minister?

(Maid A whispers to Maid B, who in turn whispers to the Second Queen.)

SECOND QUEEN: The Prime Minister has accompanied His Majesty and is now waiting for him at the entrance of the Snake God Naga's tower. He had discontinued this custom during the war, but he has resumed it today.

(Maid B whispers to Maid A, who in turn whispers to the First Queen.)

FIRST QUEEN: This is all very funny, indeed. In this royal palace there is a queen more important than the First Queen, the queen among queens, that jealous Snake Goddess, Nagi. Have you ever seen Nagi?

(Maid A whispers to Maid B, who in turn whispers to the Second Queen.)

SECOND QUEEN: No, I have not. A woman would go blind if she saw her. . . . I wonder if Nagi is still beautiful. Once, long ago, the Indian prince Kaundinya came to Cambodia and was walking along the shore when he saw a beautiful girl emerge from the moonlit waves. He was enchanted, and even though he knew she was Nagi, the daughter of the Snake God Naga, he married her. As a result, our Khmer Moon dynasty flourished, the dynasty endowed with all the noble qualities of the clear moon that rises every night—the quietness, solemnity, clarity, compassion, and melancholy. . . . Nagi may rob us of our King, but we are all indebted to her, even though she has taken the true queen's position in the reign of every King.

FIRST QUEEN: *(Ignoring the Second Queen)* Indebted? In what way? It has been said that if the King failed to visit the tower and neglected to make love to her for even a single night, a disaster would strike our country. And yet our King was away during this long war, and nothing happened in the meantime.

(Maid A whispers to Maid B, who in turn whispers to the Second Queen.)

SECOND QUEEN: Even those barbarians who invaded this capital would not dare go near that room at the top of the tower. Only a King can go in there. No one knows how His Majesty makes love to invisible Nagi in that darkness. It's a mystery, but His Majesty himself remains silent and does not tell us about it. Still, we must remember that in spite of his exhaustion from the triumphal march, because he thinks of his people, because he prays for rich harvests for this nation, our King has gone, the first thing today, to Nagi's chamber to play the husband's role. . . .

FIRST QUEEN: *(Arrogantly)* His Majesty was away during this long war, but nothing happened in the meantime.

(Maid A whispers to Maid B, who in turn whispers to the Second Queen.)

SECOND QUEEN: Nagi is a woman, too. When her man is away doing man's work, battles, she certainly can wait. But tonight. . . .

FIRST QUEEN: But tonight . . . she must be uncontrollable, having waited for so long to make love. Her thin tongue flickering madly, her scales dyed scarlet with joy and embarrassment, she won't let our King go forever and ever. He's so late in coming because of that. When he finally comes to our beds . . .

(The First Queen and the Second Queen eye each other.)

FIRST QUEEN & SECOND QUEEN: . . . he'll be dead tired.

(Music starts. The First Queen and the Second Queen rise to their feet. From the hanamichi to stage right enters the King, accompanied by the Prime Minister and pages. He stops about a third of the length of the hanamichi from the stage.)

KING: I see you have made excellent preparations. I'm sorry I've kept you waiting. For all these long months and years I've been dreaming about this celebratory banquet. Isn't that so, Prime Minister?

PRIME MINISTER: Yes, Your Majesty.

KING: *(Pointing to the sky)* The moon, the symbol of our dynasty, is clear and full tonight. Let us all drink until the moon goes down to the rim of the hills.

PRIME MINISTER: As you wish, Sire.

(The King walks on to the stage and seats himself in the throne.)

KING: Indradevi, Rājendradevi, you are both as beautiful as ever. No, I would say that after these years of watching the faces of the barbarians, your beauty is unworldly. The moons I saw in the battlefields were the faces of you two.

FIRST QUEEN: Were there two moons?

KING: Yes, there was the first moon and the second moon, the flowery moon and the pure moon.

PRIME MINISTER: Sire, their ladyships have been looking forward to hearing stirring stories of battles.

KING: You say stories of battles. We had so many kinds of battles and so many kinds of dangers I can't tell them all to you in one night. That we made it back safely at all is like a dream. When you see that all this was thanks to the protection of the Bodhisattva Avalokitesvara, you must not forget to offer prayers to him day and night. Because of him, we Cambodians were able to destroy our long-standing enemy, so that we may make ours a peaceful and prosperous country. But you say stories of battles. . . . Well, I should tell you about the exploits of our elephant battalion at a fortress in the kingdom of Champa.

Our enemy knew that we had no naval arm, and had built a formidable fortress on a shore where a precipice rose like a screen. Our elephant battalion had long advanced right to the flank of the fortress but couldn't find a chance for assault. So I sent out some scouts and had them measure the depth of the sea. And one morning, when I knew that the low tide made the sea shallow enough, I made a frontal assault on the fortress, spearheading an army of fifty elephants. What great splashes the elephants made in the blue sea, and once on the shore, what great, deep footprints they left as they dashed to the wooden structure built at the front of the fortress—and how they pushed and pushed at the fortress with their heads! The enemy fought with spears and crossbows. Some of our men climbed up the outstretched trunks of their elephants to jump into the fortress. Move! Push! I myself slashed aside the thousands of arrows that rained upon us with *(slapping the weapon he wears)* this firebrand sword. As soon as the gate collapsed, I rode my white elephant deep into enemy territory. I cut down all the enemy soldiers that jumped on my elephant from high positions. I had units of spearmen attack every strategic point. Finally I had the enemy commander's quarters set afire, retreated to the shore, and watched every bit of the fortress burn down. Reflecting the flames, or rather, reflecting the sea reflecting the flames, my elephant's ears turned into large, wavering, scarlet orchids!

FIRST QUEEN: How brave of you!

SECOND QUEEN: And you didn't even receive a single scar!

KING: It appears my mother missed my battle story. Where is she?

QUEEN MOTHER: *(The curtain is raised at the end of the hanamichi at stage left.)* Your Majesty, I am coming now.

(Music begins. The Prime Minister hurries to the stage end of the hanamichi and kneels. The Queen Mother enters, accompanied by her pages. An astrologer follows. The Queen Mother stops at a third of the way.)

QUEEN MOTHER: Welcome home, my lord. You seem so well, after performing such brilliant military exploits and destroying the fearsome enemy. No, stay, stay there. Please do not give much thought to me, but relax and continue your toasting. I'd like to watch you from here for a while. I'd like to watch my son from some distance. I'd like to see you, the way you are, with a sense of disbelief, as if you were a miracle—and after convincing myself that my joy is real, I'd like to slowly walk up to you and touch you. Prime Minister, look. The person who is resplendently shining there is my son, the god of Cambodia, the moon of Angkor, King Jayavarman. Through all his battles, he has grown manlier, sturdier than ever, and the fragrance of a man at his youthful peak is beautifully evident in his eyes, in his eyebrows. To have such a strong, beautiful King is a proud thing—not only for me, his mother, but for this country as well. Is that not so, Prime Minister?

PRIME MINISTER: *(With jealousy)* Just as you say, ma'am.

QUEEN MOTHER: *(Walking up to the stage)* Forgive me. Embarrassed by the thought of myself appearing before your beautiful self, I have made ablutions so many times since this morning, done and redone my hair, trying to make myself presentable. That is why I'm late.

(She takes the King's hand.)

KING: It is you, Mother, who are even younger, more beautiful than ever before. I will arrange to have our people prepare homage to you as the symbol of our rich country, which now has peace restored. Nothing will better show the felicity of this nation, which knows no decline.

(He leads her to her seat at stage left.)

QUEEN MOTHER: It is so kind of you. You are as gentle-hearted as ever. My teacher used to say that battles make a man gentler. Now, please return to your seat. I'd like you to see my humble gift to you in celebration of your victorious return. *(The Prime Minister stands ready by the Queen Mother's side.)* Are you ready? When I clap my hands, you dancers must start dancing, your hearts full of joy, as if invisible birds lodging in your heart suddenly begin to flap their wings.

(She claps her hands.)

   (The dancers dance the Rama part of Ramayana.)

   (As they finish, they exit.)

KING: Such a sensuous dance, light-footed music! For someone who has just returned from the battlefields, no gift could have been more timely than the one you have given me, Mother. And this delicious wine, all these delicacies from the hills and the sea, my Queens and other beautiful women of my birthplace, the luxurious moon shining in the sky, the cool breeze that comes across the fields of Angkor . . . all these things are what I dreamed about so many times on the battlefields. They are now all in front of my eyes.

FIRST QUEEN: And everything your eyes see, everything your hands touch, vies with each other, trying to come to you, like a honeybee to a flower. All excited and trembling with joy that they can receive your love.

SECOND QUEEN: And those your eyes do not reach are waiting, in modesty and shyness, for your beautiful, young visage, now in its prime, to turn to them.

FIRST QUEEN: People, grasses and trees, birds and beasts . . .

SECOND QUEEN: . . . peacocks, deer, oranges under their thick foliage, hundreds and thousands of fireflies in the jungle . . .

FIRST QUEEN & SECOND QUEEN: . . . everything is yours, my lord.

QUEEN MOTHER: That is what youth is all about, King; that is what being the golden sword to rule the world is all about.

KING: Yet, I was thinking on my way back here: this is not something that has come about because of me. My Queens, listen. This has come about, first, because of the Lord Buddha, and, second, because of our people. We must double our prayers to the Buddha, and as a token of our gratitude, we must build temples for him, while to our people we must offer alms unstintingly. This is the King's duty.

SECOND QUEEN: You are absolutely right, if you allow me to say such a thing, my lord.

(The First Queen and the Queen Mother eye each other.)

QUEEN MOTHER: Why not put off such complicated things until tomorrow? Tonight you should forget yourself in blissful ablutions.

KING: No, that won't do, Mother. There are ideas that you can move forward only when you are at the pinnacle of happiness. You can't see such ideas unless you are out boating in the sea of happiness, like the dorsal fin of a scabbard fish skimming through the waves. Prime Minister, open the royal storehouse early tomorrow morning; take out ten oxcart loads of rice . . .

PRIME MINISTER: Ten oxcart loads, Sire?

KING: Yes, and distribute them among our people. Also, open our treasury; put as much gold as you can on the back of an elephant . . .

PRIME MINISTER: As much gold as you can on the back of an elephant, Sire?

KING: Yes, you needn't parrot my words every time. Call together the people, and scatter the gold over them. That will be the miraculous rain. Then they will know that Angkor has become the paradise of this world.

PRIME MINISTER: Yes, but there is no precedent for such generous alms-giving . . .

KING: What are you saying! This is nothing, compared with the mountains of treasure, reparations, and ransoms we've brought back from the kingdom of Champa. Follow my order and do it tomorrow morning.

PRIME MINISTER: As you wish, Sire.

KING: Astrologer, I have something for you to do at once, too.

ASTROLOGER: Yes, Your Majesty. *(He kneels and bows.)*

KING: Immediately consult your astrological tables to determine an auspicious day to begin the building of the temples. In the direction of the south from here, yes—*(indicating stage right)*—so that I may see it directly to the south when I stand on that terrace, we'll build a great temple such as I have imagined all these years. Make sure to divine a good spot in that direction, understand?

ASTROLOGER: Yes . . . but, Your Majesty?

KING: What is it?

ASTROLOGER: Suppose I read that building a temple to the south of the terrace would bring bad luck?

KING: *(He laughs.)* If that happened, it would be your role to change an unlucky direction to a lucky one, wouldn't it? Do you think I've forgotten? When I set out on the campaigns against the Champa, you divined that the direction I was taking was bad. But what's happened? A great victory, if there ever was one. The barbarians were swept away from every realm you can think of.

ASTROLOGER: You might be right, Sire. But the stars . . .

KING: *(Impatiently interrupting)* Someone! Bring the Head Builder. Tell the craftsmen to come here.

QUEEN MOTHER: *(Shocked)* What are you saying? You can't allow such base people into this palace!

KING: The Avalokitesvara's compassion extends to the basest creatures. Especially, Mother, when the temple I am building will be not only for our royal family but for the people as well.

QUEEN MOTHER: But this court has no such custom.

PRIME MINISTER: Sire, may I suggest that these people be brought to the courtyard and interviewed from the terrace?

KING: In the midst of this felicitous victory banquet, you, too, try to break the wings of the phoenix flying through the sky? Have you forgotten? I am the King of Cambodia.

PRIME MINISTER: You are, Sire.

QUEEN MOTHER: Well, then, young, beautiful King, while you are talking with these base people, we'll pretend not to notice it, with our backs turned. My dear Queens, wouldn't you say that's a clever idea?

FIRST QUEEN: Let's do as our mother says.

(The Queen Mother and the First Queen turn around to face the other way. But the Second Queen does not.)

QUEEN MOTHER: *(Noticing the Second Queen)* Well, what's the matter with you, Second Queen?

SECOND QUEEN: I'd like to follow our King's wishes, if I may. *(She keeps facing downstage.)*

QUEEN MOTHER: *(Angry)* Do as you like! *(She turns her back again.)*

(Guided by a maid, the artisans in the first scene enter on the hanamichi to stage right: Head Builder, Bas-Relief Carver, Painter, Tile Maker, Gold-Leaf Craftsman, and Mason.)

KING: Welcome. I asked you to come here because I want to start a new project as a prayer for the prosperity of our kingdom and for the happiness of our people, and I need your help. Come here. You will drink, too. *(Everyone fearfully walks to the stage. The King signals with his eyes, and the maids give the artisans cups and pour wine. Everyone drinks stiffly.)*

When you have finished your cups *(indicating stage right)*, look over there. *(Everyone looks to stage right.)* Under the moonlight you can see somewhat vaguely the stone railings on the blue terrace. When I was a boy, I spent many a sleepless night there, absorbed in endless fantasies. Now I may be known as a brave warrior, but in those days I was a melancholy child. I should say, rather, that I was a melancholy, retiring boy during the day, but was a lively one brimming with fantasies at night. I say this because on that terrace over there I dreamed of myself in all sorts of forms. Myself in battle, in love, in faith. . . . Yes, fireflies flitted over the grass bushes; chameleons hid themselves in the moonlit foliage; and I could hear the breathing of small beasts of the night. But between the clouds suffused by the moonlight I saw phantom forests of silvery spears and elephant banners carried by an army of elephants flashing in a battlefield.

SECOND QUEEN: I can well imagine you in those days, milord, when you were a gentle boy.

KING: In those days you were still a baby. . . . Anyway, later on I became a brave warrior. I became exactly the kind of man I had dreamed of becoming every night, on that terrace. Now I have won the victory I once dreamed of, and I have acquired beautiful women like you. . . . *(Turning to stage right)* It's time I realized the religious imaginings I had on the terrace. Now, each one of you, step out on the terrace and construct in your imagination the kind of temple you would build beyond it. You don't need to be modest. I will not mind any amount of expenditure the building may require.

(All the artisans exit stage right.)

SECOND QUEEN: So you will acquire all three things a man can have in this world.

KING: I am greedier. For some reason I have not acquired my heir yet.

FIRST QUEEN: *(Her back still turned)* Have those base people left?

KING: Not yet. They will return soon.

PRIME MINISTER: Sire, you said you would not mind any amount of expenditure, but our kingdom must repair the scars left by the war, and that will require time and money. I am not certain that the booty you have captured and brought back is adequate for that, and the soil of our country is not rich enough to produce everything needed. May I venture to implore you, Sire, to consider this point further . . .

KING: *(Vexed)* I know, I know that. . . . *(Loudly)* Head builder! Come here. *(The Head Builder appears and prostrates himself.)*

Tell me now. What kind of temple have you thought up?

HEAD BUILDER: I have thought, Your Majesty, of an incomparably large cathedral supported by a hundred stone elephants, shaped like a lotus flower, with the frame of its gate inlaid with jewels, a peacock carved into every one of its windows.

KING: That's too conventional. Anyone can think of such a design. Besides, if all you did were to decorate it extravagantly, it would be a laughingstock next to august Angkor Wat. What I hope to build is a unique temple that is not inferior to Angkor Wat in any way. *(The Head Builder stiffens on the spot.)* . . . Bas-relief carver, come here. *(The Bas-Relief Carver appears and prostrates himself.)*

What do you think? What kinds of bas-reliefs would you like to make?

BAS-RELIEF CARVER: I have thought that I would depict your army of elephants smashing into the enemy fortress. At one end there would be a horde of dashing elephants, kicking the waves aside, with even the expression of each warrior astride an elephant vividly carved. And there would be the sea, an endless stretch of waves carved in such a lively way that if rays of sun struck them they would boil up and, if you went near enough, they might drench you with splashes. At the other end, in front of the fortress rising high, Your Majesty would be seated under the golden canopy, on your white elephant, your gallant golden armor glittering, an epitome of bravery, giving commands . . .

KING: Wait! Do you think this temple is going to be built merely to glorify my military exploits? It's intended for expressing compassion. It's for consoling the souls of the dead soldiers. It's for the people of our kingdom. It is for the exclusive purpose of praising the Bodhisattva Avalokitesvara. Do not forget that. *(The Bas-Relief Carver prostrates himself.)* . . . Where's the Painter? Where's the Tile Maker? Where's the Gold-Leaf Craftsman? *(The three men come forward and prostrate themselves.)* What do you think?

PAINTER: Yes, Your Majesty. I would use all the red and blue paints I have to depict paradise in the hall, with Garuda winging through the sky . . .

KING: An Indian deity again!

TILE MAKER: I would use great swaths of green tiles, so that the temple would resemble the jungle under the sun . . .

KING: We are talking about a temple, not a playground.

GOLD-LEAF CRAFTSMAN: I would use gold leaf even in the colonnades that Your Majesty will walk through on your way to offer prayers to create something comparable to the Land of Purplish Gold . . .

KING: It is not me, but the Lord Buddha, that we pay our respects to. Damn you all! Is that all you can think of? In my royal mind some undefinable shape has already formed and is casting its rays. But a king's idea always resembles a golden haze, and when it comes to giving form and details and completing the picture—in a military victory, for example, it's the soldiers' role to work it out, and if it's a cathedral, it's *your* duty to work out an unworldly one. A king is someone who generates an ambiguous golden haze in his mind, and it is up to his subjects to turn it into a definitive form. And the form, when it is completed, must be exactly the same as the image the King had in mind in some uncertain fashion. . . . Isn't there anyone else? Where's the Mason? Bring him here.

HEAD BUILDER: May I venture to note, Sire, that he's still an apprentice, a callow young man who hasn't had much experience?

KING: *(Smiling)* I see, you're saying that imagination is born only of experience. In that case, your experience isn't much to speak of, either, is it? . . . Mason, show yourself.

(The Mason enters and prostrates himself.)

Tell me now. You may say anything you think, without reserve.

MASON: Yes, Your Majesty. My idea has not firmed up yet either. However, Sire, when I was contemplating that stretch of land drenched in moonlight, a strange vision floated up in my mind.

KING: A strange vision?

MASON: In the pallid moonlight, a giant face of the Bodhisattva Avalokitesvara facing the four directions, eight directions—a cluster of his faces alone, one eye smiling gently, standing out calmly in unworldly mystery. . . . Such was the illusion I had.

KING: *(Interested)* You say.

MASON: I thought that if I carved a many-faced Avalokitesvara like that, as Your Majesty's agent, praying single-mindedly—if I built up those faces just like a large basket of stone fruits, then the temple would immediately rise by itself.

HEAD BUILDER: What a childish idea!

BAS-RELIEF CARVER: Because he's a skirt-chaser . . .

PAINTER: . . . he can only think up an idea that won't even make a picture.

TILE MAKER: And he's proposing a building without tiles!

GOLD-LEAF CRAFTSMAN: What in the world does he think of gold leaf?

KING: Quiet! *(To the Mason)* Tell me more. What kind of form will that temple take?

MASON: I do not have a *definite* idea yet, Sire. Only the cluster of Avalokitesvara's faces appears, and I do not have the vaguest idea of what shape the temple as a whole will take.

HEAD BUILDER: See, didn't I tell you . . .

KING: Shut up! *(To the Mason)* Your idea fascinates me. Hmmm. *(He thinks.)* Fascinates me very much. As you described your design, I think the golden haze in my mind has gradually begun to take shape. . . . I have an idea. From this moment you will be the Head Builder. You may do whatever you please.

MASON: I, the Head Builder, Sire?

HEAD BUILDER: This is going too far, Sire. . . .

KING: You, the Head Builder till now, must help the young, new Head Builder in every way, and all the other artisans, each in his own position, must follow the will of the new Head Builder. Understand? This is a royal order. You shall in no way take me lightly and sabotage his work.

MASON: *(Greatly moved)* Your Majesty, I do not know how to express my . . .

KING: *I* need no gratitude. Nothing will better express your gratitude than the result of your work.

MASON: I will design such a noble, beautiful temple without compare under the sun, that a thousand years from now people will revere, genuflecting, shedding tears of joy.

HEAD BUILDER: See, he's such a big mouth . . .

KING: What did you say?! *(Glares at him.)*

HEAD BUILDER: Sire! *(He flattens himself on the floor.)*

MASON: I make my pledge, Your Majesty: On your royal order I will build the most beautiful temple on the face of the earth, which will glow like a phantom during the day and smolder like a dream during the night. May I add one other thing, Your Majesty? As a token of my gratitude and loyalty to you, I would like to make a pledge that is most painful to myself. I have a young woman I love from the bottom of my heart. My pledge is this: I will not marry her until I complete this temple.

KING: I will gladly accept your pledge, young man. A building becomes a dream, and a dream becomes a reality. It is in that fashion that a giant stone and an illusory dream keep replacing each other eternally. This is enough for today. You may go now. Bring a rough draft within ten days.

MASON: I will, Your Majesty.

(All the artisans bow to the King and leave along the hanamichi to stage right. The Mason first places himself at the end of the file. The others try to put him at the head. The Head Builder resists somewhat, but yields, and allows the Mason to be the leader, and the group exits.)

SECOND QUEEN: That was a marvelous decision you made, my lord. I am convinced that that young man, free from traditional rules, will be able to build a beautiful temple, the like of which exists nowhere in the world.

PRIME MINISTER: No, I don't think we can say that as yet, ma'am. In the society of those lowly people, you can't tell what disastrous things may happen once you remove the pecking order. Besides, that young fellow struck me as a charlatan. . . . I don't think he has a leader's capacity.

KING: *(Ignoring him)* Mother, the base people have left now.

(The Queen Mother and the First Queen turn round to face downstage.)

QUEEN MOTHER: I heard all that went on. Wasn't I surprised that even those creatures had humanlike voices.

FIRST QUEEN: Even monkeys sometimes have humanlike faces when they peer at you from among the leaves of rubber plants.

QUEEN MOTHER: As I listened, Your Majesty's voice alone glistened like the wings of Garuda high in the sky. Ah, do whatever you want to do, King. While in the prime of your life, even what you think is impossible is always achieved, and whatever seems to you uncertain turns out to take shape as something definite and fine. . . . Long ago, I once saw a condor look down at his prey from the top of a palace tower and flap his wings sharply. The sky was blue, and the tall tree soaring before the tower had parasite orchids with blooming lavender flowers. The condor was young. He had extraordinarily sharp eyes, and his wings were powerful and sturdy. . . . As you all know, a condor always aims to get a rotting carcass. But the goat on the ground then was alive, though tottering. Perhaps it had some foul disease, and some bad smell was coming out of it. Anyway, the condor shot down at the goat like an arrow, stabbed at the white back of the goat with his beak, and as the goat rolled down on the ground, tore apart his pink belly with another sharp stab. . . . On that burning ground, under the flowers of parasite orchids, I, for a brief second, saw blood spurt out and intestines flow out. What made him do that? A young condor, bursting with youth and power, violated the natural law, the law that dictates that a condor shall eat only rotten meat. What made him do that? I thought about it many times afterward. . . . That condor knew that if he wanted to do what he dreamed of doing, such things as God and the natural law didn't mean a thing. . . . Oh, my, that I, of all people, should have told such a terrible story on a felicitous occasion like this! Your Majesty, pay no attention to me, but make as colorful a night of this victory celebration and enjoy this feast as much as you can. Pour more wine, maids. Isn't the peacock plate ready yet? The plate with a bird squatting on it with its tail and feathers spread out—is the plate with that beautiful though not too tasty bird not ready yet?

ASTROLOGER: *(He has been studying his astrological tables all this while.)* I am afraid . . .

QUEEN MOTHER: Say whatever's on your mind.

ASTROLOGER: I'm afraid I have something to tell His Majesty.

KING: What is it?

ASTROLOGER: It's about the new temple you have been talking about, Sire.

KING: What about the temple?

ASTROLOGER: Which direction is its front going to face?

KING: Let me see. Because I want to see it from the terrace over there, at first I thought the temple would face north, but it would be too irreverent to force Avalokitesvara to face this way. Besides, the front side of a temple is always equipped with a terrace, so that would mean two terraces facing each other. But you can't really have its back to us . . .

ASTROLOGER: In other words, Sire, the temple will face either east or west, will it not?

KING: Yes.

ASTROLOGER: I have been studying my astrological tables for a while, and I see that the lucky direction is west. I recommend that the temple be built facing west. We speak of the pure land to the west, and it will certainly be natural, I think, for Avalokitesvara to face west.

KING: It is a good thing that everyone longs for the west. But it is from that pure land that Avalokitesvara comes to give us mortals succor.

ASTROLOGER: That certainly is the case, Sire, but you can also think that Avalokitesvara goes west accompanied by us mortals. Also, Sire, Angkor Wat faces west.

KING: Angkor Wat faces west, indeed. Why on earth do you suggest I follow Angkor Wat down to such a detail, when I am thinking of building a temple equal to it but not the same. . . ? I will tell you: my temple will face east. Understood?

ASTROLOGER: But, Your Majesty.

KING: What is it?

ASTROLOGER: These tables say east is bad luck, as you see.

KING: Nonsense. For one thing, I wish to follow the wish of Avalokitesvara to save us all and, for another, I want to follow the tradition of Khmer, the dynasty of the moon, so I will make this temple face east. By Avalokitesvara's compassionate power, and by my own military bravery, all the demons and devils will be easily swept aside.

FIRST QUEEN & SECOND QUEEN: Brave King!

QUEEN MOTHER: *(She claps her hands)* Music! Dance!

(Music starts. An assortment of dishes, including a large plate loaded with a peacock with its tail and feathers spread, are brought in along with wine jugs. The same dancers reenter from stage left and right and begin dancing. The King leans on his left armrest as he relaxes on the throne at stage center. His left upper arm becomes exposed. The First Queen notices a red spot on his upper arm.)

FIRST QUEEN: Look!

(Simultaneous with her utterance, music and dance stop, and all the people stop moving.)

KING: What is it? Oh, you mean this?

FIRST QUEEN: What is this? A spot like a petal of a red Chinese rose is on your arm.

KING: I didn't know it was there. Perhaps I received a blow during some battle, and it has remained as a bruise.

FIRST QUEEN: Does it not hurt?

KING: It doesn't hurt, and it doesn't itch.

FIRST QUEEN: Well, then, it must be a kiss mark left by that snake, Queen Nagi. You say battle, trying to deceive us. How jealous you make us! *(The King smiles indulgently. Music and dance start all at once; people start moving and the banquet reaches its climax.)*

CURTAIN

ACT 2
SCENE 1

A year after act 1, the construction site of the Bayon. At stage right is the half-finished head of Avolaktesvara in scaffolding. Masonry stones lie on the ground. Jungle at upstage. To stage left is a stand of trees large enough to hide a couple of people. At the end of the hanamichi to stage left, the existence of the palace is suggested. It is night, with the moon out.

At stage right Young Head Builder Keo-Fa and Young Village Woman Khnūm are seated on a masonry stone, looking at the sky at stage left.)

YOUNG WOMAN: The moon is in its last quarter phase tonight, isn't it? Because the clouds are moving, the moon looks as though it's running. . . . It's like a golden boat running through the clouds, a boat made of gold with the head of Naga, which the King rides. . . . It's running. With a wonderful swiftness they're rowing the boat, splashing the waves aside. Are they taking some important news somewhere?

YOUNG HEAD BUILDER: They're taking the news of our love, Khnūm. Our love seizes us every day, and we can't bear it any more. But I made the pledge to the King, on my own, that I would not marry until this temple was completed. Ah, that was a year ago. I was an insignificant, poor mason, so I was overjoyed when the King, in his compassion, suddenly promoted me to Head Builder. I was so moved, so driven by passion for this great project, I ended up making a pledge I didn't have to.

YOUNG WOMAN: That's all right, Keo-Fa. I would never blame you for that. That's perfectly understandable in a man. A man must be able to sacrifice at any given moment the most important thing to begin work on a worthy project.

YOUNG HEAD BUILDER: Hearing you say that, I feel all the more guilty. But it was still all right that night. That night a year ago, when we celebrated the King's triumphant return, was the night I was honored for the first time in my life. But it's incredible, isn't it—that was also a fateful night for the King.

YOUNG WOMAN: Rumor has it that the first sign of the King's illness appeared that night.

YOUNG HEAD BUILDER: At first it was something we lowly people weren't informed of, but now everybody knows about it, everybody talks about it. That night, yes, right after we had an audience with him and were led away by the Head Builder, that frightening symptom of leprosy, a stain, appeared for the first time on the King's arm. And in the middle of that splendid, auspicious celebration. . . . Of course, no one knew what it was at the time, but months later it was found out to be the symptom.

YOUNG WOMAN: The first symptom is beautiful, they say, don't they? As if the petals of a Chinese rose, the smoky red of the Chinese rose, were tattooed on the King's smooth, powerful, amber arm. . . .

YOUNG HEAD BUILDER: It then scattered to many spots. Oh, even now, that incurable disease is eating into the King's body minute by minute. Just like termites eat into a beautiful palace and silently, slowly, undermine it, destroy it, irreparably.

YOUNG WOMAN: But his face remains beautiful.

YOUNG HEAD BUILDER: It's been only a year.

YOUNG WOMAN: He's always wearing a hat. His hair is affected.

YOUNG HEAD BUILDER: His hands, too. Lately he wears a loose gown of golden brocade and never shows his hands and feet to anyone. The only thing he allows us to see is his beautiful face like a pale moon. I feel so sorry for him. That of all people, such a young, such a courageous, such a great king should get it!

YOUNG WOMAN: Everybody says he got it in retribution for his sins, when he can't possibly have any sin—the King who is said to be the powerful Shiva incarnate to his enemies and the compassionate Avalokitesvara incarnate for his people.

YOUNG HEAD BUILDER: It's so cruel. Once so manly, so free, he has utterly changed. His dark eyes are always staring at some unknown place. Youthful, vigorous gestures, awesome, commanding tones are no longer his. The King's only wish now is the completion of this temple. And he has decided to call it Bayon—a place to welcome the souls of those heroes who fought along with him and were killed. Bayon. He must think he should have been killed in one of those brilliant battles.

YOUNG WOMAN: If he had, he would have left an eternally young, beautiful image with us.

YOUNG HEAD BUILDER: The only thing he thinks of is to speed up the pace of construction—faster today than yesterday. No matter how fast we do it, it will take at least two years. What worries me is what he's going to be like in two years. Our marriage, too.

YOUNG WOMAN: Let's not think about the future; let's enjoy our happiness now. Compared with our unfortunate king, we are so lucky.

YOUNG HEAD BUILDER: You may be right. *(He cheers up a little and rises to his feet.)* This is the Avalokitesvara we're working on now. It will be finished in about a month. We'll have a great many of these all over the place.

YOUNG WOMAN: *(Standing far back)* That's a beautiful face.

YOUNG HEAD BUILDER: *(He walks up to her and puts his hands over her shoulders.)* That's the famous smile Mahakashyapa is said to have smiled when Shakyamuni showed a flower. It's such a faint smile. It was very difficult to bring out those ineffable lines at the end of his mouth. . . . I thought of a moonrise. The moonrise that faintly lights up a forest like a cage, the first hint of its vague light—it's not the bright light of a full moon, but the hint of a fifth-day moon when it emerges blurred, having lost the sharp edge of the third-day moon. I think that's the smile of Avalokitesvara. I worked hard to bring it out. Once you make it, the rest is easy. You only have to make the same thing over and over.

YOUNG WOMAN: It's truly a quiet, beautiful face. It looks so generous, accommodating, forgiving all, yet somehow melancholy and lonely. . . . Listen.

YOUNG HEAD BUILDER: What is it?

YOUNG WOMAN: I . . . I have seen this face before.

YOUNG HEAD BUILDER: You mean the face of Avalokitesvara?

YOUNG WOMAN: No, but a face exactly like it. . . . I know; this is the face of our King.

YOUNG HEAD BUILDER: What?

(At that moment a gloomy chorus rises from underground.)

YOUNG HEAD BUILDER: There, that's the singing of the prisoners digging the catacombs. Now that their day's work is over, they are coming out. A woman shouldn't be seen by them. Go home.

YOUNG WOMAN: But. . . .

YOUNG HEAD BUILDER: Now, quick!

(The Young Woman exits at stage right. Out of the hole at center stage appear chained prisoners, singing, led by a Prison Guard holding a whip. The Prison Guard bows to the Young Head Builder.)

YOUNG HEAD BUILDER: It must have been a hard day's work. I see that the prisoners are tired, too. Please let them rest. Would you buy something sweet for them with this?

(He hands him some money. The Prison Guard keeps part of it for himself and gives the rest to the head of the prisoners, who falls on his knees and offers his

prayers to the Young Head Builder. Led by the Prison Guard, the prisoners enter
the hanamichi at stage right. The Young Head Builder looks at each prisoner, and
the prisoners, in turn, bow to him, one by one. The Young Head Builder stares at
the prisoner at the end of the line.)

YOUNG HEAD BUILDER: Show me your hands!

(The prisoner sticks his hands out. The Young Head Builder jumps back.)

YOUNG HEAD BUILDER: The disease has struck us! *(To the Prison Guard)*
Separate this man from the rest. Strip him of his clothes and burn them.
Don't allow him to come out to work any more, but shut him up in a
different place. If you don't do that, we'll get into serious trouble.

(The Prison Guard separates the man from the others and takes the rope off him.)

YOUNG HEAD BUILDER: I'll take care of the others.

(The Prison Guard, leading the man, exits at stage right. The Young Head
Builder, leading the other prisoners, enters the hanamichi at stage right.)

(As they leave the stage, the Old Head Builder and a number of Villagers step
out from behind the head of Avalokitesvara where they've been hiding.)

OLD HEAD BUILDER: Did you see that?

(The Villagers nod in unison.)

OLD HEAD BUILDER: Did you hear that?

(The Villagers nod in unison.)

OLD HEAD BUILDER: At last, the disease has spread to the prisoners.
What's going to happen to us now? The village residents are forced to
throw their own work aside for ten days every month to labor for the
construction of the Bayon. That alone is burden enough. But if you neglect your work a little or try to escape, you are a criminal: you get
thrown into jail and are forced to work night and day in the dark underground among the chain gang. Now you may get infected by the disease besides. In the village, you sometimes hear somebody's got the disease, and all you have to do is to stay away from him. But if you're
chained together like that, you're finished. Did you see the way the
young Head Builder blanched? He did, because he knows if the disease
strikes one of a group, it's bound to strike others, too.

(The Villagers murmur anxiously to one another.)

All this is because of the King we welcomed with such joy when he
returned in triumph. At first it was all for the better. He distributed rice
among us, showered us with gold. Everyone revered him as Buddha,
looked up to him as Avalokitesvara incarnate. But things started to go
wrong once the construction of this inauspicious temple got under way
and the talk of the King's illness reached the ears of us lowly people. He
neglected government, obsessed as he became with the building of this
temple. The villages became poor; forced labor increased. Now there's
talk that because of unexpected increases in the costs of this construction,

they're cutting the number of soldiers. Suppose the Champas rebuild
their strength and attack us now? We'd go under in a matter of seconds.
Even if they don't bother to attack us, if the construction goes on like
this, all the villages will end up buried under the corpses of people dead
of starvation and leprosy, and turn into a paradise for buzzing green bottle flies. . . . Don't you all think it's about time we reconsidered all this?
That Head Builder—I can take care of the young man any time. He's the
only man who does whatever the King tells him to do. That's because
he's blinded by his desire to advance himself. He dumped me, someone
he owes a great deal to; he was driven by gain for himself; he took the
wrong course. Because of this I work at such unimportant buildings as infirmaries and public baths. Speaking of infirmaries, have you seen any sick
person go in one of those *and* come out of it healthy?
(All shake their heads no.)

No one, right? If things go on like this, you'll end up in one of two
ways: either you'll go to one of those infirmaries or you'll be forced into
one of the underground construction sites as a criminal. The poor but
bright life in these fertile Cambodian fields is all finished now. Once you
could be as lazy as you pleased, slaking your thirst with the fruit growing on trees, filling your stomach with the fish caught in the rivers.
Those pleasant days are all finished now. . . . What can we do? Tell me.
Think about it, every one of you. And when you have put your
thoughts together, come back to me. I'll give you the kind of advice
your parents would. I will. Understand?
*(The Villagers nod, talk among themselves for a while, thank the Old Head
Builder, and leave. The Old Head Builder alone remains on stage. He looks up at
the head of Avalokitesvara, says, "Damn!" and spits at it. He looks around, takes
out a bird-whistle, and blows it. Out of the jungle emerges the Prime Minister.)*

PRIME MINISTER: Well done. I heard it all.

OLD HEAD BUILDER: I thank you, sir.

PRIME MINISTER: Take this. *(He throws to him gold coins wrapped in a cloth.)*

OLD HEAD BUILDER: *(Gratefully holding up the money)* Thank you, sir.

*(For a while night birds call incessantly. The Second Queen walks out of the stand
of trees at stage left, sees what's happening, and hides herself behind the trees.)*

PRIME MINISTER: I will take care of the King. You concentrate on incit-
ing the people to lose confidence in the King. I heard you talk now, and
I think it was wise of you not to mention my name. I see you didn't become old for nothing. If you bring up my name too early, they'll think
I'm manipulating all this. See to it that rebellious hearts spring up like
fountains, naturally, and spread among the people. It was also a clever
approach not to talk about what to do with the King. He was once so
popular, and now he has much sympathy because of his illness. You

can't suddenly divulge the intention of—*(looking around, he makes the killing gesture)*—doing this to him. Your duty is to turn the people's feelings in that direction, naturally. You understand this?

OLD HEAD BUILDER: Yes, sir. I understand that well.

PRIME MINISTER: *(Looking up at the Avalokitesvara)* First of all, you must make them neglect work on this sort of wasteful construction. There may be some fellows working out of faith and gratitude, but do your best to instill in everybody's mind hatred for this work. As more people neglect the work, the delay will increase the frustration of the sickly King, and as that happens, his heavy demands on the people are bound to become even worse. . . . That's our aim, that's what we wait for. Do you understand?

OLD HEAD BUILDER: Yes. I'll follow your instructions in everything.

(A bell tinkles at stage left. Apparently the bell on the Second Queen's armband has accidentally sounded.)

PRIME MINISTER: Wait.

(Restraining the Old Head Builder, the Prime Minister drags the Second Queen out of the stand of trees at stage left.)

OLD HEAD BUILDER: Second Queen!

PRIME MINISTER: You, get out of sight! Get lost! Get lost, you hear me?

(The Old Head Builder, in consternation, exits at stage right.)

PRIME MINISTER: What did you hear, lady?

SECOND QUEEN: Nothing. I was about to come out here to take a walk, hoping to offer prayers for the good progress made on the head of Avalokitesvara. Let me go. I will not tolerate such rude manners. I must inform our King.

PRIME MINISTER: Lately the First Queen does not go near the King. You alone serve him loyally. That's what people are saying.

SECOND QUEEN: I need not discuss such matters of royal privacy with you.

PRIME MINISTER: *(Gently)* What did you hear us say?

SECOND QUEEN: Nothing.

(The Bas-Relief Carver appears at stage right and searches for something. He picks up the tool he apparently had left behind. About to leave, he notices the Prime Minister and the Second Queen at stage right and hides himself, partly to eavesdrop.)

PRIME MINISTER: That's all right then.

SECOND QUEEN: That's no way to speak to me. You are my subject.

PRIME MINISTER: Such a haughty manner of speaking doesn't sit well with you. . . . Your only heaven-endowed virtues are that you are pure and modest, that you devote yourself sincerely to the King, rejoice in his joys, and sorrow over his sorrows. Being haughty doesn't go well with your nature.

SECOND QUEEN: You know me so well?

PRIME MINISTER: That's why I am in love with you.

SECOND QUEEN: *(Alarmed)* What did you say?!

PRIME MINISTER: But obviously, you love someone other than me, because you don't love me.

SECOND QUEEN: Who will ever love you?

PRIME MINISTER: I'm born to feel lust, lady, only for certain people—those whom I do not love or those who do not love themselves. I do not love ugly women, and beautiful women do not love me. Meanwhile I feel a desire only for those who are either extraordinarily ugly or extraordinarily pure and beautiful. I might say that my philanderous fingers don't budge for any woman who is *made* for me.

SECOND QUEEN: That is none of my concern.

PRIME MINISTER: The beautiful, red Chinese goldfish in the water container doesn't even glance at humans, being in love as it is with the beautiful, red male goldfish. That's why I'd like to hold the goldfish in my arms—her golden scales as inhumanly beautiful as you are.

SECOND QUEEN: If that is the case, why don't you hold Nagi in your arms?

PRIME MINISTER: This woman has her eyes riveted to another man. Her mind is thinking only of him. And that in my arms! When that happens, I'll be like a powerful god!

SECOND QUEEN: That must be the God of Hell.

PRIME MINISTER: It is. And you will be the appropriate Queen of Hell. . . . Look at your eyes in a mirror: they are angry, contemptuous, hateful. It's a pity that our king has never seen this pungent beauty of yours. The only one who can enjoy it is me. Your beauty, unknown to the King, has already become mine. You give it generously, only to me. You always give a gorgeous dish of cloying, lukewarm love to the King, and a pepper of stinging hatred to me. On a languid summer night like this, such pepper should be far more pleasing to the tongue.

SECOND QUEEN: For better or for worse, if I could become a cold-hearted woman, no one would make fun of me like this.

PRIME MINISTER: When have I made fun of you?

SECOND QUEEN: Just now! Just now you are speaking to a queen in such an obscene way! Be gone! If you follow me around any longer, I'll inform the King.

PRIME MINISTER: I'll now do something to you that will stop you from ever telling the King on me.

SECOND QUEEN: What did you say?!

PRIME MINISTER: From now on you will never have the courage to tell your King what you do.

(The Prime Minister attempts to violate the Second Queen. She struggles. Her decorative comb drops on the ground. While she is struggling hard, the Queen Mother enters from the hanamichi at stage left.)

QUEEN MOTHER: *(Brandishing a whip)* Stop! Stop that!

(She pulls the two apart, then whips the Prime Minister.)

SECOND QUEEN: You're whipping the Prime Minister!

QUEEN MOTHER: I have the right to do it. I am the mother of the King.

SECOND QUEEN: But stop it, please.

QUEEN MOTHER: Why do you stop me?

SECOND QUEEN: Not for me, that's . . .

QUEEN MOTHER: For you? You must be joking.

SECOND QUEEN: He's suffering so much.

QUEEN MOTHER: A queen sympathizing with somebody who humiliated her?

SECOND QUEEN: No, I don't mean . . .

QUEEN MOTHER: I see, you just want to show what an admirably gentle soul you are. You're misunderstanding the whole thing. It's you I should whip.

SECOND QUEEN: *(Struck with fear)* Me . . .?

QUEEN MOTHER: "I'm innocent, I'm untouched and pure"—your eyes are always saying that. I should whip those eyes. . . . *(She tries to aim her whip at the Second Queen's eyes.)*

SECOND QUEEN: *(Covering her eyes)* Forgive me!

QUEEN MOTHER: *(Paying no attention to her, she says to the Prime Minister)* Well, sorry about that, you're bleeding on the neck. I'll fix it for you.

(She kneels and kisses the wound on the Prime Minister's neck.)

SECOND QUEEN: *(Alarmed)* Mother, what are you doing?! *(She starts to leave.)*

QUEEN MOTHER: *(Leaping up like a leopard and grabbing the Second Queen by the sleeve)* You can't go. You've learned the truth now. You cannot go back to that pretty-pretty world of yours again. *(To the Prime Minister)* Stand up!

PRIME MINISTER: *(Rising to his feet)* I am so grateful for your ever timely lessons, ma'am. This time I believe you've whipped me more times than when I played with one of your maids.

QUEEN MOTHER: You shut up!

SECOND QUEEN: Mother!

QUEEN MOTHER: You can't go. Stay here and listen to me.

(She and the others seat themselves on a stone.)

(The Bas-Relief Carver at stage right tries to retreat quietly. A night bird flaps up from his feet with a horrible screech. The Queen Mother, the Second Queen,

*and the Prime Minister look in his direction. The Bas-Relief Carver, in conster-
nation, exits at stage right.)*

PRIME MINISTER: I saw somebody.

QUEEN MOTHER: There's always somebody everywhere. At night, evil
souls dream various dreams and walk about in the form of people. What
you saw now may have been your own soul.

PRIME MINISTER: I'll stand on guard. *(He rises to his feet.)*

QUEEN MOTHER: That's a good idea. *(To the Second Queen)* Yes, this is a
good time for this, for me to tell you my story. . . . How I am so deeply
pained by our King's illness—you certainly know that, don't you?

SECOND QUEEN: I can guess that, yes, Mother.

QUEEN MOTHER: How gentle of you! I've heard that you are taking such
good care of him, in contrast to the First Queen who's rarely seen nowadays, avoiding our King. . . . The sad truth, though, is that our king's
illness can only worsen and there's no prospect for his recovery.

SECOND QUEEN: I pray to Avalokitesvara every day so that he will recover
totally on the day this temple is completed.

QUEEN MOTHER: We can't really count on Avalokitesvara, no matter
how compassionate he may be. The disease gets worse day by day. No
other disease in the world is more terrible than this. My son—such a
beautiful body. . . . Ah, try to understand me. When he was born, he
was a pure gem. He was my pride; he was the pride of our kingdom. His
gallant beauty was from his youthful days the hope of our kingdom. . . .
But now, look what's happened! His deerlike legs are affected; his arms
as smooth as the moonlight are rotting away.

SECOND QUEEN: Your sorrow is mine.

QUEEN MOTHER: No, it can't be. My son's incomparable beauty, youthfulness, and strength are not just the treasure of this kingdom; I gave
birth to them and nurtured them. I am far more devastated than he himself. It was during a full moon that my womb gave birth to him, but the
moon has been eclipsed, never to emerge fully again. If all this is not
malice against me, an insult to me, an attempt to make a mockery of me,
what is it?

(A great many nightbirds screech terribly.)

Even nightbirds are jeering at me. Listen to me. The beautiful, glorious world I gave birth to makes its own beautiful face fester and rot with
medicinal pastes, shows it to me day and night, prevents me from sleeping all night long—and that's supposed to be an expression of gratitude
for my having given birth to it. *(Nightbirds screech again.)* And all those
jeers, uttered in unison. . . . Everything is finished now. The world has
collapsed. I must begin all over again. . . .

SECOND QUEEN: All over again?

QUEEN MOTHER: Yes, all over again.

SECOND QUEEN: *(Seized by an indescribable fear)* What do you plan to do?

QUEEN MOTHER: I've been thinking only about this. My son's illness is incurable. His body crumbles away day by day. To save at least the memory of his beautiful face, which remains untouched—to save him from his tragic fate—to make him happy once, once again. . . . To have Cambodia ruled by a beautiful, young, strong king once again. . . . There's only one thing we can do, one thing that can be done to save my son and me. . . .

SECOND QUEEN: Only one thing?

QUEEN MOTHER: Kill him, and I will give birth to him again.

SECOND QUEEN: What! *(She jerks herself away, astounded.)*

QUEEN MOTHER: You needn't be alarmed. *(The number of fireflies increase, swarming around the Queen Mother.)* I am not going to do it. I will allow you to play that honorable role.

(The Second Queen tries to run away. The Prime Minister grabs her.)

. . . What is this? So many fireflies. These must be the tears my son sheds, unknown to anyone, every night, which have floated out to appeal to me. He's pleading with me, through his tears, to kill him while some beauty is left to him. . . . Yes, indeed. *(To the Second Queen)* The King trusts you. He accepts medicine and food only from your hands. Please kill him with your own hands. *(She falls on her knees and weeps.)* With your own hands.

SECOND QUEEN: Please rise to your feet. I do not deserve such humbleness.

QUEEN MOTHER: *(Clinging to the Second Queen)* There's no other proof of motherly love that I can give him. I plead with you. Do what I tell you. *(She hands her a small medicinal bag.)* Give him this poison. One spoonful, and he will die. . . . If he remains alive for ten days, you will be killed, having broken this promise. Understand? You may want to tell this to him, but *you* will be suspected, not me. . . . If nothing happens in ten days, understand, you will die. Now, you may go.

(The Second Queen leaves toward stage left.)

QUEEN MOTHER: *(Clinging to the Prime Minister's knees, she weeps.)* I've done it, at last. At last. . . . Poor child! But I can't go on watching him any more, watching him grow uglier . . .

PRIME MINISTER: Weep your heart out on my knees. . . . Now, we will go to that secret room in the palace, so that I may soothe your sorrow to your heart's content.

QUEEN MOTHER: Forgive me. Does it still hurt?

PRIME MINISTER: No, you shouldn't show any compassion. That makes me feel strange. Compassion is supposed to be linked to cruelty, tears to murder, gentleness to ruthlessness in you.

(They leave along the hanamichi at stage left. The moon shines on the face of Avalokitesvara.)

(After a while, the King, wrapped in a robe made of golden brocade, only his pale face showing under his broad hat, appears in unsteady steps from stage left.)

KING: *(Looking up at Avalokitesvara)* Ah, the moonlight is illuminating his holy face. What purity! What a smile! . . . Only when I come here and look up at his face all by myself, do I feel peaceful.

I have lost my courage, lost the inexhaustible energy I once had. I have lost the youthfulness that made me feel as if I was winging through the skies, that enabled me to put on the world every morning freshly as if it were new underwear. My mind watches for my flesh that crumbles away day by day, and the future is no more than a temple, which embraced tightly by silk-cotton trees, slowly collapses.

Moon, symbol of our royal house. The purification of your cold light, your cold-bloodedness, your melancholy—for all that, why did you give me this painful suffering in which flesh and blood rot away while alive? What did I do? I did not do anything sinful. Did you decide to drive my flesh into precipitous decline so that you might sooner illuminate my white bones in your cool light? If that was the case, you certainly had other means. If you had had me stabbed to death in battle, you wouldn't have had to wait long before my white bones were picked clean by vultures, ready to accept your light.

Bodhisattva of Compassion, may you allow the Bayon to be completed while even one healthy piece of my flesh still remains! Until the very day when the Bayon is completed, may you allow my youthful face, facing you bathed in the same moonlight, to remain as it is.

. . . No, no. This may be part of Buddha's providence. When I think of it, the first sign of my bodily collapse appeared on the very day I thought of building this temple. The red stain like a Chinese rose that surfaced on my arm at the time may be like the morning star that appears at the top of the hills. Just as the morning star loses its light as it becomes diffused in the light that soon brightens the sky, so that stain may have been the sign spelling the end of the dark night that was our Moon dynasty and the beginning of the daylight that is Avalokitesvara's compassion. If so, my body, which everyone said was so beautiful, was nothing more than the night that allowed the moon to shine. And as dawn came, my body, the night, began to fade like this. That explains it. If not, I cannot understand why my spiritual awakening and my bodily collapse occurred on the same day, like day and night. And as my body slowly collapses, the cathedral of the Bayon nears its completion little by little. I am slowly giving my own self to the temple. Yes, that must be what Avalokitesvara, with his infinite compassion, desires. If this is the case, I will not be able to be present at the completion ceremony of the temple. When my body completely collapses, all my self will have been given away for the first time, with the temple of my soul, the temple found nowhere else in the world, the cathedral of the Bayon now completed. . . . At that moment Avalokitesvara and I will become one.

Still, I cannot help wondering: What does he, Avalokitesvara, with his enigmatic, beautiful smile, intend to do by reigning over a country where all the people are dead? There will no longer be anyone who can enjoy his compassion, will there?

Ah, noble, pure, holy Bodhisattva of Compassion! May you remove from me the worldly suffering that remains with me, the burden on my soul that I must carry every day, that increases in weight as days go by. May you pity the circumstances of my life in which I was plunged from the pinnacle of honor and glory into the lava bottom of a valley where neither grass nor tree grows. May you be understanding about my horrible days when I have to listen to my own flesh turn into beads of water little by little and drip, drip incessantly in the dark cavern of my heart where, yes, only the pulsating heart is alive in the darkness. May you allow this country, now grown destitute and poor, to spend its meager resources on this construction at least until the temple shines in glory.
(He falls on his knees. After praying, he rises to his feet and notices, on the ground below him, the Second Queen's comb. He picks it up, looks at it against the moonlight, and ponders.)

(Gay Chinese music is heard at the end of the hanamichi at stage left. The King pricks up his ears and puts the comb away. Led by several attendants, each holding a torch, the Chinese Ambassador and his wife in palanquin enter, followed by a musical band.)

(Noticing the King, the Ambassador halts the palanquin; he and his wife get down. He makes a deep bow.)

AMBASSADOR: I see, I see. It appears that Your Majesty is taking a stroll. May I introduce us? My name is Liu Ma-fu, and I have come from the court of Southern Song as ambassador extraordinary. This is my wife.

KING: Arriving so late at night . . .

AMBASSADOR: I am aware of that, Your Majesty. We stayed on a boat last night, and decided to come here as soon as possible, allowing little time for resting. As a result, we have arrived at your royal court this late at night.

KING: You must have some sort of emergency.

AMBASSADOR: Well, Sire, the kingfisher feathers of your country are noted for their incomparable beauty, and they are the rage among the ladies of the court of my country. Sadly, however, there is little trade between us, and kingfisher feathers are so scarce that they are far from meeting the demand. As a result, our Emperor commanded me to come to your glorious country, so that I may personally ask you to sell us kingfisher feathers.

AMBASSADOR'S WIFE: Look at me, if you will, Your Majesty. We use kingfisher feathers like this—for embroidery, for hair decorations, and for many other things. We value them so highly. And the only kingfisher feathers that will do are those harvested in your glorious country.

AMBASSADOR: We are ready to pay any price you name. So that we may buy thousands upon thousands of feathers, we have brought along gold as well. Show His Majesty the coffer.

(His attendants bring up the coffer to the King and open it. The gold coins inside shine forth.)

KING: Am I receiving Avalokitesvara's divine favor so fast? Perhaps he will take care of my illness as well. . . ?

AMBASSADOR: I beg your pardon, Sire?

KING: Well, first, you must rest in the palace.

(The Ambassador and his wife bow deeply. Then they leave toward stage left with their band playing again.)

SCENE 2

The First Queen's living quarters in the palace. From the window at stage right, the tower of the Snake God Naga is visible. Ten days after the previous scene.

The First Queen is lying behind the drapery at stage left. The Second Queen is at stage right. Evening glow. Among the stage props are peacocks and monkeys.

SECOND QUEEN: So you will not allow me to see you.

FIRST QUEEN: *(From within the drapery)* A terrifying evening glow. I don't want to come out there and expose myself to such an evening glow. I'm sure I'd look like a woman burned at the stake. . . . But isn't this funny—that you, the Second Queen, have taken the trouble of coming to visit me, the First Queen, in my room. That's like discarding your pride altogether. . . . Why?

(The Second Queen is silent.)

FIRST QUEEN: Why? . . . You do not respond.

SECOND QUEEN: I have come here for protection.

FIRST QUEEN: Who is after you?

SECOND QUEEN: I cannot tell you that.

FIRST QUEEN: Are you saying that there's someone within this palace who entertains harmful thoughts about you?

SECOND QUEEN: I cannot tell you that, either.

FIRST QUEEN: You, who never spoke to me directly, are now pleading with me. What am I supposed to do?

SECOND QUEEN: I'd be grateful if you could hide me here for a couple of days—and if you could tell everyone who comes to visit this room, whoever that may be, that you haven't seen me. . . . Maybe tomorrow I will have the means of escaping from this country. My maids are trying to work that out for me. . . . The other request I have is . . .

FIRST QUEEN: What is it?

SECOND QUEEN: After I leave this place, would you tend to our King, attentively. . .?

FIRST QUEEN: I . . .

SECOND QUEEN: No, I am not saying it must be you personally. You can select someone and command her to tend to him. . . . As his illness becomes worse, he is becoming very willful.

FIRST QUEEN: *(Reluctantly)* I agree to your request.

SECOND QUEEN: I thank you very much.

(Both remain silent for a while.)

(Then the First Queen gives out a deep sigh.)

SECOND QUEEN: Do you not feel well?

FIRST QUEEN: No. . . . I am looking out from here—white herons flying down in one flock onto the marshes in the evening glow. Their wings dyed scarlet, the way they move their bodies so pliantly in the red of the sun makes them look like white-clad vestals gone mad. Who is it that said, "Nature to the eye is peaceful"? Nature in its true form is madness itself.

SECOND QUEEN: When I was still a small girl, my mother pointed out a marsh and said, "That marsh is ill." Like today, it was in the sunset, the marsh lay stagnant, dyed in the five colors of yellow, scarlet, green, gray, and purple, although the colors went on shifting. A number of dead trees stuck out of it, and with wild monkeys' calls long gone, there was nothing alive anywhere.

FIRST QUEEN: This is all so strange. Since I know you are going to leave here soon, we can talk to each other like sisters.

SECOND QUEEN: May I see your face now, then?

FIRST QUEEN: Well, we will have some Chinese tea over there together. *(Tinkling a bell)* Bring some tea.

(The First Queen emerges wearing a robe with long sleeves that hide her hands. During the conversation that follows, tea is brought in.)

SECOND QUEEN: Now that I have decided to leave, I feel relaxed enough to ask you a question: Why did you begin to avoid our King altogether after his illness became known?

FIRST QUEEN: Because I love him. Because I cannot bear to see his beautiful body crumble away. You understand me, don't you? You are kind, gentle, and dedicated—and that at times makes you tougher.

SECOND QUEEN: This is because I love not his body, but his mind.

FIRST QUEEN: His mind is a conventional one, if I may say so. It's no different from that of any other man around here. The only thing that makes him superior is that noble youthfulness and beauty, that's all. All that is gone now. That is why I confine myself to my room, holding dear to my heart the memory of our King as he once was.

SECOND QUEEN: Do you not mind whatever may happen to him in the future?

FIRST QUEEN: The future? All that will happen is his flesh will collapse into a tangled heap like the roots of a mangrove tree. Tell me, what other future is there? *(Becoming furious)* We aren't talking just about our King. What future is there for Cambodia, our Moon dynasty? . . . Everything is going to be corroded like a rock constantly assaulted by the tides of time. Once our King and I were like Vishnu and Saraswati, a rare couple embodying male majesty and female sensuality. But one half of that couple crumbled. I had no choice but to hide myself.

SECOND QUEEN: I hear them again—the evening incantations of monks. *(Eerie sounds of bells and incantations come down on the wind from somewhere high.)*

(The First Queen picks up a teacup with her hands covered with sleeves. As the Second Queen watches her, mystified, the First Queen puts the teacup back on the table.)

(The evening sunlight fades, as the incantations and sounds of bells continue.)

FIRST QUEEN: It's the evening service at the Naga tower, isn't it?

SECOND QUEEN: And it continues well into the night. When it stops, our King enters Naga's room, and all the noises come to a stop.

FIRST QUEEN: Ah, I loathe the sounds and voices that come from that tower every day, every night. I loathe even more the silence of the tower that follows them. That I must give my husband to entertain the Snake God's daughter every night. . . . And what's the use? This patience so accursed, this suffering so painful, this pride trampled upon, this aimless jealousy. . . . I might be able to bear it all if it made rich harvests as it's supposed to. But in fact, all these troubles started after the King started his service: his illness, the decline of our country, the prickly irritability of people's hearts—this is all we've got as a result of his service. . . . Nagi, I'm sure, is an evil woman, and he's been carried away by her. For all this, we can't even have a glimpse of Nagi.

SECOND QUEEN: I am not going to be jealous of something I haven't seen. It would be useless.

FIRST QUEEN: You are like that. That's why everybody loves you. But I . . .

SECOND QUEEN: You are suffering.

FIRST QUEEN: Yes, I cannot get rid of Nagi from my head, night and day. I've been thinking all along that I must take our King back from her at any cost, from that invisible woman with an evil soul. . . . I hate her. I hate that woman. She controls us from a distance, messing up our love so terribly.

SECOND QUEEN: That is not true. I have loved our King in my own way, and he has loved me in his own way.

FIRST QUEEN: That is the same with me.

SECOND QUEEN: What more do you need?

FIRST QUEEN: *(Pricking up her ears)* Listen. Those sounds of bells. Those incantatory voices. From the top of the tower they slide down on the evening wind like an invisible snake. I'm sure the monks can see her. An eternally young snake woman flickering her flamelike tongue eternally. . . . She monopolizes our King.

SECOND QUEEN: She does not. First of all, you now avoid him, no longer competing for his love.

FIRST QUEEN: You do not understand. Hers is a love that captures a man entirely. It is the sort of love that leaves its imprint on every part of a man's body and heart, so he thinks of it the moment he moves any part of his body. The King's leprosy is a form of that woman's love. It makes his flesh rot, his bones dry up, so that he can't forget it for a second. . . . Imagine a man who thinks he's walking along a path in the field of his own free will. The sun sets at the end of the field. Then he knows that the sunset, the field, and the shadows of elephants feeding on grass on the horizon have all been arranged by the woman to soothe his mind. She's everywhere, like mists—in the clothes he wears, in the air he breathes. . . . Have we been able to love our King like that?

SECOND QUEEN: You sound as if you hated not Nagi, but our King.

FIRST QUEEN: Why should I hate our King?

SECOND QUEEN: Perhaps because he did not love you as you did him.

FIRST QUEEN: You are being rude.

(A maid hurries in.)

MAID: The Queen Mother is coming to see you, ma'am!

FIRST QUEEN: Why, so suddenly. *(To the Second Queen)* Come, hurry!

(The Second Queen hides herself.)

(Enters the Queen Mother.)

QUEEN MOTHER: Where is the Second Queen?

FIRST QUEEN: I don't know, ma'am.

QUEEN MOTHER: She must still be hiding somewhere in the palace. It's no good for you to try to hide her.

FIRST QUEEN: Why should I . . . ?

QUEEN MOTHER: No use pretending. Her maid already has made a confession. That she's trying to flee from this country.

FIRST QUEEN: If you know that much. . . . *(Coldly)* Well now, come out!

QUEEN MOTHER: How could you betray me. . . ?

SECOND QUEEN: *(Clinging to her knees in terror)* Forgive me.

QUEEN MOTHER: I said, in ten days, didn't I? This is the tenth day. I thought you were resigned to your fate. Instead, you've been trying to run away or hide yourself. . . . Now come with me.

SECOND QUEEN: No, spare me, Mother.

QUEEN MOTHER: Come, I said!

(She is about to take her away, when the King enters.)

KING: What is going on here?

(Everyone falls into an embarrassed silence.)

    Why do you all avoid me? The First Queen, Mother, even the Second Queen. *(Chasing each one of them)* Why avoid me? Are you afraid of me, or my illness . . . ? Why avoid me? I am King of Cambodia. Every one of you is a member of our glorious royal household. And yet. . . . Why avoid me? *(To the Second Queen)* Even you, even you. I've heard from your maid. Running away, are you? Without your husband's permission. . . . Even you avoid me—you who only yesterday leaned to me and wept so sadly while changing my bandages. . . . You, the only woman I knew who was gentle of heart. . . . *(To the Queen Mother)* You, too, Mother. . . . You avoid me, the son you yourself gave birth to, as if I were some accursed thing. As if the Cambodian King shining bright as gold were a dead goat on the roadside swarming with flies. . . . Don't you feel guilty about it? Doesn't your heart feel some pain? *(To the First Queen)* And you. . . . As soon as your husband sank into illness, you abandoned him, paid no attention to him, and ever since have been enjoying yourself, having singers sing songs, musicians play music, every night . . .

FIRST QUEEN: That's because I was terrified of you—of your sin even I did not know that began to make your body crumble.

KING: Make no excuses. Just say it was because you are heartless, that you have a heart of ice.

FIRST QUEEN: I will say it. Yes, indeed, it was because I am heartless, that I have a heart of ice. Because I loved nothing but beautiful things, and because you are now . . .

KING: I am now . . .

FIRST QUEEN: . . . neither beautiful nor youthful. You are just another leper. You say, love me, but that is just not possible.

KING: So you avoided me, because you didn't love me.

FIRST QUEEN: Yes, because I did not love you.

KING: That's a lie.

FIRST QUEEN: A lie? Are you still so confident of yourself?

KING: That's a lie. *(He approaches her, grabs one of her arms, and rolls up its sleeve. A horrible hand with crooked fingers appears.)* Because of this! *(She screams, pulls her hand back, and hides it immediately. The Queen Mother and the Second Queen are appalled.)*

QUEEN MOTHER: So you, too, have been struck by the illness.

KING: Mother, she, too, has become a leper. *(To the First Queen)* Now, tell me, why did you hide it? If you hadn't hidden it, I might have had some tender feelings for you.

FIRST QUEEN: Why should I need your pity?

KING: You and I are now on the same footing. Now you have become my true queen.

FIRST QUEEN: *(Covering her face)* No!

KING: What do you mean, no?

FIRST QUEEN: No! If I am a leper, I need no one else. If you're a leper, you need no one else. Two lepers loving each other—no! that's too revolting.

KING: Why should we hate each other?

FIRST QUEEN: We do not hate each other. It's simply that I hate you. To prevent a leper's love from drenching me like a rain of fire, I dodge. Dodging, I try not to look at you. I avoid you. If I do, you become more and more of a leper, and when you have become a complete leper . . . do you understand, I will no longer be a leper.

KING: How incredibly self-centered you are! Suppose I said I'd love you even if your beautiful form had crumbled away?

FIRST QUEEN: I wouldn't want you to love such a crumbled me! But I'm sure you would, wouldn't you? I'd rather you hate me while I'm beautiful. Every morning I look at the mirror and tell myself with a sigh: I am still beautiful, still beautiful; while I'm beautiful, I can torment the King.

KING: Ah!

FIRST QUEEN: Look into yourself. Ever since you knew of my illness, you have not been suffering. You try to hide it, but you have regained joy, you have regained light in your eyes! Cruel intimacy—that's love between lepers. I can no longer love you.

KING: You loved me before, then.

FIRST QUEEN: Yes, while I was able to torment you.

KING: And I could not torment you.

FIRST QUEEN: You did, your nightly lovemaking with the Snake God's daughter, Nagi . . .

KING: Are you jealous?

FIRST QUEEN: I can never be jealous of something that's invisible to the eye.

KING: Are you jealous? *(He laughs.)*

FIRST QUEEN: Why do you laugh?

KING: Nagi is the only woman who doesn't avoid me, whether I'm a leper or not. *(He prepares to leave.)*

FIRST QUEEN: *(Running after him)* Where are you going?

KING: Where, did you say? The set hour of the day has come, that's all. Nagi is waiting for me in her bed. I must go. You know she's my only queen. *(He hurries away.)*

FIRST QUEEN: King!

SCENE 3

Immediately following the previous scene. The shrine on the top floor of Naga's tower. A high flame rises at center stage.

The King enters. He lies down in the bed at one end of the stage, loosens his robe from his chest and waits.

In a while there is the sound of a slithering snake, hissing.

KING: Here you come. Don't be shy. My lovely Nagi. My bride who is always young. Come up here. . . . You who were born of the ocean tide, so beautiful, so smooth, of such brilliant green. Let that tide wrap around me. . . . You are my consolation. You are the only woman in the world, the only one who trembles with joy, just being with me . . . Nagi. Do not burn my body so with your tongue of flame. Oh, Nagi, do not purr so with such joy. . . . Lovely, pure, gentle Nagi. Wrap me up in the waves of your cold, green scales, and tonight, too, take me away infinitely far from the shore, to the country at the end of the great ocean, where there is no sorrow or anger, no suffering or worries. . . . You know no sympathy, no jealousy. Only with love, the unfathomable love of a gentle sea, you soothe me . . . Nagi. How could I, in a condition like this, be a consolation to you? . . . Don't let your throat hiss so, like a meadow pipe; don't pant so much. Why do you drown yourself in such joy? Nagi. . . . Aren't you afraid of me? Don't you find me loathsome? You, with your eternally maidenly pliant shiny neck, Nagi. My bride forever and ever. . . . Gentle, gentle, gentle Nagi.

(For a while, the slithering and hissing sounds continue.)

(Suddenly the door squeaks open, and the First Queen runs in.)

KING: *(Astounded)* You can't come here! The divine punishment will strike you! A terrible calamity will fall upon you!

FIRST QUEEN: The divine punishment has already struck me. A terrible calamity has already fallen upon me. What other thing is there I should be afraid of?

KING: Be gone! This place is forbidden to women.

FIRST QUEEN: You have a woman there, in your bed.

KING: She is a divine woman. An invisible woman. Human females are forbidden.

FIRST QUEEN: I am not human. *(She pulls her hand out of the sleeve. It looks like a dragon's claw.)* Look at this. My hand has become like the Snake God's.

KING: Be gone! Be gone!

FIRST QUEEN: No. *(She throws herself onto the bed.)* I love you. From tonight on I will not let you go. I will never let you go. I will become an eternally young daughter of Naga's. . . . I won't let you go.

(She wraps herself around him. The King pushes her away and rises to his feet.)

KING: What are you doing?

FIRST QUEEN: Do you avoid me? Because I'm a leper?

KING: You have violated Nagi's holy rite.

FIRST QUEEN: *I* am the Nagi. I *am* the Nagi. Tonight the former Nagi is destroyed, and the new Nagi will serve you in your bed night after night. I will embrace every part of your body to make you wholly my own. . . . Now I will become Nagi, right in front of your eyes. . . .

(The First Queen retreats step by step, then leaps into the flame at stage center. With a scream she burns up and turns into ashes.)

(The King, astounded, falls. The sounds of slithering scales and hissing grow loud in the room.)

(Opening the door, the Queen Mother and the Prime Minister rush in.)

QUEEN MOTHER: King, where's the King?

PRIME MINISTER: The Queen should be here, too . . .

QUEEN MOTHER: *(Finding the King)* Ah . . . he's not dead. He just fainted and fell. I wonder what he saw.

PRIME MINISTER: *(Slowly drawing his sword)* If we killed the King now, everybody would think the Snake God killed him. We could also blame the First Queen for the crime. There will be no better chance. To kill him with a single stab while he lies unconscious will be a kindness, too. Look the other way. I can take care of it in one second. Afterward, all the happiness and prosperity will return to us, and with the construction of the Bayon suspended, we can bring our kingdom back to its former glory. Then, you can give birth to a King who is far more beautiful, far stronger than this one. All because of me.

QUEEN MOTHER: *(Crying)* Do whatever you like. That's what I wanted after all. My poor child. . . . I will revive you in time.

(The Queen Mother turns her back. The Prime Minister prepares to stab the King. The Queen Mother suddenly turns around and stabs the Prime Minister in the back. The Prime Minister falls down with a scream. The scream revives the King.)

KING: Nagi . . . Nagi . . .

PRIME MINISTER: *(Mustering his last strength)* Your Majesty . . .

QUEEN MOTHER: I have saved you, King. This man was about to stab you. Look, he's clutching his rebellious sword.

KING: Mother, my queen has . . .

PRIME MINISTER: Your queen allowed me to take away her chastity.

KING: *(Shaking the Prime Minister)* Which queen, tell me! Which . . .

PRIME MINISTER: It is the Second Queen. In front of the half-built Avalokitesvara in the temple, I violated her one night. . . .

KING: So the comb I picked up that night. . . . Tell me! Tell me! How did that happen!

(The Prime Minister dies.)

QUEEN MOTHER: *[Aside]* He died without saying anything bad about me. He was a terrible villain, but he stuck to the rules he made for himself. *(To the King)* And what about the First Queen . . . ?

KING: *(Dazed)* She has turned into Nagi.

CURTAIN

ACT 3
SCENE 1

A year after the preceding act. Daytime.

The terrace of the Leper King with the palace in the background. At its center is a resplendent golden palanquin. The Leper King, his face wrapped up so that only his eyes peer out, is seated in it. Surrounding him are the Young Head Builder, some soldiers and maids. Somewhat apart from them stands the Second Queen.

As the curtain rises, there's the soft clonking of wooden oxen bells in the distance. Everyone is listening to it. Amid the mooing of oxen is the sound of masons carving stone.

SECOND QUEEN: Look at this. *(She points in the direction of the audience.)* It's almost finished. It's just a year since the First Queen threw herself into the fire, but I'm sure she'd be overjoyed to see this. When the Prime Minister passed away, the signs of rebellion also ceased, and the country has enjoyed a quiet, though weakened, peace ever since. The villagers ran away one after another, and now you see fewer people walking up and down the boulevards of the capital. But thanks to you, Head Builder, the construction people are working hard. Everyone has now come to bet his dreams on the completion of the Bayon. Still, you say it will take another year, Head Builder? Isn't that so?

YOUNG HEAD BUILDER: We're having them work day and night, ma'am, but yes, it will take another year.

SECOND QUEEN: So in a year we will have the fulfillment of the Cambodian tradition of devaraja worship—where the King who built the temple becomes one with the temple and later on the same king comes to be worshiped as the incarnation of the gods and Buddhas enshrined in the Bayon. Then, our King will become one with the Buddha, and those who pay their respects to the Bayon will no longer be able to tell our King from Avalokitesvara. In other words, our King will become Avalokitesvara. And all that depends on you, Head Builder.

YOUNG HEAD BUILDER: Yes, I'm aware of it, lady. My duty is to fulfill the King's dream at any cost.

KING: *(In a hoarse voice)* What's that sound? The sound I hear? In between the sounds of hammers I hear cheerful bell-like sounds that I seem to remember from the past.

YOUNG HEAD BUILDER: It's natural, Sire, that your higher self does not immediately recognize the sounds. Those sounds come from the wooden bells hung on the necks of stone-carrying oxen by their owners. Because of the lovely sounds, the owners can tell where their oxen are even if they wander off into the woods during the rest periods.

KING: I see. Lovely sounds, indeed, as you say. . . . I see black-humped oxen moving among the stones. The sides of the stones that have been cut dazzle in the sun. Everything has a vigor—yes, the way those working lustily increase their delight in the work itself—that's the atmosphere I sense here as well. I came out here to see my mother off. It's a good thing that I did.

SECOND QUEEN: Still, you shouldn't stay out in the sun too long. Your doctor says so.

KING: *(Without responding to her)* It's good I came out, something I haven't done for a long time. I'm bored with the darkness; bored with the moon, too. The bright daytime winds that come through the palms and coconut trees are so pleasant. The wing beats of insects hovering near my ears are pleasant. *(To the Young Head Builder)* What happened to your predecessor, the Head Builder who tried to block your work all the time?

YOUNG HEAD BUILDER: He fled the country when the Prime Minister passed away.

KING: He did, did he? That must have made your work easier. . . . That reminds me: I haven't seen the palace astrologer for a long time, either . . .

SECOND QUEEN: He, too, ran away a long time ago.

KING: *(Furious)* I told you not to speak to me directly!

SECOND QUEEN: *(Falling on her knees)* Please forgive me!

KING: You ought to be grateful that I allow you to stay near me. I do so because you asked me to. If you want to make up for the sin you committed, you must follow the rule laid down. You can't speak to me directly. Don't ever act familiar with me again.

SECOND QUEEN: I will not, my lord.

KING: So what about the Astrologer?

YOUNG HEAD BUILDER: I'm told he ran away.

KING: He did? I wonder why he did. A stupid fellow. He said building the temple facing east would be bad luck. His prediction has proved right. He could have taken credit for that and boasted about it.

YOUNG HEAD BUILDER: Sire, I have a request to make. . . .

KING: What is it?

YOUNG HEAD BUILDER: We lowly people have no way of surmising whatever circumstances there may have been, but our Second Queen is so deeply concerned about your health, and all our craftsmen say she's a model of chastity—that there cannot be any other person like her in the entire world. And yet, you seem so cruel to her. I beg you, Sire, to try to understand how our queen feels. . . .

KING: Shut up! Shut up! What presumption! You, a mere craftsman, dare comment on the personal affairs of our royal house! A word more, and I will . . .

YOUNG HEAD BUILDER: I know of no excuse to make, Sire.

SECOND QUEEN: Head builder, I know how you feel, but you must not act above your station.

YOUNG HEAD BUILDER: Forgive me, lady. It wasn't proper of me.

KING: You had best concentrate on your construction work. Oh! *(Staring hard)* The side of that stone has suddenly spurted fire and crumbled! What happened? Look, there, too, and there. . . .

YOUNG HEAD BUILDER: What do you see, Sire?

KING: The stones are crumbling. I can't tell them from the ground. Look, the humped oxen are melting away. Their shapes are becoming vague, spreading . . .

YOUNG HEAD BUILDER: King! Hold yourself firm! Nothing has changed. The oxen are walking about, swaying their heads; the masons are wielding their hammers vigorously; the green ivy and grass are being cut . . .

KING: Is that the truth?

YOUNG HEAD BUILDER: Yes.

KING: So now it has reached my eyes.

(Everyone falls silent, in dark thought.)

(A band approaches. The music is a mixture of Cambodian and Chinese tunes and is quite boisterous.)

SECOND QUEEN: Now the Queen Mother is ready to leave—along with the Chinese Ambassador.

(Everyone kneels. The Queen Mother, the Chinese Ambassador and his wife appear, followed by musicians and a large number of people carrying coffers.)

AMBASSADOR: Your Majesty, allow me to congratulate you on being in a much greater state of health and vigor than usual. That you should have come out this far to see your mother off not only shows your profound filial piety but also is a great honor for us. May I express our deep gratitude once again for allowing me, as well as my wife, to stay here for a year, and for treating us in an incomparable fashion every day. Your mother shows a deep interest in our country. Once we return home with her, it is our sincere desire to accord her the best treatment our country can offer, so that she may become the bond of friendship between our nations. Allow me, finally, to express our hope that the Bayon will be completed safely and that your kingdom will continue to prosper more than ever.

AMBASSADOR'S WIFE: Being a woman, I'll be casual in offering farewells. I was fascinated by every product of your country. Would you look at those coffers—two of them contain the feathers of one million two thousand kingfishers; I hear that there are no more kingfishers in Cambodia because of this. But you can imagine how delighted our Emperor and all his many queens will be. Also, a staggering quantity of elephant tusks, rhinoceros horns, honey wax, resin, gamboge—the pigment you can't do without for the beautiful paintings that decorate the palaces—as well as a great quantity of tortoise shells. . . . I shall not forget your country's strange way of tortoise-hunting during the dry season when no rain falls.

AMBASSADOR: Yes, indeed, watching that was one of the most pleasant moments during this trip.

AMBASSADOR'S WIFE: You drive the tortoise out of his hiding hole with fire and smoke, and your dog brings it to you in his jaws. It's the same as rabbit-hunting. *(She laughs merrily.)* That was so funny! The way the tortoise clumsily struggled in the dog's jaws!

AMBASSADOR: You shouldn't laugh so immodestly.

AMBASSADOR'S WIFE: Oh, pardon me! But enjoying life is the hallmark of our country. Yes, there is unhappiness everywhere. The world is brimming with unhappiness. But eating fine food, getting fat, and laughing loudly doesn't mean being contemptuous of somebody else's unhappiness. I'm not afraid of illness, either. I have brought a great number of talismans from my country. Besides, I believe only those people fall ill who turn their eyes away from the joys and happiness of this world and yearn for and dream about things outside this world.

AMBASSADOR: Come, come! Be careful what you say.

AMBASSADOR'S WIFE: Oh, pardon me! But please don't forget that there have been travelers who stayed in your country for a year and saw only good things, beautiful things, and happy things. The landscape and seasons of your country are beautiful; the people of your country are kind-hearted. Everything you eat here is delicious. There's an abundance of fruits. You can have fun riding an elephant wherever you're going. The dancers who soothe your eyes are so pretty. All this will stay with me for the rest of my life. Thank you very much indeed!

AMBASSADOR: Now, that's enough. That's enough. It also gives us great pleasure that because of the opening of trade between us, we were able to help the building of the Bayon, which means so much to the King. *(Looking in the direction of the audience)* Oh, you've made so much progress. It looks quite different from the way it did when we arrived here. I'd like to give some gifts to the craftsmen to mark our farewell. Head Builder, would you be kind enough to call together some of the principal people?

YOUNG HEAD BUILDER: Yes, sir.

(He leaves.)

QUEEN MOTHER: King, the time for us to part has come. I beg you to forgive me. Because of Ambassador and Mrs. Liu's kindness, I have decided to live in China. I'm sure you think I'm a cruel mother. But Ambassador Liu's kind offer will enable me to save myself from madness—I'd go mad if I went on like this. You might say it's a mother's duty to stay with her son even in madness. But when I think how much sorrow you'd feel to see your mother deranged, I'd rather that you see me off like this, in a healthy state. I can no longer stay still. *(She cries.)* I don't have the courage to go on watching you, King, no, I'd rather call you my lovely son. Please forgive me for my weak heart.

KING: It is of course better—that you go. That you go away, live a happy life in a foreign country, forgetting all. . . . The leper's consolation lies in being forgotten.

(During this exchange, the Bas-Relief Carver and other craftsmen are brought out by the Head Builder and line up.)

QUEEN MOTHER: *(Falls on her knees and weeps.)* Forgive me, my child. I'm not abandoning you. I have fought with myself for quite some time. But in the end I've found there's no other way for me to go on living than to hold dear the phantom, the image, of the beautiful, powerful King, once my life. For me you must remain that youthful, resplendent King Jayavarman on the day of his triumphal return.

KING: Mother, don't you believe in Avalokitesvara's compassion?

QUEEN MOTHER: I don't. No matter how I try, I can't. Because the unhappiness of this country started on the day when the building of the temple began.

KING: But suppose . . . suppose I am Avalokitesvara.

QUEEN MOTHER: *(Looking far into the audience)* Yes, all those faces of Aval-okitesvara do look like your face when it was beautiful. But—*(She laughs a long, empty laugh)*—it can't be. . . . It can't be. . . .

KING: May I ask you, Mr. and Mrs. Ambassador—may I ask you to take good care of my mother in every way, so that she may spend the rest of her life happily?

AMBASSADOR: Please rest assured that we will.

AMBASSADOR'S WIFE: Leave it to us.

KING: I'm relieved to hear it. Mother, stay well.

QUEEN MOTHER: Wait! I have one thing I must say before departing. If I didn't say it, my heart would always have to carry a burden.

KING: What is it, Mother?

QUEEN MOTHER: When I stabbed the Prime Minster to death in Nagi's room, I said to you, didn't I, that I stabbed him because he was about to kill you, who were unconscious, and saved your life.

KING: Yes, and I still do not forget my gratitude for your saving my life, Mother. If I had been killed at that time, I would have been saved from the sufferings of this world, but I would not have been able to fulfill the wishes of Avalokitesvara.

QUEEN MOTHER: What I said was true. The Prime Minister was plotting a revolt. He made a hasty move and, seizing that opportunity, tried to kill you with his own hand. At that instant I stabbed him in the back. That is true, too. . . . But I must say this. My motive was different, but I, too, was trying to kill you.

KING: Yes?

QUEEN MOTHER: In the end I had come to think that in order to resurrect you by giving birth to you once again, I would have to kill you while you were beautiful. *(She cries.)* Please understand me. It may be that I was already deranged by then. My mind was in chaos, and I couldn't think of any other means. A mother's deranged mind can think up anything. Such as smashing the moon in the night sky, such as turning a million elephants into salad. . . . I asked her, the Second Queen, to undertake that role. *(Startled, everyone stares at the Second Queen.)*

When the Prime Minister was trying to violate her and she was desperately struggling, I happened to come along. I threatened to kill her unless she killed you within ten days. I even gave her a drug. Ten days passed, and she tried to flee the country to escape danger. You know what happened then. Your queen has been faithful to you all along.

KING: What about the Prime Minister's words just before he died?

QUEEN MOTHER: It was just like that evil man—it was a terrible lie. Because he couldn't become king, he told you a lie to torment you forever.

KING: Why didn't you tell me this?

QUEEN MOTHER: That's the thing, my child. For this past year I've been thinking all by myself. Alone day and night, I've been fighting with a mind threatened with madness. Early on I decided to move to the kingdom of Southern Song to live, but what worried me was whether there was anyone who could care for you after I left. I couldn't leave unless I found someone to whom I could entrust your care. So, for a year since then, I have kept my eyes on the Second Queen. For her it must have been an impossible trial. She's been treated by you, King, in an unfriendly fashion for no apparent reason, and she had no means of clearing herself. She simply thought it her good luck to be allowed to stay near you, and she has cared for you behind the scenes, doing her sincere best. Finally I've decided I can leave this country without worrying. There's absolutely no need to worry as long as I entrust you, my child, to her. She's a model of chastity no ordinary mortal can even dream of emulating.

KING: I see. . . . I see. . . . But what about her comb that I came upon and picked up?

BAS-RELIEF CARVER: May I. . . .

YOUNG HEAD BUILDER: Hold it! You're in the Queen Mother's presence.

QUEEN MOTHER: Never mind. You may say whatever you wish. In the past we, too, had a class distinction between high and low; now we have only two kinds of people in Cambodia: healthy ones and lepers.

BAS-RELIEF CARVER: That night I realized I had forgotten a chisel, an important tool for me, and went back to the work site. I saw something terrible had started, and I hid myself behind an Avalokitesvara. The Prime Minister was trying to seduce the Second Queen, you see. . . . Well, you know, he was so persistent, so violent, and the Queen was resisting him for her life. Her combs flew, her garment was messed up. I watched, scared, but I can tell you she maintained her chastity. I saw the whole thing with my own eyes, so this is the truth. For the year since then I didn't see at all why Your Majesty was neglecting her, but when I heard the Queen Mother, I couldn't keep quiet. . . .

KING: I see now.

BAS-RELIEF CARVER: I can tell you more. The Queen Mother is a noble person, too. She appeared with a whip in the middle of the scuffling, soundly whipped the Prime Minister, and saved the Queen.

QUEEN MOTHER: Enough, that's enough.

BAS-RELIEF CARVER: Besides, the Queen Mother did something even more noble. She kissed the wound on the neck of the Prime Minister she had just whipped. She holds her subjects dear with her gentle heart, so a crime must be punished, but a wound must be pitied. I was truly touched to see her go as far as kissing the man. . . .

QUEEN MOTHER: That's enough. You may leave.

BAS-RELIEF CARVER: Yes, lady.

QUEEN MOTHER: So now you must have no more doubts about her, King. Well then, I will entrust you to her care and leave this country. Please do remember me, a mother close to madness, from time to time.

KING: And do forget about me. Stay well forever.

AMBASSADOR: Well now, you may be confident that your mother will remain secure in my care.

AMBASSADOR'S WIFE: Farewell, Your Majesty, farewell, Queen.

SECOND QUEEN: May you all stay well.

QUEEN MOTHER: Farewell.

(Music strikes up again, and all in the procession leave along the hanamichi. A pause.)

KING: *(After meditating a long while)* Come here, my queen.

SECOND QUEEN: Yes, milord.

KING: I hope you will continue to take care of me. I've learned we still have one sincere heart remaining with us.

SECOND QUEEN: *(In tears)* Milord, I'm so glad.

(Pause.)

KING: Now, Head Builder. Let's wipe away the sorrow of parting and turn this day into an auspicious one. Bring the girl you love at once.

HEAD BUILDER: Sire. . . . *(He hesitates.)*

KING: Don't tarry. Bring her here at once.

HEAD BUILDER: Yes, sir! Khnŭm!

(He calls out to stage right.)

YOUNG WOMAN: Keo-Fa! Am I allowed there?

HEAD BUILDER: Our king wants you to come here.

(The two of them kneel in front of the King.)

KING: Welcome, beautiful girl. The man who is to be your husband pledged not to marry the woman he loves the most until the Bayon was completed. It was a manly thing to do. I myself congratulated him on his pledge. . . . But with the completion scheduled in a year, the time is ripe. I, your King, command you to break that pledge. Right now, on this spot, before my eyes, conduct your wedding ceremony.

YOUNG WOMAN: Keo-Fa! *(She hugs the Head Builder.)*

HEAD BUILDER: What are you doing! Our King is with us!

KING: What do you mean, "What are you doing!"? You must now make an eternal vow.

HEAD BUILDER: *(Deeply moved)* Your Majesty!

KING: *(To the craftsmen)* You'll be their guests, too. Also, bring right away the Exorcist and the substitute father you trust the most. I will present the bride and the bridegroom with wedding costumes. *(To the maids)*

Come, help them change their clothes. Dress the bridegroom in a gold-hemmed robe with a red closed collar. Put on the bride a wig and, on top of it, a tiara made of beetle wings. Let us skip the ceremonies of the first and second days. Begin the ceremony with that of the third day when the bride visits her bridegroom in his house. Follow the custom in every detail. . . . And my Queen, come here. Let's watch together the joy of a young, lusty man and wife. The purest joy in this world is watching the joy of others. Is it not?

(In the next scene, the wedding ceremony of the third day is performed following Cambodian tradition. A description of the ceremony may be found in the three-volume book on Cambodian folk beliefs and rituals by G. Poree and E. Maspero, Etude sur les rites agraires des cambodgiens *[Paris and the Hague, 1962–69]. What follows is a summary of the moves and gestures to be made, as well as props used.)*

The groom sits on the straw mattress at the center of the room. With palms up, he bows three times toward the participants.

A small mattress bed is placed in front of the groom's seat. As soon as he is seated, he puts his arms on it.

Another mattress bed, this one the bride's seat, is placed at front center.

There are three trays prepared in advance: one holds a ball of cotton thread; one, betel palm flowers and a knife; and one is empty, as it is meant to receive gifts of money from the guests.

The musicians begin to play. The music concerns Lady Nekua, Nagi's first daughter. The male dancer starts his part. First, he kneels. Someone places a sword in front of him, and two metal bowls with lids—one to his left, the other to his right. The dancer picks up the lids and makes a motion as if to strike them; actually, he does not. He then rises to his feet and sings. He picks up the sword and dances, brandishing the sword and singing. At the end of his dance he approaches the bride's room and opens the curtain.

The bride comes out accompanied by several women. Dressed as described by the King, she takes her seat wordlessly. The bride and the groom are seated face to face and remain looking at each other: knees bent, upper bodies leaning forward, hands held together, elbows placed on the mattress bed. (When the bride is a clever woman who is likely to dominate the household, her head will be held higher than that of the groom's.)

The music played now refers to the "entwined snake-god." The participants surround the bride and the groom, forming a circle. The exorcist hands the ball of cotton thread to the substitute father, who, in turn, hands it to the participants, but holding onto the end of the thread. The ball is passed around among the participants until the thread circles the newlyweds.

The exorcist then gives three candles to the substitute father. These are put on the tips of the petals of the metal bowl shaped like a lotus flower. The bowl is then moved on the thread surrounding the couple as each participant, upon receiving it, waves the candle flames toward the newlyweds.

This done, the couple rise to their feet and hold out their wrists toward the exorcist. The exorcist, intoning congratulatory words, ties two cotton bracelets around the wrists of the bride and the groom. He takes betel palm flowers from the tray and sprinkles them on the couple. The music heightens.

(Suddenly a young soldier bursts in. He is wounded and bloodied.)

SOLDIER: *(Panting)* Sir! All your soldiers have deserted! I resisted, and see what happened! If it goes on like this, your country will perish!

KING: Don't worry. We don't need a single soldier. Avalokitesvara will protect this country with his compassion.

SOLDIER: Long live the King! *(He dies.)*

KING: *(He clasps his hands and prays.)* You'll be enshrined in the Bayon as one of the glorious war dead. Now, carry on. Carry on the happy ceremony. Don't be cowed by anything. Fill the world with joy and celebration! *(The ceremony continues.)*

The participants congratulate the newlyweds as they untie the bracelets and put them on their arms and sprinkle betel palm flowers on them. They also put gifts of money in the empty tray.

The music continues to become louder at a faster tempo. The dancer deftly rolls up with his feet the mat on which the couple have been sitting, puts it on his shoulder, and calls out, "Buy this mat and you'll be a rich person. Will anyone buy it?" The groom buys it.

The newlyweds finally retire to an inner room. As they do, the groom holds one end of the shawl of his wife who precedes him—in a manner reminiscent of the way Cambodia's first King did as he followed the snake-princess into her bedchamber.

Light dims to darkness.

SCENE 2

A year after the preceding scene. Daytime.

The same terrace, but the positions of things appear reversed, with the suggestion that the Bayon is upstage. However, for now the view of it is closed off with a curtain.

At one end of the stage is placed the same palanquin as that in the previous scene, though this time its back faces the audience. Of course who is in the palanquin cannot be seen. The Second Queen stands next to it.

SECOND QUEEN: It's been another year. The Bayon has finally been completed. What a wonderful temple. There's no temple in the world so beautiful, so unique.

KING'S VOICE: *(A voice comes out of the palanquin, hoarse, very feeble)* But I die. I'm dying.

SECOND QUEEN: Please keep your spirits up. I am with you. I care for you. How can I possibly allow my King to die?

KING'S VOICE: I know—I'm dying.

SECOND QUEEN: *(Touching her eyelids to restrain tears)* No, milord, such weak-heartedness will merely make your illness even worse. After all, you have lived long enough to see the completion of the Bayon. In the face of that strong willpower, the illness will defeat itself. Now that the temple has been finished, Avalokitesvara's compassion will increase its light, and the illness will fall away, one layer after another, day by day. I have been rewarded for my care.

KING'S VOICE: No, I am dying. I knew all along that the day of the Bayon's completion would be the day of my death. . . . My Queen, what saddens me is that my eyes cannot see the completed temple—that my eyes, blinded half a year ago, cannot see the temple in its finished splendor. . . . There is only darkness in front of me. There's no color, no shape. Death, when it meets me, will not feel it's meeting me for the first time, because it is merely a darkness continuing from this world. . . . I beg you, my Queen. I'd like to borrow your eyes. Please paint with your words every detail of the great cathedral of the Bayon as if I were looking at it with my own eyes—please detail it as if I were looking at it myself.

SECOND QUEEN: Yes, my lord. Our King will now inspect the Bayon. He will inspect a temple to which there is nothing remotely comparable in the rest of the world, a Bayon that people will talk about, along with the illustrious name of Jayavarman, for generations, far into the future.

(Music starts. Calls of tropical birds. The curtain upstage opens.)

(The Bayon in its splendor rises.)

SECOND QUEEN: Behold! The faces of Avalokitesvara rising in great numbers, etched in subtle shades by the glorious sun, one upon another like clustered flowers, they show their exquisite smiles, casting the light of compassion, each in its own direction. Each of the fifty towers has one hundred seventy-two large faces of Avalokitesvara, with a columnar tower in their midst soaring into the sky to show to the world the greatness of this temple. Each Avalokitesvara has on his pure forehead a small crown in bas-relief, and carved into each crown is a line of Amitabhas. Attached to each tower is a steep stairway, like an erect comb, which sometimes you can see, sometimes not, as it disappears behind Avalokitesvara's cheek. You see a green lizard dozing on a stairway, another on the smiling lip of Avalokitesvara. The temple as a whole is like kindling made of stone, stacked up to be lit by the fierce midday sun; in its dizzying complexity it has a single principle, every part so made as to introduce fire and air. Yes, indeed. This mysterious complex form is most skillfully constructed to ignite a fiery faith, which, once ignited, can never be extinguished. A parrot is perched on the crown of an Avalokitesvara, and a butterfly is wandering in the darkness of the entrance to a colonnade. Since this temple was made, the landscape has changed in every way. This unworldly mass of delicately carved stones has changed the sky into the Sky over the Pure Land, the forest into the Forest of the Pure Land. You cannot believe that this temple has been made by human hands. Like a cluster of white corals of joy left when the tidal wave of great sufferings has receded, it constantly evokes in people's minds the sound of waves that are the Buddha's pledge of salvation.

KING'S VOICE: Yes, exactly as you say. I can hear that sound of waves in my ears. Perhaps now only the two of us listen to it. . . . Isn't everyone gone?

SECOND QUEEN: Yes.

KING'S VOICE: All my soldiers, all my dauntless elephant units.

SECOND QUEEN: Yes.

KING'S VOICE: All the multitude of people, all the liveliness and noise of the market every morning.

SECOND QUEEN: Yes. The market ground has only a swirl of faint dust now.

KING'S VOICE: All those numberless attendants and maids.

SECOND QUEEN: Yes. There's no one but me. The royal bedchamber in the palace has become a playground for monkeys.

KING'S VOICE: I let that healthy, faithful Head Builder go, too.

SECOND QUEEN: Carrying many a gift from you, the young couple set out on a happy journey, filled with joy and satisfaction that his pledge to you to complete the Bayon had finally been kept.

KING'S VOICE: That's good. And all the people who worked on the building . . .

SECOND QUEEN: All the prisoners of war were freed and went back to their own countries.

KING'S VOICE: *(Moans)* Ah . . .

SECOND QUEEN: Does it hurt, my lord?

KING'S VOICE: The suffering will be gone in a moment. I have a request to make.

SECOND QUEEN: Please say it; it will be done.

KING'S VOICE: I must ask you to carry out this request.

SECOND QUEEN: I do not think I have ever gone against any of your wishes.

KING'S VOICE: Listen. I'd like to die alone. I know your profound feelings; I know your immeasurable gentleness. But please let me die alone. Please leave this place at once.

SECOND QUEEN: What are you saying? I can't . . .

KING'S VOICE: This is a King's request. Your husband's order. Leave this place now.

SECOND QUEEN: How can I abandon you?

KING'S VOICE: Be understanding. I'd like to face the Bayon, I'd like to die face to face with the Bayon. Leave me alone. That is the last act of love you can perform for me.

SECOND QUEEN: *(Crying)* I cannot do that. I can't.

KING'S VOICE: Hurry! Death has pressed close now. I can clearly hear death's galloping hoofs. Go. Hurry! If you don't, everything you've done for me will be wasted; my anger just before death would follow you. Wouldn't you mind that?

SECOND QUEEN: King . . .

KING'S VOICE: Go, now.

SECOND QUEEN: Yes. . . .

(Crying, she leaves. Pause. Bird calls.)

KING'S VOICE: *(Painfully)* Bayon. . . . My Bayon. . . . My . . .

(The Bayon begins to turn. Its back side also has a great array of statues of Avalokitesvara. Just as the turning stops, the King, leaning against the top of the Bayon, suddenly comes into view. Wearing nothing but a golden loincloth, his nude Body has a glittering beauty brimming with youthfulness, freshness. It is the Body of the King, as opposed to the feeble voice coming out of the palanquin, which is his Soul.)

BODY: King. Dying King. Can you see me?

SOUL: Who's that? Calling down to me? That youthful, vibrant voice calling to me from the top of the temple—I certainly have heard it before. Who are you? Calling to me like this?

BODY: It's me. Can't you tell? Can't you see me?

SOUL: How can I see you? My eyes are blinded.

BODY: Both eyes? But how can a soul need eyes? Isn't it a soul's pride that it can see without eyes?

SOUL: Such unsympathetic words. Who are you?

BODY: King Jayavarman.

SOUL: Don't be silly. That's my name.

BODY: We share the same name. King, I am your Body.

SOUL: What am I, then?

BODY: You're my Soul. The Soul that decided to build this Bayon. You're just that. What fades away in the palanquin is not the King's Body.

SOUL: My Body has rotted away, faded away. What's proudly giving forth such a youthful, pleasant voice high in the blue sky is no longer my Body.

BODY: Nonsense. Your Body has not once been ill, wounded, or shapeless. Your Body is just like this—brimming with youthful brilliance, powerful, and as eternal as a statue molded out of gold. The repugnant disease was nothing but the Soul's fantasy. The victorious King, the youthful warrior—how can this Body of his be affected by a disease?

SOUL: But what could the Body do? Could it make anything eternal? What planned the Bayon, what built the Bayon, what placed on this earth something that will retain its name for countless generations and will continue to make beholders' minds tremble in wonderment a thousand years from now; what created this beauty, this solemn splendor, is not stone. The stones are mere material. What created this is the Soul.

BODY: *(He laughs loudly, cheerfully)* And that very Soul can no longer see the Bayon. Because the Soul counted on the Body's eyes.

SOUL: I don't mind that I can't see it. The completed Bayon is already shining in the Soul.

BODY: Shining in the Soul? It's no more than candlelight in the dark, about to be blown out. Just think. If all you need is to have it shine in the Soul, what was the use of spending so much time, employing so much manpower, simply to make these stupendous lumps of stone?

SOUL: No, the Soul always yearns for some form.

BODY: That's because you don't have any form. And a form is always modeled on a beautiful Body like mine. Did you model this temple on a leper's Body?

SOUL: Don't be silly. A leper's Body is nothing.

BODY: Nothing? You suffered so much because of it.

SOUL: Nothing. The Soul is everything.

BODY: What has crumbled, what is shapeless, what has become blind. . . . What do you think *that* is? It's the way the Soul is. You weren't afflicted with leprosy. Your being itself was leprosy. Soul, you were a born leper.

SOUL: Clarity and sharpness, the ability to see to the end of this world, to the bottom of this world—that was the power that built the Bayon. The

Body doesn't have that power. You're merely a slave imprisoned in the cage called the Body.

BODY: Are you trying to say you're freer than I? Are you trying to say you are free because you can't run, can't jump, can't sing, can't laugh, can't fight?

SOUL: I run through time, a thousand years. You merely run through space.

BODY: Space has light. Flowers bloom; honeybees buzz. One beautiful summer afternoon is eternal. In comparison, what you call time is a wet, dark underground path.

SOUL: Oh, Bayon, Bayon, my memento, my love. . . .

BODY: Why leave it for the future? Why turn it into a memento? The Bayon is the present. The present that always shines and glitters. Did you say "love"? Have you ever been beautiful enough to be loved, even just once?

SOUL: I'm dying. . . . My voice, each word I utter is a painful burden. Oh, my Bayon. . . .

BODY: Go ahead and die. Fade away. The fresh morning breath, the morning wind you inhale into your capacious lungs—thus begins the day for the Body. Then the Body bathes, fights, runs, loves, gets drunk on every one of the best wines of the world, competes to see which form is more beautiful, compliments, and so on—until it lies down with another Body to sleep at the end of the day. The Body, in short, runs through each and every day with its sail filled with the fragrant winds of the sea. Planning something—that was your disease. Making something—that was your disease. My chest, like a ship's bow, glistens in the sun, as I plow the water with youth's ruthless oars. I reach nowhere. I aim nowhere. I simply keep beating my five-colored wings like a hummingbird staying in midair. Not following my example—that was your disease.

SOUL: Bayon. . . . My . . . my Bayon.

BODY: The Soul perishes—like a kingdom.

SOUL: What perishes is you—the Body. . . . The Soul . . . is deathless.

BODY: You die.

SOUL: . . . .Bayon.

BODY: You die.

SOUL: Oh . . . B-a-y-o-n.

BODY: What happened? . . . .What happened? . . . .No response. He must have died.

(The bird calls suddenly become noisy.)

BODY: *(He raises his hand proudly.)* Look. The Soul has died. Dazzling blue sky, betel palms, birds with beautiful wings, and Bayon protected by these! I rule this country again. Youth never perishes, the Body is deathless. . . . I've won. Because I am the Bayon.

CURTAIN

THE FLOWER OF EVIL: KABUKI

Mishima Talks at the National Theatre

In 1970 the Kokuritsu Gekijō (National Theatre), which the government established in 1966 to promote traditional performing arts, started a kabuki trainee program. *Aku no Hana—Kabuki* (The flower of evil: Kabuki) is a transcript of the speech Mishima gave to the first group of ten trainees on July 3 of that year. Mishima, who had by then written four one-act kabuki plays and the full-length kabuki *A Wonder Tale: The Moonbow* (this last he also directed), was on the theater's board of directors. For some reason, the transcript of the speech was not published until January 1988 when it was printed in the monthly *Shinchō* (New tides).

Among the people Mishima mentioned in his talk was Faubion Bowers (1917–99), Gen. Douglas MacArthur's aide-de-camp and personal interpreter when the Occupation began. After working for the Supreme Commander for the Allied Powers for two years, he resigned his military commission to take on the civilian post of theater censor in order to ease the censorship; he worked to restore to the stage such kabuki plays as *Chūshingura* and *Kanjinchō,* which the Occupation had banned as "feudalistic." He had fallen in love with kabuki during his one-year stay in Japan just before the Pacific War.

Later, whenever kabuki came to the United States, Bowers served as simultaneous interpreter and narrator. For his work he was called "the savior of kabuki" and Matsumoto Kōshirō VII presented him with the name Hōbu, Phoenix Dance. In 1985 he was decorated by the Japanese government with the Order of the Sacred Treasure. Okamoto Shirō's book, *The Man Who Saved Kabuki* (University of Hawaii Press, 2001), is a biography of Bowers. A Julliard graduate who studied to be a pianist, Bowers was also a devoted student of the Russian mystic composer Aleksandr Scriabin (1872–1915) and published *Scriabin: A Biography* (2d ed., Dover, 1996).

Mishima spoke without notes and with expressive gestures; he enchanted his audience. The transcript, as is normally the case in a situation like this in Japan, is faithful to the original speech and conveys, I think, Mishima's remarkable memory and narrative skill, though whether I have managed to do the same in translation is in question. Because this is a prelude to *A Wonder Tale: The Moonbow*, which has many footnotes, I have closely annotated the talk.

THE FLOWER OF EVIL: KABUKI

I did not come here today with the intention of giving anything like a lecture. How I came to be introduced to kabuki, how I came to like it—that's the sort of thing I'd like to talk about.

As I look at you, I see you are all very young. If you hear how, in the days when I was young, I came close to kabuki, I thought you might learn, though indirectly, what I got from kabuki.

When I was a child, my parents and grandfather and grandmother were all strange people. Kabuki is no good for a child's education, don't see it, they said. It has obscene things in it, so don't see it. Movies are all right. Movies are healthy, so go right ahead and see them. I didn't know what was healthy about them, but thanks to all that, after I was a second or third grader, I saw most of the Hollywood movies; a university student living with my family[1] would take me. The Hollywood movies weren't as sensual as they are today, but they had kissing scenes, and those were far more direct than the love-making scenes of kabuki.

Still, partly because of the worship of the West in those days, they felt, I think, that whatever the Westerners did was all right. But kabuki was no good.

My grandmother loved kabuki and frequently took my mother to it. So when they returned, I would look at the program and feel envious. Now, at this National Theatre, they sell the programs at a high price, but in the old days they gave them to you free. Each had a woodblock print of a scene, with an outline of the play and a cast, that's all.

Some of the older programs had a colored woodblock print on the cover. If you look at them now, they seem to have museum value. As I looked at such things, I began to have longings for kabuki as something that might be fascinating, though antiquated, with odd things about it.

When I was thirteen years old, they must have decided, Well now, now he's in junior high school, it should be all right to show him kabuki. So my grand-

---

1. *Shosei:* See *The Rokumeikan,* act 2, n. 2.

mother took me, for the first time. And it turned out to be *Kanadehon Chūshin-gura.*[2] Today you think of a large cast for this play, but in those days *Chūshin-gura* was called a "noncast play," and its casting was said to be extremely poor. I saw it, I think, at the Kabuki-za, in 1938, when Uzaemon XV played Yura-nosuke and played Kampei. Also Nizaemon XII. Nizaemon is the actor who was resented and murdered right after the war, when food conditions were ter-rible indeed, for not feeding his disciples. And Ōtani Tomoemon VI played Moronao. He is the father of today's Jakuenmon.

So it was a play with very few actors. Nevertheless, when I think of it now, I feel as if there has never been such a great kabuki. The Lady Kaoyo played by Nizaemon, the Moronao by Tomoemon, the Kampei by Uzaemon—they were all great. The thing is, in those days the grouping of Uzaemon, Nizae-mon, and Tomoemon wasn't considered a fancy cast.

I watched it from a corner near the hanamichi of the Kabuki-za, so I saw the hanamichi right in front of me. At the time I was a first-year student in jun-ior high school, and I was all excited because I had a lunch box, and there were many other kinds of food to eat. In time the play began, and a mysterious per-son emerged on the hanamichi. It was Lady Kaoyo. Lady Kaoyo comes out barefoot, that's the rule; she isn't supposed to wear *tabi* socks. For some reason she must come out barefoot; it's always been that way. So the barefoot Lady Kaoyo passed right before my eyes. And the feet were all wrinkled. And you couldn't even imagine that she was the beauty who would touch off the great event called *Chūshingura.* Besides, she suddenly voiced an utterance, and I was shocked. How could a man utter such a voice; I was simply amazed as I

2. Originally a jōruri composed by Namiki Senryū (1695–1751), Takeda Izumo (1691–1756), and Miyoshi Shōraku (1696–1772), it was first performed as kabuki in 1748. It is based on the vendetta carried out in 1703 by forty-seven samurai. In *Seiyūki* (Travels to the West), the physician traveler Tachibana Nankei (1753–1805) reports the immense popularity of *Chūshingura* in Ryūkyū (today's Okinawa) toward the end of the eighteenth century: "In their country they do plays, except that they only learn about the play of *Chūshingura* in Satsuma [today's Kagoshima] and stage it in their home country, I'm told. Large numbers of viewers crowd together, and everyone is moved to tears as they watch it. All other plays appear to puzzle them; they aren't moved by them, and attract no view-ers, I'm told." In his preface to *Chūshingura: Studies in Kabuki and the Puppet Theater,* ed. James. R. Brandon (University of Hawaii Press, 1982), Donald Keene tells us that the play "was first adapted into English by John Masefield, as *The Faithful,* in 1915, and the story is variously known in English as *The Forty-Seven Ronin, The Loyal League, The Treasury of Loyal Retainers,* and, in this book, *The Forty-Seven Samurai.*" "The Treasury of Loyal Retainers" is the title of Keene's own translation in his *Chūshingura* (Columbia University Press, 1971). The original jōruri version is included in *Jōruri Shū, Jō,* in Iwanami Shoten's classics series known as Nihon Koten Bungaku Taikei (NKBT), vol. 51.

watched. And I think, though I was still a young boy, I felt that kabuki had an indescribably mysterious flavor. Like the dried fish of Kusaya, it has a strong smell but has a strangely delicious taste.

The *Chūshingura* that I saw must have lasted very late into the evening, until about ten-thirty. Then I went home. For a boy it was something to be very proud of to see a play until so late at night. I felt I had finally seen what I had wanted to see since childhood.

Now I became a kabuki-maniac. And my family decided, Well, we allowed him to see it once, so he should be able to see it as often as he wants. I begged my mother to the best of my ability and began to see kabuki regularly. This, I think, lasted until after the war, to 1949 or 1950. During those ten years I saw kabuki with great dedication, with complete absorption.

How absorbed was I? Those were the days when the war was becoming more and more terrible, and good books stopped coming out. The military control had become severe, and books became scarce. In this period I often went to secondhand book dealers and read jōruri. Jōruri are somewhat difficult for today's young people to read, but in those days, in part because there wasn't much else to read, I began to read them, and once I did, they were all very interesting. I read all Chikamatsu Monzaemon,[3] then I read Takeda Izumo, and then I read Chikamatsu Hanji.[4] Then, though I did not read all the works, I read the major works of principal authors, such as *Shinrei Yaguchi Watashi* in the case of Hiraga Gennai,[5] and this or that when it comes to Ki no Kaion,[6] and so on. In the end I read most of jōruri.

Once you read jōruri, you know the text when you see kabuki, so you begin to wonder how this or that scene is going to be done. Once I became a kabuki-maniac, I took a notebook to the theater, fascinated as I was to see how an actor made a move at this or that point. In those days Miyake Shūtarō[7] used

3. The playwright (1653–1724) whom W. G. Aston, surveying Japanese literature toward the end of the nineteenth century, called "unquestionably the most prominent figure in the history of Japanese drama." W. G. Aston, *A History of Japanese Literature* (Tuttle, 1972), p. 275. The book was first published in 1899.

4. Playwright (1725–83).

5. Gennai (1728–79), whose pen name Fūraisanjin means "Windy Wanderer," was a man of many talents. He pursued botany, zoology, mineralogy, and studies in Dutch and classical Japanese literature and was the first Japanese to experiment with electricity—yes, he was a contemporary of Benjamin Franklin—and to construct a thermometer. As a man of letters, Gennai wrote some jōruri plays that used the Edo, rather than the standard Osaka, dialect, and as a result proved very popular in Edo. *Shinrei Yaguchi Watashi* was one of them.

6. Poet and dramatist (1663–1742). Chikamatsu Monzaemon, his rival, is thought to be indebted to him in many of his plays.

7. A theater critic (1892–1967) devoted to jōruri and kabuki, he was known for his lucid style and high integrity.

to write a great deal about such things, which I read, and I began to understand that kabuki is a matter of beauty *in a flash,* that a movement in the flash of a second determines all.

They talk about inheriting *kata,*[8] but those kata are not like in gymnastics, raising your right hand, raising your left hand this way. The time it takes for a hand to move to this point here, I don't know, it may be one-tenth of a second or something, but in that duration it can be very beautiful. In the time taken for the hand to move to this point, there can be a great variety, depending on the actor. I began to understand such things well.

I don't know if you have seen a play called *Sanemori Monogatari (Gempei Nunobiki no Taki),*[9] but Uzaemon XV played it often and it was said to be his masterpiece. Its "show-off scenes"[10] have of course to do with the story about Sanemori, but the story line is that the Heike official who comes to investigate a Genji warrior fugitive is in fact sympathetic to the Genji side and saves him.[11] He hears that a child is born, and because the child is a Genji descendent, he must capture him at any cost, and that's how he comes to look into the matter. Now people on the warrior's side decide to lie, wrap a man's arm in swaddling cloth, and show it to the inspecting official. And they bring out the bundle of swaddling cloth and put it here, whereupon there's this *chobo,*[12] "This is most shocking!"

There, Seno'o and Sanemori stand side by side—I can't imitate them, but Seno'o looks simply surprised. Sanemori is startled at first, but he senses there must be some kind of scheme, so after the initial surprise, he lifts his leg, slaps it, sticks his hand into the sleeve, and that's all he does. He turns away from Seno'o and, in a manner she will not notice, gives a light slap on his knee, and that's all he does. Those simple movements possess something indescribable, something that makes you feel so good.

Performance on the *chobo*—Hazaemon had done it over and over again, so he could do it very refreshingly, deliver his lines refreshingly. In such move-

8. For a discussion of *kata,* see "A Small Scar on the Left Knee" in "Backstage Essays."

9. A jōruri by Namiki Senryū and Miyoshi Shōraku (1696–1772)—although it is said to have been first produced as kabuki in 1833, sixteen years before it was produced in a puppet theater. The story traces its origins to "Sanemori," vol. 7, of the *Heike Monogatari* (The tale of the Heike), which describes the final battle and death of Saitō (Minamoto no) Sanemori (1111–83). The jōruri writers turned the simple, affecting story about an old warrior's final show of valor and the enemy commander's compassion into a typically convoluted story line. The jōruri is included in *Jōruri Shū, Ge,* NKBT, vol. 52.

10. *Miseba.*

11. *Heike* is a Sinified reading of two characters meaning "Taira house" and *Genji* that of "Minamoto clan." The Taira and Minamoto were rival military houses that fought a five-year civil war, from 1180 to 1185, in which the Minamoto prevailed.

12. A jōruri narrator's interjection to explain a character's movement or emotional reaction.

ments, the actors in the Otowaya line[13] were splendid indeed. I've seen many performers do Sanemori since then, but I have not seen a movement as beautiful as the one of Sanemori's on that *chobo.*

I gradually came to realize that in kabuki the scripts are of course important and so are the psychological descriptions, but that kabuki is not kabuki unless it can intoxicate you instantly.

On the whole, college students intellectualize everything. They want to think that kabuki is the theater of the feudal period. It depicts the tragedies of personalities, and these people must commit double suicide to resist the terrible morality of the feudal age. Death was the only way of resistance. When you are analyzing kabuki plays as literature, that should be all right, there ought to be such an approach. But kabuki as a performance art doesn't exist in any such analysis. It doesn't follow the method of Western theater, which tries to make the audience understand, move them intellectually, through the clashes of words or the contents of the words. Everything is done through the senses.

For example, *Kanjinchō*[14] has scenes where two characters jostle, pushing and pulling. Also, in the *yamabushi* dialogue,[15] the scene looks like a debating class. But no one is listening to what is being said in the dialogue. *"Kashira ni itadaku tokin ya ikani"* (What about crowning your head with a *tokin*[16]?)—that's one of the lines, but today no one cares what covers the head of a *yamabushi*. Benkei hurriedly responds to this by using a plethora of mystifying Buddhist terms. And Togashi's queries grow ever more urgent. When Benkei says, *"Ideiru iki wa a'un*

---

13. The line of kabuki actors that started with the first generation Onoe Kikugorō (1717–83).

14. The most popular and famous kabuki play, written by Namiki Gohei III (1790–1885), that is said to have spawned the kabuki repertoire of "eighteen classics." Directly based on the nō play *Ataka,* which is attributed to Kanze Nobumitsu (1435–1519), it describes the legendary warrior monk Benkei (d. 1189) beating up his master Minamoto no Yoshitsune (1159–89) as a ploy to escape a crisis. The famous actor Ichikawa Danjūrō IX (1838–1903)—mentioned later in this talk—played the role of Benkei sparingly, only nineteen times in his lifetime, but Matsumoto Kōshirō VII (1870–1949) played it eighteen hundred times. The play is included in *Kabuki Jūhachi-ban Shū,* NKBT, vol. 98. Kurosawa Akira's *Tora no O o Fumu* (Stepping on a tiger's tail) is a movie version of the story.

15. *Yamabushi,* "mountain sleeper," is someone who seeks Buddhist enlightenment through rough training, which includes living in the mountains without proper shelter. *Ataka* and therefore *Kanjinchō* are based on the contemporary rumor that Yoshitsune and his loyal vassals escaped the network of police set up by his brother Yoritomo (1147–99) by disguising themselves as *yamabushi*. See Hiroaki Sato, *Legends of the Samurai* (Overlook, 1995), p. 153. The group's passage blocked by Togashi Saemon, the chief of the Ataka Barrier, Benkei offers to hold a service before execution in which he explains what a *yamabushi* is; he then engages in questions and answers with Togashi on what he does.

16. A round black cloth cap worn by a yamabushi. This is one of the questions Togashi asks in an effort to expose Benkei's true identity.

no niji" (The breath that comes out and goes in is *a* and *un*[17]), he strikes a grand dramatic pose,[18] very proud as he is of his knowledge. The dialogue itself does not appeal to today's audiences, and it is doubtful whether people in the old days understood it. You cannot understand those questions and answers unless you happen to know Shugendō,[19] and unless you study Buddhism in depth, you can't hope to understand all the terms that appear there. But the audience is delighted because the two people for some reason clash in deadly earnest; they are clashing not merely through words but through kata, not through their personalities, but through kata, and that's what moves everyone.

And each of those kata is marvelously polished. Even a quarrel isn't a quarrel that's ugly to see. If it's a quarrel with someone saying, "You, son-of-a-bitch," you can show it anywhere.[20] Everything has a set kata, whether you are lifting your arm or hitting somebody.

Without appealing to that sensory charm, kabuki won't be able to convey anything to us. You can't expect anyone to understand kabuki without sensual fascination. Through that narrow path of sensory charm, kabuki slides out in front of you. If you close that path, none of what lies behind it will come out.

Today, there's a tendency to overwhelm kabuki with analysis and pettifogging speculation, thereby closing the mouth from which that charm spurts out. That's why there are people who say they can't understand kabuki no matter how often they see it.

Partly, this is the actors' fault. Kabuki has its own techniques. It requires basic training in Japanese-style dance and basic training in *gidayū*.[21] There are a variety of techniques—you must learn the kinds of movement you can make by lowering your hips, the kinds of voice you can make by vocalizing from your belly—but there are also things you can't do anything about with techniques alone. For example, there's aging, experience. In no other theater can you show your real worth only by growing old. The beauty of a young actor is of course important, but at the same time an actor who's seventy years old can play the role of an eighteen-year-old without looking funny. Shirai

---

17. In the original, this statement is divided between Togashi and Benkei. A'un ("*a* and *un*") is the Buddhist equivalent of alpha and omega.

18. Called *mie*—"a strong physical pose [which] is unique to kabuki theater. There are hundreds of different *mie,* but typically the actor plants his feet in a firm position, sets his torso, cocks his arms outward, rotates the head, and freezes motionless for several seconds." James R. Brandon, *Chūshingura: Studies in Kabuki and the Puppet Theater* (University of Hawaii Press, 1982), p. 132.

19. A school of Buddhism that seeks enlightenment through rough training. It was started by En no Ozuno, whose dates are uncertain but who is known to have been exiled to Izu from 699 to 701. The yamabushi is a typical follower of this school.

20. The original of this sentence isn't clear in meaning.

21. Jōruri. So called because Takemoto Gidayū (1651–1714) developed and perfected it.

Gompachi, in *Ukiyo-gara Hiyoku no Inazuma,*[22] is supposed to be seventeen or eighteen, but we have always been impressed to see it played by a man who is sixty or seventy years old. The role of this young gay man, Gompachi, is not interesting in itself. What is interesting are the techniques that actors of the past brought into the delivery of each line. For example, the famous line *"Kiji mo nakazuba utaremaini, yakunai sesshō o itashiyashita"* (A pheasant may not be shot if it doesn't cry; I ended up committing a senseless murder),[23] contains all the phrasing Iwai Hanshirō V[24] devised for it. The voice prolonging the pronunciation of *ki* of *kiji* [pheasant] must have the high-pitched call of a pheasant. It is a phrasing for an *oyama,*[25] and it is very sinuous. It goes, *na, ka, zu, ba, utaremaini, yakunai sesshō o itaashashita.* All the movements are entwined with the hands. That's the sort of thing that's fun about Gompachi.

Into such phrasings go each actor's ideas, which are constantly being polished. This means that each phrasing—for example, the phrasings in the Kichiemon line tended to be very prolonged—always aims not so much at literary meaning as at dramatic effect.

Nakamura Kichiemon of the previous generation (I) was an outstanding master of delivery. Just listening to his words would enchant you. But he did not simply deliver his lines; he delivered them always for stage effect. I remember the play *Kago-tsurube Sato no Eizame,*[26] in which he played (Sano) Jirōzaemon.[27] After the scene of "the first encounter"[28] is over, Jirōzaemon, a hick, a *pock-marked* merchant, realizes that in all his life he has never seen such a wonderful woman and, umbrella in hand, stands there, watching her walk away on the hanamichi. His servant is behind him, but, he, his mouth agape, keeps watching the end of the hanamichi, as if he'd been robbed of his soul. His *haori* coat starts sliding down, so his servant calls out, "Master, sir." Jirōzaemon says, *"Yado e kaeruwaa."* As you know, the complete line is, *"Yado e kaeru wa iya ni natta"* (I no longer want to go back to my inn). But saying, *"Yado e kaeruwaa,"* he continues to watch the end of the hanamichi, entranced. He's holding an umbrella, you see, and he will drop it, but he doesn't do it for a

---

22. Written by Tsuruya Namboku IV (1755–1829) in 1823. The protagonist of the play, Shirai Gompachi, is a samurai of the Tottori fiefdom toward the end of the seventeenth century; he killed a prostitute by the name of Komurasaki and was executed.

23. *Kiji mo nakazuba utaremaini* has become a proverbial saying.

24. Iwai Hanshirō V (1747–1800) excelled as a female impersonator; as a result, the Iwai line of actors have specialized in female roles.

25. Also, *onnagata:* The actor who plays a woman's role. This came about following the government ban on women's kabuki during the Kan'ei era (1624–44).

26. By Kawatake Shinshichi III (1842–1901).

27. A farmer of the early eighteenth century who, out of sheer jealousy, murdered Yatsuhashi and many other prostitutes of Yoshiwara. Namiki Gohei and Tsuruya Namboku also wrote kabuki plays based on this incident.

28. *Misome;* in this instance, the first love-making between a prostitute and her customer.

long, long time. The audience keeps watching. *"Yado e kaeruwaa"* having been said, the audience is waiting to see what comes next. Then the umbrella drops with a thump. The wooden clappers give the first clap, then comes *"iya ni natta,"* the clappers continue, and the curtain falls. That's kabuki, you see.

In kabuki you act by grasping the audience's attention. If you act simply as you are taught, you won't improve at all in such scenes. Some actors dislike such approaches. They say Kichiemon is vulgar because he's too concerned about his audience. Why not just do, "I don't like to," thump, clap, curtain? But there are a number of acting styles, and you can't really say which is good and which is bad.

While I was watching kabuki the way I was, I came upon Sōjūrō of the former generation (VII). We no longer have a film of him, and if you look at him in photographs, you won't be able to imagine this, but he had a face like one of those exaggerated faces that used to be painted in *nishiki* prints, though his voice wasn't that good. If you saw a face like that on the street today, I guess everybody would be shocked. Now, he, with that kind of face, would play, say, the role of Kyūkichi in *Kamagafuchi Futatsu-domoe.*[29] And just before the curtain fell, he would emerge, after the cloth blind of the palanquin was raised with a flourish, reeling, drunkenly, in his brocaded formal wear with extra-long trousers,[30] and stand quietly there, center stage, and, hands stuck in these parts of the *hakama,*[31] he would give a quick glare in the direction where Goemon had disappeared—that's all, that's all he'd do, but that would be so unforgettable. That would move you so, with a marvelous sense of beauty.

On the whole, kabuki is like that; it has roles in which an actor gains a lot of points just by putting in a brief appearance. Marubashi Chūya,[32] of Horihata *(Keian Taiheiki*[33]*)*—there are a number of plays about Marubashi Chūya—but the role of Matsudaira, governor of Izu,[34] who appears at the end, is one such role.

29. A jōruri by Namiki Senryū. It concerns the great robber Ishikawa Goemon (1557–94), who is reputed to have been boiled to death in a large iron tub after capture, hence the name given to the iron bathtub directly heated, *Goemon-buro.* It was first performed in 1737. The kabuki version was staged in 1756. The revised kabuki version, first staged in 1861, is a pastiche of various plays about the same man.

30. *Naga-kamishimo:* Samurai's formal outfit for visiting the shogunate quarters.

31. Trouserlike wear.

32. A master spearman who joined the revolt against the Tokugawa government led by Yui Shōsetsu (1605–51). The revolt failed; Yui committed suicide; Marubashi was captured and executed.

33. *Keian Taiheiki* is the title of many of the stories, narratives, and plays based on Yui Shōsetsu's revolt.

34. Matsudaira Nobutsuna (1596–1662). Serving the third and fourth Tokugawa shogun, Iemitsu and Ietsuna, as ranking administrator, he handled the Christian uprising known as the Shimabara Rebellion in 1637–8, Yui Shōsetsu's revolt in 1651, and the great fire of Meireki in 1657, which lasted for three days, burned down most of Edo, and killed 100,000 people. Because of his administrative prowess, he was accorded the sobriquet Chie Izu (The wise Izu).

He appears in ordinary formal wear,[35] spreads an umbrella above Chūya, and that's all he does, but that act alone determines his weight, his importance.[36]

The audience, the spectators, of kabuki always said they were bored, the whole thing was dull, things like that, but I gradually discovered that that wasn't it at all. In kabuki, silly things go on and on in front of your eyes, and you may begin to wonder how long will this thing go on, when in an electric flash you see something marvelous. The moment you realize it, it's gone. Then again, dumb, dull things resume and continue. In another ten or fifteen minutes, there's another flash.

Where does this electric flash come from? It is an effect brought about by multiple factors. There's first the actor. You can say it's the accumulation of traditions that lie behind the actor. Then there's something that I say is very internal—what you can only conclude to be a divine act, a marvelous moment of an act, which the actor who has completely thrown himself into his role flashes forth, something no ordinary mortal can accomplish.

When you see kabuki in our new age, in a place like the National Theatre, all the lighting equipment is perfect; all the stage sets are wonderful; all the costumes are brand-new; all the things that would please the audience are fully worked out. Everything, in short, is perfect, mechanically.

Mechanically perfect it may be, but the actors don't look as impressive as they should. This is because as a result of mechanization what used to move the audience so profoundly in the old days—in the midst of imperfect lighting equipment, imperfect stage sets, and costumes that had become soiled—has begun to atrophy.

For example, you may place a spotlight, but you may not be able to create any outstanding beauty, and that's what is mysterious about kabuki. This isn't the case with movies. A beautiful face appears in a close-up, spotlighted—in the movie trade they call it "lighting makeup," and by changing the lighting, you can make a face that isn't that good look beautiful. By good camera work, you can make some moments of an actor very beautiful indeed.

You can't do this on stage. Without internal accumulation, without an accumulation of a long career, you can't make that mysterious moment come out. This isn't something you can work out with logic.

---

35. *Asa-gamishimo:* a light gray garment made of hemp.

36. In *Keian Taiheiki: Marubashi Chūya,* by Kawatake Mokuami (1816–93), this takes place at the end of the first act of the two-act play (short for a kabuki). Happening on a scene where Chūya, feigning drunkenness, is measuring the depth of the moat of Edo Castle, Nobutsuna holds up an umbrella over him. It's raining. The suggestion is that he sees through Chūya's intent to revolt. Such scenes, pregnant with meaning but with no words spoken, abound in Kabuki. The play is included in *Mokuami Meisaku Sen,* vol. 2 (Sōgen Sha, 1952).

As I saw more and more kabuki, I began to feel, I couldn't help feeling, that kabuki was heading toward a shabby, desolate end.

Now, you may think I just talk about the good old days—I say the former Kichiemon was like this; Kikugorō VI was like that; Hazaemon was like this; and so forth. When I say things like that, old men who know things much older make fun of me. You talk about the sixth generation, you talk about Haz-aemon, but that's all nonsense, we saw Danjūrō IX, we saw Kikugorō V, they were far more marvelous, they say. The world we live in today is a world of progressivism, so people say, "These guys only talk about the golden age of the past, these are all nonsensical dreamers." But I think kabuki is something that was always better in the old days. Kabuki can continue its strange life because in every age it was better in the old days.

I'd like you to understand this clearly. Because, you see, you are making a big mistake if you started thinking, "Kabuki makes progress; it was so primitive in the old days; now it's getting better." Unless you have the sense that kabu-ki today is at its worst, it will end with you, you won't be able to carry kabu-ki forward into the future.

What is fortunate about this is that since the old days people have always ar-gued that kabuki is about to die. You can't count how many times the death of kabuki has been talked about since Meiji. People have kept saying, "Kabu-ki is about to die," but in the end a big theater like this has been built. With this kind of building you might think kabuki will never die, but it will die any moment. It is getting ready to die.

Every age had a number of factors that could kill kabuki, as this one does. You are all young, but have decided to enter kabuki. That means you have pledged your loyalty to something that is about to die. You have in front of you all sorts of much newer things. You can work with computers. You can work with videocassettes. In Japan today all sorts of jobs are demanding your attention. Going into something that is bound to die requires a great deal of determination. Kabuki is something of which everybody says it was good in the old days but is no good today.

But you can approach something that used to be good and lose yourself in it—that's what's mysterious about human beings. Kabuki were all written in the past, but you can lose yourself in the ideals of the past or you can find the soul of an actor of the past lodged in yourself without any effort on your part. When that happens, kabuki revives itself, regardless of the age or the period.

Even now I can remember the Tokyo right after the war that was pock-marked with burned-out places. Even Ginza and its neighborhood were all va-cant, with burned buildings standing here and there. Today it's difficult to see Mount Fuji from Tokyo, but in those days you could see it from anywhere.

The Tokyo Theater first opened with kabuki. The Kabuki-za was burned down and no good.

As I recall now, I think it was probably November of the year that the war ended that in the Tokyo Theater Kōshirō of the former generation (VII) and Utaemon of this generation (VI), who was called Shikan in those days, danced in the Michiyuki[37] of Mount Yoshino *(Yoshitsune Sembonzakura).*[38] It was, I thought, the first flowering after the war was over, that a peaceful age had arrived. In the midst of the stage set with cherry blossoms in full bloom, the Tadanobu played by Kōshirō rose up—it was a wonderful Tadanobu. Kōshirō wasn't too skilled an actor, they say, but this Tadanobu was wonderful. And the Lady Shizuka played by Shibagan was beautiful indeed, and when the two of them danced the Michiyuki of Mount Yoshino, I was ecstatic that kabuki had returned.

Toward the end of the war the Kabuki-za was burned down, and so were other theaters, so kabuki was staged at the Shōchiku-za, of Asakusa, and the Hōgaku-za, which was where the Piccadilly Theater stands now. At the Hōgaku-za *Chūshingura* was staged. Jukai of today (III) did a quick change of roles, playing Yoichibê, Kampei, and Sadakurō all by himself in this *Chūshingura*—it was quite a show.

Following this period, a theater was finally built. But the American Occupation Forces began to say certain things in kabuki were feudalistic and were no good. This gave everybody a headache.

For example, they'd say, "A scene with a beheaded head is cruel and is no good," or "Somebody sacrificing herself for somebody else is no good," and so on and so forth. It was during that period that a gentleman named Faubion Bowers firmly stood on our side. He's a good friend of mine. He came to this country as a commander or something of the Occupation Forces. He also became a good friend of Kichiemon, whose art he respected.

Kabuki is by no means simplistic propaganda for feudalism of the kind that military men assume it to be. A beheaded head may look cruel at a glance, but hidden behind it is a deep human sorrow. Things like these must be allowed to be staged gradually. The Occupation Forces may say *Chūshingura* encourages revenge and is therefore no good, but aside from the theme of revenge, this play has all the elements that make up kabuki. Or so Mr. Bowers insisted.

37. "Going along the road": A scene in which a couple, often in love, walk, sometimes dancing.

38. The most famous jōruri related to Minamoto no Yoshitsune, written by Takeda Izumo, Namiki Senryū, and Miyoshi Shōraku. A typically convoluted story.

Some years later *Chūshingura* was staged. Before then *Ichinotani Futaba Gunki*,[39] which is famous for the Kumagae Jin'ya scene[40] and which was banned for quite some time, had been allowed to be staged because of Mr. Bowers's exertions. It was about that time that the entire repertoire of kabuki was revived.

In addition, plays that were banned during the war began to be staged. For example, *Ami-moyō Tōro no Kikukiri*,[41] which was staged in this theater this past June. This was never, ever done during the war. It's so obscene; besides, a lady-in-waiting serving in Edo Castle, who is supposed to be absolutely chaste, is raped by a robber on a riverbank. You can't allow such a play. Eventually, all the plays that you couldn't stage during the war and during the American Occupation began to be allowed. Then things quite blatant began to be allowed in everything, so that the kind of eroticism you see in kabuki came to mean nothing to ordinary people.

I hear that a play called *Oh, Calcutta!* is on in New York now in which a great many people appear totally naked, and in a play called *Che!* there's an on-stage performance of a sexual act, and I'd like to see them one of these days. So far I haven't had the chance.

To suggest a sexual act in kabuki, a man puts his hand in his sleeve, feigning to think, and a woman goes close to him hiding her face with a sleeve—that's all the suggestion there is. In certain cases, the two of them go into a room set off with papered sliding doors.[42] When they reappear—it was Michitose *(Kumo ni Magō Ueno no Hatsuhana)*,[43] wasn't it; no, it wasn't Michitose, but O-Tomi *(Yo wa Nasake Ukina no Yokogushi)*[44]—Baikō of the former generation

---

39. Based on the passage in the *Heike Monogatari* describing Kumagae Jirō Naozane's killing of the teenage enemy commander Taira no Atsumori, the story is typically convoluted. Namiki Senryū died after writing the first three sections; Asada Ittō wrote the rest.

40. *Jin'ya* means "field command post." This is where Yoshitsune inspects what is supposed to be the head of Atsumori brought back by Naozane and finds that it is instead the head of Kojirō, Naozane's son. Naozane, correctly interpreting Yoshitsune's desire to save Atsumori because of his imperial blood, had sacrificed his son. Having killed his son, Naozane reveals his decision to take Buddhist vows. This "head-inspection" scene was too morbid for democracy, one judges, in the eyes of the Occupation Forces. This scene is included in *Bunraku Jōruri Shū*, NKBT, vol. 99.

41. By Kawatake Mokuami.

42. Called *shōji yatai*. Normally constructed on a platform, which itself is made to suggest the floor of a house.

43. By Kawatake Mokuami. The protagonist is Kōchiyama Sōshun who was arrested for extortion and died in jail in 1823. He and the company he kept spawned a number of narratives. Michitose is a courtesan in the play.

44. By Segawa Jokō III (1806–81). Commonly known as *Kirare Yosa*, it entails a daimyo's in-house political entanglements, but the focus is on the love affair between Izuya Yosaburō and a yakuza gambler's mistress O-Tomi.

(VI) came out with his sash tied differently. When the audience saw it, they had a very erotic stimulation, they say.

In kabuki, eroticism is a very big factor. In the old days when people didn't have movies or TVs or striptease shows, they sought the greatest sensual stimulation in kabuki. It may sound odd to you, but the story goes that after the love scene with Hazaemon XV and Baikō, there used to be a great deal of crumpled tissue around the feet of female spectators. It appears *that* was enough to excite them. Also, because the audience was sensitive to such things, you didn't have to show anything so explicitly for the audience to sense the indescribable sensuality in kabuki. Today you don't have to seek sensuality in kabuki; it is flooding everywhere. Does this mean there's less of it in kabuki? Not necessarily.

The first reason I was fascinated by kabuki was, I'm sure, that, even though I didn't understand it as a child, I must have felt there was something terribly erotic in it. This eroticism was made in the feudalistic period, so it is never straightforward. It's hidden in layers and layers of things and appears before your eyes only after going through skillfully twisted pathways.

This eroticism is different from the kind of stripped-down eroticism you see in the rest of the world. It's something mysterious that you can't describe in a word. The sensory attraction of kabuki surely has something like that, and that's why, I think, it attracts people. For example, if an actor appears barefoot, you don't feel anything, but if he gives a glimpse of his foot powdered white at the skirt of his kimono, that would stimulate the audience very much.

There's a play called *Narukami*[45] in which an actor gradually puts his hand into the sleeve of a princess, holds her breast, then goes farther down below her navel to see what's down there. That's as far as he goes, but this used to please the audience immensely. That is to say, the audience of kabuki has felt "the attraction of kata" in all this—the tragic element that makes them cry, the comic element that makes them laugh, and the kind of erotic stimulation I've just described.

The attraction I've always felt to kabuki, as I've been saying, is not something that can be easily explained. Colors, music, light, and sensual attraction. The combination of all this is hard to explain to people.

Except, when it comes to music; kabuki music is, I think, extremely modern, using, as it does, the methods used in movies and TV dramas.

---

45. One of the kabuki repertoire of eighteen classics. Like many other kabuki plays, it gradually acquired its present shape without any specific author. The Holy Man Narukami ("Thunder God") commits a transgression, his carnal desire stirred by Princess Taema ("Where Clouds Part"). Eager to make love to her, he offers to abandon the priesthood. When asked what his name will be when he does so, the actor playing Narukami is required to say his own name, followed by the word *sukebê*, "the lecher," so if Ichikawa Danjūrō played the role, he had to say, in effect, "Ichikawa Danjūrō the Lecher." This comic play is included in *Kabuki Jūhachi-ban Shū*, NKBT, vol. 98.

I mean, in realistic theater, if there's the sound of a river somewhere, the sound must stay there all the time; otherwise, it will be odd. If there's a river flowing on the stage, if its sound is one of the elements of the drama, you might think the river stopped flowing unless there's the constant sound of it.

In kabuki, however, the sound of water, say, swish, swish, swish, is skillfully used if you listen carefully. For example, if you see the "mountain section" of *Imose-yama Onna Teikin*,[46] there's the sound of water at the curtain's rising. But as the play begins, the sound disappears. Midway in the play, when people come out of the houses on both sides and go down to the river, the sound of water becomes audible. The way it's done, the sound is used according to the subjective feelings of the audience and the actors. The audience would think it strange if there were no sound when the river appears on stage, so when the river does appear, the sound also does. Aha, here's a river, the water's flowing, the audience thinks. Once that's taken care of, the audience would not want to hear the noisy sound all the time. So the sound disappears.

But, then, when the scene moves from what's happening in the houses to the river, the audience remembers the river. There's a large river right in front of them, but the audience has forgotten about it; now they remember how important the river is for this drama. So as the actors go down to the river, the sound reappears. From the viewpoint of the psychology of the actors as well, it's natural that the sound be there as they approach the river. That's the way the sound is used.

Kabuki also has techniques similar to cuts in movies. For example, in kabuki, when an actor is waiting for his turn to come—not being the focus of attention at a given moment—he may not change his expression, to make himself nonexistent. In *Benten Kozō (Aotogi Zōshi Hana no Nishiki-e)*[47] there's a "revealing-himself" scene.[48] Benten Kozō is disguised as a woman till then, but as the fact that he's there for *extortion* is finally exposed, he takes his kimono off to show his tattoo. Only then, the head store manager expresses his surprise and says, *Sate wa onna to omoishini katari de atta ka, yaa yaa yaa* (I thought you were a woman, but you are an extortionist. Oh! Oh! Oh!).[49] By then, however, right in front of him, Benten Kozō has finished showing his tattoo.

---

46. A jōruri by Chikamatsu Hanji and others.

47. By Kawatake Mokuami. Act 2, Scene of the Line-Up at the Inase River, opens with the gorgeous spectacle of "the Five Men of White Waves" (i.e., five robbers) appearing on stage in force to introduce themselves in a fancy declamatory style. Included in *Kawatake Mokuami Meisaku Sen, I,* the play has been adapted in English as *Benten the Thief* by Earle Ernst.

48. *Miarawashi.*

49. In the original text the store manager *(bantō)* Yokurō says *"Sate wa"* etc., and then "all others" say, *"Yaa yaa yaa."*

In realistic theater the other actors must act surprised the moment Benten Kozō reveals his true identity. They must be nudging one another or something. But in kabuki an actor or actors must remain *unperturbed* until their turn comes. The reason for this is that their showing any reaction at the wrong moment would detract from whatever the lead actor might be doing.

For that's where the lead actor performs. In a movie, this would be where the lead actor's face is shown in a close-up. It is here that Benten Kozō changes himself from woman to man. While he's doing that, he's being shown in a close-up shot, and the close-up doesn't include the faces of the manager and clerks who are *at the fringe* of the action. In kabuki, they are on the stage, but the audience is supposed to think they do *not* exist. Then, in the next cut or scene, they are shown.

So, when the lead actor's scene is over, the cut moves to the other side, and when that side is shown, first the head manager is shown, chest up, and he says, "I thought you were a woman, but you are an extortionist. Oh!" The moment he says "Oh!" the cut moves to the many clerks, who for the first time act surprised, saying "Oh! Oh!"

This means that, even though Benten Kozō's identity has become all too obvious to the audience, if the other players were to say, "Look at him, my, my," or some such thing, among themselves, kabuki would cease to exist. In this sense, you can say that kabuki, unlike ordinary Western theater, unconsciously began to use long ago what might be called new methods, which closely resemble those of movies and TV dramas. In the process, the actors realized the need to focus the attention of the whole audience on themselves and devised a number of ways to do so.

A group of young people are scheduled to stage *Chūshingura* pretty soon. If you see the role of Sadakurō in it, you know, if you read the original play, that it is a terribly miserable, uninteresting role. This is true in bunraku. Sadakurō is a very unpresentable evil man.

The actor named Nakamura Nakazō (I) thought about it and turned the role into something dazzling and straightforward. In my view, the most advantageous role in scenes five and six is that of Sadakurō. First of all, you have practically nothing to do. You put in an appearance only briefly, cut a terribly impressive figure, and disappear. This impression stays with the audience forever.

Kampei, there's no question about it, is a handsome man. But he has a lot of work to do. Besides, the kata for Kampei in the sixth-generation tradition are all fixed, down to the scene where his psychological state is depicted through the drop of tobacco from the tip of the pipe he's holding, and you can't change any of them.

So actors have devised all sorts of things for every phrase, every word of a kabuki text, turning it this way or that way. Unless you understand this, you can't say you've really seen kabuki.

I was absorbed in kabuki in that fashion for ten years, as I said before. And I memorized the important lines of many of the plays. I memorized them so well that I'd notice if an actor made a mistake. And I also retained in my memory how each actor would speak certain lines. When you reach that point, you begin to have pleasure in seeing the same play again and again. Then you begin to notice how an actor might speak the same line in the same scene somewhat differently from the previous time and create a different effect. And that excites you. In that way I gradually began to understand kabuki. After ten years, though, little by little, I began to sober up from my complete indulgence in kabuki. Why did I sober up?—this is something important to you, too.

To explain, I must tell you the kind of notion I'd had of what kabuki was. It was a very beautiful flower. But this beautiful flower has something lurid about it. There's something weird about it. Pretty, yes, and it would be all right if it were a tulip or a rose. But it's a somewhat mysterious flower, such as the peony, or some eerie insectivorous flower, an eerie flower of the kind you find in South America, along the Amazon. That was the feeling I had.

If that is the case, it must have some fertilizer that nurtures it. Where does the fertilizer come from? It must be from the soil. Is there anything buried in the soil? Perhaps the horrible-looking corpse of an animal is buried in it. Or perhaps eerie corpses of insects are piled up there. Or else the corpse of a human being may be buried there. Kajii Motojirō[50] has an odd short story in which the protagonist says, Sure, cherry blossoms are beautiful, but whenever I see them, I feel there have to be corpses of human beings buried under them. That is the kind of fantasy you have about kabuki.

The fertilizer for kabuki is the backstage. And the backstage of kabuki is the sort of place that makes us nonactors prisoners if we get into it unthinkingly and become familiar with its way of life.

You are going to learn about backstage life soon enough. You will also come to know the strange customs of kabuki society. It has a great many things that are, on the face of it, unthinkable to the modern way of thinking. It has contradictions. It has conventions. And a mountain of incomprehensible things. It has ugly things. Of course, this being human society, even if you work in the most modern office, you'll find ugly things. So you can't say kabuki is particularly ugly, but here you have to compete with other people for more than twelve hours a day, in the same backstage space, bumping into each

50. A short-story writer (1901–32). The story mentioned here is *Sakura no Ki no Shita niwa* (Under cherry trees), which begins: "Under cherry trees corpses are buried! / This is something you can believe, I tell you. Why, cherry blossoms blooming so splendidly is something you can't believe, isn't it? Because I can't believe their beauty, I've been uneasy for the last couple of days. But now, finally, I've come to understand it. Under cherry trees corpses are buried. This is something you can believe."

other all the time, taking your clothes off, putting them on, and taking them off again.

It is a world in which such people make a swirl of themselves and are swirling. And it's not only that people are entangled with one another. Each of the actors is entangled in the old institution of kabuki hierarchy.

To the modern eye, hierarchy may look like something premodern and full of contradictions, but both from the viewpoint of transmitting acting and from the viewpoint of theory, hierarchy in kabuki has often worked as a positive factor. If you removed all that and suddenly modernized everything, what would come out? Wouldn't that annihilate kabuki? Because of this fear, family factionalism still remains in kabuki.

To put it clearly, kabuki in itself is an evil. In the old days, a kabuki theater used to be called an *akusho,* "evil place." From the Edo period (1603–1868) to the end of the war, kabuki theaters and brothels were alike, both being "evil places." Even my parents had the sense that a child shouldn't be allowed to go to kabuki because it was an evil place.

You are right in the midst of that evil. Unless you recognize evil, kabuki can't exist.

There are evils and evils. Power is evil. Conventions, which I mentioned earlier, are evil. There is also the evil of sensuality. You may simply tell a lie or be a sycophant, and that's also evil.

Kabuki is the flower that has bloomed from a solid mass of such human evils. I don't understand why the government uses people's taxes to support something like this. Except, of course, I myself get paid to work here. I don't really understand why they have built such a wonderful theater like this for this mass of evils, boasting to anyone who cares to listen that it is a cultural asset.

In any event, kabuki is a nest of evils. Suppose you purge all such things from kabuki and turn it into something morally beautiful, something clean, to make it something you can show in any part of the world without embarrassment, something beautiful that depicts human beings only the way they ought to be—now, if you want to do that, you can. But the moment you do, kabuki will disappear.

As I said earlier, kabuki has a mysterious charm that transcends morality. Where does this morality come from? I think it comes in the end from the tradition of *kawaramono,* "riverbed people."[51]

Government officials all represent morality, represent correct humanity. They behave as if they were the paragons for mankind, yes, sir, and, dammit,

---

51. Beggars, vagabonds, and the untouchables in medieval Japan. Originally such people performed kabuki; in particular, early kabuki was staged on the riverbed at Shijō, Kyoto. During the Edo Period, kabuki people called themselves so in defiance or were so called in denigration.

we are riverbed people. But let's see which of us women will choose; none of them will go to government officials, but all of them will fall in love with us and come to this. You see, kabuki actors had this defiant confidence and that's why they could *relax*.

And when it comes to popularity among the ordinary folks, they will act like sycophants to government officials, but we are the people they love. The government may make it their business to arrest robbers. If a robber named Benten Kozō appears, they must catch him and throw him in jail. But we are on the side of robbers, and robbers are the foundation of our art; that's why we do dramas about them and show them how beautiful they are, how attractive *extortions* and *frauds* can be. Because riverbed people had this resolve, kabuki could link itself with antisocial elements. The attraction of beauty started to create something mysterious that no moralistic concept could regulate.

But, then, what about *gidayū kyōgen*,[52] which describe dying for loyalty? Isn't it odd that you side with robbers while at the same time siding with loyalty? But that is what is mysterious about kabuki, and that is what the ordinary folks are all about.

Ordinary folks like robbers, but they also like loyal samurai. Kabuki makes you cry with loyalty and delights you with robbers. It shows that no matter how denigrated a man may be by his society, there's always a grain of truth in him—and therein lies its fascination. That's what makes kabuki what it is.

What is interesting to me is that kabuki is so free of biases that it is different from, for example, today's underground theater. Underground theater people today call themselves riverbed beggars, and someone like Tō Jūrō[53] deliberately sets up tents to stage his plays. But if kabuki had been only anti-establishment, it wouldn't have made it so far. Kabuki is like a *nue*,[54] and is shapeless and malleable, so it fawns on and panders to the government.

---

52. Kabuki scripts heavily influenced by jōruri. Though kabuki and jōruri frequently interacted, kabuki preferred *spectacles* with sword-brandishing and impressive posturing to psychological subtleties. *Kyōgen* here does not mean a literary genre but is used in the general sense of "imaginary literary product."

53. Born in 1940, Kara is "a seminal figure in the new theater that emerged in the 1960s. Classified by Japanese critics under such rubrics as 'underground' *(angura)* and Little Theater Movement *(shōgekijō undō),* the new theater found a new audience: the young." Robert T. Rolf and John K. Gillespie, *Alternative Japanese Drama: Ten Plays* (University of Hawaii Press, 1992), p. 251. Kara Jūrō is a nom de plume that, through Chinese characters, puns on the great kabuki actor Sakata Tōjūrō I (1647–1709), who worked with Chikamatsu Monzaemon and excelled in love scenes *(nuregoto).*

54. An imaginary monster who has a monkey's head, a badger's body, a tiger's limbs, and the cries of the thrasher, a species of thrush. In the *Heike Monogatari* Minamoto no Yorimasa (1104–80) famously shoots it down because it gives the Emperor nightmares. The bird sings during the night.

Kabuki also advertised the ethics promoted by the Tokugawa government and staged plays about genuine loyalty, which would greatly move the samurai and make them cry.

Kabuki people had the stubbornness of riverbed people somewhere in their minds, the sense that they were on the side of robbers, but at the same time they also felt good, being part of the ordinary folks as they were, about playing a tragic hero who would sacrifice his son to demonstrate his loyalty. The actors of old were simple-minded, and they would believe they *were* loyal samurai when they played them.

Take even Ichikawa Danjūrō IX. He was reluctant to perform the role of Moritsuna in the play called *Ōmi Genji Senjin Yakata*,[55] even though it does make you look very good indeed. He said he didn't like it because Moritsuna was a samurai serving two masters.[56] He had the simple desire like a child to play a loyal samurai at any cost.

So, playing loyal samurai on one hand and playing robbers on the other, kabuki actors have succeeded in creating a large chaotic world where you find both evils and virtues. When I said earlier that kabuki is a solid mass of evils, I was exaggerating a little; I was joking. I did that because I wanted to say that you can't deprive kabuki of all its evils, leaving only good things.

In any event, to say something more delicate, closer to reality, I gradually began to feel that it was difficult to remain in contact with kabuki in human terms. Now I maintain the principle of never going backstage, because of my strong dislike of going there and getting involved in human entanglements there.

Today, at this moment, I am the speaker and you are the audience, so you are unlikely to come to me and say, "Mr. Mishima, would you give me a good role in the next play?" But if we carelessly go backstage and become friends, we are bound to start saying, "Hi, how are you?" "Well, I haven't had a good role for some time. Would you find one for me?" That's human. And if someone keeps saying that to me, I, being human, would begin to pity him. I didn't like that happening to me, so I gradually separated myself from the backstage of kabuki.

55. A jōruri by Chikamatsu Hanji and others.
56. Sasaki Moritsuna in the play is modeled after Sanada Nobuyuki, the warlord who switched allegiance to the Tokugawa. He is often contrasted with his brother Yukimura (1567–1615), who stuck to his original allegiance to the Toyotomi and was killed in the Summer Battle of Osaka, the Tokugawa's last and successful attempt to annihilate the remnants of the Toyotomi sympathizers. It is known, however, that the split allegiance was worked out between the two brothers for the Sanada family's survival. For similar moral reasons, Danjūrō IX never played the role of the Holy Man Narukami. *Kabuki Jūhachi-ban Shū*, p. 43.

I know I am extremely selfish in saying this: I do love kabuki no matter what, but I would like to stay in the audience or remain a director and love only the flower that comes out of it. I know that there's something horribly murky and dark behind the flower, but I'd like to leave that dark and murky thing alone, as it is, as an important fertilizer. I feel this strongly.

Of course, I do not totally deny the idea of improving kabuki, but because I believe that kabuki is linked to evil, the only thing I can say is, Well, sure, go right ahead and clean it up as much as you can; but think very hard what you might lose if you clean it up.

Now that you have entered this world of kabuki, I think you need to have considerable determination, because you have to accept the kind of evil, the kind of irrationality, that I have talked about. Unless you incorporate that irrationality into yourself, there will be no point in performing the drama called kabuki.

Should you decide to stick to rationalism alone, I can tell you you would soon be frustrated and break down. I could bet on it.

In the old days, in the military that was packed with irrationalities, new recruits would cry every night. Today, in the Self-Defense Forces, everything has become rational. In the Self-Defense Forces, training is continuous, from morning to night, yes, but in none of the units is there any more personal punishment or hazing. If you do anything irrational, the soldier will sue you and get you in hot water. In the case of kabuki, irrationalities are quietly hidden in layers of things. The Diet is unlikely to make an issue of it.

I was once subjected to an unbearable insult backstage. You are bound to encounter something similar in the coming years. But even if you are subjected to an unbearable insult, if you take it to the Diet, the Diet will merely laugh. They will tell you that the Diet isn't the sort of place where such things are deliberated on. But if you tell them you are a serviceman in the Self-Defense Forces and your officer beat you, they'll take it up today.[57]

Some of you might ask, Well then, in kabuki don't we have any human rights, aren't we protected at all? The constitution guarantees basic human rights. Regardless, you have made your own decision to enter this world, so you must recognize that irrationality and understand that the mystery of kabuki lies in the linkage between the most irrational and the most beautiful. The mystery of kabuki lies in the linkage between the most evil and the most virtuous. If you cut the linkage, it will lose its life.

I have made this speech today because I thought I had to tell you this so that you may make a firm commitment.

---

57. Mishima participated in a training session of the Self-Defense Forces for the first time in April 1967, later making the participation periodic. The prewar Japanese military, before it was disbanded in 1945, was notorious for the beating and slapping of new recruits, the physical abuse often extending to the officer ranks.

A WONDER TALE: THE MOONBOW

The Original Tale by Kyokutei Bakin

Chinzei ("the Pacifier of the West") Hachirō Minamoto no Tametomo (1139–70?), the protagonist of Mishima's kabuki play *Chinsetsu Yumiharizuki* (A wonder tale: The moonbow), was a warrior on the losing side in a brief internecine clash that resulted from a conflict within the imperial family, with the involvement of the principal aristocratic family, the Fujiwara, which was itself split.

Sutoku (1119–64)—officially the first son of Retired Emperor Toba (1103–56) but actually a son of Toba's father, Retired Emperor Shirakawa (1053–1129) because Shirakawa made Shōshi pregnant *after* he married her to his son—was installed as emperor when he was four, but was tricked into retirement by Toba in 1141, before ever having a chance to exercise real imperial power. His actual father, Shirakawa, had started the *insei,* a political arrangement in which the retired monarch wielded far greater power than the ruling one. As a result, he hoped to be reinstituted as emperor or to have his son ascend the throne at the death of Toba's feeble son, Emperor Konoe. But when Konoe died, in 1155, at age sixteen, Toba installed Masahito—his "fourth" son—as Emperor Goshirakawa and Masahito's son Morihito as crown prince, thereby snuffing out Sutoku's hopes for running the government either as emperor or retired emperor.

After Toba's death, on the second day of the seventh month 1156 (the first year of the Hōgen era), Goshirakawa (1127–92) provoked the discontented Sutoku, prompting him to assemble warriors, among them the leader of the Minamoto clan, Tameyoshi, and many of his sons, including Tametomo (the name Hachirō suggests he was the eighth son). But Goshirakawa had many more soldiers at his disposal, among them Tameyoshi's first son, Yoshitomo (1123–60), and the leader of the Taira clan, Kiyomori (1118–81). Before daybreak of the eleventh of the same month, following the tactics Yoshitomo recommended, Goshirakawa's soldiers attacked Sutoku, setting fire to his residence, and trounced his forces in a half-day battle.

The triumphant Goshirakawa exiled Sutoku to Sanuki (today's Kagawa), thereby creating a thrice-maligned, embittered figure, who in the tale based on the incident, the *Hōgen Monogatari,* is made to vow in fury and despair, "I shall become the great demon of the Japanese nation, turn the Emperor into an ordinary man, and turn an ordinary man into an Emperor." Indeed, the deaths of some important people and the great fires and other disasters in the years that followed Sutoku's exile were readily attributed to his vengeful ghost, as well as that of Minister of the Left Fujiwara no Yorinaga (1120–56) who died of the wounds he received during the battle. Consequently, in 1177 the court took the first step to appease their souls, presenting them with posthumous titles, and in 1184, in the midst of a great civil war, built Awata Shrine for them. Nearly seven hundred years later, in 1866, Emperor Kōmei planned a new shrine to appease Sutoku's soul. His son, Emperor Meiji, completed the plan and built Shiramine (White Peak) Shrine in Kyoto and transferred Sutoku's soul from Sanuki to it.

After the upheaval, Goshirakawa—actually his wily scholar deputy Fujiwara no Michinori, better known by his Buddhist name, Shinzei (d. 1159)—reinstated the long-suspended practice of executing warriors on the losing side, forcing Yoshitomo to behead, among others, his own father, Tameyoshi, and at least five of his own brothers. He also exiled Tametomo, after disabling his arms at the shoulders, to Ōshima, an island off the eastern coast of Izu Peninsula.

The incident, later called the Hōgen disturbance in reference to the name of the era, famously ushered in the Age of the Warrior *(musa no yo),* as Jien (1155–1225) put it in his history of Japan, *Gukanshō* (A fool's view). This is because the military clash and the harsh measures taken in its aftermath hardly ended the schisms within the ruling class. In four years they erupted in another half-day war in the capital, this time with a more open conflict within the two military houses, the Taira and Minamoto. And following that clash, called the Heiji disturbance, again in reference to its era, Taira no Kiyomori, a samurai, quickly dominated the aristocratic court, becoming, by 1167, prime minister. This eventually led to the five-year civil war directly pitting the two military houses against each other (from 1180 to 1185) and to the establishment of the first *bakufu,* military government, by the leader of the victorious Minamoto, Yoritomo (1147–99).

Much is known with some accuracy about the major players in these dramas, but most things "known" about Tametomo himself hover between fact and legend. This is best shown by the discrepancy between the descriptions of the man in Jien's account and in the *Hōgen Monogatari,* which began to be put down on paper in the early fourteenth century and continued to be refined until the end of the sixteenth. (The *Hōgen Monogatari* can be read in English translation in William R. Wilson's *Tale of the Disorder in Hōgen,* Sophia University, 1971.)

In *Gukanshō* Tameyoshi, in explaining to Sutoku the impossibility of putting up a fight against Goshirakawa's far superior forces, is quoted as saying, "I have only two small men." We assume that the "two small men" are two of his sons, one of them Tametomo, and that Tameyoshi was being deprecatory because he was talking about his own sons. Even so, the Tametomo conjured up by the composers of the *Hōgen Monogatari* is a different man, a warrior of heroic proportions who favorably compares with any of the renowned stalwarts in the military narratives of ancient China:

He was a man truly intimidating in talent, build, and visage. Because he was about seven feet tall, he towered over ordinary men by two to three feet. A born bowman, his bow-arm was longer than his horse-arm by four inches, enabling him to draw an arrow to the length of fifteen grips, and his arrows were eight feet and five inches long, besting the pole for carrying a long cabinet. . . . The way he swayed forward adjusting his court headgear, armor worn lightly, forearm and leg protectors looking smallish, bow held underarm, he vividly reminded one of the Vaisravana in his furious manifestation to subjugate the demons. It was awesome.

This image, together with the contemporary reports that Tametomo as a teenager made such a disturbance in Kyūshū, Japan's westernmost region (hence the epithet *chinzei,* "Pacifier of the West"), that his father Tameyoshi, in Kyoto, was relieved of his post as lieutenant of the Outer Palace Guards, Right Division (fifth rank), helped spawn many legends about him. From a few facts and various legends, Tametomo's life may be summed up as follows.

During his Kyūshū days, Tametomo married Princess Shiranui, the local chieftain Aso no Saburō Taira no Tadakuni's daughter and an accomplished warrior herself. He also acquired a group of loyal and highly capable men, among them the Takama brothers and Kiheiji, who was renowned for his ability to throw a pebble three (or eight) hundred yards. In Kyoto, during the war council Tametomo recommended an immediate preemptive attack, but the ranking courtier Yorinaga rejected it out of his concern for appearances. Yorinaga was famous for his formidable erudition but evidently knew nothing about the practical aspects of warfare. In fact, the rejection, which infuriated

Tametomo, is said to have been one cause of the swift and ignominious defeat of Sutoku's forces.

After his exile to Ōshima, Tametomo regained much of his ability to use the bow and arrow. He took as his wife Sasarae, the island magistrate Tadashige's daughter, with whom he had two sons, Tamemaru (later Tameyori) and Tomowaka, and a daughter, Shimagimi. In time he seized control of Ōshima and several islands nearby. A benevolent and enlightened ruler, he traveled to Ryūkyū (Okinawa), then an independent nation, and had a son with the royal princess Nei. That son would eventually ascend the throne as King Shunten.

Back at Ōshima, Tametomo faced a naval assault ordered by the emperor for his illegal possession of the islands that rightfully belonged to the lord of Izu. He sank the lead boat with a powerful arrow, then killed himself by disembowelment—or so one legend tells us. According to another legend, he went back to Ryūkyū. Still another says he escaped to Hachijō-jima, an island seventy miles south of Ōshima, where he faced another naval assault and killed himself. Yet other legends have him living to a ripe old age in various locations.

Toward the end of the Edo period Kyokutei Takizawa Bakin (1767–1848) wove together a number of legends, creating new ones along the way, to write *Chinsetsu Yumiharizuki,* a fantastically convoluted account of Tametomo's life, with one theme being Tametomo's loyalty to the exiled Sutoku and his own wish—perpetually thwarted—to follow him in death by committing suicide. Hokusai (1760–1849) illustrated the story. The publisher Iwanami's two-volume edition, annotated by Gotō Tanji, 1958–62 [NKBT 60–61], reproduces Hokusai's illustrations.

Mishima's play is based on Bakin's grand, complicated romance. In it he retains the principal theme but necessarily whittles down some of the original plots and subplots, while compressing several of them into a few scenes. Because of this I have given at times lengthy footnotes in this translation. Mishima was steeped in kabuki and used some of the terms unique to the genre. I have also explained these in the footnotes.

To re-create the atmosphere of traditional kabuki, Mishima uses classical language and 7–7- /7–5-syllabic patterns in a number of places in this play. However, as often happens in kabuki (and jōruri), these syllabic patterns are frequently loose, in part because vocalization often determines the syllabic effect. Where such patterns are discernible and sustained for a while, I have tried, though not consistently, to use lineation, often treating 7–7- or 7–5-syllables as a "line," simply to indicate that such passages are written in verse. In this play Mishima displays his fabulous command of the Japanese language, and I can hardly argue that I have managed to bring across any of the complicated rhetorical effects in my translation.

Mishima completed *A Wonder Tale: The Moonbow* on the first of September 1969. It was published in the November issue of the monthly *Umi* (The sea) and staged at the National Theater from November 5 to 27, with Matsumoto Kōshirō playing Tametomo and Mishima himself directing. As he notes in one of his commentaries on this play, a single person writing and directing a kabuki play is a rare occurrence.

Mishima also wrote a bunraku (jōruri) version of this play. It was incomplete but staged at the National Theatre from November 14 to 28, 1971.

A WONDER TALE: THE MOONBOW

The Original Tale by Kyokutei Bakin

SUTEMARU *(left)*, played by Kanbe Akira (aka Ichikawa Komazō), and KIHEIJI, played by Ichikawa Chūsha VIII. Kokuritsu Gekijō (National Theatre), November 1969. *Courtesy of Japan Actors' Association.*

Catalog
  Upper Volume
    Scene on Ōshima, Izu Province
  Middle Volume
    Scene at Shiramine (White Peak), Sanuki Province
    Scene in the Mountains of Kihara, Higo Province
    Scene in the Mountain Fort, Same as Above
    Scene in the Sea South of Satsuma
  Lower Volume
    Scene at the Ritual Site in Kitadani (North Cliff), Kingdom
    of Ryūkyū
  Scene at the Inn for Couples Only in Kitadani
  Scene at the Unten Seacoast on the Eve of a Festival
Role Names
  Chinzei Hachirō Minamoto no Tametomo
  800-yard Pebble Thrower Kiheiji Tayū
  Takama no Tarō Motoakira
  His wife Isohagi
  Sasarae
  Princess Shiranui
  Butōta
  Sutemaru Kanja
  Prime Minister Riyū
  Royal Prince
  Royal Princess Nei
  Tō Shōju
  Kumagimi
  The ghost of Retired Emperor Sutoku
  The ghost of Minister of the Left Yorinaga
  The ghost of Tameyoshi
  Tametomo's son, Tameyori
  Ditto, Shimagimi
  Tsuru
  Kame
  Vestals
  Fisherman Tashichi
  Ditto, Gengo
  Ditto, Yazō
  Ditto, Iwaji
  Ditto, Tamaichi
  Ditto, Taizō
  Ditto, Sabata

Ditto, Ikahachi
Hunter Sampei
Ditto, Rimpei
Ditto, Takihei
Chambermaid Chigusa
Ditto, Yamaogi
Ditto, Konomi
Ditto, Katsuragi
Ditto, Shiinoha
Village Chief
Soldiers
Ninja
Many young men
Many soldiers
Many crow-tengu

UPPER VOLUME
SCENE IN ŌSHIMA, IZU PROVINCE

Main stage,[1] *a volcano in the distance at stage left.*

A rock formation at stage center has a cave, which has a small shrine in it; before it stands a small torii. At an appropriate place on the rocks is a pine tree, from which hangs a large bow.

All upstage is a distant view of the ocean, with a cactus growing on a rock in the sea (with a contraption hidden inside), everything suggesting the appearance of Ōshima, Izu Province.

Minamoto no Tametomo is seated below the shrine, wearing military attire in gold brocade, a wide hakama, purple armor that grows darker toward the lower edge, and a sword in a golden scabbard.

To his left and right squat 800-yard Pebble Thrower Kiheiji and Takama no Tarō.

Before them is the light blue curtain.[2]

With the sound of waves and a "plover flute" the curtain is drawn open.

Immediately the jōruri on the floor[3] *starts.*

---

1. *Hon-butai:* the main or central section of the stage, which excludes such subsidiary setups as the hanamichi, *hashigakari* (bridge way), and *waki-butai* (side stage). The name derives from the fact that the kabuki stage was originally patterned after the nō stage.

2. *Asagi-maku,* which indicates day.

3. *Yuka no jōruri;* also called *degatari.* A jōruri narrator and a shamisen accompanist are given their own section either as an addition to the stage or part of the stage—either way at stage left. The narrator plays the role of chorus.

[Chants] Who says the ruler's way is easy,
they say the vassal's probity is hard to keep.
Once, defeated in the Hōgen disturbance,
the ruler was exiled to White Peak's eightfold goose grass,
his vassal to Ōshima's eightfold waves,
one deceased, one alive, like an abandoned skiff,
drawn up like a strong bow in vain, to no end.
The time is the fall of the second year of Kaō;
Pacifier of the West Hachirō Tametomo
holds a service for the Retired Emperor.
Those who serve him, too, are driftwood,
800-yard Pebble Thrower Kiheiji Tayū,
Takama no Tarō Motoakira,
both deeply reverential.

(When the jōruri comes to "eightfold waves," there is the sound of waves, and the light-blue curtain is "cut" and drops to the floor. A plover-flute, the sound of waves. Everyone is in a meditation posture, eyes closed. Each raises his face when his name is mentioned by the chanter.[4])

KIHEIJI: It is presumptuous of me to say this, sir,
but even in exile you do not forget your old loyalty
and on the twenty-sixth of the eighth month,
the anniversary of the Newly Retired Emperor's death,[5]
you dress up resplendently in fighting gear
and hold a memorial service.

TAKAMA: Timeless and unchanging are the pine and oak.
Should the Retired Emperor see your offerings,
it would dispel his deep bitterness.

TAMETOMO: No, I would not say that.
Unable to help dispel his bitterness,
to decay and die on an island for exiles
is the shame of disloyalty unfit for a warrior.
Since hearing the Newly Retired Emperor passed away,
my only wish has been to go to his grave
at White Peak and after offering prayers
to rip my belly open right on the spot

[Chants] and to die gallantly.

---

4. *Yobi:* a way of introducing the characters.
5. Because Toba had already "retired," Sutoku after his abdication was often called *shin'in,* "Newly Retired Emperor."

To me, at a distance, in exile, for ten years,
valor is of the past, exploits in vain.
Hmmm, this is all such a bleak world, isn't it?

[Chants] Master and his vassals, hand in hand,
are sunk in melancholy thoughts, when,

[Chants] brought up on the beach,
her skirts soaked by turbulent waves,
Tametomo's plover Sasarae
comes along the shore,[6] accompanying
the city bird yet unfamiliar with the tides,
Takama Tarō's wife Isohagi,
and speaks boastfully to the islanders
carrying for her large fins and fish.

SASARAE: Come, island people, look at him.
The island chief you're used to seeing every day,
to observe his lord's death once a year,
decks himself out in armor and warrior robe,
he's so splendid, he's so chivalrous,
I can hardly call him my own.
Isohagi, haven't you fallen in love with Mr. Takama once again, the way
he looks like a real lord?

ISOHAGI: No, no, I am used to seeing him in warrior attire. I just feel as
if we're back in the old days.

SASARAE: You grew up in a warrior house, you are stubborn.
Wives in love should act like wives in love,
telling amorous bits, that's more fun, I must say!
(The two of them look at each other and laugh. All come to main stage.)
Hello, hubby, oh, no,
Great General, Lord Tametomo,
for the shrine festival,
offerings from all the island,
though without mountain products,
we've plenty of sea products and this song,
which to sing to console his soul,
we've brought the best of them all.
Come, everyone!

EVERYONE: Yes, ma'am.

6. Sasarae and her group approach the stage from the hanamichi.

[*Chants*] *Yattokona!*[7]
lobster scarlet as armor thread,
  snapper light-pink as armor thread,
  yattona!
swordfish for the sword,
  conger eel for the quiver,
perch for the powerful bow,
  we list all the arms
as we sing to celebrate the great catch.
  Yattokona, yattosei!
(*Singing, they carry the fish and other offerings to the shrine.*)
[*Chants*] We've made a mountain of divine offerings,

TAMETOMO: and this, too, must be from our late Retired Emperor's posthumous virtue. Sasarae, would you offer this divine sake to the village folk.

SASARAE: Yes, sir, yes.
[*Chants*] So responding, she, busily,
along with Isohagi, entertains the folk.

FISHERMAN TASHICHI: Though not something to say in front of Lady Sasarae, her father the magistrate, scared by Lord Tametomo's mighty power, bolted from this island, Ōshima,

FISHERMAN GENGO: with the exiled general sitting in his position, a bizarre incident unheard of since the Age of Deities.

FISHERMAN YAZŌ: All this because to the islanders
Lord Tametomo is so benevolent.

TASHICHI: His rule so different from the previous one,
the people's worries are all gone, calmed,

GENGO: the taxes so light, we live in peace.

YAZŌ: For this once-a-year festival

TASHICHI: we'd like to express our gratitude; we'd like to console him in his boredom. Isn't there some way

ALL: to do both?

SASARAE: Oh, that's just what I had expected you to say. I'll pull the rope, too, my young friends, so will you help me?

ALL THE YOUNG PEOPLE: We will, lady.
[*Chants*] Whispering to each other they pull out
marionettes on a festival cart.

---

7. A shout of encouragement, one of the set phrases used in any of the *aragoto* (action) scenes, such as one in which a sword is brandished. Here, the phrase may be close to "yo-heave-yo."

Even the mooring rope Sasarae pulls
is made of rouge-adorned beach cotton.
Behold, Tameyori and Shimagimi,
degrading themselves as marionettes.
Tametomo, startled . . .

TAMETOMO: You are my children.

TAMEYORI, SHIMAGIMI: Father. *(They bow.)*

SASARAE: Oh, no, come now.

Today you are marionettes,
you can't talk, you can't move.
Ladies and gents, here we have
the scenes from fifteen years ago
where by imperial command Lord Tametomo,
while trying to find the crane with a golden tablet
in Mount Kyūkyū,[8] in Ryūkyū,
came across Royal Princess Nei,[9]
exchanged his treasured ball
for the crane he wished to have,[10]
a story as told by Lord Tametomo,
turned into a play for fun.

Now, all you people, watch. Here we go.

(A jōruri exchange on the floor begins.)

MARIONETTE ROYAL PRINCESS NEI: For you, it is no more than a ball;
for me, it is an imprimatur equal to the rank of a thousand chariots.[11] Of

8. *Kyūkyū* means something like "ancient dragon."

9. The daughter of King Shōnei's secondary wife, Lady Ren, according to Bakin's story. Shōnei's principal wife, Chūfukimi (which means "queen," Bakin notes in *Zokuhen*, vol.2), was "nymphomaniac and jealous" but had no children. In Ryūkyū a king's daughter ascended the throne when he had no son. Royal Princess Nei, "as she grew up, became incomparable in her facial appearance and, if I may add, her filial devotion far surpassed what was standard in society; and in her wisdom even a full-grown man often did not come close." *Zokuhen*, vol. 2.

10. According to Bakin, while still in Kyūshū, Tametomo once rescued a crane, which he found to be one of the many cranes his great-grandfather Yoshiie (1041–1108) was said to have released after attaching golden tablets to their legs. After the crane regained its health, he let it go. But Retired Emperor Toba, hearing about it, demanded that Tametomo recapture it and present it to him. Learning by divination that by then the crane had flown away to Ryūkyū, Tametomo set out for the island nation disguised as a merchant. Among the things he took with him were valuables with which to buy back the crane, in case someone had the bird, and a "ball" that he found in the jaw of a giant snake he had slain. Not long after his arrival in Ryūkyū, however, he was robbed of all his valuables, except the ball, by Ryūkyū's "National Teacher" Mōun, who was endowed with magical powers.

11. The kingly position. During the Chou dynasty, each duke was required to provide the ruler with a thousand chariots.

the two balls of *ryū* and *kyū*,[12] if one is lost, the country is thrown into chaos. That is exactly the ball that was lost. Please bless me by giving it to me.

MARIONETTE TAMETOMO: This ball is something I obtained in my native country and cannot be the royal imprimatur you are looking for. I am a merchant from Japan. I have lost all my valuables, with only this one ball left me. Should I give this to you, what would I use in exchange for what I seek?

MARIONETTE ROYAL PRINCESS NEI: I'll give you whatever you are looking for.

MARIONETTE TAMETOMO: It's none other than what you have on your arm.

MARIONETTE ROYAL PRINCESS NEI: A what?

MARIONETTE TAMETOMO: A golden tablet on the crane's leg that I seek.
    [Chants] The sky suddenly darkens,
    and with the rumbling of the ground
    the Holy Mountain spews fire.

SASARAE: Just another, familiar eruption of the Holy Mountain. It's the water's role to sober us up. The fire can't end our fun. My dear sons, don't stop your acting.
    [Chants] So warning, she turns to look:
    A swelter of smoke from the Holy Mount
    depicts a dragon in the empty sky.
This is all mysterious, the smoke turning into a dragon; born on this island, I divine. . . .
    [Chants] For some reason troubled,
    she stands there, heartbroken.

MARIONETTE ROYAL PRINCESS NEI: This is just a crane that flew down to our garden this morning. It's so tame it wouldn't leave us though we tried to chase it away. If this is what you are looking for, come and get it.
    (So the marionettes gladly exchange the ball for the crane.)

12. *Ryū* of Ryūkyū means "polished round stone" and *kyū*, "ball." As Bakin has Lady Ren explain: "Once in the long past there lived a hornless dragon *(mizuchi)* in the sea facing Mount Taihei, which constantly stirred up storms and brought forth tsunami, many times damaging the five grains and harming the people of the state. Our ancestral king was deeply concerned about this, prayed to Heaven and Earth, immersed himself in the tides, slew the dragon himself, and buried it in the eastern peak of Mount Heika. . . . When he slew the dragon, he tore apart its jaws and obtained two balls, one called *ryū* and the other *kyū*. . . . These balls have been handed down from king to king, and they are equal to the imperial imprimatur transmitted in China. As is the custom of this country, when there is no royal prince, the royal princess inherits the throne. When Royal Princess Nei established herself in the Middle Castle a few years ago, the first thing King Shōnei did was to entrust her with these balls. Yet in no time one of them was lost." *Zenpen*, vol. 3.

TAMETOMO: Enough, stop that. Stop all that, children.

   [Chants] Because of these island people, I have refrained from
   speaking up until now, but a warrior's children mimicking
   puppets, this is something about which I can make no excuse
   to my ancestors.

   [Chants] Degrading yourselves to be actors, the way you have your
   eyebrows drawn, only to repeat what I said long ago, all this is
   shameless, makes me furious.

That Sasarae, an old wife now, can't understand my sentiments because
she was brought up on an island, I can't do anything about that, but even
for festival amusement,

   [Chants] the boy is a Genji descendant,

at the least he's a Genji warrior. To put makeup on him and place him
in a show is an act of indescribable stupidity, which I cannot possibly
overlook.

   [Chants] He takes the heavy rattan bow[13] hung from the pine and
   moves towards Sasarae, when she speaks in her gentle way.

SASARAE: Sir, please do forgive me. For the sole purpose of soothing your
   heart, I came up with this brash amusement. I wondered if I ought to
   ask some islanders, but because I myself gave birth to them, feeling more
   comfortable with them,

   [Chants] though they are my master the warrior's children,
   I turned them into puppets and manipulated them;
   this is all my grievous mistake.

Come to think of it, having turned against my immoral parent notorious as an evil magistrate, I sincerely hoped to be the formal wife[14]

   [Chants] of an illustrious warrior, but having been brought up in a
   lineage no effort can undo,

   I am mortally ashamed of myself.

ISOHAGI: I know it is forward of me to say this, sir, but all this is a result
   of her gentle thinking. I beseech you to forgive her.

---

13. *Shigetō (no yumi)*: a bow with heavy rattan bindings both for reinforcement and decoration. Normally used by a commanding officer.

14. *Kita no kata*, "the northern quarter": formal wife. So called because an official or
principal wife's residence was located in the northern part of a mansion. Tametomo's formal wife is Princess Shiranui, whom he married in Kyūshū.

[Chants] She tries to stop him, but he is a stubborn, strong-willed general. Tameyori rushes forward.

TAMEYORI: Father, please forgive mother. It was me, Tameyori, who went against the warrior's way. Punish me, sir, instead of mother.

TAMETOMO: I see, you ask for punishment yourself on behalf of your mother. This is interesting, interesting. Listen, here, Tameyori.

I'll tell you my reasons for giving
part of my name "Tame" to you.
Defeated in the Hōgen disturbance,
the Newly Retired Emperor's wish not fulfilled,
I was unfilial to father Tameyoshi as well.
The muscles of my bow-arm
famed for its strength severed,
I was exiled to Ōshima. For ten years
I haven't spent a day without thinking
of raising the banners to reestablish the Genji,
but with Kiyomori's might still in full force,[15]
I have no means of leading assault forces

[Chants] up along Capital roads full of red banners.[16]

Parted alive as I am from Sutemaru,
the one son I had with dead Shiranui,
my hope is to install you as a warrior
so you may carry forward my wish.
Understand these thoughts
and take my beatings of love.

[Chants] He soundly whips him, whips him,
with a great bow seven feet, five inches long,
the father-son love and duty disturbing even the rattan.
Everyone's in tears, exclaiming, "This is all
understandable, both so courageous!" Among them,
800-yard Pebble-Thrower Kiheiji
finally manages to brave a few words.

15. In both the Hōgen disturbance and the Heiji disturbance, in 1159, the leader of the Taira house, Kiyomori, was on the victorious side. Following the Heiji conflict, he managed to kill off the leaders of the rival Minamoto clan, including Yoshitomo, Tameyoshi's first son (who was on the opposing side during the Hōgen war), or exile them. Kiyomori then went on to concentrate enormous power and brought in the rule of the Taira house. Not until 1180 did Yoritomo, Yoshitomo's first son, raise war banners against the Taira rule. He eventually prevailed after five years of war.

16. The Taira famously used red banners, the Minamoto white banners.

KIHEIJI: That should be enough for now, sir. The simple, brave offer to accept the punishment has revealed his true worth as a warrior. Be at ease, sir. From now on, Lord Takama and I, Kiheiji, will take on Master Tameyori's training in martial arts.

[Chants] His dependable guarantee softens
the Lord General's mien, allowing everyone
to heave a sigh of relief, when
[Chants] pulling and shoving a man, fishnet workers
(These words turn into batabata[17] as Fishermen Iwaji and Tamaichi enter on the hanamichi holding a suspicious man by the arms.)

FISHERMAN IWAJI: Here, here, look at this.
On the shore where we cast our nets a skiff
drifted by and we found this man in it.

FISHERMAN TAMAICHI: Exposed to the sun he was just like a dried fish. We helped him out and nursed him, and he, instead of spitting out water,

IWAJI: was found to have this secret letter on his chest.

TAMAICHI: Absolutely no doubt he is a spy.

IWAJI: Here, for Lord Tametomo

TAMAICHI: to investigate.

[Chants] They offer the secret letter, which Kiheiji accepts.
(Shoving the spy forward, the two fishermen offer the secret letter. Kiheiji takes it and deferentially tries to hand it over to Tametomo. With his eyes Tametomo tells Kiheiji to read it, and Kiheiji reads it.)

KIHEIJI: Let's see now. "Tametomo as an exile ostentatiously wields power. He robs various islands and halts the annual tributes. As to those above him, he is not even afraid of Heaven's Son; as to those below him, he does not pity the ordinary people. He feels free to mete out punishment and has penalized Island Chief Tadashige. His violent, evil deeds are beyond compare. Here we issue an imperial command and in no time government forces will head for Ōshima. The chiefs of neighboring islands are absolutely required to side with them. For adequate work rewards will be given as desired." I see, this is certainly an imperial command telling the chiefs of neighboring islands to side with the forces to subjugate Tametomo. And as to the fleet of the government forces, let's see, "Former Magistrate Saburō Tayū Tadashige shall be its leader. . . ."

SASARAE: Oh, no, then my father. . . .

[Chants] Sasarae is astounded.
[Chants] The spy's expression changes visibly,
he spits blood and falls face down.

---

17. A kabuki term: a pair of wood clappers are struck noisily, in quick succession, to emphasize the footsteps of someone running.

KIHEIJI: Damn, we let him die. He must have bit his tongue.

    [Chants] All the islanders are now perturbed.

TASHICHI: If they attack us with a fleet,

GENGO: in no time we'll be like trash fish boiled in a pot,

YAZŌ: and we'll be eaten and swallowed with tea rice,

IWAJI: and fall to the pit of the stomach, Hell's Third Street.

TAMAICHI: How can we wipe our tears

ALL: with scales.

    [Chants] All are confused and no wonder.

    Tametomo bursts out laughing merrily.

TAMETOMO: Come now, my fellow islanders. Which is harder, the boulder rising at the water's edge or your flesh? Try to answer that.

TASHICHI: That is a very baffling question, sir. Our body has less resistance than the shellfish removed from its shell or the turtle that has left its carapace behind. How can it compare with a boulder, sir?

TAMETOMO: Now, look.

    [Chants] He picks up a *kabura* arrow,[18] draws the bow sharp, full–length,

    and shoots, shwoop, hitting directly

    the rock that looks like a cactus,

    and the rock instantly splinters into bits,

    the tide of shattered rock pieces

    flooding as if to overwhelm the shore.

TASHICHI: Well done, Commanding General!

GENGO: This gives us a hundred times more courage

YAZŌ: as if aboard a giant ship

IWAJI: with sculls and oars as our weapons

TAMAICHI: we'll help you in battle.

TASHICHI: Please, we are all

ALL: at your service, sir.

TAMETOMO: With determination to pierce a rock,

    what should a horde of enemies mean to you?

    Though you are soldiers instantly made,

        come, Takama Tarō,

    command these men in my place.

TAKAMA: Yes, sir!

    [Chants] Following the order, he arranges the instantly trained fishnet casters into a troop formation.

---

18. An arrow equipped with a turnip-shaped (hence the name *kabura*) tip, which is made of wood or horn, with a hollow in it. When shot, the arrowhead makes a great sound. These arrows were used for the first round of shooting, a ritual face-off, when two armies confronted each other.

TAKAMA: Soldiers!

ALL FISHERMEN: Yes, sir!

TAKAMA: *(Attuning himself to the shamisen rhythm)*[19] To begin with the very beginning, to be a soldier,

    you must first have loyalty, second righteous bravery,

    third the will to do your best

    [Chants] by drawing the net on the same boat-shore,

    by holding down the leaping fish,

    grabbing the ones that try to get away,

    striking down the ones that bite at you,

    working with your friends and colleagues.

    [Chants] So he taught.

TAMETOMO: That's splendid! That's splendid!

    [Chants] The Lord General's eyebrows show his joy.

    At that moment, in the offing gulls rise in flocks,

    in no time arriving above their heads to flap and wheel.

    Kiheiji looks sharply at the sky.

KIHEIJI: All that commotion on the surface of the sea suggests .that the enemy troop ships are approaching fast. Look out! Look out!

    [Chants] He picks up a pebble by his side and throws it up with admirable skill,

    and instantly a gull drops before him,

    now revealing the reason for his great fame

    as 800-yard Pebble Thrower.

    Takama Tarō rushes up the rocks.

    (Takama climbs up the rocks and looks out.)

TAKAMA: I see, that's an abundance of troops coming. The enemy has more than five hundred horsemen, I estimate, with twenty-five to twenty-six troop ships. The ship that's coming, rowing ahead of the pack, has a butterfly crest on the canvas.

SASARAE: That's exactly like my father's ship. That he's spearheading an army to kill his son-in-law, this is such an effrontery!

    [Chants] She becomes visibly agitated. Tameyori bows to
      Tametomo, his hands on the ground.

TAMEYORI: Father, the enemy may be my grandfather, but I am a Genji warrior and would like to have the honor of being the first to lead the troops, sir.

---

19. *Nori:* delivery of a heightened speech to the rhythm of the accompanying shamisen.

TAMETOMO: Well said. I understand your excitement. Should the enemy come deep into us, you would then be acting commander and would not sully my military record. I will first shoot at the troop ships and annihilate the enemies who swim to the shore. Kiheiji, follow me. Takama, you and your wife[20] lead your troops to the eastern shore. Tameyori, you stay here to protect your mother and sister. So the first to come is Tadashige. It's a bit too far for an arrow, but I'll give it a try.

(Tametomo, followed by Kiheiji, goes behind the rock formation. Takama Tarō and Isohagi lead the fishermen, exit stage left.)

> [*Chants*] With Kiheiji, he places himself behind the rock.
> Takama, seeing him off, courage surging,
> leaves, stomping his way to exit.
> Sasarae, left behind, feels anew
> the waves and winds between father and husband
> rising over the sea within her view,
> when the great *karimata* arrow[21] Tametomo shoots
> pierces through the troop ship, just like that,
> and water gushes in through the two holes it makes,
> the ship beginning to sink in no time. *(The ship in the distance sinks.)*

SASARAE: Oh, oh, oh! Father's ship is sinking. He may be an immoral man, but he's my own father who shares my blood. He's drowning, but what can I do? My husband, for his part, faces an overwhelming enemy that renders him utterly defenseless. Though a bowman known under heaven, his ferocious fighting may prove in vain, he perishing in the end. My father drowning is better than the miserable fate of these two facing and killing each other. Hear me, Lord Sun, Lord Mountain *(She offers prayers to the volcano):*

> Think of it, think of it, in my childhood
> a diviner made a prophesy to me:
> The day the smoke from the Holy Mountain
> clearly forms the figure of a hornless dragon
> will be the day when my life ends.
> That is exactly the sign of my death.
> Because of what karma was Lord Tametomo
> exiled to this island?
> [*Chants*] First glance at him and she was in love;
> behind the demon official's eyes,
> she took particular, loving care of

---

20. According to Bakin, Takama Tarō's wife Isohagi was also a warrior.
21. An arrowhead that opens outward like a goose's crotch *(karimata)*.

the tendon of his injured bow-arm.

When this came to light, she was scolded severely

and I turned against my father right then

[Chants] which has led to today's dead end.
Having grown up on an island,
she's been eager to be called Lady North,[22]
the shame of being not so called magnifying,
though she's admonished herself about it,

all, pitifully, has come to naught.

[Chants] while she's so lamenting, Shimagimi speaks:

SHIMAGIMI: Mother, Grandfather's there.

SASARAE: What, you say Grandfather? (She picks her up and looks behind the rock formation.) Oh, my! I thought he had drowned, but he, with his stout heart, swam to shore and now is engaged in one-to-one combat with Lord Tametomo. Father and husband fighting for life or death—seeing this is living hell!

[Chants] Seeing, she can't stand seeing, the shellfish,
the seaweed tangled up by the briny storm,
she cries, crazed, so piteously.

SHIMAGIMI: Mother, what to do? Grandfather was cut down by Father. Father's surrounded and in great difficulty.

SASARAE: Oh, come, come. I can be calm now. Lord Tametomo, for me to maintain filial piety and remain a woman dedicated to you, I have no other option. Please at least do me the favor of complimenting me for dying like a warrior's wife. I am taking two of my children so that I may meet you in intimacy in the netherworld. I hope you'll forgive me. Come, now, Tameyori, Shimagimi, your mother will take you to a good place. We'll wait for Father over there. Don't fret. Follow me.

SHIMAGIMI: Mother, where?

SASARAE: Well, as always, we'll play on the beach.

SHIMAGIMI: Will we have lots of top shells and shrimp?

SASARAE: Not only that, starfish stars will shine on our dark path so brightly it will be almost blinding. Tameyori, come along.

TAMEYORI: No, no, I am a warrior's son. I intend to die, doing battle in a way people will say, "He was deservedly a Genji descendant."

---

22. At this point the fate of the official wife, Shiranui, is unknown.

SASARAE: What are you saying? You are just a child. This is a battle even your father is having difficulty with. You can't hope to be in it.

TAMEYORI: No, no, no! It would be sad to be scolded for forgetting my father's admonishment, Be always a samurai.

SHIMAGIMI: Mother, be quick and take me to the beach to play.

[Chants] She pulls and is pulled by the cord of compassion,

tears overflow, clouding the tides,

obliterating patches of the sun.

Enemy foot soldiers leap forward before them.

ENEMY SOLDIERS: Ho, ho! You may disguise yourself in shabby clothes but you can't deceive us. Here's Tametomo's wife Shiranui to take now!

TAMEYORI: You can't, you can't!

(A sword fight ensues. Trying to protect his mother and sister, Tameyori fights bravely. Gradually he sustains many wounds and enemy soldiers are about to capture Sasarae and Shimagimi, when Sasarae, Shimagimi in her arms, manages to slip under their arms and throws herself beyond the rock formation. At that moment the smoke from the volcano vanishes. Still fighting, Tameyori follows in Sasarae's direction, but surrounded by the foot soldiers, he determines his end has come and disembowels himself at the top of the rock formation and falls forward.)

(From stage left enter Takama and his wife followed by fishermen. The fishermen and enemy foot soldiers snap up the fish dedicated to the shrine deity and fight using them as swords. They exit stage right. Takama and his wife, while fighting with a new set of foot soldiers, jump up on the cart stage and pretend to be marionettes, thereby escaping capture. An amusing scene ensues in which the soldiers, unable to detect the couple, go about in confusion. At this point, from behind the rock formation)

VOICE: Princess Shiranui threw herself to her death. This is unmistakably her corpse. Come here! Come here!

(In response, the soldiers exit stage right and left. Takama and his wife jerk out of their stance)

TAKAMA: What! They said Princess Shiranui's corpse?

ISOHAGI: No, that can't be. She already passed away, in Dazaifu,[23] when your father was killed in battle, I thought.

TAKAMA: That's peculiar, that they're investigating the matter here, again.

ISOHAGI: She can't possibly have died here.

TAKAMA: The reason they mistook a corpse for hers

ISOHAGI: is that she's surely alive somewhere. Because the government force knew it

---

23. Government's military headquarters in Kyūshū, in today's Fukuoka. At an early period it became a place of exile for ranking government officers, the most famous among them Minister of the Right Sugawara no Michizane (845–903). In 1186 Minamoto no Yoritomo restored its military and administrative role.

TAKAMA: they chased her as far as this place.

ISOHAGI: If a deceased mistress still lives in this world

TAKAMA: not knowing it is being disloyal. We'd like to go

ISOHAGI: as soon as possible to where she is.

>[Chants] Routing foot soldiers, the Lord General
>comes forward to face Takama and his wife.

(From stage left enter Tametomo and Kiheiji, disentangling themselves from those trying to get them.)

TAMETOMO: I heard over there that my wife Shiranui turned up as a corpse.

TAKAMA: Yes, sir.

TAMETOMO: Kiheiji, come with me.

>[Chants] So says he, dauntless,
>and climbs the rocks, surveying the scene.

That certainly is Sasarae's corpse. She threw herself down, along with Shimagimi. Damn, that I allowed them to die!

>[Chants] While so aggrieved,
>he notices the pampas grass rustle.

Are you Tameyori? Tameyori. Tameyori.

TAMEYORI: Are you my father?

TAMETOMO: Yes.

TAMEYORI: I can no longer see. Please help me to die, sir. I never went against your admonishment, but battled like a samurai and disemboweled myself.

TAMETOMO: Yes, well done. Well done. That proves you to be a Genji descendant.

>When we reestablish the Genji House,
>we'll wait for your soul clad in vermilion
>to come back to join us all.

TAMEYORI: I'm glad to hear you say that, sir. Be quick and help me to die, sir.

TAMETOMO: Agreed, son.

>[Chants] The sword he lifts, like dead pampas grass,
>merely wavers, unable to fall,
>when, struck by a melancholy shore wind,
>it suddenly sways, the head rolls;
>taking it up in his arms, he stands, crying.
>[Chants] Surmising how he must feel, Kiheiji
>deliberately raises his salty voice.

KIHEIJI: Matters having reached this point, milord,
>for now you ought to abandon this place
>to plot to reestablish yourself, that is best.
>Meanwhile Lord Takama and his wife

should set out to find Lady Shiranui.

Now the tides are fortunately up.

Every one of you, to his own destination.

Come, hurry.

(A sheet of cloth indicating waves[24] *is brought out on the hanamichi with an abandoned boat carrying some dead bodies of foot soldiers; there is also an abandoned boat at stage left.)*

TAMETOMO: Farewell.

TAKAMA: Farewell, sir.

(They part, two toward the hanamichi, two others toward stage left. Kiheiji kicks the corpses out into the sea and invites Tametomo aboard. Takama and his wife get on the boat at stage right. The boat at stage left exits.)

(Tametomo rows the boat with his bow. The boat reaches the seven-three point[25] *of the hanamichi.)*

(Butōta shows up with foot soldiers.)

BUTŌTA: Tametomo, I won't let you go.

KIHEIJI: He's the one who originally brought suit against milord, that heinous Butōta. He's dared to come this far. Damn that coward! Milord, shoot him dead with a single arrow.

TAMETOMO: Oh, I'm damned! I'm out of arrows.

[Chants] Though within shooting range,

oh, to his chagrin, he's out of arrows;

but with the heavy rattan for paddle, with a tail wind,

faster than an arrow.

(The boat exits the hanamichi.)

CURTAIN

MIDDLE VOLUME
SCENE AT SHIRAMINE (WHITE PEAK), SANUKI PROVINCE

At stage right is Retired Emperor Sutoku's grave. The atmosphere is one of mountain depths in a dark valley. Insects chirp uninterrupted.

As the curtain rises, Tametomo enters from the hanamichi.

TAMETOMO: *(Stopping at the seven-three point)* Oh, how glad I am! That must be the Newly Retired Emperor's mausoleum. *(He runs to main*

---

24. Called *nami-nuno.*

25. *Shichisan:* When the actor entering from the hanamichi is required to make some kind of flourish, he stops after covering 70 percent of the length of the runway, hence the expression.

stage, prostrates himself before the grave, and is unable to stop his tears for a while)
I have missed you, Sire, I am so sorry for you. As Holy Prince of Ten
Virtues and Ten Thousand Chariots,[1] Your Majesty had brocaded curtains glittering in the moonlight above the Northern Gate,[2] but now you
are a soul missing your land and yearning for your home, mired as your
jeweled body is among the vulgar of the Southern Seas. How chagrined
you must be! I, your negligible vassal Tametomo, having lost momentum, having run out of strength, do not even have the means of dedi-
cating myself in solitary loyalty[3] to you, Sire, and have come here so that
I may at least make up for my lateness in accompanying you in death.

I accepted Kiheiji's recommendation
that I try to reestablish myself,
and abandoned Ōshima for that.
Ashamed of my miserable military fortune,
I plan to die before Your Majesty's mausoleum
by ripping my stomach apart.
On my way here, to Sanuki,
I somehow lost sight of Kiheiji,
because your soul wanted no obstacle.
The more I think of it, I, a warrior,
have served loyally, to no avail.
In apology I die at Li Kuang's[4] death spot;
forgive me for sullying it with blood.

*(He opens the front of his clothes and positions his sword to stab his belly, when
there's dorodoro,[5] his hand suddenly becomes numb, and he cannot stab himself.
Bewildered, he drops his sword and leans against the stone fence.)*

*(In the clouds and mist at stage left, there is a moon faintly shining. A sudden
gust of wind down the mountain.)*

*(From a height at stage left, upstage, a procession of dolls appears on a bank
of clouds: two warriors as forerunners, crow-tengu[6] carrying a palanquin, and crow-*

---

1. *Jūzen banjō no seishu:* Both "ten virtues" and "ten thousand chariots" are honorific
names for the Emperor. The term "ten thousand chariots" derives from the understanding
during China's Chou dynasty that set at ten thousand the number of war chariots the Emperor should be able to produce from the lands under his direct control.

2. Another name for the imperial palace.

3. *Kochū:* See the headnote to *The Decline and the Fall of the Suzaku.*

4. Li Kuang (d. 119 BCE): an outstanding commander of Han. Appointed the Pacifier
of the North by Emperor Wu, he was feared by the Huns as "Flying General."

5. An onomatopoeic stage term: the low drum sound effected when a ghost, a monster, or a magician appears or the presence of one of them affects the stage proceedings.

6. *Tengu:* fabulous beings with a human body, an extremely long nose that is said to resemble a crow's beak, and wings. Residents of woods and mountains, they can fly at will
and have magical powers.

tengu as servants, followed by warriors and courtiers, each clad in armor with white brocade and carrying a plain "white" wooden bow and arrows with white feathers. The procession descends in stately fashion from upper left to lower right. At stage right, the dolls' procession is replaced by a procession of children, counterparts to each doll, which then proceeds obliquely to stage left, where the procession is replaced by another procession that consists of adult actors. This procession moves toward the main stage.)

(The procession settles down off center, somewhat toward stage left. A crow-tengu servant lifts the blind on the palanquin. The ghost of Retired Emperor Sutoku steps out, with a terrifyingly pallid face and clad in a white robe.[7] Everyone prostrates himself.)

MINISTER OF THE LEFT YORINAGA: We had your enemy Yoshitomo[8] executed while you were alive. The question is how we can destroy the Taira House whom you regard as even more loathsome. Any one of you with a plot or scheme should apprise His Majesty of it.

TAMEYOSHI TADAMASA: Even though Kiyomori is atrocious and immoral in the extreme, Shigemori's virtuous acts[9] are so effective that the time is not yet ripe for us. But, if we wait another ten years, Shigemori's life will end. We must simply wait until then, Sire.

RETIRED EMPEROR SUTOKU: In the first place, Kiyomori forgets the decorum between ruler and subject. For this reason, if we make him think ill of the ruling Emperor Masahito and shut him up in the detached palace of Toba, exile the Prime Minister, and remove the Chancellor,[10] his

---

7. *Hōgen Monogatari* says that Sutoku, after learning in the place of exile that the court rejected the idea of according him a more proper treatment, "would not cut his hair or clip his nails, thereby taking on the appearance of a tengu while alive." He became so emaciated that he was a "terrifying" sight.

8. Minamoto no Yoshitomo was on the winning side in the Hōgen disturbance but was on the losing side in the Heiji disturbance. While on the run, he was betrayed and killed by his former vassal.

9. After gaining ascendance at the court, Taira no Kiyomori, probably Shirakawa's son like Sutoku, promoted many members of his family and clan to important positions, creating a tyrannical atmosphere where it was said, "Those who are not of this [Taira] clan must be all nonhumans." However, Kiyomori's first son, Shigemori (1138–79), was known for "his extremely beautiful heart" *(imijiku kokoro uruwashiku)*, as Jien put it in *Gukanshō*—as evinced, Jien said, by the wish he expressed to "die soon" when he discerned his father's "rebellious intent." In that milieu he became the symbol of the good conscience of the Taira clan.

10. In a power struggle with Goshirakawa, in the mid-eleventh month of the third year of Jishō (1179), Kiyomori forced Chancellor Motofusa to resign (and later demoted him to the post of acting commander of Dazaifu), fired Prime Minister Moronaga, Acting Major Councilor Sukekata, and thirty-seven other officials. Five days later he shut Goshirakawa up in Toba Palace. Even though at the time Takakura was Emperor, Mishima makes Sutoku refer to Goshirakawa as "ruling Emperor" because Goshirakawa in his "retirement" wielded actual power. Sutoku and Goshirakawa had the same mother.

popularity will immediately be swept away, and a rare, unprecedented thing will occur.[11] We'll lure all our enemies to Yashima Bay, which is right before us, and sink the infant emperor, the generals, soldiers, and all at the bottom of the ocean.[12] Oh, how good we'll feel then! If my main wish is achieved in about ten years, my rewards to you will be as you please.

Now, I am not neglectful of any one of those who perished for me, but you, Tameyoshi, above all,

TAMEYOSHI: Yes, Sire.

RETIRED EMPEROR SUTOKU: I shall never forget the loyal service you rendered to me by bringing many of your sons. All the young ones were beheaded during Hōgen, and the only surviving one now is Tametomo. Nonetheless, Tametomo,

(His name called, Tametomo puts his sword in its sheath and reels forward as if pulled by a string, but the ghosts, as if unaware of his presence, remain utterly indifferent. He walks up to Tameyoshi.)

TAMETOMO: I haven't seen you for a long time, Father.

(Tameyoshi does not notice that he is being addressed. Tametomo, coming in front of Sutoku and suddenly realizing that he is so close to the Emperor, shudders, takes a few steps back and prostrates himself.[13])

RETIRED EMPEROR SUTOKU: Nonetheless, Tametomo, resentful of the world and despairing of himself, dares to try to erase himself by committing suicide. This will never do. If he goes to Higo Province[14] this year when midwinter comes, he will unexpectedly meet some people from his past and find ways of consoling himself. Shouldn't he restrain himself from hastiness born of shallow thinking? There are certain to be good results from good causes, and his descendants will prosper, which I will assist with my spiritual power.

11. Here Mishima may be referring to the legend that Kiyomori's fever, which led to his death, was such that his body repelled water "like a hot stone or iron" and the water that touched his body "burned up in flames," as *Heike Monogatari* puts it.

12. The war between the Taira and Minamoto began in the eighth month of 1180. In the second month of 1185 the top Minamoto commander, Yoshitsune, defeated the Taira forces that had assembled in Yashima, in Sanuki (then an island; today part of a small peninsula), which, as Mishima makes Sutoku say here, was very close to where Sutoku was exiled and died. In the following month, in the Battle of Dannoura, Yoshitsune annihilated the remaining Taira forces. The Taira had taken Emperor Antoku with them as they fled Kyoto and as their defeat became certain in the sea battle, many soldiers and ladies chose to plunge themselves into the sea. One lady did so with Antoku in her arms. He was seven years old at the time.

13. Normally a warrior did not come face to face with the Emperor; they communicated with each other through an aristocratic intermediary.

14. Today's Kumamoto.

TAMEYOSHI: I, your insignificant vassal, had many sons, but Tametomo stood out among them in wisdom and courage. So I've been feeling particularly sorry for what has happened to him. In the circumstances nothing brings me greater joy than the news that his descendants will prosper. I can only express my humble gratitude to Your Majesty's magnanimous considerations, Sire.

(He expresses his gratitude. He and Yorinaga then offer a cup and pour sake. Su-toku, in turn, passes his cup to his vassals gathered there, and the cup makes the round—around Tametomo.)

(Suddenly there is the first rooster's call. Sutoku drops his cup, surprised.)

RETIRED EMPEROR SUTOKU: So it's already time for the rooster. We all have to go now.

(He gets into the palanquin with some haste, the palanquin descends under the floor, and all disappear. Tametomo remains prostrate for a while, bewildered. There are indications of the sun rising in the east. There are incessant calls of roosters now. Tametomo raises his face.)

TAMETOMO: So it's already daybreak. I see, all this has been a dream. *(So saying and looking around, he picks up the cup Sutoku had dropped.)* Lo and behold! This is an imperial cup. After all, all this was true.

(He reverentially holds up the cup and puts it in the chest fold of his robe. As he does so, there is batataba *with Kiheiji running toward him on the hanamichi.)*

KIHEIJI: Oh, you are safe and sound, milord! Congratulations! You're safe and sound! I feel this has prolonged my life!

TAMETOMO: So you've followed me, worried about me. All this is gratifying! Now then, let us together leave Sanuki Bay by boat so we may reach Higo Province as soon as we can.

KIHEIJI: To Higo Province? For what purpose, sir?

TAMETOMO: Come, now, it's the Newly Retired Emperor's *(The remark signaling the change of scene)* divine advice.

SCENE IN THE MOUNTAINS OF KIHARA, HIGO PROVINCE

In the mountains of Kihara, Higo Province. A "prop curtain"[15] *with a snowy scene painted on it comes down. From stage left enter Hunters Sampei and Rimpei.*

HUNTER SAMPEI: As we track his footsteps in the snow,
   we sense the boar will show up anytime now,

---

15. *Dōgu-maku:* any of the curtains used temporarily to suggest a scene and hide what lies behind it.

HUNTER RIMPEI: here and there are droppings, bristles;
  in the mountains of Kihara above all,
SAMPEI: there's a man-eating boar, the rumor says,
  as many as four folk of the village
RIMPEI: have perished on account of his tusks.
  If we only wounded him the wrong way,
SAMPEI: he'd be a crazy boar with wild guts
  and we'd never be able to deal with him.
RIMPEI: We'd rather leave our job to someone else.
  Should a tough-minded traveling samurai
  subdue the boar—if that happened,
SAMPEI: *(Ostentatiously shaking the sake-gourd hanging from his hip)*
  we'd reward him with this rot-gut,
  regale him with a "whale pot"[16]
RIMPEI: famous in Higo and in so doing
SAMPEI: get some meat to take back home. . . .
  There I see a man.
RIMPEI: For now let's be sure
SAMPEI: not to make a mistake.
RIMPEI: I know, I know.
  (The two exit stage left. With that as signal, the prop curtain is dropped. A bliz-
  zard starts. On the hanamichi enter Tametomo and Kiheiji in straw coats and
  hats. They stop at seven-three.)
TAMETOMO: What a snowfall, this!
  Since I received the divine advice
  at White Peak, it's already three months.
  We've been here in Higo that we aimed for,
  but we have yet to meet those from the past
  as we wander in Kihara mountains,
KIHEIJI: the day darkening in bamboo along the path,
  we never know what bandit may be hiding.
  Be careful, milord.
TAMETOMO: That hardly need be said. Come, Kiheiji.
KIHEIJI: Yes, sir.
  (As the master and servant approach main stage toward stage left, a giant boar the
  size of a bull emerges from the bamboo-grass bush and attacks the two. Tametomo
  steps aside with agility. The boar dashes as far as the hanamichi, turns around,
  and heads back toward him. Kiheiji throws pebbles at him as fast as he picks them
  up. This makes the boar hesitate a bit, but in the end he continues his head-on at-
  tack. Tametomo lifts his foot and kicks him in the flank. The boar falters. Tameto-

16. "Whale" here is a local term for "boar meat."

mo pushes him against a rock, kicks and tramples upon him, until the boar, weak-
ened and exhausted, lies flat on the ground. The master and servant then stab him
with their swords.)

    (Enter Hunters Sampei and Rimpei from stage left)

SAMPEI: He got him, he got him!

RIMPEI: A giant boar the size of a bull.

SAMPEI: Got him barehanded. Incomparable strength!

RIMPEI: In comparison, we, though hunters

SAMPEI: since our grandpas' generation,

RIMPEI: are too embarrassed for words.

SAMPEI: Yes sir, yes sir, Mr. Samurai, we are simply

RIMPEI: amazed at you.

TAMETOMO: You seem to live around here. We've been lost in this snow,
the day darkening, so this boar is our gift to you. We ask you to serve
as our guides.

SAMPEI: Well, sir, just about a couple of miles up from here, we have our
houses and we'd be happy to offer lodging.

TAMETOMO: That's gratifying.

SAMPEI: For now, though, sir, the rule here is
    to celebrate the capture of a boar
    by tasting a slice of its meat on the spot,
    exchanging a cup, that's the hunters' etiquette.
    By luck we also have sake right here.
    After warming our bodies frozen with snow
    we'll then be your happy guides.

TAMETOMO: That's interesting. What do you say, Kiheiji?

KIHEIJI: We don't know anything about these fellows. We better be careful, sir.

TAMETOMO: When in a village, do as the villagers do, they say. Come, don't
be so stiff-necked.

SAMPEI: So we've got our lordship's permission. Rimpei, make a fire. I'll
entertain them with our local brew while you prepare the meat. Now,
sirs, where are you from and where are you going?

    (He pours rot-gut from his gourd and offers it to the master and servant.)

TAMETOMO: By some guidance we came to Higo but we were lost in
these mountains and have faced some unexpected difficulties.

SAMPEI: Difficulties? No, sir, this is a rare exploit. When the villagers learn
about this, they will enshrine and worship you.

TAMETOMO: Timely sake to entertain us. Kiheiji, this is what makes travel fascinating, isn't it?

KIHEIJI: Milord, take care not to have too much of it.

SAMPEI: You, too, sir, have a cup.

(He continues to pour for them. In a while Tametomo and Kiheiji make evident that they cannot move their bodies.)

TAMETOMO: Mmm, what's this?

KIHEIJI: This, in fact, is a drugged sake.

TAMETOMO: We've been trapped.

KIHEIJI: Watch out, sir.

SAMPEI: Rimpei, don't you fail to get them!

RIMPEI: Never!

(They start to fight. Sampei and Rimpei, holding ropes, wrestle down the reeling master and servant and in the end manage to tie their hands behind them. At an appropriate moment, there's a signal for prop change and the stage rotates.)

SCENE IN THE MOUNTAIN FORT, SAME AS ABOVE

The main stage is a 3-ken-wide room with a taka'ashi no nijū platform,[17] the roof thatched with tufts of pampas grass, all the pillars and other wooden parts are "natural," unplaned, etc., although the entire structure has a palatial appearance. Toward stage left is a room closed off with papered sliding doors. The lantern-shaped door[18] at center is framed with wisteria vines and draped with quilted cotton fabric. The railings are also made of natural wood tied together with vines. Up front hangs a bamboo blind. Everything suggests a mountain fort in a snowy landscape.)

CHAMBERMAID CHIGUSA: *(From behind the blind)* The master of the mansion[19] will conduct an inspection. Bring out the captive.

VOICE: Yes, ma'am.

(The voice comes from stage left. With it Takihei, in the guise of a hunter, enters. He is leading Butōta by a rope.)

CHIGUSA: *(From behind the blind)* Explain to the master of the mansion in detail how you have managed to bring him.

TAKIHEI: Yes, ma'am. In accordance with instructions, I was standing guard on the mountain when this drug vendor came along and asked directions. I took a close look. He was a man of superior make, so I deliberately provoked him into a fight. But his strength was amazing, surely far above what you come across normally. And so pretending to make peace, I offered sake and then captured him.

---

17. *Sangen no ma, taka'ashi no nijū:* The original nō stage was a 3-*ken*-square space, one *ken* being equal to 6 feet (1.8 meters). Today, the spatial designation for the kabuki stage has not changed, but the actual width is 10.2 *ken* or 61.2 feet. *Taka'ashi no nijū* refers to the height of a structure raised from the stage floor that is equal to 2 *shaku*, 8 *sun* or 2 feet, 9 inches.

18. *Gatōguchi:* used as a door to the interior backstage in a palatial setting.

19. *O-yakata-sama.*

CHIGUSA: *(From behind the blind)* Does he seem useful?

TAKIHEI: I think he knows martial arts. After the inspection I think we can add him to our team.

CHIGUSA: *(From behind the blind)* But you say he was wandering in the snow. A drug vendor's attire is a little strange, too. Are you sure he isn't a spy?

TAKIHEI: Everything should become clear through the inspection.

CHIGUSA: *(From behind the blind)* Tell him the rules, the master of the mansion instructs us.

TAKIHEI: Yes, ma'am. *(To Butōta)* Listen to me carefully. The master of the mansion here is a lady from a high house, though I cannot reveal her name. For reasons I cannot give, she has hidden herself in these mountains to secretly gather men of arms with the intent of turning herself into a dragon rising up high into the clouds and rain.[20] We already have twenty to thirty men staying with us. As soon as you agree to be our ally, we'll untie your rope and add you to our team. Or if you do not agree, we won't let you go alive. Our rule here is that the master of the mansion herself hears your response. So make up your mind and give your response. We're ready for the lady's inspection, ma'am.

CHIGUSA: *(From behind the blind)* I understand. Master of the mansion, we are ready

ALL THE CHAMBERMAIDS: for your inspection.

(The blind rises. At center sits Princess Shiranui leaning on an armrest, dressed as a Red Princess,[21] with a deer skin draping her left shoulder. Lined up with her are Chambermaids Chigusa, Yamaogi, Konomi, and Shiinoha.)

SHIRANUI: Captive, raise your face.

(Butōta raises his face sharply. Shiranui shows surprise.)

SHIRANUI: Look at you now; you're Butōta!

BUTŌTA: I sure am!

> Princess Shiranui was thought to have died.
> but she's alive somewhere, the rumor said.
> On government order I went as far as Ōshima
> to track you down. Soldiers had taken
> a woman who threw herself to her death
> to be you, Shiranui. I inspected
> and they couldn't explain themselves.
> Then I ran around several provinces,

---

20. *Kōryō un'u o u:* a metaphor for a hero grasping the right opportunity to show his true worth.

21. *Akahime:* In kabuki a princess usually appears in a vermilion costume brocaded with gold and silver threads. Otherwise, "red" indicates evil or bravery or both.

finally coming to this province, Higo.
As soon as I heard that here on Mount Kihara
a mysterious woman maintains a fort,
I turned myself into a drug vendor
and sneaked into this area as a spy.
And yet with you, Shiranui, before my eyes,
I can't move my limbs drugged with sake,
dammit, I'm so chagrined, I'm so sour.

SHIRANUI: You're a dog, a beast in a human skin. How dare you bark like that in my face? You were a lowly man but Lord Tametomo treated you kindly. Nevertheless, when, after his defeat in the Hōgen disturbance, he was trying to heal his arrow wounds in the hot spring of Ishiyama, you were blinded by an excessive reward and turned yourself into an informer. Your crime is as clear as a mirror. The evidence is the wound on your forehead that Kiheiji gave you with a sword at the time. You sold your lord who'd done so much for you. You should have died of shame. Instead, you've searched out me even, Shiranui, meanwhile piling up one evil deed upon another. That you're captured and in my hands now is the sign that Heaven's Way hasn't decayed yet. I'm glad; I'm grateful. If you hadn't turned informer, Lord Tametomo, a man without compare in strength and bravery, wouldn't have been put to the humiliation of exile. Because of you, his family have scattered, I myself forced to the sad fate of wandering. Many of his loyal vassals have lost their lives. Those who have survived have fallen into poverty and continue to have many a difficulty. I can't loathe you enough. At the time of hot spring healing at Ishiyama, you pretended to care for him in every way, even while leading the enemy to his defenseless bathing place to capture him alive. The world hasn't seen a nonhuman like yourself.

CHIGUSA: May I say, master of the mansion,
    to punish this inhuman human being

CHAMBERMAID YAMAOGI: chopping his head off wouldn't satisfy us,
    tearing him into eight pieces wouldn't appease us,

CHAMBERMAID KONOMI: on behalf of Lord Tametomo,
    in order to mete out justice to avenge him

CHAMBERMAID KATSURAGI: we'd have to kill him slowly, cut him slowly;

CHAMBERMAID SHIINOHA: what's the best way to do that, I wonder.

CHIGUSA: Oh yes, I've just had a great idea, everyone.

ALL THE OTHER CHAMBERMAIDS: Chigusa, what is your idea?

CHIGUSA: The "wood-hammer punishment" that Higo bandits have handed down for years would be very good, I think.

ALL THE OTHER CHAMBERMAIDS: That's so scary!

CHIGUSA: Master of the mansion, what would you say?

SHIRANUI: You may decide whatever you please. I'll play the koto and sing. Chigusa, bring the koto.

CHIGUSA: Yes, milady.

(Chambermaids bring the koto and place it in front of Shiranui. They also bring out five wood hammers and a pile of bamboo nails. With Takihei's help, they strip Butōta of his clothes until he is left with only a loincloth. They then put him in a sitting position and tie him, his hands in back, to the left pillar at the end of a railing to stage right. Then with their eyes they signal Takihei to leave. While this is going on a blizzard starts, followed by incessant snow.)

CHIGUSA: Everything is ready for the punishment, milady.

SHIRANUI: Butōta, listen.

> The music I'm about to play is "Light Snow,"
> which, while I was in Dazaifu,
> I played as Lord Tametomo requested
> every intimate night we made love
> like a pair of mandarin ducks,[22]
> a tune my husband liked above all others.
> This koto song was an omen perhaps.
> Our union light as light snow,
> we parted, sadly, not sure we would meet again,
> all this because of your inhuman ways.
> Listen to it with that in mind,
> and you will know your crimes to be
> as heavy as the snow that accumulates.
> Women, never hurry in your punishment.
> Follow this music, "Light Snow,"
> at the song's every turn, tune's every twist,
> turn them, twist them, into the man,
> into every organ, every limb.

CHIGUSA: We all perfectly

ALL THE OTHER CHAMBERMAIDS: understand you, lady.

SHIRANUI: *(She plays the koto and sings)*

> Aggrieved over my fate,
> the union of light snow,
> the keepsake of my love who's left,
> the tears are all that remain.

---

22. A metaphor for uxorious love in Chinese (and therefore Japanese) tradition.

(She sings; she plays the music; and at every turn where only the accompanying music is played, the chambermaids each with a wooden hammer strike a bamboo nail into various parts of Butōta's body—the right shoulder blade, the left shoulder blade, the right arm, left arm, stomach, in that order—and each time he groans aloud. In the end he is covered with blood. As Shiranui finishes "all that remain," she and Chigusa exchange a glance, and Chigusa hammers a bamboo nail into Butōta's heart and kills him. The chambermaids untie him and show the corpse to Shiranui. She rises to her feet and looks down upon it.)

SHIRANUI: So he's breathed his last. Give the corpse to the wolves.[23]

(The blind falls.)

(From stage left enter Sampei leading Tametomo by a rope and Rimpei leading Kiheiji by a rope.)

SAMPEI: The master of the mansion's inspection will take place soon,

RIMPEI: so we might as well wait for the summons right here.

TAMETOMO: You are not hunters; you are actually samurai in disguise, aren't you?

SAMPEI: Now that we've lived so long in these mountains,
we have no worry that we'll be revealed.

RIMPEI: Together with this Sampei here,
we hunt for warriors wandering in the mountains.

KIHEIJI: For what reason do you act so rudely to my lord?

SAMPEI: We'll tell you the reason in time. Relax. We have no intention of killing you.

RIMPEI: It's entirely up to you, whether you are going to stay alive or die.

SAMPEI: Remain calm

RIMPEI: while awaiting the decision.

TAMETOMO: Listen here, Kiheiji.
For a while I've been puzzled about one thing.
I thought this was a mountain bandits' abode,
but that exquisite tune that came over the snow,
that was none other than the music "Light Snow,"
and the voice heard intermittently, singing,
"The keepsake of my love who's left,
the tears," the voice so singing was
what's stayed in my ears, unforgettably.
Yes, yes, while we were in Dazaifu,

---

23. As Bakin tells the story, Tametomo had a pair of wolves as his pets and dedicated friends during his Kyūshū days. (Wolves inhabited Japan until they were practically exterminated during the Edo period. The last known specimen was captured in Nara, in the early twentieth century.)

we nightly heard that koto song of Shiranui.

You do remember that, don't you?

KIHEIJI: You didn't have to say that, sir; for some time

I was pricking up my ears to hear what it was.

The tune was none other than "Light Snow."

Could it be, the lady's also a captive . . . ?

SAMPEI: You, shut up, you!

CHIGUSA: *(From behind the blind)* Master of the mansion's inspection.

(The blind rises. Tametomo turns sharply to look.)

TAMETOMO: You *are* Shiranui!

SHIRANUI: Milord! Is this a dream?

KIHEIJI: What in the world is this?

SHIRANUI: *(She rushes down. To Sampei and Rimpei)* Remove his ropes. I say,

quick. Who do you think he is? He's my husband, Lord Tametomo.

SAMPEI, RIMPEI: Yes, ma'am.

(Agitated, they can't easily remove the ropes. Tametomo, Kiheiji, Shiranui, Chi-gusa, Sampei, and Rimpei all get entangled, each holding the tip of a rope, to present an amusing scene. In the end the ropes become untangled all at once, and all of them fall flat on their backsides.)

SHIRANUI: Oh my, oh my! How can this be possible? How can there be

a wife who ties up her husband with a rope?

TAMETOMO: What a mysterious reunion! My dear wife, how did all this

come about?

SHIRANUI: Once I start telling you, it will be a long story.

But though a woman, I decided to raise an army

and set up camp here in these mountains

and secretly gathered together stalwart warriors.

The numbing sake is a woman's device.

Would you please forgive me, milord.

VOICE: *(From within the section closed off with papered sliding doors)* Father, you

have finally returned to us. This is a great occasion to celebrate, sir.

TAMETOMO: Whose voice is that?

SHIRANUI: That's our youthful son, Sutemaru, who will soon come of age.

Please take a look at him, milord.

(The papered sliding doors open. There sits Sutemaru, with Takama no Tarō and his wife in attendance, and other attendants. Shiranui makes an obeisance to Tametomo. With correct ceremony, the group in the room with papered sliding doors comes down to the stage floor in stately solemnity. In turn, Tametomo steps up to the raised floor and seats himself at center.)

(All on the stage floor prostrate themselves.)

TAMETOMO: What a fortunate day!

All this is because of the imperial cup

(He takes the cup out of the chest of his robe)
   the Newly Retired Emperor gave me at his mausoleum,
   which, turning round and round Meandering Water,[24]
   has achieved this mysterious union. His divine power!
I am grateful; I don't deserve this honor. Come, everyone, do partake of
the flow of this cup.
   Except, of course, we have no use for the drugged sake.
   (Chigusa and other chambermaids step out and pour sake.)

TAKAMA: We've missed you, sir. After we parted in Ōshima, we wandered
   until we reached this place where I took upon myself the role of protecting Master Sutemaru, and having brought him up, I have the humble honor of seeing you and our young master come face to face. This
   is so overwhelming I don't know how to describe it.

KIHEIJI: Now that you are here with us, sir, the two dozen stalwarts we
   have on our side can more than equal a million horsemen. When we
   raise our banners, all the landed warriors, down to the farmers, will rush
   to us uninvited. If we then drive the governor out, set up our base in
   Dazaifu, and bring Kyūshū entirely under control, we'll have no reason
   to dread the government forces.

TAMETOMO: Yes, but an army shouldn't be raised without some foundation. We'll hole up here until summer, lining up soldiers and preparing weapons, and then we'll build warships, cross over to the capital in
   a single sweep, strike Kiyomori, and crush all the red banners of the
   Taira Clan.

SHIRANUI: Yes, indeed, when that happens, I, Shiranui, will take up my
   halberd and join your army,

ISOHAGI: I, Isohagi, will carry your flag,

SUTEMARU: and I, Sutemaru, will compete with Takama no Tarō to see
   which of us can reach the enemy forces first.

---

24. *Kyokusui (no en):* a banquet at which people seat themselves at strategic points along
a meandering stream to drink and compose poems. The person most upstream composes
a poem, drinks, and puts the emptied cup in the stream; the next person downstream must
compose a poem before the cup floats down to him; he then drinks sake in the same cup
and puts the emptied cup in the stream, and so on. This drinking-cum-poetry-writing
game originated in China where Calligraphic Sage Wang Hsi-chih (c. 303–c. 361) famously describes one such banquet taking place near Mount K'uai-chi, in 353, in his
"Preface to the Gathering at the Orchid Pavilion" (see *Possessing the Past,* Wen C. Fong
and James C. Y. Watt, Metropolitan Museum of Art, 1996, p. 108). In Japan it was prac-
ticed among the Heian nobles until the ninth century or so, during the Festival of the
Peach, on the third of the third month.

TAMETOMO: You are all so brave, so brave! To wipe out the shame of
Mount K'uai-chi,[25] today's snow is the Genji's white banners,
SHIRANUI: this white cloth as it is,
KIHEIJI: the white banners to cover the whole ground,
TAKAMA: the Capital will soon be a snowy scene,
ISOHAGI: valorous exploits accumulated
SUTEMARU: by my own hand.
TAMETOMO: All so felicitous. *(He opens his fan to signal the rotation of the stage.)*
All so felicitous.

SCENE IN THE SEA SOUTH OF SATSUMA[26]

*The stage rotates from the preceding scene to a "swept-up stage"[27] covered with
white cloths to indicate waves, with a distant view of the Province of Higo. The
jōruri narrative opens with boisterous accompaniment.)*

[Chants] Familiar place to live,
Higo lies in distant haze to a distant eye,
one thing missing in the abandoned village,
the Capital bird[28] calling in solitary loyalty,
the ships gliding over quiet waves,
their masts arched in the sky with full white sails.

*(The kakiwari[29] is flipped to reveal a second painting that shows the land at a
farther distance.)*

[Chants] Heave-ho! Heave-ho!
The rowers are swift with a rowing song,
kicking up Genji's white waves so high
they overshadow Kiyomori
who rises up as a monstrous cloud,

---

25. Defeating an enemy who once defeated you or killing someone who once humiliated you. The phrase refers to Yüeh king Kou-chien's humiliating defeat in a battle with
Wu King Fu-ch'a on Mount K'uai-chi and his eventual triumph. As Grand Historian Ssu-
ma Ch'ien (c. 145–c. 90 BCE) put it: "[Kou-chien's wise vassal Fan Li], putting himself
through hardships, joining forces with Kou-chien, and conspiring with him for more than
twenty years, finally destroyed Wu, thereby avenging the shame at K'uai-chi."

26. Today's Kagoshima, southernmost prefecture in Kyūshū.

27. *Haki-butai:* stage with no human figures, though with certain props.

28. Literal translation of *miyakodori:* eastern oystercatcher. This migrant bird used to
visit Japan in considerable flocks.

29. The name of a prop made of canvas set on a wood frame. It is used to show an in-
door or outdoor scene.

who rises up as a monstrous cloud![30]

(The kakiwari is flipped to reveal a third painting to show the land at an even farther distance.)

[Chants] Now to avenge his lordship's fury,
we secretly push all the way to the Capital
to subjugate the Taira Clan,
our warships blinding upon the sea.

(The kakiwari is flipped to reveal a curtain with only waves painted on it[31] and no land.)

[Chants] Aboard the lead ship is Lord General,
Soldier Shiranui by his side,
both full of courage and bravery.

(A large ship with a white sail is raised from under the floor. Standing at the bow is Tametomo holding up his military fan; behind him are Shiranui, who holds a halberd under her arm, Sampei, Rimpei, Takihei, and other soldiers.)

TAMETOMO: We're so glad. The time was ripe; the tides were full; and we set out for the Capital over the ocean in order to prove Su Wu's steadfastness.[32] I'm convinced it's within our grasp to take the heads of Kiyomori and Shinzei[33] and offer them to the Newly Retired Emperor's mausoleum. Everyone, this is the time for loyal service.

SOLDIER TAKIHEI: Lord General, your momentum and bravery will repel any enemy running up against you. The beneficial result of your sleeping on chopped wood and licking livers[34] is obvious today in the glorious manner you set out for battle. We all

ALL IN UNISON: congratulate you, sir.

SHIRANUI: For me, too, this is the fulfillment of a long-standing wish. It's all like a dream, milord.

---

30. The original verbally plays on the fact that Kiyomori became a lay priest *(nyūdō)* late in his life and the fact that cumulus is called *nyūdō-gumo* because the cauliflower head of a cumulus is thought to resemble a priest's shaven head.

31. Called *namitesuri* in kabuki.

32. Su Wu (140–60 BCE), a general of the Former Han, went to meet the Huns as Emperor Wu's envoy and was captured. He was not swayed by the Huns and remained loyal to his country. After nineteen years of captivity, he managed to return home.

33. Fujiwara no Michinori (d. 1159), for whom see the headnote to this play. The harsh measures he took after the Hōgen disturbance was one cause of the Heiji disturbance. After the initial skirmishes he was captured while on the run and beheaded. Mishima suggests that Tametomo, having been exiled four years earlier, wasn't aware of Shinzei's fate.

34. That is, willingness to endure hardships to avenge oneself. According to legend, Wu king Fu-ch'a slept on chopped wood to constantly remind himself of the need to avenge his father who was defeated by Yüeh king Kou-chien. Kou-chien, in turn, licked bitter-tasting livers to remind himself of the need to avenge himself after he was defeated by Fu-ch'a. Some attribute both acts to Kou-chien.

TAMETOMO: This route should take us east, but we must have become confused in the early morning mist. We seem to be moving southward. Let me look at the tides.

[Chants] So saying he steps down onto the gunwale
and looks closely at the sea.

Look, this is disturbing!
The sea water has turned dirty, churning, foamy;
an abundance of jellyfish float in the water;
flocks of flying fish are suddenly flying about.

Judging by the seasonal winds that I used to know in crossing the seas around Ōshima, I see an evil wind is about to rise. Unless we deal with it quickly, our ship will be capsized in no time. Quick, pull down the sail!

ALL: Yes, sir!

(They hastily pull down the sail, then try to lay anchor, but evidently unable to hit bottom, show consternation. Then there's the sense that Sutemaru's ship has caught up with Tametomo's ship, its bow appearing at stage right, with Sutemaru standing there and 800-yard Pebble Thrower Kiheiji and Takama no Tarō and Iso-hagi in the lower section.)

KIHEIJI: We're being forced south, and the look of the sea isn't right, either. What do you think, sir?

TAMETOMO: You're quite right. We've been forced off course. I suspect that we're about a hundred miles away from Satsuma. There are signs that a foul wind will rise, but we have no harbor to drop anchor in.

KIHEIJI: Our ships are big enough that if we tie them and work together, we might avert the crisis. Come, Lord Takama!

TAKAMA: All right!

[Chants] He tries to throw a hawser, but Tametomo stops him.

TAMETOMO: You've got it wrong! For father and son to be aboard the same ship in a crisis is no way to fight. Yes, all is up to Heaven's Way, but it can't be that the fate of master and servants alike is all evil. Each of us must leave himself to his own fate. Come to think of it, we set sail on the fifteenth of the eighth month, when the tail star of the Big Dipper pointed at a typhoon, didn't we?

[Chants] Before he finishes, there come blasts of wind;
the sky suddenly darkens with clouds;
the rain pours down as if a tray were upset;
the waves rise, boiling, six, nine yards high,
dancing round and round the large ship,
dunking and rolling them, smashing waves,

(The ships are twisted by the foul winds, splashed with waves, as they rise, as they dive.)

[*Chants*] They all pitch and yaw, fall suddenly,
and Sutemaru's ship becomes separated.
(*They pitch and yaw, and the ship to stage right withdraws.*)
[*Chants*] Shiranui calls out, "Oh, my son!"
her scream drowned by the thunder god,
the ship almost overturning.
[*Chants*] Shiranui raises her voice loudly.

SHIRANUI: Prince Yamato Takeru, I hear, while sailing on his way to sub-jugate the eastern barbarians, ran into a storm, but his endangered life was saved, I'm told, when his empress, Princess Ototachibana, got into the water.[35] If I turn my body into a sacrifice and offer it to the Sea God, the wind may cease. Even without me, there's no question that our great wish will be fulfilled as long as you, milord, your soldiers, and Sutemaru remain alive in this world. Farewell.

[*Chants*] She readies herself to plunge in.

TAMETOMO: No, wait, Shiranui.

Your admirable heart aside,
I'm a wanderer with imperial wrath
and don't deserve comparison to Yamato Takeru.
If we are to die, we'll die together.
I'll tolerate no rash act.

SHIRANUI: Those words of love are our bondage.

Guided by the Newly Retired Emperor,
we, husband and wife, were reunited last winter.
The happiness of the half year since then
was a blessing wholly unexpected.
Is it a dream or reality, I've wondered.
Should I be greedy about this good luck,
I might trample upon the divine wish, I fear.
Genji's tutelary deity, Otokoyama Shō Hachiman,[36]

---

35. As described in the *Kojiki*, "When [Yamato Takeru] went out of the country and tried to cross the sea called Running Water, the deity of the strait stirred up the waves and turned his ship round and round, so the prince could not make any headway. When she saw this, his empress, whose name was Princess Ototachibana, said, 'I'll go into the sea in your place. You, milord, must complete your mission and report to His Majesty.' She then had eight reed mattresses, eight leather mattresses, and eight silk mattresses laid on the waves, and went down to sit on them. The rough waves quieted down on their own, and the prince's ship could now proceed." See Hiroaki Sato, *Legends of the Samurai*, p. 7. *Jusui*, "getting into the water," is a euphemism for drowning oneself.

36. Otokoyama ("Mount Man"), in southern Kyoto, has a famous shrine dedicated to the Minamoto's tutelary deity, Hachiman, at its top.

Newly Retired Emperor's soul
imprecating this heavenly cup,
(She reverentially holds up the cup)
looking upon us with accepting pity,[37]
Eight Dragon Kings[38] responding,
may my husband and friends aboard this ship,
along with my son's ship, be blown
to some harbor without a mishap!
[Chants] So offering prayers in a high voice,
she sweeps her sleeves aside
and throws herself toward the bottom
a thousand leagues deep, parting the waves.
Mysterious, out of the sea dances
a black swallowtail of the darkness of hell.
The butterfly flits about as if reluctant to depart
before becoming lost in the storm.

(Shiranui steps into the water. A black butterfly appears on a sashigane[39] *and soon leaves.)*

[Chants] But wind and rain show no sign of ceasing,
the waves rising unceasingly like high peaks,
the ship drawn down into the valley.
Soldiers now giving up.

(The storm worsens and the ship is gradually lowered. When it has sunk to the gunwale)

SOLDIER SAMPEI: Now we'll be

ALL THE OTHER SOLDIERS: the forerunners of death.

(The soldiers stab each other in groups of two and get into the water through the kiriana.[40]*)*

TAMETOMO: What fabulous luck Kiyomori has!
If I, Tametomo, assembled diehard soldiers
and went to the Capital in secrecy,
I could get his head, I thought.
But even the Dragon Deity[41] follows the times,
contorts himself to aid the Taira.

---

37. The original for "accepting pity," *aimin nōju* is a set phrase in prayer, as in the nō play *Dōjōji*.

38. The protectors of the Lotus Sutra.

39. A section of baleen or a wire painted black, handled by a *kōken*, stage assistant, to manipulate an object.

40. A square hole on the floor of the stage or the hanamichi. Often ghosts and monsters come out of and disappear through it.

41. The deity in charge of the sea and other large bodies of water.

When one runs out of one's luck,
there's no reason to resent society or men.
I don't know where Sutemaru's ship is,
I've lost my wife and all my soldiers.
How can I go on living like this?
     Did I ever expect
to spend a number of years on wild shores
and, just when my wish is about to be fulfilled,
to find myself buffeted by wind and waves
and sink on an eightfold briny route
in the wild, utterly unknown sea?
[Chants] When everything seems to be over now,
a dark cloud descends from heaven upon the ship,
and odd, bizarre-looking tengu.

(When Tametomo, joining his hands in prayer at the gunwale of the sinking ship, is about to get into the water, a dark cloud descends and from stage left a "wave platform"[42] *carrying many crow-tengu is pushed out at the level of the upper end of the curtain with waves painted on it. These tengu jump onto the ship and immediately set to work, bailing, steering, etc. Also, some of those on the "wave platform" make the gesture of pulling up the ship and the ship rises.)*

TAMETOMO: This is no doubt the Newly Retired Emperor's divine aid. God! I don't deserve this honor.

(He joins his hands in prayer, signaling the change of scene. The stage rotates.)

[Chants] Meanwhile, Sutemaru's ship,
tossed by the wild waves, separated,
drifts about, not knowing where,
the rudder broken, nothing to be done.
Kiheiji bows, his hands down.

(Sutemaru's ship, constructed as part of the stage floor,[43] *has a storm-battered appearance. Takama no Tarō and Isohagi flank Sutemaru to protect him. Kiheiji seats himself before Sutemaru and places his hands on the floor.)*

KIHEIJI: My hope to serve you in the first battle
of your blossoming fragrant self, ended,
now our campaign can take on as enemies
only those various fishes all in vain.
Accompanying you to the battlefield

42. Called *namidai*.
43. Called *itatsuki*, "glued to the board," in kabuki.

a thousand leagues down breaks my heart.
I feel so sorry for you, sir.
[Chants] So he tries to shout, but voice not rising,
he suddenly rolls, picks himself up,
and all his strength gone, he offers prayers
to the wild sea. Even as he does this
(As he offers prayers)
[Chants] the ship smashes into a rock,
breaks up, splintering with a crack,
(The ship breaks in two, and all aboard are thrown into the sea.)
[Chants] The sea of Eight Sufferings[44]
where life and death flow and tumble
is terrifying.
(With this as a signal for a change of scene.)

(As the ship, broken in two, is withdrawn to stage right, a large rock is pulled out from stage left. Takama no Tarō and Isohagi swim to it and, helping each other, step up onto it.)

TAKAMA: Now that Sutemaru has entered the water,
to be late in doing so is being disloyal.
I, having been born in a warriors' house,
becoming sick and dying is against my wish,
but rather than drowning for no excuse,
my heart dictates that I kill my loving wife
with my own hands, then kill myself.[45]
You think the same way, do you not?
ISOHAGI: Our marriage bond not ended,
to have my husband's sword touch me,
this must be a deep pledge in a past life,

---

44. Life, old age, disease, death, parting with someone you love, meeting someone you hate, the inability to get what you want, and "five *skandas*"—namely, form, perception, conception, volition, and consciousness.

45. The samurai ethos during certain periods held the samurai's greatest honor to be to die while fighting on a battlefield and, failing that, to kill himself. The genius of guerrilla warfare, Kusunoki Masashige (1294–1336), exemplified that idea by going into a hopeless battle and, failing to die during battle, committing suicide with his remaining men. See Hiroaki Sato, *Legends of the Samurai*, pp. 157–87. Even before Masashige took that action, at least two groups from the enemy forces committed similar mass suicides. See Eiko Ikegami, *The Taming of the Samurai: Honorific Individualism and the Making of Modern Japan* (Harvard University Press, 1995), pp. 108–9.

and I'm so glad of that covenant.
If there's anything left that I sorely regret,
it's that we don't know whatever happened
to Princess Shiranui whom I served for years,
and even our young master we attended to
has been taken away by the waves.
After all this how could we live on?

TAKAMA: A person makes his life worthwhile by his final thoughts. Before another wave overtakes us, we must hurry and catch up with him.

[Chants] One soothing the other, being soothed

TAKAMA: Be ready, Isohagi.

[Chants] the tip of his sword flashes
near her chest which is white.

ISOHAGI: Farewell!

[Chants] Husband and wife look at each other,
cheek to cheek in hopeless thoughts;
love and loyalty being two separate rivers,
their tears make splashes of waves
and while they drench the wild seaweed
Isohagi presses her chest forward,
the sword makes one penetrating stab,
a spurt of blood running alongside it.
Takama no Tarō, turning it around,
slits his stomach with a single sweep,
when a fiery red wave towers and crashes,
burying the two under it.

(The two appear unable to part, cheek to cheek, until Isohagi presses her chest against her husband's sword and dies. Takama on the rock then commits disembowelment but even as he is pulling his sword from left to right, a Hokusai-style giant wave rushes forth from stage right and crashes over the two people, and the wave, along with the rock, sinks below stage.)

[Chants] They are sinking.
Kiheiji, who is expert at swimming,
helping with his bow-arm and tugging like a boat
Sutemaru, who's dependent on a piece of wood,
swims, tries to stay afloat as long as
his string of beads[46] holds.

---

46. *Tama no o:* a metaphor for life.

(Out of the suppon,[47] Kiheiji helping Sutemaru clinging to a piece of wood rises up, then swims to main stage.)

(From stage left a monstrous fish appears and assaults Kiheiji, and they chase each other for a while until the black butterfly on a sashigane appears and makes sport of the monstrous fish. The fish, exhausted, quiets down and does whatever the butterfly wishes. Kiheiji and Sutemaru ride it, as if guided by the butterfly.)

[Chants] Guided by Shiranui's soul,
   kicking the waves aside

(At an appropriate moment, a ki no kashira[48] sounds.)

CURTAIN

LOWER VOLUME
SCENE AT THE RITUAL SITE IN KITADANI
(NORTH CLIFF), KINGDOM OF RYŪKYŪ

On main stage, a raised platform[1] whose surface is covered with stone paving. Below the stone steps that rise from there toward stage right are a fireplace and an altar. Backstage is the sea, coral reefs with white waves surrounding them. Visible between the stone pavements and the sea are summer grasses and the tops of Australian pines.[2] There is the suggestion that beyond the foreground is a cliff.

As the curtain rises, enters Prime Minister Riyū on the hanamichi protectively behind the infant Royal Prince, with a retinue of soldiers in attendance, some of them leading Royal Princess Nei and Tō Shōju, both tied with a rope. All line up.

RIYŪ: Now, Your Highness, we have no way of stopping our nation's hardships. Your father, King Shōnei, and your mother, Chūfugimi,[3] were slain by the Monstrous Monk Mōun,[4] who besides has taken possession of national power so that a monstrous air prevails under heaven. With heaven's anomalies and earth's anomalies accompanying it, our people are subjected to sufferings as if they were covered with mud and burned.[5] Worried about our nation, I have humbly asked Kumagimi[6] to come to today's rite to offer sacrifices. Come, please step forward.

---

47. The square hole on the stage floor. Also called *kiriana*, "cut hole," as noted earlier.

48. A pair of wooden clappers struck to mark certain moments, such as, as here, the curtain falling. To be exact, the term refers to the first sound made by the clappers.

1. *Nijū*, literally, "two layers."

2. *Mokumaō (Casuarina stricta)*: a species originating in Australia. Also called she-oak, beefwood, horsetail tree, and swamp oak.

3. Chūfukimi, according to Bakin.

4. *Mōun* means something like "impenetrable cloud."

5. "Sufferings" etc. An expression that appears in one of the Five (Chinese) Classics, the *Book of Documents*.

6. In Bakin, Kumakimi.

(The group moves to main stage. Riyū, protectively following the Royal Prince, steps up to the platform of stone pavements and seats himself toward stage left. The two sacrificial victims are brought to the center of the same platform and made to sit down.)

ROYAL PRINCE: Listen, Riyū.

RIYŪ: Yes, Your Highness.

ROYAL PRINCE: The kindhearted Royal Princess Nei
    is to me an older half sister, so to speak,
    and Tō Shōju is a young samurai
    who's served me with attention and care.
    Why are you offering them to a god?

RIYŪ: You are sensible to raise such doubts, sir, but Her Highness, who should have been heir to our Ryūkyū Nation, lost a ball, the imprimatur of the kingly position. That is not her least sin. She bought a counterfeit ball from a fake merchant from Japan whom she came across at Mount Kyūkyū and has ever since deceived our nation. On top of these punishable crimes, she indulged in secret talks with this fellow Tō Shōju, who has served you with a pretense of loyalty, conspiring, I dread to say, to poison you, Your Highness. This has brought down the wrath of the god. This is why we are offering them as sacrifices.

TŌ SHŌJU: Damn your evil ways, Riyū!
    Our nation's ruinous robber isn't Mōun alone,
    a pretense of loyalty describes you.
    Hoodwinking our infant lord,
    colluding with Chief Vestal Kumagimi,
    you are cruel, offering for sacrifice
    one loyal vassal after another who gets in your way.
    May god strike your heart, you're now
    even killing Royal Princess Nei herself!
    Heaven's Way will never forgive you.

ROYAL PRINCESS NEI: Your words will be all in vain, Tō Shōju.
    At this point it's up to Heaven's Command;
    we can only wait for justice in a later world.

ROYAL PRINCE: They are angry because they don't want to be sacrificed.
    I feel sorry for them. Let them go.

RIYŪ: What are you saying, Your Highness?
    You are crown prince at the least.
    To save our nation from hardships,
    you mustn't have personal feelings.

ROYAL PRINCE: No, no, I don't like it. Let them go.

RIYŪ: Come, you are being childish.

KUMAGIMI'S VOICE: Kumagimi will be right there with you.

(Kumagimi comes down the stone steps at stage right accompanied by vestals.)

ROYAL PRINCE: Here you are, *Grandma*. Come closer.

RIYŪ: Kumagimi, come.

KUMAGIMI: Having finished preparations for the divine rite, I, his nurse, shall come over and explain the reasons to the royal prince.

 Now, listen, Prince, Your Highness. Just turn your eyes toward the ocean. The shallows of the coral reefs surrounded with rings of white waves are light yellow, and the part beyond is deep green. It is at the bottom of that ocean that Kinmanmon[7] resides. If touched by Kinmanmon's wrath, the sea goes wild and the earth quakes, even hailstones fall so that no plants grow, and all the people suffer. For this reason Kumagimi offers prayers and even gives human sacrifices to appease the god in his wrath. Above all, Kinmanmon dislikes illicit affairs. Call your older sister Royal Princess Nei, and she should strike awe into our hearts, but she is crooked by nature. Since she lost her mother, Lady Ren, she has been perversely resentful that you have become crown prince. Even worse, she has been fooling with this treacherous vassal Tō Shōju, conspiring . . .

ROYAL PRINCE: What does "fooling with" mean? Tell me.

KUMAGIMI: That means for a man and woman to press naked breast against naked breast, just like this, and mimic doggy beasts, thereby defiling the god.

ROYAL PRINCE: Royal Princess Nei can't possibly do any such . . .

KUMAGIMI: Yes, she can. Outwardly, her face is like a bodhisattva's; inwardly, her heart is like a *yaksa's*.[8] With that gentle face she did illicit things with her retainer. On top of that, she wrote an oath to a god cursing you, our Royal Prince.

ROYAL PRINCE: Since *Grandma* tells me so, it must be true. If they are such bad people, make sacrifices of the two of them as soon as possible!

KUMAGIMI: Oh, you understand me so well. You are such a clever Royal Prince, Your Highness.

TŌ SHŌJU: Concocting such baseless evil stories for our Royal Prince, who understands little. I don't mind losing my life, Your Highness, but I do resent perishing like this, my name sullied with mud. Please understand how I feel. I understand how you feel.

---

7. Ryūkyū's tutelary deity. "This deity takes yin and yang forms. The one that descends from heaven is called *Kiraikanai no Kinmanmon* and the one that rises from the sea is called *Ōtsukeraku no Kinmanmon*." Bakin, *Zokuhen,* vol. 2. The three Chinese characters applied to the word seem to mean, "You are the real thing."

8. *Yasha* in Japanese: a flying monster with a ferociously convoluted face that does evil things to human beings, sometimes eating them. In a different role, he is a good demon who works as a warrior guarding the Lotus Sutra. His female counterpart is called *yaksini*. "Her face . . ." is a set phrase.

ROYAL PRINCESS NEI: Tō Shōju, you speak the truth.

KUMAGIMI: What's this yakking of doggy beasts! Your Highness, help them shut up.

ROYAL PRINCE: What can I do to shut them up?

KUMAGIMI: Look, like this *(Breaking a branch off a tree)*. A whip is best for dogs.

ROYAL PRINCE: Like this? *(He whips them.)*

KUMAGIMI: Come, harder, strike them much harder.

RIYŪ: We're getting nowhere, Kumagimi. Since we've decided to sacrifice them, let's shove them off this cliff as soon as we can, so that their bodies shattered into pieces on the rock may be eaten fittingly by Kinmanmon.

KUMAGIMI: No, no, we have a law to follow before that. We have to make a fire; we have to offer incense. Then after the god has appeared, we kill the sacrifices. That is the important part of this divine rite. Vestals, light the incense.

(The vestals light black, flat bars of incense.)

RIYŪ: Dammit, I just can't take this. Whether you kill them now or kill them later, for Kinmanmon the taste of the sacrifices will make no difference, will it? Let *me* take care of Royal Princess Nei first. . . .

(He roughly pulls up Royal Princess Nei, takes her to the cliff, and is about to shove her off it, when an arrow pierces his chest. He cries and falls, Nei faints, startling all. . . . Tametomo, holding a bow in one hand, emerges from the cliff, accompanied by two boys, Tsuru and Kame.)

TAMETOMO: On behalf of the people I have killed the treasonous vassal Riyū in punishment.

My soldierly name, if you haven't heard it in the waves
on wild shores, see it now with your own eyes.
Direct descendant of Seiwa,[9] of Great Yamato,
I am indeed Hachirō Tametomo.
Anyone of evil wisdom who puts up a fight
I'll turn into Riyū's companion to the netherworld.

ROYAL PRINCE: Kinmanmon has come out; he's out!

TŌ SHŌJU: So he's Lord Tametomo, the bowman whose reputation has reached as far as Ryūkyū!

TSURU: You killed our mother!

KAME: Kumagimi, prepare yourself to die!

(Fighting ensues. Repelling the soldiers who strike at him, Tametomo unties Tō Shōju and fights alongside him. Kumagimi, targeted by both Tsuru and Kame, manages to run off along the hanamichi, holding the Royal Prince by the hand.)

---

9. The Minamoto clan that flourished as a military house began with Prince Tadasumi, the fourth son of the fifty-sixth Emperor, Seiwa (850–80).

While all this is going on, the black butterfly appears on a sashigane *and torments the evil soldiers. In time all the soldiers leave. Left on the level stage,*[10] *Tametomo, Tō Shōju, Tsuru, and Kame look at one another.)*

TAMETOMO: The enemies have scattered.

TŌ SHŌJU: A relief for now.

TSURU: She got away.

KAME: We regret it so!

TAMETOMO: Tsuru, Kame, guided by your deceased mother as you are, you're bound to meet your enemy one of these days. So don't be discouraged. When you see Kumagimi again, I, Tametomo, will provide you with help.

TSURU: We're truly

TSURU AND KAME: grateful to you, sir.

TAMETOMO: *(Catching sight of the butterfly flitting before his eyes)* This, an unfamiliar butterfly.

TŌ SHŌJU: It's a black swallowtail that's familiar
     even to the children in all-summer Ryūkyū.

TAMETOMO: Well, come to think of it . . .
     (While he looks puzzled, dorodoro[11] *starts, and everyone falls into a drowsy trance. The butterfly flies up to the platform and onto the chest of Royal Princess Nei who lies there. She comes to with a start, raises herself, and looks around.)*

TŌ SHŌJU: *(Noticing her)* Oh, Royal Princess Nei . . .

TAMETOMO: Let's be quick.
     (As soon as all climb up to the platform, Royal Princess Nei clings to Tametomo.)

ROYAL PRINCESS NEI: I have missed you, Lord Tametomo.

TAMETOMO: As many as sixteen years ago,
     by imperial command I crossed to Ryūkyū
     where at the foot of Mount Kyūkyū
     I handed to you a ball from a dragon
     in exchange for the crane I was looking for:
     I was a merchant from Under-the-Sun[12] then,
     and I'm gratified you haven't forgotten me.
     But in these months and days of wandering
     my face has changed. Yet this sudden recognition.
     I'm puzzled, mighty puzzled.

ROYAL PRINCESS NEI: Come, don't be so formal and stiff. Have you forgotten your present wife?

TAMETOMO: What?

---

10. *Hira-butai,* as opposed to the platform.

11. See act 2, n. 5.

12. *Hi no Moto,* a different reading of the two Chinese characters given to *Nihon,* Japan.

ROYAL PRINCESS NEI: The soul of Shiranui who threw herself
 from the warship to pray to the god
 has lodged now in my humble body.
 Again meeting you, I feel like a butterfly
 fluttering about an udumbara[13] flower, don't you see!

TAMETOMO: Oh, so you say you are Shiranui.

ROYAL PRINCESS NEI: Lord Tametomo.

TAMETOMO: A mysterious encounter, this; I'm grateful. I don't deserve it.
 We ran into foul winds off Satsuma, and I alone have been washed up
 here. But having been separated from Sutemaru and Kiheiji, there's nothing I can do.

ROYAL PRINCESS NEI: Be assured. I guided Sutemaru and Kiheiji and
 they arrived in Ryūkyū without any trouble, and I'm sure you'll meet
 them soon.

TAMETOMO: I'm gratified. This, too, must be divine assistance. As for
 these boys here, they call themselves Tsuru and Kame. I rescued them
 on Mount Washisu where Riyū's soldiers were chasing them. I asked,
 and was told that they, the late loyal vassal Mō Kokutei's sons, were
 looking for their parents' enemies. I thought their filial dedication
 praiseworthy. They've just killed their father's enemy, Riyū. After they
 take the head of their mother's enemy, Kumagimi, whom they've just
 failed to kill, they'll make good soldiers for Sutemaru. Then you'll look
 after them, too.

ROYAL PRINCESS NEI: I'll take the place of their deceased mother and
 make sure they avenge her. *(Becoming formal)* Listen, Tō Shōju.

TŌ SHŌJU: Yes, milady, Royal Princess Nei.

ROYAL PRINCESS NEI: Now that you've defeated the treasonous vassal
 Riyū with Lord Tametomo's help, from today on you'll obey his commands and be always vigilant in gathering righteous soldiers so that you
 may ready an army with which to defeat and destroy Mōun.

TŌ SHŌJU: No need for those words of yours, milady. I have long been
 determined to return the favors this kingly country has given me and, in
 so doing, treat my life as lightly as a goose feather.[14] With Lord Tametomo on our side, our righteous army will be as strong as a million men.

TAMETOMO: Well then, we'll part here for now

TŌ SHŌJU: to gather again at the fort, Mount Castle.

13. Sanskrit; *udonge* in Japanese: an imaginary tree in India that is believed to flower once
every 3,000 years.

14. *Kōmō,* "a bean-goose feather," is a metaphor for something extremely light. Grand
Historian Ssu-ma Ch'ien: "A man is doomed to die once. His life can be as weighty as
Mount T'ai or as light as a bean-goose feather." The bean-goose is one of the largest geese
in Asia.

TAMETOMO: Royal Princess Nei, Your Highness,

TŌ SHŌJU: let us follow you.

ROYAL PRINCESS NEI: Well said. *(She rises to her feet, then suddenly collapses and clings to Tametomo)* Don't make fun of me, Lord Tametomo. Now, you take command.

TAMETOMO: All right. All of you, follow me. *(He opens his military fan, signaling the change of scene.)* Um, ha-ha-ha-ha!

(As they look at one another and laugh, the stage rotates.)

SCENE AT THE INN FOR COUPLES ONLY IN KITADANI

The main stage is a 3-ken-wide room with a tsuneashi no nijū platform.[15] *To stage left is a room closed off with papered sliding doors. At the egress toward backstage hangs a noren*[16] *dyed Ryūkyū style, and there is a pillow-screen.*[17] *The place where normally a Buddhist altar should be is taken up by a prayer-place for Kinmanmon. Toward backstage to stage right a couple of slaughtered pigs are hung upside down.*[18] *Outside the latticed door hangs a lantern with "Inn for Couples Only" written on it. The roof is made of Ryūkyū tiles. To stage right is a very low, rundown stone fence where grow a Chinese banyan,*[19] *plantain, Ryūkyū pine,*[20] *shell gingers,*[21] *and the rose of China*[22] *blooming red.*

As the curtain rises, Kumagimi is pressing a supper tray upon the Royal Prince while fanning him with a fan made of a plantain leaf.

KUMAGIMI: Your Highness, please eat your fill.

ROYAL PRINCE: Do I have to eat pork cubes again?

KUMAGIMI: Truly, if you hadn't been driven out by someone like Mōun, you could be living in a golden palace and jeweled tower, your tray loaded with fabulous foods from the mountains and the seas mornings and evenings, with nothing lacking. But now that both our nation and our people have been kidnapped by his monstrous magic, the electricity

---

15. *Tsuneashi no nijū* is fourteen inches high.

16. A decorative partition made of fabric.

17. A low screen used as a partition in a bedroom.

18. Ryūkyū culture was pervasively influenced by Chinese culture, and pork was regarded as quintessentially Chinese food.

19. *Kajumaru (Ficus microcarpa):* a semitropical or tropical evergreen of the mulberry family that grows in Okinawa and the Amami islands.

20. Obviously the list here is made to suggest the semitropical Ryūkyū (i.e., Okinawa), but I have not been able to identify anything called *Ryūkyū-matsu,* "Ryūkyū pine."

21. *Gettō (Alpinia speciosa):* a semitropical or tropical plant of the ginger family that grows to be ten feet tall. Also called "shell flower."

22. *Bussōge:* a species of hibiscus.

of the southern barbarians,[23] we have no way of getting rid of Mōun, the only hope for sweeping him aside being Kinmanmon. If we don't neglect our prayers and offerings to him, some day Your Highness will reign. Until then you only need to remain patient, meanwhile eating whatever we have without complaint. Come, that bowl with a lid has a soup that I, your nurse, am particularly good at. It's made of pig's ears. I was careful to taste it myself to make sure that you would like it. So try a sip.

ROYAL PRINCE: This soup is delicious. Delicious.

KUMAGIMI: My, you're such a clever child. We have too many mosquitoes this evening. Let me light a mosquito incense.

(While she lights a mosquito incense, the Royal Prince finishes his meal and looks sleepy.)

KUMAGIMI: You've finished eating and you're sleepy. You're such an innocent darling. Come, Your Highness, I'll sing a lullaby to you, so you may fall asleep now.

>Ito-yanagi
>kokoro kuni
>arashi yaba
>noyote haro mono
>kaze nite riyo ka.[24]

Oh, he's already asleep now. *(She puts the pillow-screen around him.)* Yes, yes, I had forgotten. Let me light the lantern. *(She rises to her feet, walks to the lantern near the entrance that says "Inn for Couples Only," and lights it. Insects chirp incessantly. She goes back to where she was.)* Whether we're going to have guests is up to Kinmanmon's divine wishes. Let's see now, let me find out what he thinks. *(She lights a black, wide bar of incense and prays.)*

---

23. Information on electricity was brought to Japan by Dutch traders—here called "southern barbarians"—during the second half of the eighteenth century, and Hiraga Gennai (1728–79) famously experimented with it. As Mishima noted, Bakin, while loving to flaunt his erudition, at times nonchalantly committed anachronisms, e.g., making Kumagimi say that when young she studied Yuiitu (also Yuitsu, Yuichi) Shinto, which was started three centuries later by Yoshida Kanetomo (1435–1511). (See *Zenpen,* vol. 3.) Evidently Mishima decided to make Kumagimi commit an even more flagrant anachronism.

24. In Bakin's story, this is a song that Lady Ren sings for Mō Kokutei in a scene of dalliance created by Mōun's magic to provoke King Shōnei. Bakin provides interlinear comments on the song: "*Ryūkyū-dan* reports that the venerable Sorai cites this as a Ryūkyū song in *Heishi-ki* [ref.: *arashi yaba*]. This means 'I have pain in my heart living in this world' [ref.: *noyote* etc.]. What follows is hard to comprehend. One theory has it that this is a ditty of women in the licentious quarters. If so, this may not be appropriate for the lady [i.e., Ren]." *Zokuhen,* vol. 4. *Ryūkyū-dan* is an assemblage of reports about Ryūkyū compiled by Morishima Chūryō (dates unknown), published in 1790. Sorai is the Confucian scholar Ogyū Sorai (1666–1728), and *Heishi-ki* is his report on the Ryūkyū embassy that came to Edo in 1710.

(On the hanamichi appear Tsuru and Kame wearing tsuyushiba,[25] *in the disguise of a married couple; they stop at seven-three.)*

TSURU: Kumagimi, whom we're seeking to avenge ourselves on,

    runs an inn for couples only, we were told.

    As soon as we heard that, we disguised ourselves,

    I, your older brother, in the role of husband,

KAME: and Kame, your younger brother, plays the innocent wife.

    Disguised as a married couple, we can best

    put her off guard and kill her, we thought,

TSURU: agreed, and came along to Kitadani,

    and are now deep in these mountains.

    But our clothes to repel the dew, our sleeves,

KAME: we'd hate them to get wet, being married.

    My older brother,

TSURU: Oh, come now,[26]

KAME: My dear, we feel so uncertain

TSURU: about what's coming, don't we?

KUMAGIMI: *(Smoking on a long pipe)* Even the chief of vestals needs some means of making a living. I hope I have some guests this evening, too. This is an inn for travelers, but a single man is troublesome one way or another, so I allow only married couples to stay here. As a result, they've long called this the inn for husbands and wives.

TSURU: The more I think, the angrier I become.

    Our father Mō Kokutei was slandered;

KAME: we infants, accompanied by our mother,

    were on the road, traveling, wandering,

TSURU: when we were attacked at night by Kumagimi,

    who killed our mother; even worse,

KAME: she tore her belly and stole the baby

    who was about to be born any moment.

TSURU: I don't know how wily she can get,

    but Kumagimi, be she human or beast,

KAME: how could we forget her evil ways?

KUMAGIMI: Since I started taking couples,

    I've already had as many as ten.

---

25. A type of clothing suggesting that its wearer has adopted a lower, humbler station. Ishii Tatsuhiko has pointed out that when someone like Tametomo appears in this attire (as he does later on), the material tends to be extravagant.

26. "My older brother" is a vocative; Tsuru stopped Kame because Kame forgot their disguised roles.

TSURU: Future not known on a travel-pillow,

KAME: if you pass this one, all's still like foam[27]

KUMAGIMI: which never comes back to this lodge.

TSURU: The ruddy face you visit in the morn

KUMAGIMI: swiftly turns into bones in the eve,
which make a mound below this floor.

KAME: Our anger piling up for six years now,
we brothers fake being husband and wife.

KUMAGIMI: Kinmanmon hates carnality;
hunting sacrifices is a means of salvation.

TSURU: Our vengeance is tonight at last
though the moon's clear through the clouds.

KUMAGIMI: For a sacrificial banquet to thank the god
I wait for them to go to bed and stab them.

KAME: The soul-searing scream, is that a night crow's?

KUMAGIMI: The bed dark-red as the day breaks with crows

TSURU: the fulfillment of our wish now so close.

KAME: After revenge and rain the moon in the sky

KUMAGIMI: is wet, soaked wet as a bloody feast.

THREE OF THEM: Well, now, we feel so good as we go along.
(The brothers make the gesture of noticing the lantern.)

TSURU: We were lost on the road as night came,
but how convenient, there's the lantern
that says exactly

KAME: "Inn for Couples Only."

TSURU: My dear wife, come along!

KAME: Yes, dear.
(As they come close, Kumagimi rises to her feet.)

KUMAGIMI: The insects have suddenly stopped chirping. Is it possible that
I . . .
(She opens the door.)

TSURU: We are travelers lost on the road. But luckily we're a married couple, and we'd like lodging for a night.

KUMAGIMI: Oh, why shouldn't I give you lodging? I see both of you are young. These mountain roads are tough for such a precious bride. You'll relax to your heart's content. Now, come in, come in. *(Leading them in)* You see, this is just a dewy little lodge. I can't entertain you in any way, but for those from the capital there's the poetry of a mountain hut[28] and

---

27. *Utakata:* a metaphor for the transience of life.

28. In court poetry, *yamaga* (also, *sanka, sange*), "mountain hut" or "mountain living," is a set topic associated with *fūryū,* "elegance," "poetry."

a feast of the calls of stags crying for their wives.[29] But first of all, let me take you to the bedroom. The night is deep, and young people love to hurry to bed. One virtue of an old woman is that she's hard of hearing. So, don't be shy about it. Come hand in hand, and rest to be rid of your travel fatigue.

(She puts them in the room sectioned off with papered sliding doors to stage left, then steps through the noren.*)*

   (The sound of a temple bell.[30] The sound of winds. Kumagimi steps out, offers prayers at the altar, and takes out a dagger-bag and a whetstone. She then takes an armor-piercer[31] from the bag and starts sharpening it on the whet-stone.)

   (Tsuru comes out of the room.)

TSURU: Excuse me, ma'am.

KUMAGIMI: *(Startled)* What can I do for you?

TSURU: May I have a cup of tea?

KUMAGIMI: Oh, I'm sorry; I was neglectful. I'll bring it right away. You may go back to your room and wait there.

TSURU: No, you needn't trouble yourself. I see that you don't even have a maid. I'll get it myself.

KUMAGIMI: No, you can't do that, sir. I can't allow a guest to get his own tea.

TSURU: I am the guest and I say it's all right.

(Kumagimi rises to her feet against her wishes and makes tea at stage right. Tsuru picks up the dagger on the whet-stone and inspects it.)

   So this is it.

(Noticing that Kumagimi is coming back, he puts the sword where it was.)

   So I see you were born to a samurai house, that you treasure an armor-piercer, which is unmistakably made in Under-the-Sun.

KUMAGIMI: No, not really, I thought I'd serve you slices of pork tomorrow morning and began tonight to sharpen this blunt thing that I use as a cooking knife. *(She points to the slaughtered pigs to stage right.)* I have some fat ones over there. Which one would you like to have?

TSURU: A young one

KUMAGIMI: What?

TSURU: should be just fine.

(He receives the tea set from Kumagimi and leaves to the room at stage left. Kumagimi resumes sharpening the sword. Insects chirp.)

   (On the hanamichi appear Tametomo and Royal Princess Nei in tsuyushiba *similar to those of Tsuru and Kame; they stop at seven-three.)*

29. Another favorite topic in court poetry.
30. Often precedes a horror scene.
31. *Yoroi-dōshi:* a short, fat, uncurved sword carried on a battlefield.

TAMETOMO: Pressed by the thought of avenging their mother,
pretending to be husband and wife,
those brothers Tsuru and Kame told me
they'd be visiting Kumagimi at her inn.
I wasn't sure they could really do it,
so I discussed it with Royal Princess Nei
and we're disguised as a traveling couple.

ROYAL PRINCESS NEI: No, no, we aren't disguised at all.
Traveling as husband and wife as in the past,
I'm overjoyed with our grass-pillows.

TAMETOMO: There's nothing flirtatious about this. We're helping Tsuru and Kame because I'm impressed by their filial thoughts though they're hardly grown up. You must forget about Shiranui and do the necessary work thinking like Royal Princess Nei.

ROYAL PRINCESS NEI: Yes, milord, I'll do as you say.

(As they approach main stage, Kumagimi holds up the armor-piercer she's finished sharpening and surreptitiously steps toward the room sectioned off with papered sliding doors.)

TAMETOMO: *(At the entrance)* Is anyone there? Is anyone home? We're a traveling husband and wife, and we'd like to stay here overnight.

(Startled, Kumagimi hides the short sword in her sleeve and appears to wonder for a while what to do next; in the end she goes to the entrance, turns off the lantern, and walks into the room to stage left. As soon as Tametomo destroys the entrance and steps in, she opens the sliding doors of the room she was in and strikes a dramatic pose,[32] holding up the short sword as if to protect Tsuru and Kame. At the sound of a temple bell,[33] there is a shinobi-sanjū accompaniment[34] to a danmari scene[35] where Tsuru, Kame, Tametomo, Royal Princess Nei, and Kumagimi grope about. After a while, Kumagimi steps behind the pillow-screen and stabs the Royal Prince. This is followed by another round of fighting in which Kumagimi, both of her shoulders slashed, falls down, when Royal Princess Nei lights the lantern with flints.)

Look, did we stab the Royal Prince by mistake?

ALL: This is terrible!

KUMAGIMI: I, Kumagimi, stabbed the Royal Prince, and Tsuru and Kame stabbed me with their swords. Now I have no regrets left.

---

32. Called *mie;* see "The Flower of Evil: Kabuki," n. 18.

33. *Hontsuri (gane),* "real hanging bell": a small bell; as with the large temple bell, it is struck to suggest the evening or the lateness of a night pregnant with horror.

34. *Shinobi-sanjū* is a special piece of music composed to suggest horror. It is played on a single shamisen.

35. *Danmari,* "silent, dumb": a pantomime that is supposed to take place in darkness.

TSURU: *(To Kame)* Now, give her a coup de grâce.

KAME: Glad to.

TAMETOMO: No, wait, you two brothers. There must be profound secrets behind all this. Come, Kumagimi. I am Chinzei Hachirō Tametomo. Unburden yourself to your heart's content.

(The jōruri on the floor begins.)

> [Chants] At these words of compassion
> the wounded one prostrates herself and prays.

KUMAGIMI: To disclose to Lord Tametomo what lies at the bottom of my heart before going to the netherworld—this is your grandma's great luck. Listen, Tsuru and Kame, my grandsons, for my confession to you before dying, allow me to prolong my last breath.

> [Chants] Tsuru and Kame jeer at her.

TSURU: You've grown so old you've lost your mind.

KAME: At this late moment you're trying to deceive us.

TSURU: That armor-piercer in your hand is our deceased mother's talismanic sword. As long as you possess it, you are unmistakably our mother's enemy. We have no reason whatsoever to be called

TSURU AND KAME: your grandsons.

> [Chants] Kumagimi smiles a broad smile.

KUMAGIMI: Your doubts are understandable. From the beginning I meant you to kill me, but if I had told you that you are my grandsons and I am your grandma, you wouldn't have been able to wield your swords fully, and that's understandable, even though I am your mother's enemy. Now I can tell you about my life. Lord Tametomo, please listen to my story as well.

> When still a young woman I lost my parents;
> despairing of this world I crossed to Yamato[36]
> where, staying at the Aso shrine,
> I sought the deep principles of Yuichi Shinto.
> On the eve of the festival of its deity
> a gallant youth came up and spoke to me
> and I saying No without really meaning No[37]
> we pledged ourselves in vain love.
> Ashamed, I didn't give my name, he his;[38]

---

36. An old name for Japan.

37. *Ina niwa aranu inafune no,* literally, "like a rice-boat carrying no rice." Alludes to an anonymous tanka "from the East" in *Kokin Shū* (no. 1092): *Mogami-gawa noboreba kudaru inafune no ina niwa arazu kono tsuki bakari.*

38. Mishima here alludes to the ancient custom of young people engaging in anonymous and promiscuous love-making on the eve or the night of a festival.

simply for keepsakes till our next meeting
he gave me the armor-piercer he had on him
and I gave him a Ryūkyū scroll.
The presents exchanged, we parted,
and I in time returned to Ryūkyū.
Using the one skill I acquired in Yamato,
I installed myself as chief vestal in Kitadani,
but soon to my great embarrassment,

[Chants] that one night of the Aso festival

I became pregnant through that pledged love,
and as months accumulated, my girth
could no longer be hidden though I tried.

[Chants] If this were known to society at large,
I'd violated the rule of serving the god, they'd say.

So I gave birth, without telling anyone,
to a girl who could best a jewel,
and forsook her, the armor-piercer,
the Yamato man's keepsake, attached to her.
Many a year has passed since then

[Chants] but unforgettable is my daughter.
She so reminisces, hardly able to breathe.
A ninja peers in at the entrance
and hides himself as if he has a secret.
The wounded one regains her strength
(From stage right enters Kiheiji in the guise of a ninja, eavesdrops, and hides himself in shrubbery.)
Of course I was chief of vestals
and was not allowed to have a husband.
Living unsexed was maintaining my
chastity for the man of Under-the-Sun
or so I thought, wasting my prime.
Grown old, I was bewitched by greed
when Riyū came with a flagitious scheme:
to steal a baby from a commoner
and pretend he's this nation's heir.
A woman lying ill in a field
was ready to give birth, I saw,

and I deceived her two children,
sending them away to buy medicine.
I tore the pregnant woman's belly
and took the baby out of it.
But when I robbed the dagger she held onto
until her death and gave it a close look

[Chants] it was the man's keepsake she'd never forgotten

and so the pregnant woman I killed
with my own hands was my daughter.

[Chants] She was shocked in vain, remorseful in vain

An evil result of a secret deed—
and yet my sorrow spurred my greed.
What I'd done, done, I decided to serve
my grandson till the day he'd be Ryūkyū king
and spent my days exalting the Royal Prince.
But Mōun overturned this nation,
obtaining his position through his magic.
With Riyū protecting the Royal Prince
I escaped as far as Kitadani
but after even Riyū was killed,
I prayed day and night that Heaven's Luck turn,
restoring the Royal Prince to the throne.
By luck, no one in the world knew
that the Royal Prince was a false heir.
And so I ran an inn for couples
and with sacrifices as an excuse
I killed travelers to rob their valuables.
When I welcomed Tsuru and Kame here
who sought me to avenge their mother,
at once I knew they were my grandsons.
Their courage put to shame my wicked ways,
breaking the horns of my evil thoughts.

[Chants] Grandsons leading her into Shallow River[39]

---

39. *Asase-gawa*. Mishima apparently uses this word for an alliterative effect for it is followed by *azamuki*, "dupe." I have tried to re-create a semblance of alliteration by using
the word "society" for *yo*.

To apologize both to society, to the people,
for my atrocious evils that duped society,
I killed one of my grandsons, the Royal Prince.
For the remaining grandsons, as a sign of apology

[Chants] This white-haired head is the gift.

I killed my daughter, then killed
a grandson, to be killed by grandsons;
this is retributive justice you can't escape.
Come, be quick, behead me.
And yet, now dying, I still can't forget
the face of the owner of this armor-piercer.
While piling up evils I kept my chastity;
I, Kumagimi, would like to tell him
of my devotional love, my devoted heart.

[Chants] A flower on an old tree, what a pity!
A ninja leaps in the entrance.

TAMETOMO: Who is this?

KIHEIJI: I haven't seen you for a long time, sir. *(He removes his mask.)*

TAMETOMO: You're Kiheiji. A long time, indeed.

KIHEIJI: I've been protecting Master Sutemaru with my life and he's hiding in a mountain nearby. You might see him as early as tomorrow.

TAMETOMO: Well done. But how have you managed to come here?

KIHEIJI: If I have to tell it, it's a long story.
But since I washed up here in Ryūkyū
I've heard the rumor that you washed up, too,
but have been unable to see you till now.
Now that I see your face here, sir,
I'm embarrassed even to say it,
but the man Kumagimi here talks about
is me, Kiheiji, none other.

TAMETOMO: What?

KIHEIJI: *(Taking out a scroll from the chest part of his clothes)* The scroll you gave me in Aso long ago in exchange, a map of Ryūkyū,
has been useful since I arrived in this place,
a road-guide I've never let go of.
Kumagimi, don't you remember this?

[Chants] He holds it out for her.
The wounded one opens her fading eyes,

dazzled, rolled over by a scroll of love.

KUMAGIMI: You are the secret husband of that night
[*Chants*] An old bush warbler on a scarlet plum,
her dying cheeks blushing, dyed crimson.
Meeting being the start of parting

my face, now grown so old and ugly,
I'm too mortified to keep exposing it.
Please be quick, help me die by your hand.

KIHEIJI: With what karma, it all began one night.
Since then your evil ways have been widespread,
but now your good heart returns at last.
So here again the keepsake of my blade. (He raises a sword.)

TSURU AND KAME: Grandma!

KUMAGIMI: Oh, you call me that. I'm grateful.

TSURU AND KAME: (*To Kiheiji*) Grandpa!

KIHEIJI: (*He puts down his sword and hugs them*) Oh, you courageous ones.

KUMAGIMI: To hold my grandson on one lotus flower,[40]
I'd like to die with the Royal Prince in my arms.

(*Tametomo signals with his eyes and Royal Princess Nei brings the dead Royal Prince in her arms.*)

ROYAL PRINCESS NEI: We pity the Royal Prince who was duped into believing he was the nation's heir. For making such a young, innocent one
die, we must destroy the damnable Mōun so the evil fate of my Ryūkyū
may be

TAMETOMO: terminated along with Mōun.

ROYAL PRINCESS NEI: And you will help us, Lord Tametomo.

TAMETOMO: Oh, is there need to say that? Kumagimi, you may die with
peace of mind.

KUMAGIMI: (*Taking the Royal Prince in her arms*) I am so grateful. Come,
Royal Prince. Your nurse will sing a lullaby to you so you may sleep
well and pleasantly.
Ito-yanagi
kokoro kuni. . . .
I see, you've already fallen asleep. Did I ever expect
to be surrounded by a husband and grandsons,
for the crooked tree to have a moment's
happiness of gathering blossoms to bloom.
Come, be quick.

40. *Ichiren takushō:* for two persons to be reborn in nirvana after death and sit on one
lotus flower and peacefully meditate.

(Kiheiji lifting his sword, he and Kumagimi look at each other, which signals the change of scene.)

[*Chants*] Pitiful, transient.

(At an appropriate moment a "wave curtain"[41] is dropped.)

SCENE AT THE UNTEN SEACOAST
ON THE EVE OF A FESTIVAL

Main stage is a flat-stage[42] with a view of mountains in the distance. To stage right is a large Chinese banyan. At stage ends "wave boards"[43] are put up and the hanamichi is covered with a sheet indicating waves. At stage center is a desk made of plain wood with a Shinto staff and a branch of sakaki[44] *put up erect, all suggesting the Unten Sea Coast. —In front of the* namimaku *are Fishermen Taizō, Sabata, and Ikahachi, each holding black incense, paper money,[45] and a piglet.)*

TAIZŌ: In Ryūkyū, here at its northernmost end,
the shore of Unten is a spot where
the King comes to visit once a year.

SABATA: Today's the twenty-fifth of the eighth month,
the start of autumn when the heat subsides;
tomorrow, it appears, is the anniversary

IKAHACHI: of the day the previous King died
of Under-the-Sun to which we're told
he bears some relationship.

TAIZŌ: So the King, to start with,
and Lord Tametomo, who is the King's papa,
along with Royal Princess Nei,
at this shore that is closest to Yamato
hold an evening festival,[46] we're told.
And so we've brought our offerings;
I a bundle of incense,

SABATA: I a money stringer for paper money to burn,

IKAHACHI: I a piglet here, as you see.

TAIZŌ: If the King praised us for bringing these,
that would be an honor for our houses.

---

41. *Namimaku:* a "prop curtain" *(dōgu-maku)* with waves painted on it.

42. *Hira-butai:* stage without any platform.

43. *Namiita:* a board half a foot high and three feet wide with waves painted on it.

44. A rather humble looking evergreen glabrous tree *(Cleyera japonica)* that is held to be sacred in Shinto.

45. *Shisen:* here perhaps money used for a talismanic purpose.

46. *Yoimatsuri:* preparatory festivity on the eve of a festival day.

When you think of it, seven years ago
on Mount Castle[47] Lord Tametomo killed Mōun,[48]
thereby building the stone base for peace
of the world where not even branches rustle.
We the people recommended him for King
of Ryūkyū; that certainly was our wish.

SABATA: But he firmly declined, and for two years
the King's position remained vacant,
vain as his bow in its bag, sword in its scabbard.
With his people rejoicing, he, with much
reluctance, made his son Sutemaru
King, renaming him King Shunten.

IKAHACHI: And he, the King, is a man of humanity,
with trees and grasses naturally bowing,
laden with dew of compassion and love.
So we've been concentrating on fishing,
the ovens in every cove and bay thriving.[49]

TAIZŌ: In gratitude we've brought these offerings
and we've been waiting for their visit.
But we have one worry: for the last few days
we've had rough waves we don't see normally.
Today, too, white waves rolling in from offshore
are just like white horses galloping in.

SABATA: And yesterday children sang on the shore,
"White horses are coming from the sea,"
comparing the waves to horses as they sang.

IKAHACHI: What kind of omen was it? We're afraid.
    Oh,
here comes our Village Chief.

TAIZŌ: Our village is involved in this welcoming

SABATA: and he must be very busy

IKAHACHI: with this and that.

VILLAGE CHIEF: (*Coming from stage right to the curtain front*) Oh, it's good
that I've met you here. The festival eve starts at moonrise, and tonight
appears to be good for a moonbow, which is related to Lord Tametomo.
If you stay here, you'll be in his way. Let's pay respects to him over there.

---

47. Kusuku-yama.

48. Bakin's description of the slaughtering of Mōun is a marvelous example of swift-
moving, heightened prose. *Zenpen,* vol. 4.

49. Alludes to the legend that the sixteenth Emperor, Nintoku, suspended taxes when
he saw no smoke rising from people's ovens, suggesting that his people were desperately
poor. He resumed taxes only when he saw a good deal of smoke rising again.

TAIZŌ: But, Village Chief, we've brought our offerings here and we'd like to give them to the King.

VILLAGE CHIEF: Offerings?

TAIZŌ: Incense and paper money, and a piglet, too.

VILLAGE CHIEF: What are you saying? To the deities of Under-the-Sun, incense and paper money are defilements. When it comes to a piglet, you might even be punished. This divine festival shuns four-legged beasts. Before his retainers spot you, take them away, throw them away!

ALL: Yes, sir.

(They exit. The sound of waves. At a signal, the namimaku *is dropped. In the sky to stage left is a large moonbow. At center is a palanquin, which is attended by Royal Princess Nei, Tō Shōju, Tsuru, and Kame. To stage right stands a somewhat-aged Tametomo in armor, holding a bow and arrow, with Kiheiji in attendance.)*

ROYAL PRINCESS NEI: It's already moonrise, and the festival eve is about to begin;

TŌ SHŌJU: now is the time for you to appear,

ROYAL PRINCESS NEI AND TŌ SHŌJU: Your Majesty.

(Music starts.[50] *Sutemaru, now King Shunten, emerges from the palanquin. All prostrate themselves.)*

KING SHUNTEN: Listen, Tametomo.

TAMETOMO: Yes, sir.

KING SHUNTEN: According to the rules of the world, we have
　　separated ourselves as ruler and subject.
　　But this is a festival eve of the same bloodline;
　　as long as we hold this for the anniversary
　　of our late lord, the Newly Retired Emperor,
　　this evening at least not only you
　　but I also am a Shikishima man;[51]
　　because we are father and son, related,
　　I shall follow patriarchal etiquette
　　as we face the east where roosters call.[52]

TAMETOMO: I humbly accept this honor.

KING SHUNTEN: Father, please come to this place.

TAMETOMO: With your permission, sir.

---

50. *Gaku:* music played on a flute, drum, and shamisen to indicate the appearance of a nobleman, a deity, or the Buddha.

51. Shikishima, "islands spread out," is another old name of Japan.

52. *Tori ga naku,* "where roosters call," is a *makura-kotoba,* or epithet, for Azuma, "the East."

(King Shunten deferentially moves to stage right and Royal Princess Nei, Tō Shōju, Tsuru, and Kame follow him. Tametomo seats himself in front of the desk made of plain wood.)

Well then, now we'll begin the rite.

(He takes the Shinto staff and waves it. Everyone lowers his head.)

Truly, truly, our Newly Retired Emperor must feel at ease now. This is the spring of the fourth year of Juei and the Taira clan has sunk in the waves of the Western Sea and all the plans Your Majesty made at White Peak have been achieved.

Your Majesty's enemy having been destroyed,
whom do I now have to kill as the enemy?
My bow was once compared to
the moonbow shining in the sky,
but now it is as useless as useless waves,
and if I perish at the end of the Southern Ocean,
what honor is there in being a brave man?
At least I've passed the exploit
of conquering Mōun to my son,
and my only remaining wish is in a samurai's one thought:
to end my life by paying respects
to Your Majesty's mausoleum
and dying there by cutting my belly open.
Yet wild waves allow me no passage
to the Great Eight Islands,[53] which lie way beyond my sight.
I miss you, Your Majesty, I miss my homeland.
How can you hear my wish and not accommodate it
as you lie quietly, ever so distant and eternal,
in the depths of your grave at White Peak
overgrown with goose grass?
With your Majesty's *miraculous* spiritual power,
may your Majesty understand my sincerity
and lead me to your mausoleum.

(He closes his eyes and prays. The scene turns to dorodoro.*)*

KIHEIJI: The offing suddenly stirs up

TŌ SHŌJU: thunderous eightfold waves shattering

TSURU: kicking up the white waves

KAME: even the mane a white horse shakes

ROYAL PRINCESS NEI: can't be as wild as its kicking hoofs,
    oh, look, look, look—

---

53. Ō-Yashima. Yashima is an old name of Japan.

something has leapt out of the waves

KIHEIJI: and is rushing, dashing toward us

TŌ SHŌJU: It's not a wave.

TAMETOMO: (*Opening his eyes*) Yes, exactly, that's the white horse.[54]
    (*Out of the suppon in the hanamichi a white horse holding an imperial cup in
    its mouth leaps up and trots to main stage.*)

KIHEIJI: Hurry, we must protect His Majesty.
    (*Everyone tries to protect King Shunten. Tametomo, utterly unperturbed, holds the
    horse by the rein, calms him, and takes the cup from its mouth.*)

TAMETOMO: This is the very imperial cup
    the Newly Retired Emperor gave to me,
    that sank in the sea where Shiranui threw herself.
    Now a horse emerging from the sea
    has given it back, bringing it in his mouth.
            Yes,
    this certainly is the divine horse
    sent from White Peak to welcome me.
    Let me ride astride him. . . .

KIHEIJI: I'll accompany you, sir! (*He runs up to him.*)

TAMETOMO: (*Pushing him aside and mounting the horse*) Kiheiji, forgive me.

ROYAL PRINCESS NEI: Lord Tametomo, where in the world are you going?

KING SHUNTEN: Father!

TAMETOMO: Don't anyone get upset.
    Sutemaru has already been King for seven years;
    he certainly doesn't need his father's help.
    Royal Princess Nei's soul being Shiranui,
    you care for him as your own son.
    As for Kiheiji, as his great general,
    serve him forever and ever with Tō Shōju,
    Tsuru, and Kame as your arms and legs.
    I set out on a journey, heart emboldened,
    my wish fulfilled as divine welcome has come.
    This is a parting and no parting.
    Never sorrow over this.

ROYAL PRINCESS NEI: That may all be true, but you're my husband

KING SHUNTEN: and we're losing you beyond the wild waves

KIHEIJI: as you set out on a journey along the distant briny road

TŌ SHŌJU: You are the paragon of warrior bravery.

TSURU: This nation's sorrow over losing you

KAME: can only accumulate

54. Regarded as divine in Shinto.

ALL: like water poured on waves.

TAMETOMO: Now I must go. Never grieve.

    When toward the end of Leaf Month[55]

    you see a moonbow in the evening sky,

    regard it as Tametomo's keepsake.

    Sutemaru, farewell.

SUTEMARU: Farewell, sir.

    (Tametomo goes to seven-three on the hanamichi. As he holds up his bow to wave farewell, a ki no kashira *sounds.)*

      (While everyone is seeing him off, the curtain is drawn.)

      (Outside the curtain, Tametomo leaves, riding the white horse.)

55. Another name for the eighth month.

OTHER WORKS IN THE COLUMBIA ASIAN STUDIES SERIES

TRANSLATIONS FROM THE ASIAN CLASSICS

Major Plays of Chikamatsu, tr. Donald Keene 1961

Four Major Plays of Chikamatsu, tr. Donald Keene. Paperback ed. only. 1961; rev. ed. 1997

Records of the Grand Historian of China, translated from the Shih chi of Ssu-ma Ch'ien, tr. Burton Watson, 2 vols. 1961

Instructions for Practical Living and Other Neo-Confucian Writings by Wang Yang-ming, tr. Wing-tsit Chan 1963

Hsün Tzu: Basic Writings, tr. Burton Watson, paperback ed. only. 1963; rev. ed. 1996

Chuang Tzu: Basic Writings, tr. Burton Watson, paperback ed. only. 1964; rev. ed. 1996

The Mahābhārata, tr. Chakravarthi V. Narasimhan. Also in paperback ed. 1965; rev. ed. 1997

The Manyōshū, Nippon Gakujutsu Shinkōkai edition 1965

Su Tung-p'o: Selections from a Sung Dynasty Poet, tr. Burton Watson. Also in paperback ed. 1965

Bhartrihari: Poems, tr. Barbara Stoler Miller. Also in paperback ed. 1967

Basic Writings of Mo Tzu, Hsün Tzu, and Han Fei Tzu, tr. Burton Watson. Also in separate paperback eds. 1967

The Awakening of Faith, Attributed to Aśvaghosha, tr. Yoshito S. Hakeda. Also in paperback ed. 1967

Reflections on Things at Hand: The Neo-Confucian Anthology, comp. Chu Hsi and Lü Tsu-ch'ien, tr. Wing-tsit Chan 1967

The Platform Sutra of the Sixth Patriarch, tr. Philip B. Yampolsky. Also in paperback ed. 1967

Essays in Idleness: The Tsurezuregusa of Kenkō, tr. Donald Keene. Also in paperback ed. 1967

The Pillow Book of Sei Shōnagon, tr. Ivan Morris, 2 vols. 1967

Two Plays of Ancient India: The Little Clay Cart and the Minister's Seal, tr. J. A. B. van Buitenen 1968

The Complete Works of Chuang Tzu, tr. Burton Watson 1968

The Romance of the Western Chamber (Hsi Hsiang chi), tr. S. I. Hsiung. Also in paperback ed. 1968

The Manyōshū, Nippon Gakujutsu Shinkōkai edition. Paperback ed. only. 1969

Records of the Historian: Chapters from the Shih chi of Ssu-ma Ch'ien, tr. Burton Watson. Paperback ed. only. 1969

Cold Mountain: 100 Poems by the T'ang Poet Han-shan, tr. Burton Watson. Also in paperback ed. 1970

Twenty Plays of the Nō Theatre, ed. Donald Keene. Also in paperback ed. 1970

Chūshingura: The Treasury of Loyal Retainers, tr. Donald Keene. Also in paperback ed. 1971; rev. ed. 1997

The Zen Master Hakuin: Selected Writings, tr. Philip B. Yampolsky 1971

Chinese Rhyme-Prose: Poems in the Fu Form from the Han and Six Dynasties Periods, tr. Burton Watson. Also in paperback ed. 1971

Kūkai: Major Works, tr. Yoshito S. Hakeda. Also in paperback ed. 1972

The Old Man Who Does as He Pleases: Selections from the Poetry and Prose of Lu Yu, tr. Burton Watson 1973

The Lion's Roar of Queen Śrīmālā, tr. Alex and Hideko Wayman 1974

Courtier and Commoner in Ancient China: Selections from the History of the Former Han by Pan Ku, tr. Burton Watson. Also in paperback ed. 1974

Japanese Literature in Chinese, vol. 1: *Poetry and Prose in Chinese by Japanese Writers of the Early Period,* tr. Burton Watson 1975

Japanese Literature in Chinese, vol. 2: *Poetry and Prose in Chinese by Japanese Writers of the Later Period,* tr. Burton Watson 1976

Scripture of the Lotus Blossom of the Fine Dharma, tr. Leon Hurvitz. Also in paperback ed. 1976

Love Song of the Dark Lord: Jayadeva's Gītagovinda, tr. Barbara Stoler Miller. Also in paperback ed. Cloth ed. includes critical text of the Sanskrit. 1977; rev. ed. 1997

Ryōkan: Zen Monk-Poet of Japan, tr. Burton Watson 1977

Calming the Mind and Discerning the Real: From the Lam rim chen mo of Tson-kha-pa, tr. Alex Wayman 1978

The Hermit and the Love-Thief: Sanskrit Poems of Bhartrihari and Bilhaṇa, tr. Barbara Stoler Miller 1978

The Lute: Kao Ming's P'i-p'a chi, tr. Jean Mulligan. Also in paperback ed. 1980

A Chronicle of Gods and Sovereigns: Jinnō Shōtōki of Kitabatake Chikafusa, tr. H. Paul Varley 1980

Among the Flowers: The Hua-chien chi, tr. Lois Fusek 1982

Grass Hill: Poems and Prose by the Japanese Monk Gensei, tr. Burton Watson 1983

Doctors, Diviners, and Magicians of Ancient China: Biographies of Fang-shih, tr. Kenneth J. DeWoskin. Also in paperback ed. 1983

Theater of Memory: The Plays of Kālidāsa, ed. Barbara Stoler Miller. Also in paperback ed. 1984

The Columbia Book of Chinese Poetry: From Early Times to the Thirteenth Century, ed. and tr. Burton Watson. Also in paperback ed. 1984

Poems of Love and War: From the Eight Anthologies and the Ten Long Poems of Classical Tamil, tr. A. K. Ramanujan. Also in paperback ed. 1985

The Bhagavad Gita: Krishna's Counsel in Time of War, tr. Barbara Stoler Miller 1986

The Columbia Book of Later Chinese Poetry, ed. and tr. Jonathan Chaves. Also in paperback ed. 1986

The Tso Chuan: Selections from China's Oldest Narrative History, tr. Burton Watson 1989

Waiting for the Wind: Thirty-six Poets of Japan's Late Medieval Age, tr. Steven Carter 1989

Selected Writings of Nichiren, ed. Philip B. Yampolsky 1990

Saigyō, Poems of a Mountain Home, tr. Burton Watson 1990

The Book of Lieh Tzu: A Classic of the Tao, tr. A. C. Graham. Morningside ed. 1990

The Tale of an Anklet: An Epic of South India—The Cilappatikāram of Iḷaṅko Aṭikaḷ, tr. R. Parthasarathy 1993

Waiting for the Dawn: A Plan for the Prince, tr. and introduction by Wm. Theodore de Bary 1993

Yoshitsune and the Thousand Cherry Trees: A Masterpiece of the Eighteenth-Century Japanese Puppet Theater, tr., annotated, and with introduction by Stanleigh H. Jones, Jr. 1993

The Lotus Sutra, tr. Burton Watson. Also in paperback ed. 1993

The Classic of Changes: A New Translation of the I Ching as Interpreted by Wang Bi, tr. Richard John Lynn 1994

Beyond Spring: Tz'u Poems of the Sung Dynasty, tr. Julie Landau 1994

The Columbia Anthology of Traditional Chinese Literature, ed. Victor H. Mair 1994

Scenes for Mandarins: The Elite Theater of the Ming, tr. Cyril Birch 1995

Letters of Nichiren, ed. Philip B. Yampolsky; tr. Burton Watson et al. 1996

Unforgotten Dreams: Poems by the Zen Monk Shōtetsu, tr. Steven D. Carter 1997

The Vimalakirti Sutra, tr. Burton Watson 1997

Japanese and Chinese Poems to Sing: The Wakan rōei shū, tr. J. Thomas Rimer and Jonathan Chaves 1997

Breeze Through Bamboo: Kanshi of Ema Saikō, tr. Hiroaki Sato 1998

A Tower for the Summer Heat, Li Yu, tr. Patrick Hanan 1998

Traditional Japanese Theater: An Anthology of Plays, Karen Brazell 1998

The Original Analects: Sayings of Confucius and His Successors (0479–0249), E. Bruce Brooks and A. Taeko Brooks 1998

The Classic of the Way and Virtue: A New Translation of the Tao-te ching *of Laozi as Interpreted by Wang Bi,* tr. Richard John Lynn 1999

The Four Hundred Songs of War and Wisdom: An Anthology of Poems from Classical Tamil, The Puranāṇūṟu, eds. and trans. George L. Hart and Hank Heifetz 1999

Original Tao: Inward Training (Nei-yeh) *and the Foundations of Taoist Mysticism,* by Harold D. Roth 1999

Lao Tzu's Tao Te Ching: *A Translation of the Startling New Documents Found at Guodian,* Robert G. Henricks 2000

The Shorter Columbia Anthology of Traditional Chinese Literature, ed. Victor H. Mair 2000

Mistress and Maid (Jiaohongji) by Meng Chengshun, tr. Cyril Birch 2001

Chikamatsu: Five Late Plays, tr. and ed. C. Andrew Gerstle

The Essential Lotus: Selections from the Lotus Sutra, tr. Burton Watson 2002

Early Modern Japanese Literature: An Anthology, 1600–1900, ed. Haruo Shirane 2002

MODERN ASIAN LITERATURE

Modern Japanese Drama: An Anthology, ed. and tr. Ted. Takaya. Also in paperback ed. 1979

Mask and Sword: Two Plays for the Contemporary Japanese Theater, by Yamazaki Masakazu, tr. J. Thomas Rimer 1980

Yokomitsu Riichi, Modernist, Dennis Keene 1980

Nepali Visions, Nepali Dreams: The Poetry of Laxmiprasad Devkota, tr. David Rubin 1980

Literature of the Hundred Flowers, vol. 1: *Criticism and Polemics,* ed. Hualing Nieh 1981

Literature of the Hundred Flowers, vol. 2: *Poetry and Fiction,* ed. Hualing Nieh 1981

Modern Chinese Stories and Novellas, 1919 1949, ed. Joseph S. M. Lau, C. T. Hsia, and Leo Ou-fan Lee. Also in paperback ed. 1984

A View by the Sea, by Yasuoka Shōtarō, tr. Kären Wigen Lewis 1984

Other Worlds: Arishima Takeo and the Bounds of Modern Japanese Fiction, by Paul Anderer 1984

Selected Poems of Sŏ Chŏngju, tr. with introduction by David R. McCann 1989

The Sting of Life: Four Contemporary Japanese Novelists, by Van C. Gessel 1989

Stories of Osaka Life, by Oda Sakunosuke, tr. Burton Watson 1990

The Bodhisattva, or Samantabhadra, by Ishikawa Jun, tr. with introduction by William Jefferson Tyler 1990

The Travels of Lao Ts'an, by Liu T'ieh-yün, tr. Harold Shadick. Morningside ed. 1990

Three Plays by Kōbō Abe, tr. with introduction by Donald Keene 1993

The Columbia Anthology of Modern Chinese Literature, ed. Joseph S. M. Lau and Howard Goldblatt 1995

Modern Japanese Tanka, ed. and tr. by Makoto Ueda 1996

Masaoka Shiki: Selected Poems, ed. and tr. by Burton Watson 1997

Writing Women in Modern China: An Anthology of Women's Literature from the Early Twentieth Century, ed. and tr. by Amy D. Dooling and Kristina M. Torgeson 1998

American Stories, by Nagai Kafū, tr. Mitsuko Iriye 2000

The Paper Door and Other Stories, by Shiga Naoya, tr. Lane Dunlop 2001

Grass for My Pillow, by Saiichi Maruya, tr. Dennis Keene 2002

STUDIES IN ASIAN CULTURE

The Ōnin War: History of Its Origins and Background, with a Selective Translation of the Chronicle of Ōnin, by H. Paul Varley 1967

Chinese Government in Ming Times: Seven Studies, ed. Charles O. Hucker 1969

The Actors' Analects (Yakusha Rongo), ed. and tr. by Charles J. Dunn and Bungō Torigoe 1969

Self and Society in Ming Thought, by Wm. Theodore de Bary and the Conference on Ming Thought. Also in paperback ed. 1970

A History of Islamic Philosophy, by Majid Fakhry, 2d ed. 1983

Phantasies of a Love Thief: The Caurapañcāśikā Attributed to Bilhaṇa, by Barbara Stoler Miller 1971

Iqbal: Poet-Philosopher of Pakistan, ed. Hafeez Malik 1971

The Golden Tradition: An Anthology of Urdu Poetry, ed. and tr. Ahmed Ali. Also in paperback ed. 1973

Conquerors and Confucians: Aspects of Political Change in Late Yüan China, by John W. Dardess 1973

The Unfolding of Neo-Confucianism, by Wm. Theodore de Bary and the Conference on Seventeenth-Century Chinese Thought. Also in paperback ed. 1975

To Acquire Wisdom: The Way of Wang Yang-ming, by Julia Ching 1976

Gods, Priests, and Warriors: The Bhṛgus of the Mahābhārata, by Robert P. Goldman 1977

Mei Yao-ch'en and the Development of Early Sung Poetry, by Jonathan Chaves 1976

The Legend of Semimaru, Blind Musician of Japan, by Susan Matisoff 1977

Sir Sayyid Ahmad Khan and Muslim Modernization in India and Pakistan, by Hafeez Malik 1980

The Khilafat Movement: Religious Symbolism and Political Mobilization in India, by Gail Minault 1982

The World of K'ung Shang-jen: A Man of Letters in Early Ch'ing China, by Richard Strassberg 1983

The Lotus Boat: The Origins of Chinese Tz'u Poetry in T'ang Popular Culture, by Marsha L. Wagner 1984

Expressions of Self in Chinese Literature, ed. Robert E. Hegel and Richard C. Hessney 1985

Songs for the Bride: Women's Voices and Wedding Rites of Rural India, by W. G. Archer; eds. Barbara Stoler Miller and Mildred Archer 1986

The Confucian Kingship in Korea: Yŏngjo and the Politics of Sagacity, by JaHyun Kim Haboush 1988

COMPANIONS TO ASIAN STUDIES

Approaches to the Oriental Classics, ed. Wm. Theodore de Bary 1959

Early Chinese Literature, by Burton Watson. Also in paperback ed. 1962

Approaches to Asian Civilizations, eds. Wm. Theodore de Bary and Ainslie T. Embree 1964

The Classic Chinese Novel: A Critical Introduction, by C. T. Hsia. Also in paperback ed. 1968

Chinese Lyricism: Shih Poetry from the Second to the Twelfth Century, tr. Burton Watson. Also in paperback ed. 1971

A Syllabus of Indian Civilization, by Leonard A. Gordon and Barbara Stoler Miller 1971

Twentieth-Century Chinese Stories, ed. C. T. Hsia and Joseph S. M. Lau. Also in paperback ed. 1971

A Syllabus of Chinese Civilization, by J. Mason Gentzler, 2d ed. 1972

A Syllabus of Japanese Civilization, by H. Paul Varley, 2d ed. 1972

An Introduction to Chinese Civilization, ed. John Meskill, with the assistance of J. Mason Gentzler 1973

An Introduction to Japanese Civilization, ed. Arthur E. Tiedemann 1974

Ukifune: Love in the Tale of Genji, ed. Andrew Pekarik 1982

The Pleasures of Japanese Literature, by Donald Keene 1988

A Guide to Oriental Classics, eds. Wm. Theodore de Bary and Ainslie T. Embree; 3d edition ed. Amy Vladeck Heinrich, 2 vols. 1989

INTRODUCTION TO ASIAN CIVILIZATIONS
WM. THEODORE DE BARY, GENERAL EDITOR

Sources of Japanese Tradition, 1958; paperback ed., 2 vols., 1964. 2d ed., vol. 1, 2001,
compiled by Wm. Theodore de Bary, Donald Keene, George Tanabe, and
Paul Varley

Sources of Indian Tradition, 1958; paperback ed., 2 vols., 1964. 2d ed., 2 vols.,
1988

Sources of Chinese Tradition, 1960, paperback ed., 2 vols., 1964. 2d ed., vol. 1,
1999, compiled by Wm. Theodore de Bary and Irene Bloom; vol. 2, 2000,
compiled by Wm. Theodore de Bary and Richard Lufrano

Sources of Korean Tradition, 1997; 2 vols., vol. 1, 1997, compiled by Peter H. Lee
and Wm. Theodore de Bary; vol. 2, 2001, compiled by Yăngho Ch'oe,
Peter H. Lee, and Wm. Theodore de Bary

NEO-CONFUCIAN STUDIES

Instructions for Practical Living and Other Neo-Confucian Writings by Wang Yang-ming,
tr. Wing-tsit Chan 1963

Reflections on Things at Hand: The Neo-Confucian Anthology, comp. Chu Hsi and
Lü Tsu-ch'ien, tr. Wing-tsit Chan 1967

Self and Society in Ming Thought, by Wm. Theodore de Bary and the Conference on Ming Thought. Also in paperback ed. 1970

The Unfolding of Neo-Confucianism, by Wm. Theodore de Bary and the Conference on Seventeenth-Century Chinese Thought. Also in paperback ed.
1975

Principle and Practicality: Essays in Neo-Confucianism and Practical Learning, eds.
Wm. Theodore de Bary and Irene Bloom. Also in paperback ed. 1979

The Syncretic Religion of Lin Chao-en, by Judith A. Berling 1980

The Renewal of Buddhism in China: Chu-hung and the Late Ming Synthesis, by
Chün-fang Yü 1981

Neo-Confucian Orthodoxy and the Learning of the Mind-and-Heart, by Wm.
Theodore de Bary 1981

Yüan Thought: Chinese Thought and Religion Under the Mongols, eds. Hok-lam
Chan and Wm. Theodore de Bary 1982

The Liberal Tradition in China, by Wm. Theodore de Bary 1983

The Development and Decline of Chinese Cosmology, by John B. Henderson 1984

The Rise of Neo-Confucianism in Korea, by Wm. Theodore de Bary and JaHyun
Kim Haboush 1985

Chiao Hung and the Restructuring of Neo-Confucianism in Late Ming, by Edward T. Ch'ien 1985

Neo-Confucian Terms Explained: Pei-hsi tzu-i, by Ch'en Ch'un, ed. and trans. Wing-tsit Chan 1986

Knowledge Painfully Acquired: K'un-chih chi, by Lo Ch'in-shun, ed. and trans. Irene Bloom 1987

To Become a Sage: The Ten Diagrams on Sage Learning, by Yi T'oegye, ed. and trans. Michael C. Kalton 1988

The Message of the Mind in Neo-Confucian Thought, by Wm. Theodore de Bary 1989